Forests: Fresh Perspectives from Ecosystem Analysis

Forests: Fresh Perspectives
from Ecosystem Analysis

Proceedings of the 40th Annual Biology Colloquium

Edited by
Richard H. Waring

Oregon State University Press
Corvallis, Oregon

Library of Congress Cataloging in Publication Data

Biology Colloquium, 40th, Oregon State University,
    1979.
    Forests, fresh perspectives from ecosystem analysis.

    1. Forest ecology—Congresses.   I.   Waring,
Richard H.   II.   Title.
QH541.5.F6B56   1979   574.5'2642   80-14883
ISBN 0-87071-179-2

Preface

Over the last decade a new perspective on how forest ecosystems operate has emerged. Ecosystems appear much more flexible than we once thought. Even the most persistent is still evolving in composition. Yet for all their diversity, very similar processes are seen as operating in all forests, providing a point for comparative studies. A more balanced time perspective brings a greater appreciation of the infrequent but dominating events that shape the course of ecosystem development. Through joint studies of forests and streams we see new roles for living and dead components of both ecosystems.

For the 40th annual Biology Colloquim held April 27-28 1979 at Oregon State University, a select group of scientists was invited to share this new perspective on forest ecosystems with a wider audience. The colloquium papers are grouped into three sections within this volume. The first section (chapters 1-3) revises classical theories on community structure, succession, and ecosystems. The second section (chapters 4-8) examines in detail how forest canopies, soil microbes, and root systems operate as almost independent subsystems. The final section (chapters 9-12) focuses on the impact of the different materials-- logs and leaves, soil and sediments, water and minerals--that move through forests and into stream ecosystems. Although each section is distinct in scope, they share a common link of matter and energy flow.

For permitting us the opportunity to share these ideas, we are indebted to the late Ralph Shay, who originally suggested the topic and helped arrange the colloquim. To him we dedicate this volume.

Richard H. Waring

Contributing Authors

Daniel B. Botkin
Department of Biological Studies
University of California
Santa Barbara, California

George C. Carroll
Department of Biology
University of Oregon
Eugene, Oregon

Kermit Cromack, Jr.
Department of Forest Science
Oregon State University
Corvallis, Oregon

Kenneth W. Cummins
Department of Fisheries and Wildlife
Oregon State University
Corvallis, Oregon

Jerry F. Franklin
U. S. Forest Service
Forest Science Laboratory
Corvallis, Oregon

W. F. Harris
Environmental Sciences Division
Oak Ridge National Laboratory
Oak Ridge, Tennessee

James A. MacMahon
Department of Biology and Ecology Center
Utah State University
Logan, Utah

D. McGinty
Department of Biology
Huntingdon College
Montgomery, Alabama

R. V. O'Neill
Environmental Sciences Division
Oak Ridge National Laboratory
Oak Ridge, Tennessee

Dennis Parkinson
Department of Biology
University of Calgary
Calgary, Alberta

D. E. Reichle
Environmental Sciences Laboratory
Oak Ridge National Laboratory
Oak Ridge, Tennessee

Dan Santantonio
School of Forestry
Oregon State University
Corvallis, Oregon

Wayne T. Swank
Coweeta Hydrologic Laboratory
U. S. Forest Service
Franklin, North Carolina

Fredrick J. Swanson
Pacific Northwest Forest and Range
  Experiment Station
Forestry Sciences Laboratory
Corvallis, Oregon

Frank J. Triska
U. S. Geological Survey
Menlo Park, California

Jack B. Waide
Environmental Sciences Division
Oak Ridge National Laboratory
Oak Ridge, Tennessee

Richard H. Waring
Department of Forest Science
Oregon State University
Corvallis, Oregon

Contents

Section I: Ecosystem Theory

A Grandfather Clock down the Staircase: Stability and Disturbance in
Natural Ecosystems 1
    Daniel B. Botkin

Dimensions of Ecosystem Theory 11
    R. V. O'Neill and D. E. Reichle

Ecosystems over Time: Succession and Other Types of Change 27
    James A. MacMahon

Section II: Terrestrial Ecosystems

Distinctive Features of the Northwestern Coniferous Forest: Development,
Structure, and Function 59
    Jerry F. Franklin and Richard H. Waring

Forest Canopies: Complex and Independent Subsystems 87
    George C. Carroll

Aspects of the Microbial Ecology of Forest Ecosystems 109
    Dennis Parkinson

The Dynamic Belowground Ecosystem 119
    W. F. Harris, Dan Santantonio, and D. McGinty

Vital Signs of Forest Ecosystems 131
    R. H. Waring

Section III: Watershed and Stream Ecosystems

Interpretation of Nutrient Cycling Research in a Management Context:
Evaluating Potential Effects of Alternative Management Strategies on
Site Productivity 137
    Wayne T. Swank and Jack B. Waide

Geomorphology and Ecosystems 159
    Frederick J. Swanson

The Role of Wood Debris in Forests and Streams 171
    Frank J. Triska and Kermit Cromack, Jr.

The Multiple Linkages of Forests to Streams 191
    Kenneth W. Cummins

A Grandfather Clock down the Staircase: Stability and Disturbance in Natural Ecosystems

Daniel B. Botkin

BASIC CONCEPTS

In a small village in New Hampshire, an elderly lady lives in an old red brick house crammed with antiques that her parents bought at the turn of the century. At the top of the staircase stands a wonderful grandfather clock, whose pendulum had swung rhythmically to and fro for many years. Several years ago two grandchildren discovered the clock and, in the process of investigating it with all the empirical skills known to small children, managed to edge it over to the staircase. With a push, they watched it tumble down the stairs with a marvelous series of noises. With considerable effort, friends and neighbors eventually returned the clock to its former position, but the disruption had been too great for its internal mechanisms and it has stood silent since, outwardly intact, a sad image of mechanical frailty.

Nature's biota sometimes seem like that clock -- able to withstand small disturbances but unable to survive major perturbations.

In ecological systems, perturbation and stability seem to oppose one another. In both scientific literature and in popular discussions of the effects of civilization on the environment, stability is referred to as resisting disturbance and perturbation as a disruption of the stability of nature. We call an undisturbed forest stable and a highly perturbed one unstable.

Are ecosystems, in these terms, stable or unstable? Is perturbation common and, in some sense, natural, necessary, or desirable? Or is perturbation always the product of human interference in nature, and bad -- something to be avoided in our management of natural ecosystems?

In regard to these questions, we seem to believe simultaneously in contradictory views. On the one hand, we tend to agree with George Perkins Marsh, who wrote more than one hundred years ago in his classic book, Man and Nature, that "nature, left undisturbed so fashions her territory as to give it almost unchanging permanence of form, outline, and proportion, except when shattered by geologic convulsions; and in these comparatively rare cases of derangement, she sets herself at once to repair the superficial damage, to restore as nearly as practicable, the former aspect of her dominion." We tend also to agree with Marsh that an undisturbed wilderness forest, the kind that he referred to as occurring in "new countries," meaning those not yet subject to civilization's heavy hand, is characterized by a single, permanent equilibrium condition -- the climax forest of twentieth century ecology. In Wildernesses, Marsh wrote, "the natural inclination of the ground, the self-formed slopes and levels, are graded and lowered or elevated by frost and chemical forces and gravitation and the flow of water and vegetable deposit and the action of the winds until, by a general compensation of conflicting forces, a condition of equilibrium has been reached which, without the action of man, would remain, with little fluctuations, for countless ages" (Marsh, 1864).

On the other hand, we also seem to agree with Lucretius, who in the first century B.C. wrote in De Rerum Natura that all things are subject to mutability and change; that "time does change the nature of the whole wide world; one state follows from another; not one thing is like itself forever, all things move, all things are nature's wanderers, whom she gives no rest, ebb follows flow." Lucretius used the erosion along riverbanks in forests as an example of the mutability of nature. Here the forests, Lucretius said so long ago, are "shorn, gnawed by the current" (Humphries, 1968).

We acknowledge, as did Lucretius, that nature is subject to change, that forests change: trees have mast years when, for reasons we do not now understand, a single species will produce an abundance of seeds over a large geographic area.

Well, which is it? Is the truth as Marsh saw it? Does Mother Nature set herself at once to repair superficial damage and restore the former aspects of her dominion, creating an equilibrium that remains for countless ages? Or is the truth with Lucretius, that the earth is both "our mother" and "our common grave," and that all things, even undisturbed forest wildernesses, are always changing?

These two ideas can be brought together -- they only appear to be contradictory. The contradiction occurs because of the restricted way that we define stability -- a definition we have used during the last 200 years. In this paper, I will attempt to show that perturbation and stability are linked together in truly natural ecosystem processes. What appears to be contradictory can be shown not to be, but this requires a basic change in our conception of natural ecosystems as well as changes in our concept of stability. These basic changes may seem quite disturbing at first, but as we pursue the topic they will seem quite natural.

This discussion is not merely academic: it is crucial to our management of our natural biological resources. Our attitudes toward stability and perturbation have influenced our methods of managing our biological surroundings, sometimes to their, and to our, detriment. I will concentrate on forest ecosystems, because forests are composed of long-lived organisms and should be more likely to demonstrate long-term constancy than most other ecosystems. However, I believe the points that I make will be general.

In the twentieth century, the favorite metaphor among naturalists for the stability of a forest, or any ecosystem, is the stability of a pendulum. This is the stability of a strictly mechanical system, a stability that I have referred to elsewhere as "static stability" (Botkin and Sobel, 1975). In the 1920's Alfred Lotka stated this metaphor in his Elements of Mathematical Biology (Lotka, 1956). The Australian ecologist Graeme Caughley used the metaphor in a recent review on the effects on ecosystems of the introduction of ungulates into new habitats (Caughley, 1970). According to this view, a stable system has two attributes: an equilibrium state, and the ability to return to this equilibrium state following a disturbance. Thus a pendulum, when "disturbed" with a push, will oscillate. Theoretically, a pendulum can demonstrate three possible kinds of stability: that of a frictionless

(idealized) pendulum, which will oscillate indefinitely with a constant frequency and amplitude; that of a dampened (idealized) pendulum, which will oscillate with a continually decreasing amplitude around its central point but never come to complete rest; and that of a real pendulum with friction, which will oscillate for a while but eventually stop at its original rest point.

This concept of stability underlies the classical twentieth century ideas of forest succession. According to this classical concept, an undisturbed forest is unchanging and a disturbed forest "recovers" to its prior condition. The forest proceeds through a well-defined series of stages and eventually reaches a fixed single state, the climax, which is that permanent condition referred to by Marsh.

Early twentieth century ecologists like William S. Cooper believed in this idea of forest stability. In the first decade of this century, Cooper made a classic study of forest succession on Isle Royale in Lake Superior. He saw that island, little disturbed by Indian or European culture, as an excellent place to learn about the real characteristics of forest ecosystems. After a careful study of the forests of Isle Royale, Cooper concluded that one forest type, the boreal forest, was the island's natural condition. This forest, he wrote, is the "final and permanent vegetation stage, toward the establishment of which all other plant societies are successive steps." He believed that regardless of the condition of the starting point -- be it bare rocky summit or open water bog, the final condition, given enough time, would be the same single state. "Both observational and experimental studies have shown," Cooper wrote, "that the balsam-birch-white spruce forest, in spite of appearances to the contrary, is, taken as a whole, in equilibrium; that no changes of a successional nature are taking place within it" (Cooper, 1913).

Accepting this idea of stability, we tend to think of a perturbation as destabilizing a forest in two senses: first of all, a mild perturbation removes the system (pendulum or forest) from its equilibrium point. Strictly speaking, this is not a change in the stability of the system, merely a change in the system's current state, but we often confuse equilibrium state with stability. Second, a large perturbation, as when the two small children knocked a grandfather clock down the staircase, throws the system far enough from the equilibrium that a return to that original equilibrium is no longer possible. Even today, the idea still predominates that ecosystems in general and forests in particular are characterized by this static stability.

In the last decade, ecologists have divided static stability into different stages and found it useful to refer to these different stages and their different attributes. For example, C. S. Holling, using this concept of stability, described the resistance and resilience of an ecosystem (Holling, 1974). The resistance is like mechanical inertia -- the ability of the pendulum to resist the forces that tend to cause it to leave its equilibrium. The resilience is, loosely speaking, the rapidity and ease with which the system returns to its original equilibrium state. Although these are new terms, they refer to -- and accept -- the static concept of ecosystem stability. This static stability is readily defined mathematically, as has been done in physics for a long time, and can be found in many recent ecology texts and articles (May 1973; Jordan et al., 1972; Krebs, 1972).

If this static definition of stability for ecosystems is correct, then the natural condition of an ecosystem like a forest must be one of "rest" -- a static equilibrium point. Furthermore, a forest that is changing is therefore not in its natural state, and a manager whose job is to maintain a forest in its natural condition would seek to restore the forest to its equilibrium as quickly as possible. He would also attempt to remove the possibility of subsequent perturbations in the future.

Evaluation of the stability of a system must involve a definition of stability and a variable of interest, whose stability is measured according to the accepted definition. In a simple system like a pendulum, the measure of interest is obvious. In an ecosystem, however, the appropriate measure is not obvious. We tend to think that nature will provide us with the appropriate measure, but ecological studies of stability use a variety of measures including species composition, relative abundance of species, total organic matter, and the rate of flux or the stored amount of specific chemical elements.

To summarize, a system characterized by static stability has a single equilibrium state and will return to that state along a well-defined pathway following disturbance. Also, it has generally been argued that perturbation is "bad" and an equilibrium is "natural."

A FOREST DOES NOT HAVE A
SINGLE EQUILIBRIUM STATE

In order to apply static stability to a forest or other natural ecosystem, we must be able to identify the equilibrium state. Before the theory of continental glaciation was well established, which was before our century, it was possible to believe with George Perkins Marsh that the equilibrium condition of a forest could persist for "countless ages." But by the beginning of the twentieth century, it was well recognized that severe changes in climate had occurred during the last two million years. Earlier in the century, it was believed that there had been four major periods of glaciation, that the changes accompanying these periods had been most marked at high latitudes, with little or no effect at low latitudes, and that the climate during the glaciations represented relatively short, anomalous climatic episodes.

Once the theory of continental glaciation was accepted, it was clear that, at least in temperate zones, the climate had changed markedly over periods of thousands of years and these long-term climatic changes were accompanied by changes in the kind of ecosystem at a particular location. Earlier in this century, ecologists attempted to resolve the problem of ecosystem stability and long-term climate changes by talking about a climatic climax for an ecosystem -- a single state or condition that would persist without change as long as the climate did not change. This constancy is usually described in terms of the species composition, the relative or absolute abundance of species, and the total amount of organic matter in the ecosystem.

Throughout most of our century, it has been generally believed that enough time has elapsed since the end of the last glaciation to allow most natural ecosystems to obtain an equilibrium, and that the presettlement landscape in North America represented an equilibrium state of the vegetation communities. During the past two decades our knowledge of the history of the Pleistocene climate and ecosystems has increased greatly. Forest history is particularly well known for the Northeastern forests of North America, those that extend from Maine to Minnesota and from Ontario to the southern Appalachians in Georgia. What does the evidence from such areas tell us about the equilibrium conditions of a natural forest?

Consider a forest in Minnesota and a manager whose job is to restore that forest to its equilibrium condition. What vegetation assemblage would he choose? The obvious answer appears to be to choose a forest similar to the natural, original presettlement vegetation of that area.

Recent pollen studies indicate that the forests of this area have undergone major

changes in species composition since the
last glaciation. For example, a study in
Minnesota indicated that the last glaciation
was followed by a tundra period, then by a
spruce forest that was replaced about 9,200
years ago by a forest of jack and red pine.
About 8,300 years ago paper birch and alder
migrated into this forest, and about 7,000
years ago white pine entered. Afterward
there was a return to spruce and jack pine.
These changes reflected fluctuations in
climate, periods of cooling and warming,
and the differential migration of the species
as they returned north following the melting
of the continental ice sheet. The study
indicates that, on a time scale of 1,000
years, major changes have taken place in the
species composition of the forests (Craig,
1972; Swann, 1972).

Which of these forests represents the
natural state? If one's goal were to return
northern Minnesota to its "natural" condition, which of these forests would one
choose? Each appears equally natural in the
sense that each dominated the landscape for
a rather long period, approximately 1,000
years, and each occupied a landscape at a
time when the influence of human beings was
nonexistent or slight. The range of choice
is great, representing kinds of vegetation
communities now distributed thousands of
miles apart.

The desire to return a particular spot
in Minnesota to its natural state leaves us
in a quandary, because as the glaciers
receded and the climate changed, the vegetation communities also changed. Thus we do
not find constancy in the abundances of
forest tree species over time at a particular location, at least in mid-latitudes of
North America.

A thousand years seems to be a long
time. One might argue that changes in
forest composition are slow and that an
equilibrium state might be obtained in
periods of less than 1,000 years. However,
one would expect that the effects of a
marked change in climate would influence an
ecosystem for at least a few generations.
Because the lifetimes of some of the tree
species in northern hardwood and coniferous
forests are on the order of 400 years, an
equilibrium state would not have had time
to develop in northern Minnesota. What
alternatives are left to us?

Throughout the first half of the
twentieth century, it was generally believed
that glaciers caused a great displacement in
the location of vegetation communities, but
these communities remained intact and merely
migrated north and south with changes in the
climate. The location of a community and
its migration across the landscape were
believed to have the same relative abundances of species as are observed today in

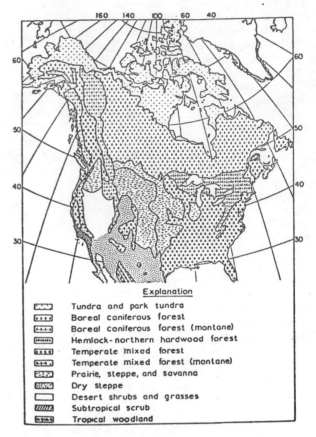

Explanation

- ▭ Tundra and park tundra
- ▭ Boreal coniferous forest
- ▭ Boreal coniferous forest (montane)
- ▭ Hemlock-northern hardwood forest
- ▭ Temperate mixed forest
- ▭ Temperate mixed forest (montane)
- ▭ Prairie, steppe, and savanna
- ▭ Dry steppe
- ▭ Desert shrubs and grasses
- ▭ Subtropical scrub
- ▭ Tropical woodland

*Figure 1. Natural vegetation zones in North
America today, much generalized (from
Flint, 1971).*

each forest type. For example, in Flint's
standard work on the Pleistocene geology
(Flint, 1971), the vegetation communities
are pictured as having been pushed south,
but still intact (Figs. 1 and 2). Figure 1
shows the modern distribution of vegetation
zones and Figure 2 shows the distribution
that was assumed to have occurred during
the ice age. In Figure 2 we see a tundra
border just below the edge of the ice,
spruce forests south of the tundra, and
temperate mixed species forests to the
south of the spruce. If this were true, one
could then argue that the communities have
had a continuous existence throughout the
Pleistocene, merely migrating back and
forth along the landscape in response to
the climate. Then the natural condition of
a particular locale would be the entire
biological community that was characteristic
of the existing climate and had followed
that climate across the landscape in ages
past. The natural forest would be the one
that existed under a particular climate
prior to the influence of human beings.
Under this interpretation, each community
has retained its integrity and has a climate-
determined equilibrium state. Its structure,
in terms of the relative abundance of its

constituent species, has remained constant.

Recent evidence suggests that this idea is false. Studies of pollen deposits from 26 sites scattered across the eastern and central United States allow us to piece together the paths of migration of the major tree species as they returned north during the last 13,000 years as the North American continental ice sheet melted (Davis, 1976). The trees migrated at different rates, depending on the size and mobility of their seeds. Light seeds, like those of poplar, are readily blown long distances by the wind, and these moved northward most rapidly. Heavy seeds, like those of beech, are moved by squirrels and other small mammals, and these migrated much more slowly. Not only did the different species move northward at different rates, but the species appear to have moved northward from different directions, as illustrated in the accompanying maps (Fig. 3). Hickory moved toward the northeast from some refuge in the southern midwest or west, while chestnut moved eastward from a refuge east of the Carolinas, an area that now is covered by the ocean but would have been dryland during the glaciation. In recent times, just prior to the chestnut blight of the early twentieth century, hickory and chestnut were two of the major trees of the forests of the mid-Atlantic states, and botanists classified the forests of this region as chestnut-oak-hickory, believing that, without disturbance, these species would dominate the landscape indefinitely.

According to their interpretation, this oak-chestnut-hickory forest would have remained intact during the maximum extension of the continental glaciers, merely occupying an area south of its present location.

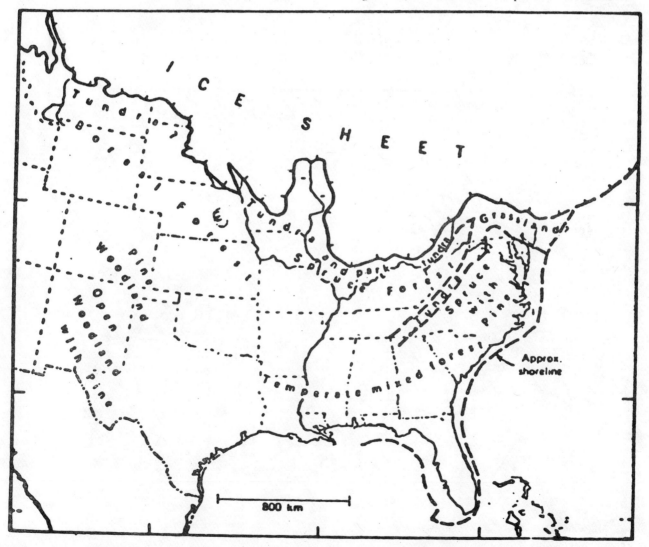

Figure 2. Sketch map suggesting possible pattern of vegetation in eastern and central United States at the Late-Wisconsin glacial maximum. Although controlled at a few localities, the sketch is very speculative (from Flint, 1971).

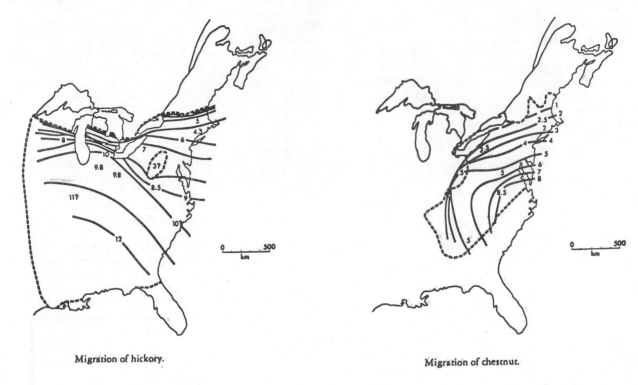

Migration of hickory.

Migration of chestnut.

Figure 3. *Migration of hickory and chestnut interpreted from pollen records (from Davis, 1976) following the last glaciation. Each line represents in thousands of years the first occurrence of the species. Figures show the direction and temporal sequence of migration.*

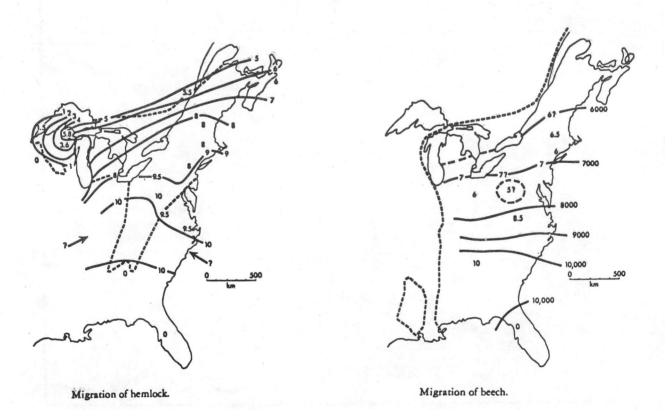

Migration of hemlock.

Migration of beech.

Figure 4. *Migration of hemlock and beech interpreted from pollen records (from Davis, 1976) following the last glaciation. Each line represents in thousands of years the first occurrence of the species. Figures show the direction and temporal sequence of migration.*

But Davis's study indicates that the forest composition itself changed markedly. The species that are most important in the modern forest scattered in different directions, forming forest communities that no longer exist.

But there is still another possibility that would allow us to believe in the existence of a single equilibrium state in a forest. One could argue that, although the individual species separated for a part of the glacial period, they returned rapidly enough to the present location to form an interglacial forest that would be constant throughout its entire range for most of the interglacial period. However, the maps of tree migration routes indicate markedly different rates of return (Fig. 4). Hemlock reached Massachusetts 9,000 years ago, approximately 2,000 years before beech, although now beech and hemlock are assumed to occur in similar climates, with the beech occurring on slightly warmer, better drained soils and the hemlock in cooler, moister valleys, streamsides, and ridges.

Beech is also found in much of the present range of hemlock, but the process has not yet reached an equilibrium. Hemlock reached the upper peninsula of Michigan 5,000 years ago and moved westward slowly, reaching the western shores of Lake Superior 1,000 years ago. Beech, on the other hand, is still migrating westward, with its present western boundary in the middle of Michigan's upper peninsula.

We need not abandon the possibility that an equilibrium forest condition will be reached during the present interglacial, and we could argue that such an equilibrium forest would be the true natural state of nature of this region. It might be that we are still seeing a recovery and, if the interglacials are truly very long in comparison to the period of continental glaciation, a true equilibrium of the distribution of the forest trees may yet be reached.

However, studies of the migration rates of trees during the present interglacial and during previous ones show that such a floristic equilibrium is never reached at the mid and high latitudes. Furthermore, according to Davis, "In this sense, the interglacials are unstable interruptions in Pleistocene history" (Davis, 1976). Soils also show continuous development throughout interglacial periods, indicating that interglacials are too short for attainment of a soil equilibrium and therefore of an ecosystem equilibrium.

A FOREST IS NOT CHARACTERIZED BY A SINGLE DETERMINISTIC PATTERN OF RECOVERY

When a pendulum is given a push and displaced from its equilibrium, it follows a strictly determined pathway back and forth until, if it is subject to friction, it eventually stops at its original rest point. The position and velocity of the pendulum can be calculated precisely if the position, velocity, and frictional and gravitational forces are known at any one time. Can forests be characterized by similarly exact patterns?

Even if we admit that over a long time forests change in composition, does this mean that we must also abandon the idea of static stability for a short time period? Suppose we consider a time period short enough so that the species that make up a forest, including all of the forest's successional stages, do not change. It was frequently argued earlier in this century that a particular forest type, that is a particular assemblage of forest tree species, would follow a strictly determined one-way pattern of recovery following a disturbance. Clearly this is not true at very small spatial and temporal scales. Whether a seed germinates and survives, whether a tree grows well or poorly, whether it dies in any one year, depend in part on chance events. The success of any one tree or population in a small area can be predicted only in terms of probabilities. What of large temporal and spatial scales?

A Lesson From Bogs

In his study of forest succession at Isle Royale, William S. Cooper argued that there was a single climatic climax that would be reached, given enough time under a constant climate, regardless of the starting point. He believed that both a bare rocky ridgetop and the open water of a bog would proceed, through different but equally specific successional patterns, to the same final equilibrium forest. Moreover, he and others argued that the pattern of succession from each of these starting points was exact: like a pendulum returning from disturbance, one stage inevitably followed another.

A recent study of one of these kinds of succession -- that of freshwater bogs -- suggests that this is not true. The classical successional pattern would be development from dominant green plants, phytoplankton, and submerged macrophytes on open water to a stage of floating leaved macrophytes, to a reedswamp, to fens and various fen stages, and finally to dryland. Walker (1970) recently analyzed the available published pollen records concerning changes in bogs in Britain. From these he identified twelve different stages in bog development. He made a transition table, listing each stage and the percentage of times that one stage led to each of the others. Although one pattern that Walker called the "central tendency" predominated, a variety of patterns actually occurred. In 17 percent of the cases the transitions were reversed; that is, the succession went in the direction opposite to what was assumed to be natural.

This study of bogs is particularly important because, as Walker concluded, "in a system which has often been considered one of the most unvarying in plant ecology, the variety of courses actually taken is remarkable." The evidence demands, he concluded, that "predictions be made only in terms of probabilities."

Of course, one could argue that the lack of predictability is due merely to the uncertainty of our understanding of causal mechanisms, and we would be able to make exact predictions if we studied enough. This is a belief that nature is actually deterministic, and only the limits of our observational techniques prevent us from learning the exact processes.

However, Walker also found that the transitions from one bog state to another depended in part on the level of the water table, and since this in turn depends on rainfall, which is a stochastic phenomenon, there is some inherent, underlying unpredictability or risk about this successional process. Thus bog succession is stochastic, not deterministic, in its inherent nature.

Other recent studies suggest that forest succession is a stochastic process. In some recent studies researchers have attempted to investigate what kinds of stochastic processes best characterize these patterns (Horn, 1976). A model based on population dynamics of individual species can, if stochastic events are included, provide realistic projections of the central tendency and the variation around this central tendency (Botkin et al., 1973).

The graph of the central tendency can be mistaken for the path of a deterministic system following static stability. To make such a mistake would cause a forest manager difficulty.

CHANGE IS NOT ALWAYS UNDESIRABLE

Forests are not characterized by either attribute of static stability: a single equilibrium or a single, deterministic pattern of recovery from perturbations. In spite of this conclusion about natural forest ecosystems, a manager could still argue that it is always desirable and possible to maintain a forest in a fixed condition, and to remove or suppress perturbations. This was the belief regarding forest fires earlier in this century.

In the nineteenth and early twentieth centuries, severe fires followed intensive logging in eastern and central areas of the United States. For example, in Michigan, where 19 million acres of white pine were cut, the great amount of slash left on the ground and the careless treatment of logged-over areas led to extremely devastating fires. These left the landscape in a condition from which recovery to a mature forest would take a long time, if it were to occur at all. As a consequence of these devastating fires, many concluded that the proper policy for forest management was to prevent fires in all cases.

We know now that such a policy of fire suppression can lead to quite undesirable results in some cases. One of the most famous cases is the attempt to prevent fires in the jack pine forests of central Michigan. Jack pine (Pinus banksiana), as every good naturalist of the east knows, is a fire-successional species. It has serotinous cones that open after a fire; it reproduces well after burning, grows rapidly, lives a short time, and cannot compete with those species which tend to appear in a forest after several decades. Jack pine is, in this sense, an early successional species. If fire is prevented, jack pine decreases in abundance and eventually disappears.

In central Michigan, jack pine was the home and habitat of Kirtland's warbler (Dendroica kirtlandi), and this species was threatened with extinction because of the elimination of jack pine by fire suppression. Only the activity of a few conservationists led to the maintenance of jack pine stands -- by allowing change to occur -- and to the persistence of Kirtland's warbler. Here is a case where change was required to allow the continuation of what was desirable. Change and stability, at least in terms of the preservation or the persistence of Kirtland's warblers and jack pine forests, were linked.

Disturbances are Required for Some Desired Forest Conditions

The preservation of Kirtland's warbler required that jack pine forests in Michigan be allowed to burn. Other evidence indicates that change may be necessary to achieve certain desirable states for some forests. For example, Heinselman (1973)

studied the history of fires in the Boundary
Waters Canoe Area in Minnesota, an area
where presettlement landscape was characterized by jack pine and red pine forests. His
work indicates that the intentional suppression of fire can produce two trends, both
undesirable. In the first, "dry matter
accumulations, spruce budworm outbreaks,
blowdowns and other interactions related to
the time since fire increases the probability
that old stand will burn." The probability
of a fire increases with the amount of time
since the last fire. Furthermore, because
fuel accumulates on the forest floor, the
severity of a fire increases with the
amount of time since the last fire (at
least in terms of the area burned). Second,
the successful prevention of a fire leads to
a change in the forest composition: in the
Boundary Waters Canoe Area, jack and red
pine decrease and are replaced by cedar.
Thus, the intentional suppression of fire
did not lead to a maintenance of what was
found in the presettlement forests. In
these forests, fire can be seen as an
intrinsic part of the system; change must
be viewed as part of this system.

    Other evidence suggests that short-term
perturbations are crucial factors in maintaining ecosystems in what are thought to be
their natural state. For example, the
Serengeti Plains in Tanzania are often cited
as the last true wilderness of the big game
animals: wilderness in the sense of a lack
of human influence and a lack of disturbance.
However, Talbot (pers. comm.), one of the
most knowledgeable wildlife scientists about
the Serengeti, has investigated the history
of fires there. He believes that the great
majority of fires are caused by people and
that the fires are important in the maintenance of the great abundance of large
mammals.

    These are a few of many examples that
suggest to us that change may be necessary
to create the desirable conditions in many
ecosystems. Then what can be meant by
ecosystem stability?

ALTERNATIVE CONCEPTS OF STABILITY

    If a forest does not have a single
stable equilibrium and does not recover
from disturbance along a deterministic
pattern of successional stages, what is
meaningful to say about stability? How can
we compare the relative stability of different forests, or of the same forest type
under different management policies? Without static stability we are left in an un-
comfortable position as managers or
scientists. Nature no longer tells us when
a forest is stable or in a desirable state.

    It is tempting, therefore, to continue
to use the idea of static stability, argu-
ing that although it may not be quite right,
it is a good enough approximation. However,
we have seen that an insistence on maintaining a forest in a single state can lead
to undesirable consequences. Then what can
we do?

    We must first recognize that underlying
our concern with the stability of forests
and all ecosystems is a concern with the
probabilities that they will persist on the
landscape, and with a concern about the
impact of natural and human influences on
such probabilities. Reconsider a forest of
jack pine. To persist it must change, but
the changes must be bounded. If the abundance of mature jack pine becomes too low,
then the forest may not recover following
a fire (that is, it may not be maintained
as a jack pine forest). If the abundance
of jack pine becomes too great, the
accumulated fuel in dead limbs on live
trees and dead organic matter on the forest
surface may lead to a fire so severe that
recovery would be extremely slow.

    This suggests two concepts. One is that
of a manager who allows the forest to vary so
that particular states come and go and recur;
and the second is that the recurrence of
desirable states depends on the total amount
of variation (the total number of possible
states), and this total amount of variation
must be bounded. This suggests the concepts
of ecosystem persistence within bounds and
the recurrence of specific ecosystem states
(Botkin and Sobel, 1975).

    A manager's actions can affect the
range of variation (the number of possible
states), the rate of recurrence of particular
states, and the average time that the ecosystem is in any of the possible states. A
manager can compare different policies on
the basis of these concepts. He can compare
the effects of different policies on the
bounds within which the forest persists, the
average time spent in desirable states, and
the time between the recurrence of desired
states.

    With jack pine forests, he would find
that a policy of removing all fires would
decrease the rate of recurrence of desirable
states in comparison to a policy that pro-
moted relatively frequent and light fires.

    The cases discussed in this paper con-
cern abundance and species composition of
forest ecosystems. Similar arguments can
be made for ecosystem processes, such as
mineral cycling. Similar evidence about the
linkage between change and stability, persistence within bounds, and recurrence of
specific states can be applied to other ecosystems. Such a review obviously would
require a much longer discussion.

CONCLUSIONS

Throughout the history of ecology, including the most recent decades, ecologists have tended to believe that the stability of natural ecosystems was metaphorically like the stability of a simple mechanical system. This metaphor has been used in a mathematically formal way in a great many discussions of ecosystem theory and management. In this paper I have attempted to show that this metaphor is incorrect and can lead to undesirable management policies. Clearly, if this view of stability is wrong in practice, it must be wrong for ecosystem theory. An ecosystem, like a jack pine forest, is more likely to persist on the landscape with certain rates of disturbance than with others, and it will disappear altogether without perturbation. The persistence of biota on the landscape is a central concern of discussions of stability in ecology and is clearly central to many ecological investigations.

I have attempted to show that we must abandon the concept of static stability in both theory and management of natural ecosystems. There may be a variety of alternative concepts, but I have suggested that we replace the concept of static or mechanical stability with two others: (1) the persistence of an ecosystem within bounds and (2) the recurrence of specific ecosystem states. With these concepts we can focus on our real concern: the probability that ecosystems will persist on the earth's surface. By recognizing the real nature of our concerns, we recognize that change and stability are linked together, and that the ideas of Lucretius and George Perkins Marsh can be brought together in a certain way.

LITERATURE CITED

Botkin, D. B., and M. J. Sobel. 1975. Stability in time-varying ecosystems, Amer. Nat. 109:625-646.

Botkin, D. B., J. F. Janak, and J. R. Wallis, 1973. Some ecological consequences of a computer model of forest growth. J. Ecol. 60:849-872.

Caughley, G. 1970. Eruptions of ungulate populations, with emphasis on Himalayan Thor in New Zealand. Ecology 51:53-72.

Cooper, W. S. 1913. The climax forest of Isle Royale, Lake Superior, and its development. Bot. Gaz. 55:1-44, 115-140, 189-234.

Craig, A. J. 1972. Pollen influx to laminated sediment: a pollen diagram from northeastern Minnesota. Ecology 53:46-57.

Davis, M. B. 1976. Pleistocene biography of temperate deciduous forests. Geoscience and Man 13:13-26.

Flint, R. F. 1971. Glacial and Quaternary Geology. New York: John Wiley and Sons, Inc.

Heinselman, M. L. 1973. Fire in the virgin forests of the Boundary Waters Canoe Area, Minnesota. J. Quat. Res. 3:329-382.

Holling, C. S. 1974. Resilience and stability of ecological systems, In Annual Review of Ecology and Systematics, Vol. 4, edited by R. F. Johnston, P. W. Frank, and C. W. Michener. Palo Alto, Calif.: Annual Reviews, Inc.

Horn, H. S. 1976. Succession, in Theoretical Ecology, edited by R. S. May, pp. 187-204. Oxford: Blackwell.

Humphries, R. 1968. Translation of De Rerum Natura, by C. T. Lucretius. Bloomington: Indiana University Press.

Jordan, C. F., J. R. Kline, and D. S. Sasscer. 1972. Relative stability of mineral cycles in forest ecosystems, Amer. Natur. 106:237-253.

Krebs, C. J. 1972. Ecology. New York: Harper and Row.

Lotka, A. J. 1956. Elements of Mathematical Biology, reprint. New York: Dover Publ., Inc.

May, R. M. 1973. Stability and Complexity in Model Ecosystems. Princeton, N.J.: Princeton University Press.

Marsh, G. P. 1864. Man and Nature, reprint, edited by D. Lowenthal, 1967. Cambridge, Mass.: Belknap Press.

Swain, A. M. 1972. A fire history of the Boundary Waters Canoe Area as recorded in "Lake Sediment Naturalist." J. Natur. Hist. Soc. (Minnesota) 23:24-31.

Walker, D. 1970. Direction and rate in some British postglacial hydrospheres. In Studies in the Vegetational History of the British Isles, edited by D. Walker and R. G. West. Cambridge: Cambridge University Press.

Dimensions of Ecosystem Theory[1]

R. V. O'Neill and D. E. Reichle

INTRODUCTION

The study of ecosystems, forests in particular, had its origin with early naturalists who classified the occurrence and distribution of a wide variety of ecosystems (Kerner, 1863; Schimper, 1903). At the turn of the century, ecologists perceived the dynamic nature of ecosystems--growth, reestablishment, succession, and persistence were themes that provided a qualitative framework for research (Cowles, 1901; Clemens, 1904). In the late 1950's the use of radiotracers initiated analyses of the fluxes of materials among functional compartments of ecosystems. In recent years systems analysis has begun to synthesize disparate principles of growth, persistence, and metabolism into a holistic theory of ecosystem function.

Recognition of the functional, energetic basis of ecosystem organization is commonly credited to Lindeman (1942), who developed the concept of the trophic-dynamic structure of ecosystems (Cook, 1977). This approach quickly led to a new theoretic basis for examining the structure and interconnectiveness of aquatic and terrestrial ecosystems (Juday, 1940; Elton, 1946). The trophic approach to an understanding of ecosystem dynamics soon associated the flows of materials between components of the system with overall ecosystem metabolism (Odum and Odum, 1955; Odum, 1957; Smalley, 1960; Teal, 1962; Macfadyen, 1964). These studies resulted in an understanding of the quantitative, functional relationships between producers, consumers, and decomposers in ecosystems. Unresolved were the interdependencies of mineral pools, biomass, and environmental constraints--and how ecosystems evolved homeostatic, self-regulatory mechanisms to optimize use and exchange of resources.

Large, empirical data sets on mineral cycles and energy flow did not appear until the advent of the International Biological Program. For the first time it was possible to compare quantitatively different strategies of ecosystem metabolism (Reichle et al., 1973a; Wetzel and Rich, 1973; Odum and Jordan, 1970; Woodwell and Botkin, 1970; Reichle and Auerbach, 1972). The first comparative analyses of forest metabolism over a wide geographic scale appeared in 1975 (Reichle, 1975; Reichle et al., 1975a).

This paper reviews and extends our earlier attempts at ecosystem theory (O'Neill et al., 1975; Reichle et al., 1975c; O'Neill, 1976a). We will (1) define the dimensions of a theoretic construct of ecosystems, (2) propose some elements of an ecosystem theory, and (3) where possible, compare the predictions of this theory with ecosystem data.

AN APPROACH TO ECOSYSTEM THEORY

A theory is a logical construct within which a class of phenomena can be predicted and explained. By use of theory, available data are synthesized and new research is focused with minimal predispositions and assumptions. Indeed, the ratio of experiments explained plus new experiments stimulated to assumptions determines the appeal of a theory. The dimensions of a theory are defined by the phenomena it seeks

[1] Research supported jointly by the National Science Foundation's Ecosystem Studies Program under Interagency Agreement No. DEB 77-25781 and the Office of Health and Environmental Research, U.S. Department of Energy, under contract W-7405-eng-26 with Union Carbide Corporation. Environmental Sciences Division. Publication No. 1355, ORNL.

to explain. In the present case, we focus on the observation that ecosystems persist, i.e., in the face of environmental perturbations, the system maintains its functional integrity. To understand what we mean by ecosystem theory, the terms "ecosystem" and "persistence" must first be clarified.

The Ecosystem Concept

The ecosystem is a functional unit. It is important to clarify this concept, because the term is used in other contexts in ecology (O'Neill, 1976b). For example, the monarch butterfly avoids the toxic effects of secondary plant substances by concentrating them in body tissues. In addition to avoiding toxic effects, this mechanism renders the butterfly unpalatable to predators (Price, 1975). The physiological mechanism is inexplicable if the population is viewed in isolation from its food supply, its competitors, and its predators. An explanation requires reference to the "ecosystem" in which the population occurs, but primarily focuses on the population.

In contrast, our concept of an ecosystem emphasizes general system properties, such as total biomass, productivity, and nutrient cycling, and minimizes consideration of taxa. The difference in viewpoint can be clarified by considering the ecosystem as it undergoes succession (Odum, 1969). Although populations change as succession proceeds, productivity is a property of the system measurable through time. Succession is not a sequence of different systems, but a single system which exchanges transient species and populations through time.

This concept of the ecosystem as a functional unit has analogies in community analysis. Root (1973) introduced the concept of a "guild" as a group of species that occupy "equivalent" niches in a community. Members of a guild have the same trophic function in the community and are seldom, if ever, found together. Each plant, or group of plants, may harbor a member of the guild but the specific species will differ from plant to plant. Thus, the guild has properties that transcend its component populations.

The Concept of Persistence

The phenomenon of primary interest is the ability of the ecosystem to maintain functional integrity when subjected to environmental changes. In other words, the ecosystem is stable in some sense of the word. Because of ambiguity in the use of

the term "stability" (Botkin and Sobel, 1975), it is necessary to clarify our use here.

It is seldom appreciated that the concept of stability depends upon definition of the system of interest. A system is stable if it remains within some bounded "state" or returns toward some reference (e.g., equilibrium) "state" following perturbation. The concept of stability strongly depends upon the definition of this state. If the system's reference state is defined specifically (e.g., species composition + relative numbers of each species + spatial arrangement of species), then every ecosystem is inherently unstable and every perturbation causes irrevocable changes. If the reference state is defined in terms of total biomass, then the ecosystem may show bounded behavior and be considered highly stable. Thus, an ecosystem may be either stable or unstable, depending solely upon the definition of its reference state.

Different definitions of ecosystem state are influenced by intrinsic values and can lead to dilemmas in management of ecological systems. In one respect, society needs the ecosystem for life support. The ecosystem's ability to absorb CO_2, release O_2, and process wastes is unaffected as long as the overall properties of the system persist. For these functions, species composition per se has little relevance. In other value systems, the ecosystem is viewed as a support system for values species, e.g., sports fish or wildlife. The dilemma arises when the ecosystem responds to perturbation by shifts in species composition. Such shifts result in the persistence of the ecosystem, but also may result in the elimination of valued species.

A classic example of such a dilemma concerns the construction of the Indian Point Power Plant on the Hudson River. The use of river water as a coolant should result in a stable response by the total ecosystem (Van Winkle, 1975). There will still be an intact living system in the river following the perturbation, but this stable response may be achieved by a critical species replacement. A highly valued sports fish, the striped bass, which uses the Hudson River as a spawning ground, may be replaced by less desirable species such as white perch. In this respect, the ecosystem is not stable as a support system for this valued species, and many elements of society regard this as an unacceptable alteration.

In the present discussion, persistence refers to total ecosystem properties (i.e., total biomass, productivity). The "state" of the system is defined by these properties, and a system is considered persistent or stable if these properties remain within reasonable bounds following perturbation.

ELEMENTS OF AN ECOSYSTEM THEORY

A theory of ecosystem persistence must contain a definition of the state of the system and its relevant components. Since persistence is a dynamic property, we stress the functional components of the system. At least three components are needed to explain ecosystem persistence: producers, heterotrophs as rate regulators, and a large storage component with slow turnover (O'Neill et al., 1975; Reichle et al., 1975c; O'Neill, 1976a).

Primary Producers: The Ecosystem Energy Base

The fixation of solar energy is essential to all ecosystems. Autotrophic populations provide the energy base which supports secondary trophic structure. To persist in an unpredictable environment, the system must be capable of flexibility in its energy-capturing function. This flexibility may be achieved by two alternative "strategies."

One strategy is to maximize resistance, i.e., the system becomes imperturbable, which results from producer organisms with very large biomass and slow turnover. In this case, response to short-term environmental changes is minimal. Mature forests illustrate this strategy. These systems are usually dominated by "K-selected" species. The resistance strategy requires that energy fixed exceed total metabolic needs, so that net energy is available for structural elaboration of large organisms.

The second energy-capturing strategy is that of resilience, i.e., a system maximizes its ability to recover rapidly in response to perturbations. To maximize resilience, the system consists of small biomass units with rapid turnover. Pelagic phytoplankton-based systems illustrate this strategy. Such systems are usually composed of "r-selected" species. Resilience can be achieved either by a collection of species which are resilient to perturbations or by a collection of species, each of which is relatively nonresilient, but together can respond to a wide range of perturbations.

Heterogeneity in spatial pattern, species composition, and genetic information are common elements of both resistance and resilience strategies. For the resistance strategy, the development of large biomass consumes time and energy and, therefore, is risky if persistence depends on a small number of species. For the resilience strategy, heterogeneity is required to ensure a large number of producer species, so that no single perturbation is likely to destroy the entire species array.

Few systems rely exclusively on a single strategy. Forest ecosystems include an herbaceous layer capable of rapid growth and reproduction (Taylor, 1974). Forests also contain saplings in the subcanopy strata capable of rapid growth if a canopy opening occurs. Lake ecosystems with a dominance of phytoplankton production also may contain a zone of rooted or floating macrophytes. Thus, the persistence of an energy base in a fluctuating environment relies on the opportunism afforded by the mix in that ecosystem of "fast" and "slow" turnover populations of autotrophs.

The mechanisms by which ecosystems establish a persistent energy base translate into competitive interactions among primary producer populations. A given number of populations, with limited light, nutrients, and water, will interact and tend to pack the niche space to support the maximum primary production that can be sustained by available resources. The ecosystem strategy is simply the result of the population processes.

Whichever strategy characterizes a specific ecosystem, a stable energy base requires high rates of material (or energy) processing. Odum and Pinkerton (1955) postulated that the ability of the ecosystem to persist is directly related to its ability to process energy. The larger the ratio of energy fixed to standing crop, the more resilient the ecosystem. The validity of this relationship was tested (O'Neill, 1976a) by comparing the rates of recovery after a 10 percent reduction in the standing crop of autotrophs in models of six ecosystems. The deviations from equilibrium were summed over time (25-year simulations), and each deviation was divided by the standing crop at equilibrium. The square root of the sum was compared to the energy processing capabilities of the system (Table 1). An increased ability to process energy is associated with a decreased index of recovery. The comparison (Table 1) indicates that recovery from perturbation is related to the capability of the ecosystem to process energy. This reinforces our emphasis on the energy base of the ecosystem as a critical ingredient in ecosystem persistence.

Storage Capability: Nutrient Recycling and Ecosystem Resistance

Despite strategies to maintain a stable carbon base, environmental extremes may disrupt the energy-capturing capability of an ecosystem. Since ecosystems are persistent, some alternative to the energy-capture component must exist to provide a reserve energy supply. This reservoir must

Table 1. *Comparison of ability to recover from perturbation (10% decrease in primary producers) with energy-processing capability.*[1]

Ecosystem type	Index of Recovery[2]	Power[3]	Reference
Tundra	7.9×10^{-2}	0.018	Whitfield, 1972
Tropical forest	1.4×10^{-2}	0.92	Odum and Pigeon, 1970
Deciduous forest	1.3×10^{-2}	1.22	Reichle et al., 1973a
Salt marsh	1.3×10^{-2}	1.28	Teal, 1972
Spring	1.9×10^{-3}	8.69	Tilly, 1968
Pond	5.8×10^{-5}	32.2	Emanuel and Mulholland, 1976

[1]From Odum and Pinkerton, 1955. The comparison was made with a simple ecosystem model (O'Neill, 1976a) quantified for each of the systems.

[2]Mean error sum of squares of deviations from equilibrium, divided by equilibrium values and sum over all compartments (see O'Neill, 1976a).

[3]Primary production/standing crop of active tissue.

Table 2. *Comparison of biomasses of detritus-based and plant-based heterotrophic food webs in terrestrial ecosystems.*[1]

Forest system	Country	Plant based	Detritus based	
			Animals	Microflora
Temperate deciduous[2]	USA	0.640	34.60	270.0
Tropical rain[3]	Puerto Rico	34.4	79.8	0.2
Temperate deciduous[4]	Belgium	205.0	300.0	---
Subalpine coniferous[5]	Japan	2.6	50.0	280.0
Tropical deciduous[6]	Zaire	1.0	74.29	---
Temperate deciduous[7]	England	3.0	360.0	890.0
Broadleaf evergreen[8]	Japan	3.0	1,680.0	---
Temperate deciduous[9]	Denmark	0.5	1,435.0	---

[1]All values are in units of kg ha^{-1}.

[2]Edwards et al., 1974.

[3]Odum and Pigeon, 1970 (assuming 5 kcal/gm).

[4]Denaeyer and Duvigneaud in Reichle et al., 1973b.

[5]Kitazawa in Reichle et al., 1973b.

[6]Malaisse in Reichle et al., 1973b.

[7]Satchell in Reichle et al., 1973b.

[8]Shidei in Reichle et al., 1973b.

[9]Thamdrup in Reichle et al., 1973b.

Table 3. *Nitrogen fluxes in terrestrial forest ecosystems.*[1]

System	Country	Inputs	Losses	Ratio input/losses
		$kg\ ha^{-1}\ y^{-1}$		
Temperate deciduous[2]	USA	13	109.5	0.12
Temperate deciduous[3]	Belgium	8.7	79	0.11
Tropical rain[4]	Puerto Rico	46	160	0.29
Coniferous[5]	Sweden	8	58	0.14
Tropical dry[6]	India	51	133	0.38
Mediterranean evergreen oak[7]	France	1.47	72	0.02
Montane coniferous[8]	USA	5.1	12.3	0.41

[1] Inputs include atmospheric inputs and nitrification minus denitrification. Losses indicate total N lost from vegetation through litterfall, mortality, consumption, root death.

[2] Henderson and Harris, 1975.

[3] Denaeyer and Duvigneaud in Reichle et al., 1973b.

[4] Odum and Pigeon, 1970.

[5] Anderson in Reichle et al., 1973b.

[6] Bandhu in Reichle et al., 1973b.

[7] Lossaint in Reichle et al., 1973b.

[8] Stark, 1973.

be large (perhaps compensating for its sub-optimal quality) and must exhibit slow response times so short-term fluctuations in environmental conditions would have minimal effect. Most ecosystems have a pool of inactive organic matter with the required characteristics of large size and slow response.

This pool of inactive organic matter serves as an alternate energy base. In fact, for many systems, organic matter supports a larger community of heterotrophs than living plant materials (Table 2). The advantages of stability in the food base appear to more than compensate for the disadvantages of difficult energy extraction.

This large, slow component plays a role more important than supplying energy -- it is fundamental for effective nutrient recycling. Large pools of organic mass provide capability to store nutrient elements; slow turnover maximizes the probability that elements will be retained within the system. The importance of nutrient recycling can be

seen in the data for nitrogen shown in Table 3. If elements were not recycled, growth of new tissue would depend solely upon the input of nutrients from outside the system (i.e., atmospheric and weathering of parent materials). Therefore, production would be reduced (by a factor of 0.5 to 0.1) to the rate of incoming nitrogen.

If our storage hypothesis is correct, we would expect soil organic matter and wood components to be more important as temperature and moisture conditions for growth become more favorable. Under these conditions, growth would more likely be limited by nutrient availability and there would be greater advantage to developing the organic pool for nutrient conservation.

A climate index combining temperature and moisture can be derived to test this hypothesis. Potential evapotranspiration, PE, is proportional to the sum of daily mean temperatures over $10^{o}C$. Average growing season temperature, G, multiplied by the length of the growing season, L, should approximate the summation. The exact relationship is given by Budyko (1956):

$$PE = 0.18 \; G \cdot L.$$

By dividing PE into the actual precipitation during the growing season, P, we arrive at an index of moisture stress. We combine this index with average annual temperature, T, to derive a measure of climatic conditions (O'Neill and DeAngelis, in press), π (higher values indicate more favorable climatic conditions),

$$\pi = T \frac{P}{PE} \; .$$

This climatic index, π , can be compared with the ratio of biomass of active leaf tissue to reservoir size (bole and branch biomass plus soil organic matter) for 16 stands in the International Woodlands Data Set (Reichle, in press). Testing this hypothesis for forests depends heavily on the Woodlands Data Set. This data set is composed of 117 sites which were involved in coordinated efforts to measure the structure and function of woodland ecosystems as a part of the International Biological Program. With the conclusion of the program, these data are becoming available in synthesized form (see Table 4) and represent a unique resource for the analysis of forest ecosystems.

Values of π are correlated with size of the hypothesized nutrient reservoir (Fig. 1). Although it may be an artifact of the small number of sites, the relationship approximates a straight line. The boreal forests lie toward the origin and tropical systems at the upper right, with temperate deciduous and broadleaved evergreen forests occupying intermediate positions. The comparison confirms the prediction that systems in more favorable conditions accumulate organic matter to store and retain nutrients.

Rate Regulation: The Role of Heterotrophs

The role of heterotroph regulation of ecosystem processes is essential to the persistence of ecosystems. Herbivore populations may exert more control than would be indicated by the small amount of organic matter actually consumed (O'Neill, 1976a). While consumption in forest canopies may be only a few percent of net primary production, the impact on photosynthetic potential can be more substantial (Reichle et al., 1973b). Episodic outbreaks of populations (Mattson

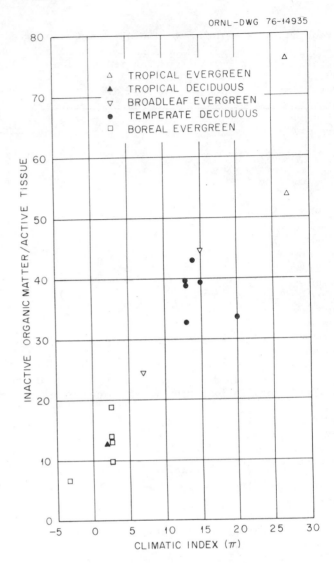

ORNL-DWG 76-14935

Figure 1. The ratio of inactive organic matter (branch and bole biomass plus soil top organic) to active leaf tissue as a function of the climatic index, π. The index is calculated as average annual temperature times precipitation during the growing season divided by potential evapotranspiration calculated according to the approximation of Budyko (1956).

and Addy, 1975) maintain ecosystem heterogeneity. Wiegert and Owen (1971) and Lee and Inman (1975) have also discussed the stabilizing influence of heterotrophs. The role of heterotrophs in nutrient dynamics has recently been summarized by Kitchell and others (1979).

The role of heterotrophs as regulators is apparent from the proportion of total ecosystem respiration represented by heterotrophic activities. Heterotrophic respiration may account for between 35 and 55 percent of total ecosystem respiration (auto-

trophic plus heterotrophic respiration)
(Reichle, et al., 1975b). Thus, a substantial portion of maintenance respiration
energy of ecosystems is accounted for in
heterotroph activity. While consumer
organisms may play a role in rate regulation
of producers, Table 2 indicates that heterotrophic effects are greatest in decomposer
processes. In a forest ecosystem, 95 percent of total heterotrophic respiration is
contributed by decomposers (Reichle et al.,
1975b).

Decomposer organisms increase the rate
of release of nutrients from organic matter
above that of simple physiochemical processes. While this increase may be un-
important for highly mobile elements, it is
critical for nutrients tightly bound in
organic tissue (e.g., nitrogen). Simple
increase in release rates, however, is insufficient for ecosystem utilization, since
the rate of release must be commensurate
with the ability of soil and roots to absorb
the nutrients. If the release is too slow,
the demands of plant growth are not met.
If the release is too rapid, much of the
nutrient could be lost from the system by
leaching. Thus, the heterotroph community
performs an important function in controlling the fluctuations in the rate of release.
This concept of control is important to
understanding the complexity of interactions
within the decomposer community, particularly the interactions of microflora and
saprophagous animals.

The evolutionary mechanisms resulting
in the nutrient control system can be easily
envisioned. Mortality of plants provides
an energy base which can be exploited by
animal populations. Those populations
which evolved saprophagy, possibly to avoid
competition with herbivores, begin to interact with the microbial opportunists already
present in the dead organic matter. The
resulting interaction stabilizes nutrient
releases and results in more efficient
recycling. Controlled nutrient availability
permits sustained plant productivity and
continued inputs of dead organic matter.
The result is a gradual buildup of the
stable organic matter food base.

In contrast to the view presented here,
consumers have often been considered
simply as consuming excess production and
playing a minor role in the maintenance and
persistence of the ecosystem. If such a
view were correct, then the biomass of
heterotrophs should be directly related to
the productivity or energy input into the
system, or else to the productivity rate or
energy input per unit of autotrophic standing crop. Figures 2 and 3 demonstrate that
this relationship does not hold.

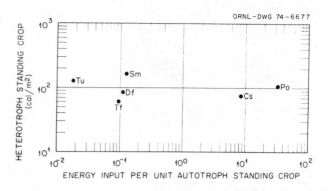

Figure 2. Heterotroph biomass as a function
of net primary production per unit plant
biomass. Data from O'Neill, 1976a. The
six points represent ecosystem types:
Tu: tundra; Po: pond; Sm: salt marsh;
Df: deciduous forest; Cs: cone spring;
Tf: tropical forest. References to the
original articles are given in Table 1.

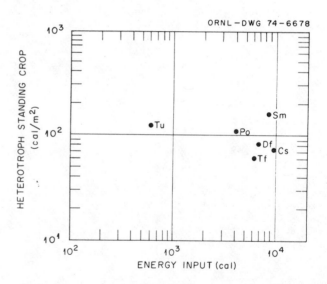

Figure 3. Heterotroph biomass as a function
of net primary production. A key to the
abbreviations is given in the legend to
Figure 2. References to the original data
are given in Table 1.

Table 4. Forest characteristics taken from the International Biological Program, Woodlands Data Set (Reichle, 1979). Forest classification is taken from Burgess (1979). Means were calculated for stands more than 50 years old. Outliers were eliminated from the calculation if they were more than 2 standard deviations from the mean.

| | BOREAL | | TEMPERATE | | | | | |
| | Needle-leaved | | Broad-leaved | | | | Needle-leaved | |
Characteristics	Evergreen (Plantation)	Evergreen (Natural)	Deciduous (Beech)	Deciduous (Natural)	Evergreen (Natural)	Evergreen (Plantation)	Evergreen (Natural)	Deciduous (Plantation)
Number of sites	5	9	9	19	1	5	5	1
Mean temperature (°C)	6.6	0.25	7.4	9.9	21.5	13.6	6.1	10.2
Mean precipitation (mm)	913	514	1073	917	2630	1338	935	1806
Leaf area index		7.6	5.2	5.2	6.0		8.8	6.7
Basal area ($m^2 ha^{-1}$)	46.2	32.8	30.6	23.7	47.9	34.5	68.8	37.3
Stand height (m)	25.8	17.2	23.9	20.8	12	15	21	19.4
Aboveground biomass ($g\ m^{-2}$)	24452	13917	25123	17352	19328	11918	21437	16938
Aboveground productivity ($g\ m^{-2}\ y^{-1}$)	1128	516	1218	918	1368	1249	1159	939
Leaf biomass ($g\ m^{-2}$)	1371	964	334	350	770	647	932	359
Wood biomass ($g\ m^{-2}$)	23081	12443	24686	16249	18558	11249	22496	16080
Ratio branch/bole biomass	0.13	0.18	0.30	0.27	0.36	0.24	0.37	0.11
Ratio bark/bole biomass	0.09	0.07	0.05			0.15		
Wood productivity ($g\ m^{-2}\ y^{-1}$)	699	135	777	359	983	743	382	580
Ratio branch/bole productivity	0.22	0.11	0.34	0.50		0.23	0.57	
Root biomass ($g\ m^{-2}$)	6005	3810	3842	3799		3116		3794
Leaf litterfall ($g\ m^{-2}\ y^{-1}$)	344	230	308	342	385	348	201	359

Table 4. *Forest characteristics taken from the International Biological Program, Woodlands Data Set (Reichle, 1979). Forest classification is taken from Burgess (1979). Means were calculated for stands more than 50 years old. Outliers were eliminated from the calculation if they were more than 2 standard deviations from the mean.*

Characteristics	TROPICAL			MEDITERRANEAN
	Deciduous (Plantation)	Broad-leaved Deciduous (Plantation)	Evergreen (Natural)	Broad-leaved Evergreen (Natural)
Number of sites	14	2	4	3
Mean temperature (°C)	27.5		26.5	12.9
Mean precipitation (mm)	1158	1058	1851	908
Leaf area index	9.2		8.9	4.3
Basal area ($m^2 ha^{-1}$)	29.4	26.3	29.8	41.3
Stand height (m)	14.3	13.8	37.8	17.1
Aboveground biomass ($g\ m^{-2}$)	15200	17200	43266	28753
Aboveground productivity ($g\ m^{-2}\ y^{-1}$)	1631	1304	1549	748
Leaf biomass ($g\ m^{-2}$)	834			694
Wood biomass ($g\ m^{-2}$)	14355	16494	37126	27825
Ratio branch/bole biomass	0.16	0.41	0.27	0.10
Ratio bark/bole biomass				0.19
Wood productivity ($g\ m^{-2}\ y^{-1}$)	1009	747		
Ratio branch/bole productivity				0.44
Root biomass ($g\ m^{-2}$)	3459	2908		
Leaf litterfall ($g\ m^{-2}\ y^{-1}$)	639	496	654	217

If heterotrophs actively participate in the functional dynamics of the system and play a role in rate regulation, we would expect that greater heterotrophic biomass would be supported per unit of autotrophic biomass as the need for regulation increased. That is, as the potential for rapid fluctuations in autotroph biomass increases, the need for rate regulation also increases. O'Neill (1976a) found this relationship by comparing different ecosystems ranging from tundra through forests to pond ecosystems. This hypothesis can also be tested with data summarized by Whittaker and Likens (1973). Figure 4 (from O'Neill and DeAngelis, in press) clearly shows that as turnover times (total above-ground biomass/net primary production) increases, the heterotroph/autotroph ratio decreases.

Figure 5 shows that the expected relationship also exists for four of the Woodlands Data Set sites (Table 4). These analyses reinforce the concept that consumers play an active role in ecosystems, and the more rapid the turnover of the system, the greater the heterotroph biomass required to maintain and regulate energy flow through the system.

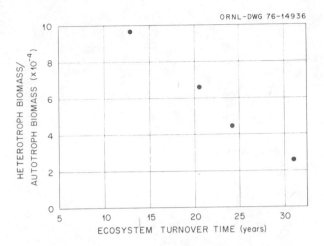

Figure 5.   *Ratio of heterotroph to autotroph biomass as a function of total ecosystem turnover time with data from the Woodlands Data Set.   Only four sites have sufficient information to permit inclusion in the figure.   Calculations are based on aboveground biomass only.*

Population Interactions and
Ecosystem Dynamics

Discussion of the dynamic properties of ecosystems leads to a consideration of how these properties are related to interactions among populations in the ecosystem. Lindeman (1942) showed that the energy-processing structure of the ecosystem resulted in a layered trophic structure. Heatwole and Levins (1972) have shown that this trophic structure is more consistent than the taxonomic entities which compose the trophic levels. Levins (1974) and others have shown that populations can be stable only in specific configurations. Fager (1968), Evans and Murdock (1968), and Teraguchi and co-workers (1977) all found that species may change in different systems, but a basic underlying trophic structure appeared consistently. O'Neill and Giddings (in press) argued that resource competition among phytoplankton populations would result in relatively constant total production, no matter what the mix of species. These studies lead to interesting questions about ecosystem properties and underlying population configurations.

Populations competing for a limited resource, such as light or nutrients, are essentially functioning in a parallel configuration (Fig. 6). In this case, dis-

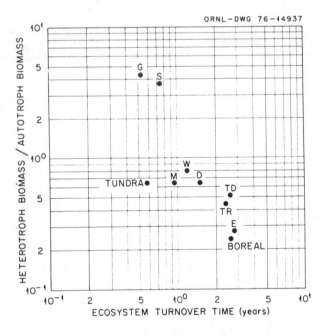

Figure 4.   *Ratio of heterotroph to autotroph biomass as a function of total ecosystem turnover time.   Data from Whittaker and Likens, 1973.   System turnover time is calculated as total aboveground biomass plus litter divided by aboveground net primary production.*

turbance to a single population would free other populations from competition, enabling them to use the available resource. Consider a system parameter such as total photosynthesis or total respiration which results from the summation of the activity of the individual populations. Since the limited resource constrains the entire system, the expected result of a disturbance to a single population is that the system parameter would remain relatively constant even though the populations changed.

If populations operate in a cyclic configuration (Fig. 6), then each population must process a resource before it can be utilized by other populations in the system. Such a configuration would be expected in nutrient cycling or in decomposition of complex substrates. In this case, a perturbation in any part of the cycle will affect the overall process.

Ecological systems can be expected to contain both parallel and cyclic configurations. Examination of Figure 6 suggests, however, that if the system is disturbed, some parameters (e.g., rates of nutrient cycling) will be relatively sensitive. To test this concept, unpublished data of Ausmus and E. G. O'Neill on CO_2 efflux and leaching of NO_3, NH_3, and PO_4 from soil core microcosms were analyzed. By comparing the variability in the time series of respiration and nutrient loss data, it was possible to test whether an ecosystem parameter which results from the summation of individual populations activity (CO_2 efflux) is relatively constant compared to a parameter based on successive processing of a resource (N and P cycling).

Three indices were developed to determine whether CO_2 efflux was less variable through time than nutrient loss. The first index was the coefficient of variation (standard deviation divided by the mean for the entire time series). Table 5 shows that the coefficient of variation was smaller for the respiration rates in all replicates.

A second index, Z, is given by

$$Z = \frac{100}{n} \sum_{i=1}^{n} \frac{X_i - X_{i+1}}{\min (X_i, X_{i+1})}$$

where X_i is the ith observation, n is the total number of observations, and min ( ) indicates that the smaller of the two values X_i and X_{i+1} was taken as the divisor. Z measures the average percentage difference between successive measurements. Table 5 shows that Z was always lower for the CO_2 efflux data.

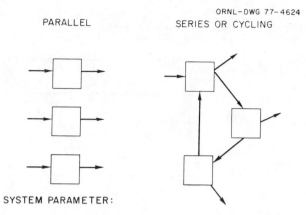

PARALLEL   SERIES OR CYCLING

SYSTEM PARAMETER:

ENERGY FLOW   NUTRIENT CYCLING
(e.g. TOTAL RESPIRATION)   (e.g. NUTRIENT LEACHING)

Figure 6. Two possible configurations for population interactions. The parallel configuration corresponds to populations in the same trophic level, performing similar ecosystem functions and interacting with each other primarily through a limited resource. The cyclic configuration might correspond to populations involved in cycling of a nutrient or breakdown of a complex organic compound.

The third index of variability, K, was the number of times that successive values differed by more than 100 percent. Table 5 shows that, again, K was always smaller for the respiration values.

Table 5 shows unambiguously that the CO_2 efflux was more constant in the microcosm system than was nutrient loss. With a single exception, the difference was always greater than a factor of 2 and frequently greater than an order of magnitude. Thus, the analysis confirms the hypothesis that a system property resulting from the sum of the activities of populations (respiration) is less variable than a system property which depends on the cyclic processing of a resource (N and P cycling).

The potential lack of stability of cyclic configurations leads us to ask whether one can predict the sensitivity of ecosystem processes based on their underlying structure. A sensitive process probably would involve multiple populations interacting in a cyclic configuration. Because cyclic interactions depend on continuity of rate processes, a perturbation may not be sufficient to eliminate a population, but it may be enough to move the system into a new, unstable state. Controlling variables might determine the magnitudes of flows between populations and the timing and synchronization of the process. Such an ecosystem process might be more sensitive than individual populations.

Table 5. *Comparison of variability in CO_2 efflux and nutrient leaching for six replicate soil cores.*[1]

	Replicates					
	1	2	3	4	5	6
Coefficient of variation[2]						
CO_2	0.24	0.25	0.27	0.24	0.27	0.26
NO_3	0.68	0.58	0.69	0.63	0.97	0.72
NH_3	2.86	2.62	0.54	1.30	0.88	0.55
PO_4	2.37	1.94	1.50	1.36	1.95	2.42
Z[3]						
CO_2	30	250	20	13	21	19
NO_3	876	291	106	1,404	148	113
NH_3	15,325	1,626	159	501	258	64
PO_4	3,850	1,391	1,200	425	1,250	2,500
K[4]						
CO_2	0	1	0	0	0	1
NO_3	6	8	4	7	6	5
NH_3	9	11	2	6	4	3
PO_4	9	12	10	10	9	15

[1]Data are presented for three indices of variability (CO_2 efflux N = 38; NO_3, NH_3, PO_4 N = 18.

[2]Standard deviation/mean.

[3]Average percent difference between successive measurements. See Equation 1.

[4]Number of time successive measurements differed by more than 100 percent.

Nutrient cycling involves a significant number of populations operating in a cyclic configuration. Consequently, increases in nutrient loss from the system might occur irrespective of which specific organisms or processes are being affected. Indeed, physiological changes in response to some perturbation might affect the rates and timing of processes in the nutrient cycle without detectable changes in populations. Shugart and others (1976) have suggested that a nutrient in soil solution (i.e., calcium) would have excellent properties as a monitoring point for overall system control.

This hypothesis has been tested with data from microcosm experiments (O'Neill et al., 1977). The experiment consisted of six boxes of an intact soil, each containing a red maple sapling approximately 2 m high,

with associated herbaceous ground cover. The surface of the soil was contaminated by adding litter collected adjacent to a lead smelter. This litter contained high concentrations of several heavy metals (Jackson and Watson, in press) that subsequently leached into the intact soil.

After nine months of monitoring, no significant differences could be detected in the tree growth (Table 6). However, mean values for Ca concentration in soil leachate were significantly higher ($p < 0.05$) for treated microcosms. Similar sensitivity of the nutrient cycling parameters were also seen in small soil core microcosms and in field sampling in forests adjacent to the lead smelter (O'Neill et al., 1977).

These studies do not demonstrate, of course, that sensitive population parameters

Table 6. *Population and system level parameters from microcosms of Emory silt loam soil containing Acer rubrum seedlings (values represent means ± S.E.)*

Treatment (Pb mg/cm^2)	Population parameter Annual branch growth (cm)	System parameter Ca concentration in leachate (µg/ml)
0	347 ± 42.8	6.6 ± 0.4
12	346 ± 67.7	10.0 ± 0.8

do not exist. However, it is not apparent which populations should be chosen a priori as indicators of stress. The experiments demonstrate that nutrient cycling processes are relatively sensitive and changes can be detected in these processes before significant increases in mortality of the populations are evident.

Heterogeneity as a Mechanism
for System Persistence

Heterogeneity, the final element of the theory, may appear in a variety of ways: diversity of species, spatial heterogeneity, or genetic heterogeneity within populations. Such heterogeneity is apparent in the natural system and the search for patterns in this heterogeneity is a major field of investigation for community ecologists.

In stating that heterogeneity is essential for ecosystem persistence, we do not imply any simple relationship between species diversity and stability. The complexity/stability question at the community level has been discussed, and it has been argued elsewhere (Van Voris et al., 1978) that there is no reason to believe that the relationship should hold at that level. Increased stability with increased numbers of species has been difficult to demonstrate experimentally, and theoretical studies (May, 1973) indicate that stability should be expected to decrease. On the other hand, Van Voris and others (1978) present data that suggest complexity may be related to stability at the total ecosystem level.

Heterogeneity can be viewed in terms of redundancy in function and pattern. Redundancy is essential so that any single perturbation is unlikely to destroy all capability for performing a critical function. If the system contains multiple species capable of similar functions (i.e.,

guilds in the sense of Root, 1973), environmental changes simply shift competitive advantages. If the perturbation is localized (e.g., forest fire), spatial heterogeneity ensures that some individuals will escape. In these and other ways, redundancy in the system prevents catastrophic consequences due to perturbations.

There are also detectable patterns of distribution which must be considered. Thus, the spatial distribution (clumping) of prey affects the rate of feeding by a predator (Pielou, 1969). The effect of patterning along a gradient on ecosystem stability has been investigated by Smith (in press). The patterning may not necessarily be spatial, since there are distinct patterns (i.e., "J-shaped" frequency distributions, Pielou, 1969) in the distribution of species abundances within communities. There also appear to be distinct patterns of interactions among populations (Teraguchi et al., 1977; Heatwole and Levins, 1972) in the form of underlying trophic relationships and guild patterns. Since these patterns are discernible within the system structure, we hypothesize that pattern plays some role in the persistence of the total system. Consideration of patterns of heterogeneity as a component of ecosystem stability is intuitively appealing to the ecologist but has received little attention at the ecosystem level of resolution. Many of our present environmental problems will require us to view the ecosystem in a broader context, i.e., as an element in a landscape or regional mosaic.

SUMMARY

Various dimensions of ecosystem structure and behavior seem to develop from the ubiquitous phenomena of system growth and persistence. While growth and persistence attributes of ecosystems may appear to be simplistic phenomena upon which to base a comprehensive ecosystem theory, these same attributes have been fundamental to the theoretical development of other biological disciplines. We explored these attributes at a hierarchical level in a self-organizing system and analyzed adaptive system strategies which resulted. We have taken causative relations previously developed (Reichle et al., 1975c), expounded upon their theoretical implications, and tested these assumptions with data from a variety of forest types. Our conclusions are not a theory in themselves, but an organization of concepts contributing towards a unifying theory, along the lines promulgated by Bray (1958). The inferences drawn rely heavily upon data from forested ecosystems of the world and have yet to be validated against data from a much more diverse range of ecosystem types. Not all of our interpretations are logically tight, and other explanations will provide fruitful grounds for further speculation.

LITERATURE CITED

Ausmus, B. S., and M. Witkamp. 1973. Litter and soil microbial dynamics in a deciduous forest stand. EDFB/IBP-73/10. Oak Ridge National Lab., Oak Ridge, Tenn.

Botkin, D. B., and M. J. Sobel. 1975. Stability in time-varying ecosystems. Amer. Nat. 109:625-646.

Bray, J. R. 1958. Notes toward an ecological theory. Ecology 39(4):770-776.

Budyko, M. I. 1956. The Heat Balance of the Earth's Surface, trans. by N. I. Stepanova, 1958. U.S. Weather Bureau, Washington, D. C.

Clements, F. E. 1904. The development and structure of vegetation. Bot. Surv. Nebr. 7:1-175.

Cook, R. E. 1977. Raymond Lindeman and the trophic-dynamic concept in ecology. Science 198:222-226.

Cowles, H. C. 1901. The physiographic ecology of Chicago and vicinity. Bot. Gaz. 31:73-108, 145-182.

Edwards, N. T., W. F. Harris, and H. H. Shugart. 1974. Carbon cycling in deciduous forest. In The Belowground Ecosystem: A Synthesis of Plant-Associated Processes, edited by J. K.

Marshall. Stroudsburg, Penn.: Dowden, Hutchinson and Ross, Inc.

Elton, C. 1946. Competition and structure of ecological communities. J. Amer. Ecol. 15:54-68.

Emanuel, W. R., and R. J. Mulholland. 1976. Linear periodic control with applications to environmental systems. Int. J. Control 24:807-820.

Evans, F. C., and W. W. Murdock. 1968. Taxonomic composition, trophic structure, and seasonal occurrence in a grassland insect community. J. Anim. Ecol. 37:259-273.

Fager, E. W. 1968. The community of invertebrates in decaying oak wood. J. Anim. Ecol. 37:121-142.

Heatwole, H., and R. Levins. 1972. Trophic structure stability and faunal change during recolonization. Ecology 53:531-534.

Henderson, G. S., and W. F. Harris. 1975. An ecosystem approach to the characterization of the nitrogen cycle in a deciduous forest watershed. In Forest Soils and Forest Land Management, edited by B. Bernier and C. H. Winget. Quebec: Laval University Press.

Jackson, D. R., and A. P. Watson. Disruption of nutrient pools and transport of heavy metals in a forested watershed near a lead smelter. J. Env. Qual. (in press).

Juday, D. 1940. The annual energy budget of an inland lake. Ecology 21:438-450.

Kerner, A. 1863. Plant Life of the Danube Basin. Trans. by H. S. Conard, 1951, The Background of Plant Ecology. Ames: Iowa State University Press.

Kitchell, J. F., R. V. O'Neill, D. Webb, G. W. Gallepp, S. M. Bartell, J. F. Koonce, and B. S. Ausmus. 1979. Consumer regulation of nutrient cycling. BioScience 29:28-34.

Lee, J. J., and D. L. Inman. 1975. The ecological role of consumers -- an aggregated systems view. Ecology 56:1455-1458.

Levins, R. 1974. Qualitative analysis of partially specified systems. Ann. N.Y. Acad. Sci. 231:123-138.

Lindeman, R. L. 1942. The trophic-dynamic aspect of ecology. Ecology 23:399-418.

Macfadyen, A. 1964. Energy flow in ecosystems and its exploitation by grazing. In Grazing in Terrestrial and Marine Environments, edited by D. J. Crisp, pp. 3-20. Oxford: Blackwell.

Mattson, W. J., and N. D. Addy. 1975. Phytophagous insects as regulators of forest primary production. Science 190:515-522.

May, R. M. 1973. Stability and Complexity in Model Ecosystems. Princeton, N.J.: Princeton University Press.

Odum, E. P. 1969. The strategy of ecosystem development. Science 164:262-270.

Odum, H. T. 1957. Trophic structure and productivity of Silver Springs, Florida. Ecol. Monogr. 27:55-112.

Odum, H. T., and E. P. Odum. 1955. Trophic structure and productivity of a windward coral reef community at Eniwetok Atoll. Ecol. Monogr. 25:291-320.

Odum, H. T., and C. F. Jordan. 1970. Metabolism and evapotranspiration of the lower forest in a giant plastic cylinder. In A Tropical Rain Forest, edited by H. T. Odum and R. F. Pigeon, pp. I165-I190. USAEC, Division of Technical Information, Washington, D.C.

Odum, H. T., and R. F. Pigeon, eds. 1970. A Tropical Rain Forest. USAEC, Division of Technical Information, Washington, D. C.

Odum, H. T., and R. C. Pinkerton. 1955. Time's speed regulator, the optimum efficiency for maximum power output in physical and biological systems. Amer. Sci. 43:331-343.

O'Neill, R. V. 1976a. Ecosystem persistence and heterotrophic regulation. Ecology 57:1244-1253.

O'Neill, R. V. 1976b. Paradigms of ecosystem analysis. In Ecological Theory and Ecosystem Models, edited by S. A. Levin, pp. 16-20. Office of Ecosystem Studies, The Institute of Ecology.

O'Neill, R. V., W. F. Harris, B. S. Ausmus, and D. E. Reichle. 1975. A theoretical basis for ecosystem analysis with particular reference to element cycling. In Mineral Cycling in Southeastern Ecosystems, edited by F. G. Howell, J. B. Gentry, and M. H. Smith, pp. 28-40. ERDA Symp. Series (CONF-740513).

O'Neill, R. V., B. S. Ausmus, D. R. Jackson, R. I. Van Hook, P. Van Voris, C. Washburne, and A. P. Watson. 1977. Monitoring terrestrial ecosystems by analysis of nutrient export. Water, Air, and Soil Pollution 8:271-277.

O'Neill, R. V., and D. L. DeAngelis. Comparative analysis of forest ecosystems. In International Woodlands Synthesis Volume, edited by D. E. Reichle. Cambridge University Press (in press).

O'Neill, R. V., and J. M. Giddings. Population interactions and ecosystem function. In Systems Analysis of Ecosystems, edited by G. S. Innis and R. V. O'Neill. Fairland, Md: Internat. Coop. Publ. House (in press).

Pielou, E. C. 1969. An Introduction to Mathematical Ecology. New York: Wiley-Interscience.

Price, P. W. 1975. Insect Ecology. New York: John Wiley and Sons, Inc.

Reichle, D. E. 1975. Advances in ecosystem analyses. BioScience 25:257-264.

Reichle, D. E., ed. International Woodlands Synthesis Volume. Cambridge University Press (in press).

Reichle, D. E., and S. I. Auerbach. 1972. Analysis of ecosystems. In Challenging Biological Problems, edited by J. A. Behnke, pp. 260-280. New York: Oxford Press.

Reichle, D. E., B. E. Dinger, N. T. Edwards, W. F. Harris, and P. Sollins. 1973a. Carbon flow and storage in a forest ecosystem. In Carbon and the Biosphere, Proc. 24th Brookhaven Sym. on Biology (CONF-720510), edited by G.M. Woodwell and E.V. Pecan, pp. 345-365. Springfield, Va.: National Technical Information Service.

Reichle, D. E., R. V. O'Neill, and J. S. Olson, eds. 1973b. Modeling Forest Ecosystems. EDFB/IBP-73/7. Oak Ridge National Lab., Oak Ridge, Tenn.

Reichle, D. E., J. F. Franklin, and D. W. Goodall. 1975a. _Productivity of World Ecosystems_. Washington, D.C.: National Academy of Sciences.

Reichle, D. E., J. F. McBrayer, and B. S. Ausmus. 1975b. Ecological energetics of decomposers in a deciduous forest. In _Proc. 5th Internatl. Colloquia of Soil Zoology_, Prague, Czechoslovakia, October 1973.

Reichle, D. E., R. V. O'Neill, and W. F. Harris. 1975c. Principles of energy and material exchange in ecosystems. In _Unifying Concepts in Ecology_, edited by W. H. van Dobben and R. H. Lowe-Connell, pp. 27-43. The Hague: Junk.

Root, R. B. 1973. Organization of plant-arthropod associations in simple and diverse habitats: the fauna of collards (_Brassica oleracea_). Ecol. Monogr. 43:95-124.

Schimper, A. F. W. 1903. _Plant Geography upon a Physiological Basis_. Oxford, U.K.: Clarendon Press.

Shugart, H. H., D. E. Reichle, N. T. Edwards, and J. R. Kercher. 1976. A model of calcium-cycling in an East Tennessee _Liriodendron_ forest: Model structure, parameters, and analysis in the frequency domain. Ecology 57:99-109.

Smith, O. L. The influence of environmental gradients on ecosystem stability. Amer. Nat. (in press).

Stark, N. 1973. _Nutrient Cycling in a Jeffrey Pine Ecosystem_. Institute for Microbiology, University of Montana, Missoula.

Taylor, F. G., Jr. 1974. Phenodynamics of production in a mesic deciduous forest. In _Phenology and Seasonality Modeling_, edited by H. Lieth, pp. 237-254. New York: Springer-Verlag.

Teal, J. M. 1962. Energy flow in the salt marsh ecosystem of Georgia. Ecology 43:614-624.

Teraguchi, S., M. Teraguchi, and R. Upchurch. 1977. Structure and development of insect communities in an Ohio old-field. Environ. Entomol. 6:247-257.

Tilly, L. J. 1968. The structure and dynamics of Cone Spring. Ecol. Monogr. 38:269-197.

Van Voris, P., R. V. O'Neill, H. H. Shugart, and W. R. Emanuel. 1978. Functional complexity and ecosystem stability. Oak Ridge National Lab. Rep. ORNL/TM-6199. Oak Ridge, Tenn.

Van Winkle, W. 1975. The application of computers in an assessment of the environmental impact of power plants on an aquatic ecosystem. In _Proc. of Conf. on Computer Support of Environmental Science and Analysis_, pp. 85-108. Albuquerque: ERDA.

Wetzel, R. G., and P. H. Rich. 1973. Carbon in freshwater systems. In _Carbon and the Biosphere_, Proc. 24th Brookhaven Symp. on Biology (CONF-720510), edited by G. M. Woodwell and E. V. Pecan, pp. 241-263. Springfield, Va.: National Technical Information Service.

Whitfield, D. W. A. 1972. Systems analysis. In _Devon Island IBP Project, High Arctic Ecosystem_, edited by L. C. Bliss, pp. 392-409. Dept. of Botany, University of Alberta, Edmonton.

Whittaker, R. H., and G. E. Likens. 1973. Carbon in the biota. In _Carbon and the Biosphere_, Proc. 24th Brookhaven Symp. on Biology (CONF-720510), edited by G. M. Woodwell and E. Pecan, pp. 281-300. Springfield, Va.: National Technical Information Service.

Wiegert, R. G., and D. F. Owen. 1971. Trophic structure, available resources and population density in terrestrial vs. aquatic ecosystems. J. Theoret. Biol. 30:69-81.

Witkamp, M. 1971. Soils as components of ecosystems. Ann. Rev. Ecol. Syst. 2:85-110.

Woodwell, G. M., and D. B. Botkin. 1970. Metabolism of terrestrial ecosystems by gas exchange techniques. In _Analysis of Temperate Forest Ecosystems_, edited by D. E. Reichle, pp. 73-85. New York: Springer-Verlag.

Ecosystems over Time: Succession and Other Types of Change

James A. MacMahon

INTRODUCTION

Biologists discussing change in ecosystems or communities generally subdivide their discussion based on the time interval over which change takes place. Short-term changes are thought to involve both internal ecosystem dynamics and the effects of allogenic perturbations, both of which cause fluctuations in various ecosystem attributes (Rabotnov, 1974). Ecosystem change over moderate intervals is termed succession, while long-term change is generally defined as community or ecosystem evolution. For a more detailed presentation of the kinds of ecosystem change over time, see Major (1974).

Part of all change in the organization of the organisms occupying a plot of ground is caused by very similar and fundamental processes, regardless of the time scale involved. That is, the evolution of communities and ecosystems, ecological succession and short-term ecosystem or community fluctuation are all similar processes, differing only in the time scale of the observer's mental reference system.

To approach these complex anastomosing and overlapping relationships I shall focus on the part of the time scale which emphasizes succession. I will attempt to discuss succession in terms of its historical development as a concept, its universality, and details of the types of successional changes thought to occur, along with the causes of the observed changes. Finally, I will compare succession with the other types of ecosystem change mentioned above.

My definition of ecological succession, for simplicity, is merely the change in the biocoenosis (sensu Hutchinson, 1978) of a plot of the earth's surface over a moderate time period, i.e., tens to a few hundreds of years. Unlike many, I assume no inherent order to the process and no closely defined time schedule.

HISTORICAL OVERVIEW

Before the word "succession" had even been applied to biological systems, many observers referred to changes of plant species composition of plots of ground, over time. Golley (1977) mentioned a very early paper (King, 1685) which presented observations of successional change in an Irish bog without reference to the general concept or use of the specific term.

I do not attempt to totally review the history of the concept of succession here, only to point out that the process was so "obvious," especially where trees were involved, that ecological historians can interpret writings as far back as Theophrastus (300 B.C.) containing discussions of succession. Indeed, such empiricists as Thoreau (1860) used familiar interpretations of succession in a discussion of pines occurring in the hardwood zones of New England (see Spurr, 1952).

The formalization of the concept, by application of a term, may be attributed to Dureau de la Malle (1825). From 1870 onward, European ecologists implied succession in their observations of vegetation while attempting to develop classifications (Warming, 1909).

In the United States the work of Cowles (1899) expressly emphasized that, given enough time, vegetation would converge through succession to the same species mix within a broad geographic area. As Whittaker (1974) points out, this involves the assumptions that the end result of the convergence is (1) stable and self-maintaining, (2) the terminus of the convergence process, and (3) the characteristic and prevailing plant community in that geographic (assume climatic) area.

The result of these early studies was the presentation of a plethora of observational studies to verify the successional trends and the climaxes of various areas, particularly those culminating in forested sites in North America. Clements (1916, 1928, 1936) codified successional observation by developing a lexicon to describe variations in the process and endpoints of succession. His system used an analogy between the community and the individual organism, where succession was akin to the ontogeny of the individual. This approach was rapidly assaulted (Gleason, 1926, 1927, 1939; Whittaker, 1951, 1953, 1957, 1962). It is now fairly clear that despite numerous detailed data presentations, many workers have misunderstood the philosophical position from which Clements' arguments emanated (Johnson, 1979). For details of the early history of the concept of succession in North America and an evaluation of the various philosophies expressed, see Cooper (1926).

While in its extreme form the analogy between an organism and an ecosystem has disappeared from ecological thinking (cf. Morrison and Yarranton, 1974; Williams et al., 1969), there have been recent attempts to review the emergent properties (see Salt, 1979, for comment on the use of this term) of ecosystems over time (Margalef, 1968; Odum, 1969). Currently, more workers are considering succession as the outcome of interactions of individual species with the environment, including the biota (Connell, 1972; Connell and Slatyer, 1977; Drury and Nisbet, 1973; Grime, 1977; Horn, 1974, 1975, 1976; Pickett, 1976; Van Hulst, 1978). Thus, the concept of a general convergence to a single species mix, over successional time, is often rejected; for example, see the detailed study by Matthews (1979a) of 636 sites of known age. While these are more robust approaches, they hardly differ from the ideas of Gleason (1917, 1926, 1927, 1939), except in detail and mathematical sophistication.

Part of the intellectual underpinnings of older succession theory paralleled the development of the theory of evolution. Initially biologists were inundated by variety without seeing pattern. Then, when geologists developed earth science generalities, the light went on for biologists and they followed the earth science lead. Instead of a Lyell-Darwin combination as in evolution, ecology has its Davis-Cowles/ Clements symbiosis. Davis over a period of years discussed the "Geographical Cycle" (Davis, 1899, 1909), an idea which appealed to a geologist-turned-ecologist like Cowles, who applied this perspective to changes in sand dune vegetation.

Since succession occurs over time intervals of moderate duration, it has seldom been observed directly (Drury and Nisbet, 1973). Rather, most successional

knowledge is actually inferred from analysis of spatial variation in vegetation, where various plots supposedly represent different stages in a chronosequence. Such an assumption is obviously forced by the long-time interval required by many seres and the short observation period of most investigators. That this short observation period is a fact is humorously obvious from Horn's (1971) definition of climax as "...that stage when no significant change occurs during the lifetimes of several research grants."

After the word "succession" was first applied, the "concept" developed as an important part of a whole system of ecology by Clements. Despite the philosophical objections of workers like Gleason directed to the mechanism causing change, the cataloging of examples of succession from many situations was enthusiastically implemented. A gradual falling away from Clementsian views followed, replaced by the "ecosystem" approach of Odum and Margalef. Currently there is unrest and a search for a mechanism(s) to explain the phenomenon of ecological succession. Details of the ecosystem development scheme were challenged by Drury and Nisbet (1973), whose work renewed interest in succession. Contemporary workers have masses of detailed data (e.g., Bormann and Likens, 1979) that can be used to address successional questions. These data have permitted new models, both mathematical and verbal in nature, to be developed. Despite these developments, succession continues to defy careful classification into a meaningful system, underlain by known cause and effect relationships.

Throughout the rest of this paper I will discuss various levels of successional relations, from the world pattern of where succession may or may not occur, to changes in single plots over short time periods (tens of years). The history of some aspects of successional theory, particularly since Odum (1969), was consciously omitted in the terse treatment above and will emerge in these subsequent considerations.

WORLD PATTERN OF SUCCESSION

Even though many authors catalogued supposed successional changes in their favorite vegetation type, some ecosystem types seemed, on the surface, to be devoid of successional changes. Succession was most obvious on sites where the climax contained trees--whether this was in a temperate or tropical climate. On the other hand, succession seemed less obvious in certain vegetation types, most notably deserts and tundra (Muller, 1940, 1952). Since succession is usually characterized as a change through time of species composition and community structure of a site (see Pickett, 1976), then the <u>obviousness</u> of succession must relate to the difference in percent composition of species of initial and climax stages of disturbed plots or by differences in ecosystem structure. A common structural feature used to emphasize change in ecosystems is physiognomy or lifeform. This approach is implicit in <u>the use</u> of attributes to measure successional change such as stratification, size, and growth changes; see Odum (1969).

The recognition of differences in the obviousness of succession in different ecosystems is most common in terrestrial systems, where the majority of succession studies have been conducted. The same variation in the assessment of whether or not succession occurs has also been applied to aquatic communities (Blum, 1956; Wautier, 1951). The most detailed assessment of the obviousness of succession seems to be Whittaker's (1974), wherein he specifically

plots the position of different ecosystem types, separating those characterized by "differentiated" and "undifferentiated" succession (Fig. 1). He further subdivides the undifferentiated succession on the basis of his inferences about the specific reasons for the lack of succession (Fig. 1). The four he recognizes are: <u>Aclimaxes</u>, which contain dominants having generation times which are short compared to environmental change and which are in "incessant" community fluctuation; <u>Cycloclimaxes</u>, where "generations are timed to annual environmental fluctuations"; <u>Cataclimaxes</u>, which may or may not show succession, but where "generations correspond to irregular intervals between destructions"; and <u>Superclimaxes</u>, where "generations are long relative to environmental fluctuation" and where a dominant's self-replacement is more or less continuous, but the environmental modifications are small. These names designating climax "types" are not meant to be formal terminology.

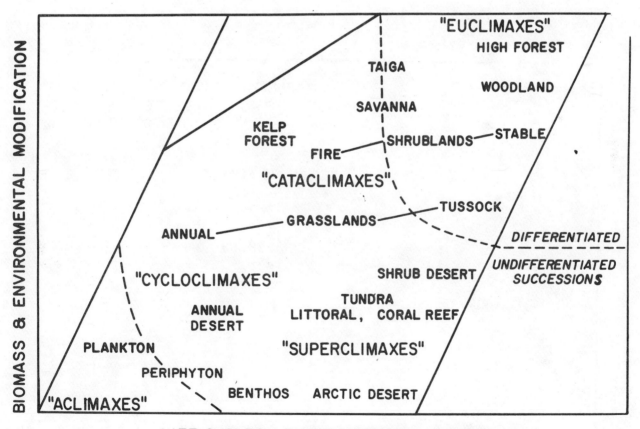

Figure 1. Whittaker's (1974) scheme relating characteristics of climaxes and successions to one another and other community characteristics. Effectiveness of the distinction of climax from non-climax, and utility of the climax concept, increase obliquely upward to the right (redrawn by permission).

While considering the lack of apparent succession in some ecosystems, I asked the following question: "What property of tundra and desert environments, two biomes where succession is often not conspicuous, is similar and might potentially be related in a cause and effect manner to succession of plant species?"

An obvious answer is that biomes are frequently differentiated on two-dimensional graphs, using mean annual temperature and mean annual rainfall as the axes (Fig. 2). While I realize that three or more axes of environmental factors give better resolution (Holdridge, 1967) and have even field evaluated such systems (MacMahon and Wieboldt, 1978), increases in resolution through increasing dimensionality are not required. Since tundra and desert differ so vastly in temperature, their similar low moisture regimes is one apparent common feature.

As mean annual rainfall decreases, the variance around that mean increases (Goudie and Wilkinson, 1977). We can conceive of evolutionary adaptation of organisms to extreme values of environmental factors (e.g., low annual precipitation) if these extreme values occur in predictable ways.

On the other hand, the combination of extreme values of an environmental factor and the unpredictable variation obviously taxes the adaptive suites of most organisms. In the context of succession then, I suggest that the only species that can survive in extreme environments are the ones that are already there. Thus, disturbance of a climax area opens up a plot of ground, but the only viable colonists are members of the same species mix; the result is auto-succession (Muller, 1952). Thus, low desert and tundra precipitation plus the extreme variability of precipitation may greatly limit the number of species capable of adapting to these conditions.

Specifically I suggest that, as a worldwide pattern, low annual precipitation, but more importantly its unpredictable variation, limits the species pool and their effects on the environment so that succession is "telescoped" (Whittaker, 1974). I believe that succession occurs in these areas and that the mechanism is the same, but that the results of the process are not obvious to casual observation.

Even in ecosystems where classical succession seems not to occur, minor species

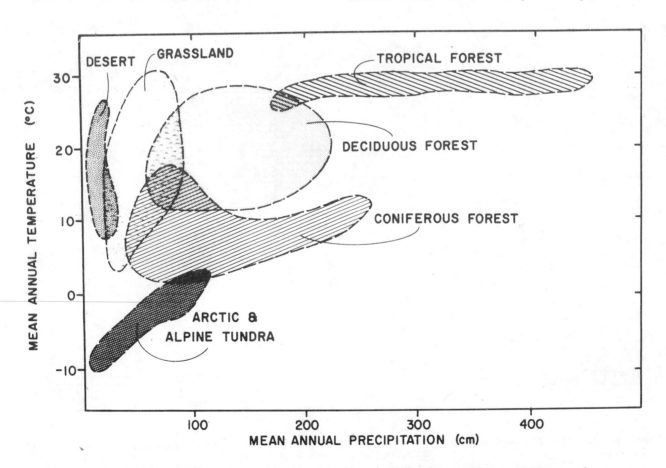

Figure 2.   Depiction of the differentiation of biomes on the bases of temperature and rainfall (redrawn from Hammond, 1972).

changes may take place following some types of disturbance. For some desert examples, see Beatley (1976), Shields and Wells (1962), Wells (1961), and the reviews of desert succession by MacMahon (1979), MacMahon and Schimpf (1980), and MacMahon and Wagner (in press), but these should not be mistaken for directional changes in desert species composition (e.g., Shreve and Hinckley, 1937).

To test the precipitation predictability hypothesis, Smithsonian world weather records (Clayton, 1944; Clayton and Clayton, 1947) were used to calculate mean annual precipitation and temperature for a variety of localities, as well as to calculate the coefficient of variation of mean annual precipitation. All localities were plotted on the background of a hypothetical, two-axis world biome graph (Fig. 3). From the position of that weather station on the biome graph, a biome name was assigned to each locality. Half of the weather stations used were checked for appropriateness of the biome designation by referring to published vegetation descriptions.

The mean annual precipitation data were used to calculate variance. Additionally, log transformed values of mean annual precipitation (+ 1 mm to remove zero values) were used to calculate variance, which represents a measure of intrinsic variability (Lewontin, 1966). All sites, with their arbitrary biome designations, were plotted on graphs of variance versus mean annual rainfall (Fig. 4). Since there are no differences in log transformed or nontransformed data, I present only one data set. The shape of the curve, the lack of data scatter, and clarity of the breakpoint are striking. More striking is that the biome types (desert and tundra) implied to lack obvious succession group together on the ascending arm of the graph. Those biomes exhibiting conspicuous succession fall on the horizontal arm.

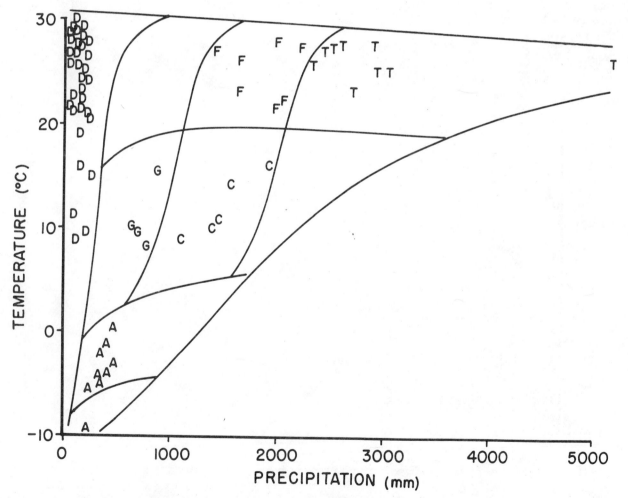

Figure 3. Plot of weather data (taken from Clayton, 1944; Clayton and Clayton, 1947) from various world localities on an overlay of biome limits (adapted from Whittaker, 1975, p. 167). D = desert; F = deciduous forest; T = tropical rain forest; G = grassland; C = coniferous forest; A = tundra.

I suggest that this separation, based on unpredictability of the annual precipitation, is in fact the cause and effect relationship explaining the conspicuousness of succession. Thus, there are limits to the number of species, plants in this case, that can withstand the combination of low and unpredictable water, and that these species, in the general sense, succeed themselves. The environment is never sufficiently moderated by the effects of organisms to permit a new biota, adapted to the changed environment, to become established. Conversely, in favorable invariate environments (equable) more species can "make it" and temporal turnover of species, each adapted to narrow subsets of the changing environment, is to be expected. Thus, succession of species will be more obvious.

The unpredictability and lack of precipitation are not the only factors determining the conspicuousness of succession. For tundra sites, temperature extremes may also limit succession in some areas. Some tundra sites show successional trends (Peterson, 1978), as do some relatively more mesic desert sites. I predict that the arrangement of such sites on Figure 4 would place those of most conspicuous succession closer to the origin and those of least conspicuous succession farther up on the ascending arm of precipitation variance. The overlap of the precipitation variance of some tundra sites with other biome types implies that some tundra sites should show equally conspicuous species changes--not necessarily physiognomically obvious. Additionally, the areal extent of disturbance and the presence of certain toxic compounds may also alter successional dynamics and enhance autosuccession. At the level of a global pattern, precipitation represents a surprisingly good fit and offers a first approximation of how conspicuous succession might be expected to be.

Succession is likely to be most obvious where sites have environments with two characteristics. First, the difference between early and late succession environments, in this sense the abiotic factors,

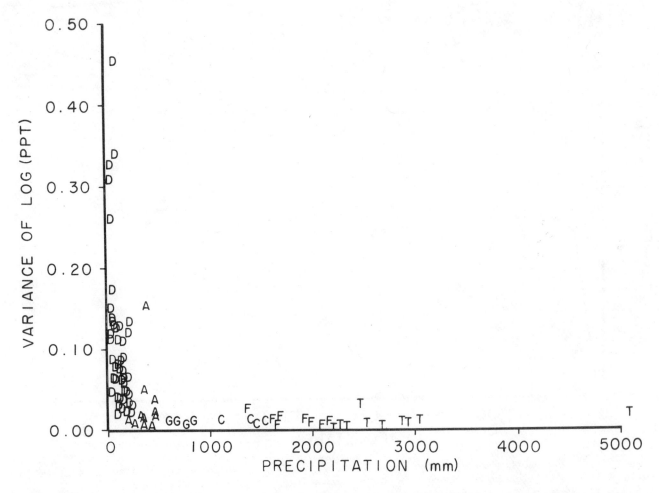

Figure 4. A plot of the variance, the log of mean annual precipitation versus mean annual precipitation. See Figure 3 for data and biome designations.

must be great. Secondly, all of the environments along the sere must be benign for organisms. These two conditions present ideal _conditions_ for species turnover. Acceptable environments permit or even foster high species diversity and a high degree of change (early to late succession) selects out a continuously changing mix of species over the time axis.

Thus, deserts or tundra, with their harsh environments, are so dominated by abiotic factors that the "reaction" effects of the biota on the environments are minor and relatively little environmental change occurs. Add to this the limited number of adapted species and succession is not conspicuous. In contrast, the tropical situation is such that the environmental differences between a clearing and a closed canopy are great, yet the differences are contained within the context of an equable environment so that the species turnover rate is great and rapid. This same relation, the steepness of the environmental gradient from openings to canopy coverage, has been proposed as a factor accounting for enhanced species diversity in tropical ecosystems (Ricklefs, 1977).

CHANGES IN SPECIFIC PLOTS DURING SUCCESSION

The biotic changes which occur on any plot of ground during succession have been the topic of literally hundreds of scientific articles since the turn of the century. Workers have documented changes occurring during primary succession (e.g., on granite outcrops -- Burbank and Platt, 1964), but more commonly those changes associated with secondary succession are detailed. Of particular significance in the American literature are the studies of two seres, one commencing with a fallow field (old field) which progresses to a forest-dominated climax, the other a prairie sere. I infer that such changes involve ecosystems (MacMahon et al., 1978).

Much of the history of the concept of succession, and perhaps even the basis of some divergent interpretations of the processes involved, may be attributable to the ecology of the ecologists, rather than to the processes themselves (Sears, 1956; McIntosh, 1975). The vast difference between Clements and Gleason may represent such an experimental bias:

"It is tempting to speculate how Clements' views may have been formed by his location, early in his career, near the center of the grassland (Nebraska), while Gleason,

located on the prairie-forest border (Illinois), arrived at diametrically opposed views. These were substantially retained by both men, in spite of subsequent extensive experience in diverse areas. Is there an imprinting phenomenon in ecologists?" (McIntosh, 1975)

This is a particularly important consideration because many of the "synthetic" attempts to predict trends in specific attributes of seral ecosystems are undoubtedly attempts drawing on a body of literature biased toward temperate forest areas.

Of the attempts at a synthesis directed to changes in communities over successional time, by far the most widely quoted work is a seminual paper by E. P. Odum (1969). Collating results from his own experiences and drawing on the information of Margalef (1963a, 1963b, 1968), Odum postulated changes in 24 ecosystems attributes which might be expected during succession from the "developmental" to "mature" stages (Table 1).

Many workers have failed to recognize that Odum, in fact, was attempting to demonstrate a parallel between a "model for ecosystem development" and "development of human society itself." I shall not discuss those parallels here; rather, on the basis of recent data, I will attempt to assess some of Odum's ecosystem predictions and, perhaps more importantly, show problems with some predictions in terms of their verifiability.

It is instructive to reread Odum's exact words, describing his view of succession at the time he wrote the paper.

"Ecological succession may be defined in terms of the following three parameters (i) It is an orderly process of community development that is reasonably directional and, therefore, predictable. (ii) It results from modification of the physical environment by the community; that is, succession is community-controlled even though the physical environment determines the pattern, the rate of change, and often sets limits as to how far development can go. (iii) It culminates in a stabilized ecosystem in which maximum biomass (or high information content) and symbiotic function between organisms are maintained per unit of available energy flow. In a word, the 'strategy' of succession as a short-term process is

Table 1. A tabular model of ecological succession: expected trends in the development of ecosystems.[1]

Ecosystem attributes	Developmental stages	Mature stages
Community energetics		
1. Gross production/community respiration (P/R ratio)	Greater or less than 1	Approaches 1
2. Gross production/standing crop biomass (P/B ratio)	High	Low
3. Biomass supported unit energy flow (B/E ratio)	Low	High
4. Net community production (yield)	High	Low
5. Food chains	Linear, predominantly grazing	Weblike, predominantly detritus
Community structure		
6. Total organic matter	Small	Large
7. Inorganic nutrients	Extrabiotic	Intrabiotic
8. Species diversity--variety component	Low	High
9. Species diversity--equitability component	Low	High
10. Biochemical diversity	Low	High
11. Stratification and spatial heterogeneity (pattern diversity)	Poorly organized	Well organized
Life history		
12. Niche specialization	Broad	Narrow
13. Size of organism	Small	Large
14. Life cycles	Short, simple	Long, complex
Nutrient cycling		
15. Mineral cycles	Open	Closed
16. Nutrient exchange rate, between organisms and environment	Rapid	Slow
17. Role of detritus in nutrient regeneration	Unimportant	Important
Selection pressure		
18. Growth form	For rapid growth ("r-selection")	For feedback control ("K-selection")
19. Production	Quantity	Quality
Overall homeostasis		
20. Internal symbiosis	Undeveloped	Developed
21. Nutrient conservation	Poor	Good
22. Stability (resistance to external perturbations)	Poor	Good
23. Entropy	High	Low
24. Information	Low	High

[1]Taken from Odum, 1969, by permission.

basically the same as the 'strategy' of long-term evolutionary development of the biosphere--namely, increased control of, or homeostasis with, the physical environment in the sense of achieving maximum protection from its perturbations."

Odum's superorganism leanings are clear in the above statement.

One or another of Odum's postulates have been criticized for specific taxa by various workers. General reviews of the model suggest that many of the predicted ecosystem trends are the result of the "passage of time rather than of internal control" (Connell and Slatyer, 1977). See general critiques in Drury and Nisbet (1973), Colinvaux (1973), Horn (1974), and Mellinger and McNaughton (1975). A myriad of studies have demonstrated excellent agreement with many of Odum's predictions for some components of some ecosystems, but herein lies part of the confusion concerning the robustness of Odum's postulates. There is precious little data including both plants and animals from one sere or even a broad taxocene considered over a variety of seres which is directed to testing the model. This is even true of the extremely careful and significant Hubbard Brook ecosystem studies (Bormann and Likens, 1979), which challenge Odum mainly on the basis of plant data. A partial exception is the work of Hurd and others (1971).

A group of workers at Utah State University has been attempting over the last five years to meld animal and plant data from a subalpine forest sere in northern Utah to address Odum's postulates in a coordinated way, using a site which shows the classic species replacement chronosequence. This is not the place to present all of the data generated from this program. However, some preliminary results, gleaned from my various colleagues, seem especially appropriate to the topic of this symposium.

I will discuss some of Odum's postulates, not so much to accept or reject them at this time, but to comment on problems associated with an ecosystem approach to the postulates. The details of the sites studied, the sere(s) involved in developing to Engelmann spruce forests in northern Utah, and the relation of northern Utah to the subalpine Rocky Mountains are contained in Schimpf and others (1980, in press).

Community Energetics

Odum divided his 24 ecosystem attributes into six somewhat related groups (Table 1). The first group -- Community energetics -- seems easy to test. While our analyses are not complete, the general results suggest that we accept Odum's prediction for animals, at least the vertebrates, and reject them for the plants (Fig. 5). This specific case of conflicting tendencies, i.e., whether to accept or reject the hypotheses, will be used to elucidate a problem of Odum's, as well as many other authors', ecosystem-wide hypotheses.

Since most vertebrates are relatively small and not embedded in the substrate, they are tractable research subjects and have been used for numerous laboratory and field studies of their metabolism and movements. Thus, for bioenergetics topics we can make good approximations of values necessary to calculate production/respiration, production/biomass, biomass/growth ratios, and even yield. In fact, for most vertebrates we can guess tissue caloric content or resting metabolism for an unknown species more accurately than we can measure field population densities for common species. Aboveground plant parts are likewise relatively amenable to study because they are sessile and generally accessible. The belowground component is much less tractable and generally represents anywhere from one-sixth (trees) to nine times (some desert shrubs) the biomass of the aboveground parts. Additionally, we have few respiration data for the whole tree on any species.

The size, habitat, and numerical abundance of invertebrates causes a problem because many of them are soil forms that are difficult to sample and difficult to know in regard to critical aspects of their natural histories--data which are required for energetics analyses such as foods, feeding rates, and reproductive rates. The result of these problems is that ecologists' assessment of successional community energetics is biased toward aboveground plant parts and vertebrates, especially birds and mammals. This problem is demonstrated in our own work by the lag in filling in Figure 5 for invertebrates and some plant components. None of this is to overlook many studies of invertebrates of various seres, including classics such as Shelford (1912) or recent studies of adaptive syndromes of species as related to succession (Cates and Orians, 1975; Duffey, 1978; Hurd and others, 1971; and Otte, 1975).

Even when dismissing all of the above data problems, the present results are still troublesome. The vertebrates (we have only

ATTRIBUTE:		Herbs	Trees	(Plants)	B.G.Inverts	A.G.Inverts	(Inverts)	Birds	Mammals	(Verts)	(Animals)	(Ecosystem)
Community Energetics												
P/R Ratio	approaches 1	R	R	N	N	N	A	A	A	A		
P/B Ratio	decreases			N	N	N	A	A	A	A	A	A
B/E Ratio	increases							A	A	A		
Yield	decreases	A	R	R				A	A	A	A	
Community Structure												
Organic Matter	increases	R	A	A	A			R	R	R		A
Species Diversity												
Variety	increases	R	R	R	A		A	A	A	A	A	A
Equitability	increases	R	R	R	R	R	R	R	A	R	R	R
Life History												
Size of Organism	increases	R		R	R	R	R	R	A			R
Selection Pressure												
Growth Form	r→K		A					R				

Figure 5. *A status report of an assessment of* some *of Odum's (1969) ecosystem attribute changes during succession. R = data suggest rejection of postulate; A = accept; N = not applicable; blank means data as yet are too incomplete to hazard an opinion. Notice that those categories across the top of the figure in parentheses are summaries of various groups to their left. For invertebrate columns, B.G. = belowground; A.G. = aboveground; The abbreviations in the attribute column are: P = total photosynthesis; R = total community respiration; B = biomass; E = energy flow, approximated here by growth.*

birds and mammals on our plots), essentially without exception, follow the postulated trends of ecosystem energetics (Figs. 6 and 7) as mentioned. But they represent a small portion of the total ecosystem complement, and they "handle," as a group, only a few percent and seldom more than 15 percent of the Net Annual Primary Production (see Andersen et al., 1980, in press). On the other hand, trees continue to have P/R (total photosynthesis/ecosystem respiration) ratios greater than 1; yield does not decrease in our oldest stands (≈ 300 years), nor in 1,000-year-old conifer stands in the more favorable climate of the Pacific Northwest of the United States (Waring and Franklin, 1979; see also Franklin elsewhere in this book). This is indirectly shown for our site by the lack of an asymptote to the litter/duff accumulation data (Fig. 8) and continuously increasing (albeit at a lower rate) leaf production in "mature" spruce stands (Fig. 9).

How does one integrate the data obtained from various diverse taxocenes to test the postulates? If the majority of species fit the supposed trends, shall the hypotheses be accepted? If so, Odum's postulates are correct for our site, i.e., most species, in this case, animals, follow the trends. Or does one accept or reject the postulates on the basis of the energetically dominant organism, the plants, in which case we would reject the propositions?

While a modeling approach might be of value in this area of study, we must find less expensive and less data-demanding methods to assess the postulates, i.e., a type of benchmark measure which would suggest ecosystem-wide status. For most processes these are not yet available, but clearly some interesting, and perhaps suggestive, diagnostic measurements are now available (see Waring elsewhere in this symposium for a summary of some creative uses of tree cores and their ecosystem-oriented interpretation).

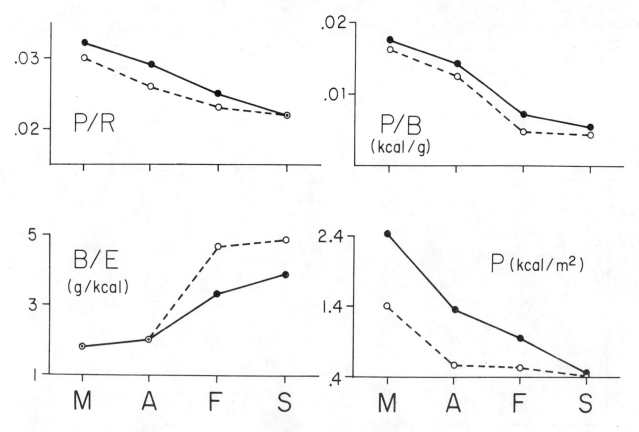

Figure 6. *Changes in the mammalian component along a spruce-fir sere in northern Utah (M = meadow; A = aspen; F = fir; S = spruce; B = biomass). Total energy flow (E) = secondary production (P) plus respiration (R). Solid lines and circles represent 1976; broken lines and open circles, 1977 (taken from Andersen et al., 1980, in press).*

Community Structure

The postulates about community structure (Table 1) have a mixed acceptance-rejection record also. Again, addressing particular taxocenes we can calculate species diversity metrics for variety or equitability components. Here, we find additional problems. While we have calculated a diversity measure (H') that follows Odum's predicted trends for mammals (Fig. 10), we had to make certain simplifying assumptions. It is difficult to pick one population density (number per area) and one species density (species per area) value to calculate an integrated seral stage diversity. The problem rests with the extreme seasonal flux in measures of diversity (e.g., insects, Fig. 11) or diversity components (e.g., insect richness, Fig. 12) where taxocenes of seral stages do not maintain the same position relative to one another. For example, in our study insect and plant diversity of aspen as compared to meadow seral stages switch seasonally as to which stages contain the higher diversity, or particular diversity components (Figs. 11, 12, and 13B). In addition to the sea-

sonal problems, the year-to-year variations in many of these same attributes add additional complexity.

All of the above comments can be made for what appear to be straightforward measurements, such as total organic matter. Clearly the dominance of trees in the "climax" provides more grams of organic matter in later stages, and thus one accepts Odum's postulates on the basis of accumulation of the inedible plant parts, i.e., bole biomass. For other plants (Fig. 13A) or animals (e.g., birds, Fig. 14), seasonal and yearly changes in the system components make calculation of "averages" difficult.

While ecosystem-wide data for various taxocenes, collected intensively over time and space, are difficult to integrate into single representative metrics, the data are valuable for considering some hypotheses. For example, on our site 1976-1977 was a "drought" year (≅ a 90 cm maximum snowpack depth) as compared to either 1975-76 or 1977-78 (220 cm). During the drought year bird species density (not species composition) and integrated daily biomass (Fig. 14) remained more constant in fir and spruce seral stages compared to meadow or aspen.

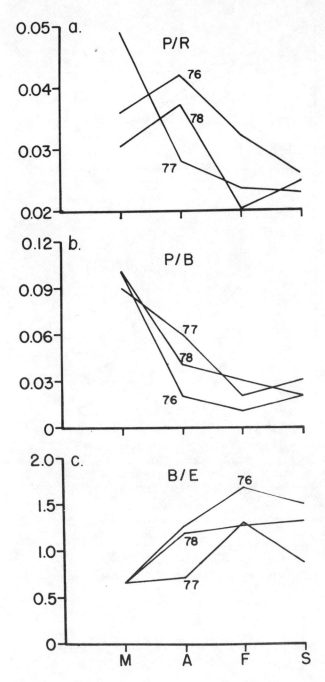

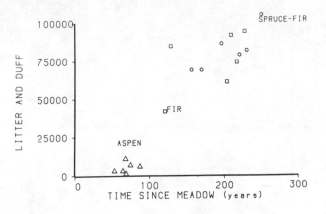

Figure 8. Total organic matter (kg/ha) in form of litter and duff contributed by trees to spruce-fir successional stages in a spruce-fir sere in northern Utah. Triangles = aspen stage; squares = fir plots; open circles = spruce plots (data provided by J. Henderson, G. Zimmerman, and S. Williams).

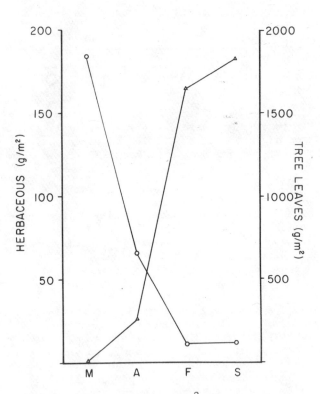

Figure 7. Annual energetics relationships for the avian communities in each seral stage of a spruce-fir sere in northern Utah for 1968 through 1978 as calculated by a modification (Innis and Wiens, 1977) of the bird energetics model of Wiens and Innis (1974). a.   Total annual secondary production divided by total annual respiration. b. Total annual production divided by total annual biomass present. c.   Total annual biomass present divided by total production plus respiration ("energy flow" of Odum, 1971). Note the general decrease in a and b and the general increase in c (data from Smith and MacMahon, mans. submitted).   See Figure 6 for abbreviations.

Figure 9.   Production (g/m^2) of herbaceous vegetation and tree leaves (aspen, subalpine fir, and Engelmann spruce) along a subalpine spruce-fir sere in northern Utah. M = meadow stage; A = aspen; F = fir; S = spruce. Data are for 1977 field season. Triangles = tree leaves; open circles = herbaceous vegetation (data from N. West, G. Reese, and J. Henderson).

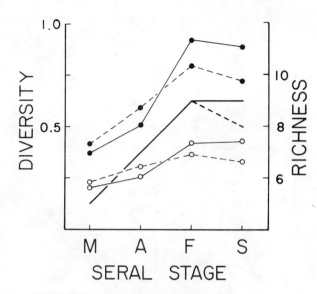

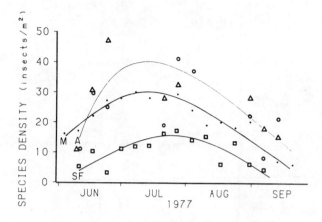

Figure 10. Changes in diversity and richness of herbivorous mammals between seral
stages. General diversity is measured as
the Shannon-Wiener index, H' (closed
circles), with equitability measures as J'
(open circles). Richness is represented by
the heavy line. Data are for 1976 and 1977
(data from Andersen et al., submitted).

Figure 12. Insect species ($\bar{X}$ no./m^2) in the
herbaceous vegetation layer throughout the
1977 sampling period. Trend lines fitted
by eye: A = two aspen replicates (△) and
(○); M = meadow (•); SF = conifers (□).

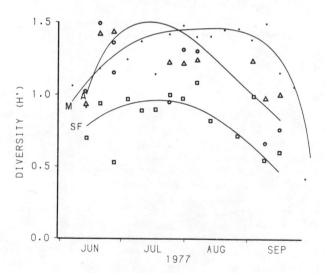

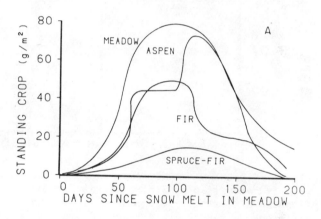

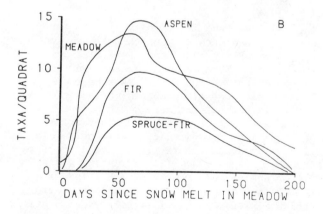

Figure 11. Mean Shannon diversity index
H'/m^2 for insects of the herbaceous vegetation layer during the 1977 sampling period.
Trend lines fitted by eye: A = two aspen
replicates (△) and (○); M = meadow (•);
SF = conifers (□).

Figure 13. Seasonal changes in the daily
standing crop (A) and species richness (B)
of the herbaceous vegetation of four stages
of a spruce-fir sere in northern Utah for
1977 (data provided by G. Reese and N.
West).

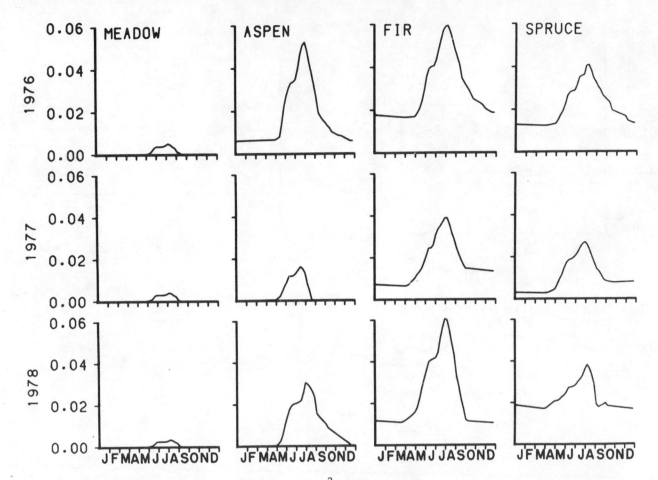

Figure 14. Daily amount of avian biomass (g/m²) present in each seral stage for 1976 through 1978 as calculated by a bird energetics model (Innis and Wiens, 1977). The meadow is significantly different from the other stages in all years, and the meadow is significantly different from both the fir and the spruce in 1977 and 1978 (Smith and MacMahon, in prep.).

The same was true for mammals. It is perhaps a better natural test of "climax" ecosystem stability than some artificial perturbations. Thus we might accept, on this narrow criterion and for these specific taxa, Odum's postulate about increasing stability through the sere. Other taxa, other perturbation types, and other criteria of stability might lead to different conclusions. Hurd and others (1971) found increasing species diversity (approximating a seral difference) but found that trophic levels varied in their stability response to perturbation, in this case a fertilizer augmentation.

Hypotheses about organic matter increasing with time, when based on trees (as are most succession studies), are uninteresting. We should readily admit that organic matter will increase if a plant is long-lived, inedible, and continues to grow. In fact, it is the organic matter persistence, in the form of standing trees, that has deluded us into believing that the climax is an equilibrium state. Part of the "stability" is illusory. That is, the "stable" forest is changing its plant species composition by significant percentages yearly. For example, Holland (1978) found that while species density per quadrat remained the same in two hardwood forest study sites, there was a 20 percent and 14 percent species replacement or turnover over an eight-year period. Even over relatively short periods, tree species are replaced, but the "forest" and the associated illusion of stability remains. See for example Forcier's (1975) climax microsuccession of Acer saccharum, Fagus grandifolia, and Betula allegheniensis and Fox's (1977) data on tree species alternation and coexistence. Most species in an ecosystem are varying widely, season to season, year to year, each responding, often independently, to the vagaries of a somewhat unpredictable world. It is clear to most ecologists that the vegetation we see may not be adapted to the environment we measure. For example, current conditions may not permit reproduction, merely persistence of resilient adults until their death and re-

placement by other species. Such persistence, or as Gorham (1957) termed it, "biological inertia," causes time lags in ecosystem change which confound ecologists'
analyses. A confounding relationship is
that between size and generation time (see
Fig. 1 in Bonner, 1965), i.e., larger
species, animal or plant, have longer generation times. Thus the largest, most obvious members of a biota take longer to
develop and turn over, while the smaller,
often more numerous, less abundant forms
may be turning over yearly or even during
shorter time intervals (e.g., microbes).
The actual variation of species composition
shifts will be discussed later.

The above discussion points out the
problem of addressing some of Odum's postulates; others are equally difficult to
demonstrate. In many cases, it "all depends
on exactly what you mean." And what is
"meant" varies from worker to worker.
Examples of these problems of interpretation,
i.e., the lack of specificity in the original model, are given for nutrient cycles

by Vitousek and Reiners (1975) and for
several of the postulates by Bormann and
Likens (1979) (see also Whittaker, 1975b).

Other Trends

In addition to postulates concerning
community structure and flows of matter and
energy, Odum also posits (Table 1) about
adaptive aspects of life histories, changes
in selection pressures, and a catchall
termed "overall homeostasis." Since 1969
knowledge of "r" and "K" selection strategies has burgeoned to the point where a
simple two-ended continuum of selection
strategies seems inappropriate either
empirically (Grime, 1977, 1979; Whittaker,
1975b; Wilbur et al., 1974), or even in the
theoretical sense, as in the outcome of a
computer simulation (Whittaker and Goodman,
1979). Similar caveats can be made to
some extent about other attribute changes.

In addition to our reinterpretation
and expansion of the "r" and "K" life

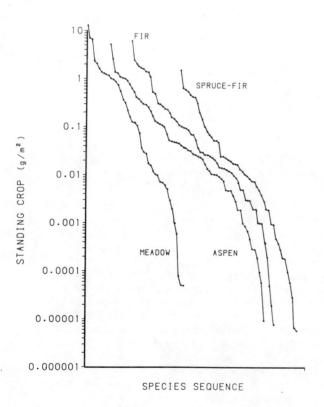

Figure 15. Dominance-diversity curves for
herbaceous species along the subalpine sere.
Log of mean daily aboveground standing crop
for each species is plotted against descending species sequence (data courtesy of
G. Reese).

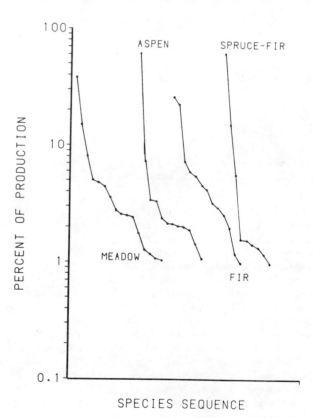

Figure 16. Dominance-diversity curves for
plant species along the subalpine sere.
Log of proportion of total plot primary
production (tree leaves plus herbaceous
shoots) for each species is plotted against
descending species sequence (data courtesy
of G. Reese, J. A. Henderson, and S.
Williams).

Table 2. A. *Number of species within each successional stage of a subalpine spruce-fir sere, adapted for various types of dispersal. (Data from D. Schimpf).*

B. *Number of non-anemophilous species within each seral stage in four categories of flower color. (Data from a subalpine, spruce-fir sere in northern Utah, provided by D. Schimpf and R. Bayn).*

A. Dispersal adaptation types	Meadow	Aspen	Spruce-fir
Animal	4	6	5
Wind	6	6	8
Other	15	10	10

$$x^2 = 1.99, \text{ n.s.}$$

B. Flower color	Meadow	Aspen	Spruce-fir
Red, orange, or pink	6	2	0
Yellow	7	7	7
Blue or purple	4	3	1
White	6	6	12

$$x^2 = .05 < P < .10$$

history strategy concepts, some other very interesting successional trends in life history traits have been suggested. For example, the rather standard species rank-dominance curves are turning out to be interesting in the context of succession. Whittaker (1975a), Bazzaz (1975), McNaughton and Wolf (1973), and May (1976) all point out how such curves move to the right over successional time. An example of this from our own data shows the shift where dominance is measured as standing crop (Fig. 15), but less so when dominance is measured as percentage of annual production (Fig. 16). Such trends seem generally true even though various forest types, including tropical wet forests, have different curves. The difference among forest types, moving from less equable temperate montane forests to tropical wet forests, parallels the shift (see Fig. 8 in Hubbell, 1979). This quantitative difference does not negate the qualitative similarity of dominance-diversity patterns in a variety of ecosystems.

There are also interesting trends (perhaps local, perhaps more general) in attributes of taxocenes within seral ecosystems. Some authors have suggested a succession from wind-dispersed to animal-dispersed plants (Dansereau and Lems, 1957). While this may be true for other systems, we could find no such trend in our data (Table 2A). On the other hand, we found a significant increase in white flowers and a concomitant decrease in reds and blues along the sere (Table 2B). This correlation adds to the growing body of data relating floral colors to ecosystem characteristics (Daubenmire, 1975; Moldenke, 1976; del Moral and Standley, 1979; Oster and Harper, 1978).

Recently, a general model relating plant strategies to vegetation processes has been proposed and elaborated upon (Grime, 1977, 1979). In addition to many other vegetation processes, this model describes the changes expected on a plot of ground during succession. The crux of Grime's approach is that one can classify

the strategies of vascular plants on the
basis of the "intensity of disturbance" of
the environment and the "intensity of
stress." Stress in this context "...con-
sists of conditions that restrict production...," while disturbance "...is associated with the partial or total destruction
of plant biomass..." (Grime, 1977). Grime
sets up a two-by-two matrix, representing
two levels of each factor. Grime terms the
low-stress, low-disturbance strategies
"competitive"; the low-disturbance, high-
stress strategies "stress tolerant"; and
the low-stress, high-disturbance strategies
"ruderal." For the strategy of high stress
and high disturbance, there appear to be no
viable strategies.

Grime suggests that the three strategy
types are the result of selection pressures
favoring these strategies. Using the short-
hand "C," "S," and "R" for the three axes
of a triangle, Grime (1977, 1979) shows in
a series of graphs, the positions where his
data suggest various plant types should
cluster. Figure 17 depicts, in a summary
manner, where various types of plants might
fit onto such triangular graphs.

Grime also suggests a possible path of
vegetation succession under different conditions of potential productivity (Fig. 18B).
A plot of data from our studies (Fig. 18A)
does not show clear-cut vectors. Rather,
our data suggest that early successional
stages ("M's" representing the meadow seral
stage) show a broad suite of strategies
represented by the vascular plants present,
and that as succession proceeds there is a
contraction of the spectrum of adaptive
suites present. These data should not be
taken as a critical test of Grime's model;
however, they suggest some alternative interpretations, consistent with existing
literature.

A reasonable interpretation is that
after moderate disturbance at many sites,
the environment is acceptable for the establishment of a variety of plants, representing various adaptive suites. As time
passes, and the environment changes as a
result of biotically mediated alterations,
only a subset of the original spectrum of
adaptive suites are viable. Thus, there is
an apparent contraction of the successful
plant types occurring on a plot. A point
similar to this was made by Drury and Nisbet
(1973), who summarize data suggesting that
many species, even climax forms, establish
early and are suppressed (not conspicuous)
until "climax" is approached. (See also the
relay floristics vs. initial composition
arguments of Egler, 1954.)

When trees are part of the climax,
their suppression (inability to establish or
ability to establish but grow only at below

average rates) early in succession may very
well be related to their lack of adaptation
to stress. Thus, other forms are more obvious until the trees are repressed in the
relatively more equable environments of
later succession. When individual trees
occur as early successional species, they
differ in many ways including morphogenesis
(Marks, 1975) from the same species in the
climax. This is not inconsistent with
Grime's approach, merely an addition of
detail. While Grime formalizes the role of
stress, Woodwell (1970) clearly approaches
the relationships of woody plants to stress
gradients in a way that is compatible with
Grime's original model (1977), but is overlooked in that article and the subsequent
book (1979). I will develop my approach to
Grime's general model later in this paper.

It is clear that some predictable
changes in vegetation and animals occur on
some plots of ground following disturbances.
Our ability to predict exact species series
and proportions of each species through time
is not good. In fact, I believe there are
reasons to doubt that we will ever be able
to do this very precisely. On the other
hand, the biological characteristics of the
sequence of organisms must fit within the
constraints of the environment and the
environmental changes occurring over successional time. Insofar as these changes
of environment are predictable and direc-

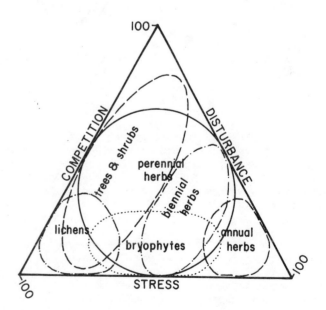

Figure 17. A model, modified from Grime
(1977, Fig. 3a-f), depicting the various
equilibria between competition, stress, and
disturbance in vegetation. Axes are the
percentage of each strategy. Plant "life
form" positions are approximated from
Grime's specific point data for a large
number of species.

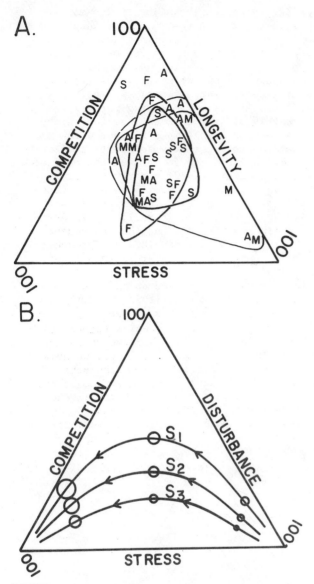

Figure 18. A. An attempt to place species
from a subalpine sere in northern Utah on a
graph representing Grime's (1977) model of
plant strategies. Data for exact positions
of species were derived from the literature
and from a questionnaire addressed to local
plant biologists familiar with the flora in
question. Positions are difficult to assign
on a three-axis graph, so data represent a
best attempt. M = meadow stage species;
A = aspen; F = fir; S = spruce. Lines en-
close only herbaceous species since the
three trees (aspen, subalpine fir, and
Engelmann spruce) cluster near the apex of
the triangle.

B. Grime suggested paths of vegetation
succession under high (S_1) to low (S_3)
potential productivity. The figure is
modified from Grime's (1977) Figure 4a.
The size of plant biomass at each stage of
succession is indicated by the size of
circles.

tional, so also will be the biological
characteristics of the component organisms,
without regard to their taxonomy. Details
of this proposition (shown in Fig. 21) will
be discussed later.

MECHANISM

The causes of succession, or the underlying mechanisms related to the change of
species composition of the biota, and/or
physiognomy of a plot of ground, have been
variously interpreted. Among ecologists,
succession is variously thought to be allogenic or autogenic in its controls, predictable or unpredictable in its consequences, and an important scientific theory
or a phenomenon of no value to generalized
ecological thinking.

Amazingly, Clements' (1916) idea that
the mechanism-producing succession was composed of six processes has been accepted by
some workers to the present time, despite
much contrary data (Colinvaux, 1973; Connell,
1972; Drury and Nisbet, 1973; Egler, 1954;
Gleason, 1917, 1939; Horn, 1974; McCormick,
1968; Niering and Goodwin, 1974). Clements'
(see 1916, 1928 for details) view was that
first an area was opened to invasion (nuda-
tion process). If the substrate had not
been occupied before, this was called primary succession; previously occupied substrates underwent secondary succession.
Once opened, an area was invaded by the
propagules of species (migration process).
He also clearly states the role of propagules remaining after the disturbance,
entities I term "residuals." The migrants,
being a somewhat random assortment of
species proximate to the opened site, had to
survive the conditions of that site, i.e.,
establish and grow (ecesis process). Resulting from the successful establishment
and growth was an increase in the size and
number of plants leading to competition for
various resources (competition process).
All of the activities of plants up to this
point, including deaths, had effects on the
environment, which changed various abiotic
parameters (reaction process), which in turn
favored a different set of migrants and so
on, in a mechanistic repetition of the
processes until the species admixture was
able to maintain itself (stabilization process) as a climax. The six processes described were grouped into three phases of
succession: initiation, continuation, and
termination (Table 3).

Clements' approach is so pervaded by
orderliness and laced with parts appealing
to biological intuition that it remains
represented, in essence, by one of the three
models of succession recently proposed by
Connell and Slatyer (1977). One model they

Table 3. Clements' (1916) three major
phases and six basic processes of
succession.

---

1. Initiation

    Nudation

    Migration

    Ecesis

    Reaction

2. Continuation

    Competition

3. Termination

    Stabilization

---

recognize is the facilitation model, which
is essentially the Clementsian approach cast
in the context of the ecosystem by Odum
(1969). The second (tolerance model) "...
holds that succession leads to a community
composed of those species most efficient in
exploiting resources, presumably each
specialized on different kinds or proportions of resources" (Connell and Slatyer,
1977; Connell, 1975). Finally, the inhibition model simply states that "...no species
necessarily has competitive superiority over
another. Whichever colonizes the site first
holds it against all comers" (Connell and
Slatyer, 1977). In essence, this is site
preemption by species which have long-lived
individuals or other biological characteristics leading to persistence. Figure 19
depicts the Connell-Slatyer model.

Recently, Horn (1971, 1974, 1975, 1976)
has represented succession as a Markovian
replacement process. Generally, his approach
is to assume tree by tree replacement as a
probability function of the stand composition, using linear models but also finding
interesting nonlinearities. Horn is not the
only one to use this general approach,
though others have sometimes not explicitly
stated the use of nonlinearities in the
past (Botkin et al., 1972; Leak, 1970;
MacArthur, 1958; Shugart et al., 1973;
Waggoner and Stephens, 1970) nor apparently
in the future (Van Hulst, 1978). I will
return to Horn's approach later.

Additional contributions to mechanisms
of succession have involved reasoning about
the role of life history strategies by
Grime (1977), as described above. Grime's
system emphasizes the identification of his

proposed strategies based on a number of
characteristics including morphological features, resource allocation, phenology, and
response to stress. While Grime reasoned
from empirical data gathered from plants, a
recent theoretical exploration by Whittaker
and Goodman (1979) produced essentially the
same three strategies. Grime represents
succession as a vector across a triangle
whose axes are degrees of his three strategies (Fig. 18b). Other approaches to succession emphasize adaptive strategies in
one sense or another (Auclair and Goff,
1971; Bormann and Likens, 1979; McNaughton,
1974; Newell and Tramer, 1978; Pickett,
1976; Pielou, 1966; Shafi and Yarranton,
1973; Tramer, 1975; Van Hulst, 1978).

Recently, in a very lucid presentation
of the data obtained during the 15 productive years of research at Hubbard Brook,
Bormann and Likens (1979) presented their
view of the bases of successional change
after clearcutting a northeastern hardwood
forest. Their emphases on the importance
of various factors in determining the
course of succession is not much different
from mine. I will include some of their
points in my discussion rather than present
a separate analysis of their data.

If one allows some "wobble" in applicability, one can represent succession,
using recent wisdom, in a manner not unlike
Clements. Such an admission is particularly hard for me because I have frequently
declared myself a staunch Gleasonian (e.g.,
MacMahon, 1976, 1978). For this discussion,
assume that I am tracking through time the
fate of a plot of ground, including the
whole ecosystem (biotic and abiotic components). Generally, I will write only
about changes in the biota, especially
plants, despite inclusion of the substrate
in the model (Fig. 20).

The model (Fig. 20) looks at the
states $S_{0...3}$ of the plot through time. It
must always be assumed that cycling can
occur back through a process, say $S_3 \rightarrow S_1$,
and when that occurs a new state exists,
S_1 , which I will not formally indicate.
See the caption for Figure 20 for details
of notation.

Since a system must have initial conditions I start, arbitrarily, at a point
where a plot has substrate available for
colonization (S_0). In successional terms,
this original state is the beginning of
either primary or secondary succession.
There is no qualitative difference among
plots which are to undergo primary as
opposed to secondary succession except that
secondary succession plots may contain
residuals, i.e., plant or animal propagules
(seeds, spores, bulbs, cysts) remaining
from the predisturbance period. There are

similar residual effects on the chemical
and physical properties of once-inhabited
sites. It would be hard to differentiate
plots on a mobile sand dune, which were
never vegetated (undergoing primary succession) from those undergoing revegetation.
Thus, to my mind the subdivision into primary and secondary succession serves no
useful purpose, except to define extreme
situations.

The importance of the residuals cannot
be overemphasized; their effects on the plot
might completely determine the vector of the
subsequent successional changes. The number
of buried viable propagules can be quite
high. In northern Saskatchewan, Archibold
(1979) found 456 propagules per square
meter; 87 percent of these were seeds and 13
percent were remnant roots or rhizomes that
produced aerial shoots. Tree species
accounted for 42.9 percent of the total pro-

pagules. Since there are differences in the
amount of viable seeds in different vegetation types (Thompson, 1978), the relative
importance of these precursors may vary
geographically and altitudinally. The
importance of the residuals is such that
Egler (1954) specifically referred to them
as the "initial floristic composition."
They formed a critical part of his discussion of succession mechanics, incorporated
successively into papers by McCormick (1968)
and Drury and Nisbet (1973), all of which
purport to deal with the mechanisms of succession. Residuals were pointed out as
especially important at Hubbard Brook
(Bormann and Likens, 1979).

As the residuals survive (valve in
Fig. 20), endure the environment (environmental driver, E in Fig. 20), including the
subsequent disturbance of the plot (disturbance driver in Fig. 20), and have their

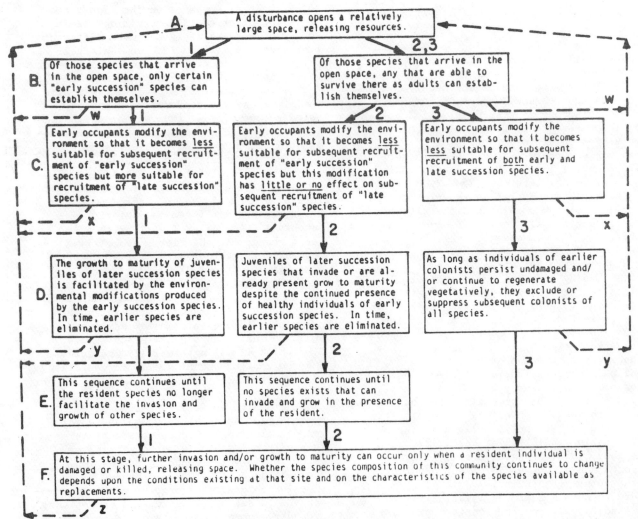

Figure 19. Three models of the mechanisms producing the sequence of species in succession.
The dashed lines represent interruptions of the process, in decreasing frequency in the
order w, x, y, and z (taken from Connell and Slayter, 1977, by permission).

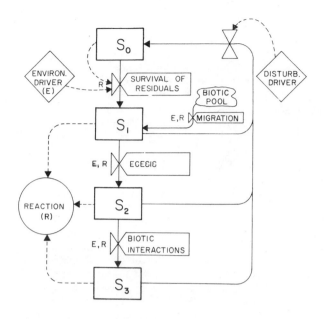

Figure 20. A model of the change in the
status of the components of a plot of ground
over time. Boxes are states of the plot at
any instant. Diamonds are system drivers.
The circle is an intermediate variable.
Dashed arrows show information flows.
Letters next to control gates replace dotted
lines from that point to the control for the
sake of graphic simplicity.

effect on the plot (Reaction (R) in Fig.
20), they are joined by a series of migrants
from the available biotic pool. The exact
nature of the events during this early
period of succession determine the ultimate
successional vector. Which species get to
a particular plot depends on a number of
factors. Perhaps the two most significant
are the distances various species are from
the plots and the relative vagility of each
species' propagules. A species distant
from a disturbed plot without good dispersal
potential is not likely to be a part of
early succession. Conversely, highly vagile
and proximate species are likely to establish rapidly when a plot is available,
assuming none of their environmental
tolerance axes are violated on that plot.
Notice in Figure 20 that the process of
migration is itself affected by both the
environmental driver and the reaction intermediate variable.

The prevalence of annuals or herbaceous
perennials in early succession of plots in
many different vegetation types is partly
related to their small, numerous, readily
dispersed seeds. Also, at least a few individuals occur around the countryside,
providing seed sources uniformly across the
landscape. An obvious example is the presence of dandelions in the most out-of-the-
way places, e.g., in a spruce-fir forest

opening where a single tree has fallen.
Such species have localized reservoirs forming a landscape mosaic, where each "patch"
goes to extinction as the site develops.
This approach is explicit in a review of the
adaptive nature of seed size and shape
(Baker, 1972; Harper et al., 1970) and oil
content (Levin, 1974) and in the general
theoretical discussion of mosaic phenomena
by Whittaker and Levin (1977).

Given a longer time, the larger, less
vagile propagules of other species stand a
statistical chance of eventually getting to
the open plot. Thus, if a late successional species is not proximate to the plot, it
may not occur on that site until late in
succession because late succession species
have less vagile propagules and greater
dependence on vegetation reproduction.
However, if a late successional species does
occur proximate to the plot, it may very
well be present in early successional
stages, though not obvious because of slower growth rates or even because its growth
is initially suppressed by other species.
It is through this very phenomenon that the
size of a disturbed area can affect succession. If 100,000 ha are burned, tree
seeds may have less chance to be in the
middle of that area until the plot is very
old. On the other hand if a one-quarter
hectare gap is created in a forest canopy,
trees are much more likely to reoccupy that
site rapidly, "shortening succession."

The specific nature of the species
occupying the plot during these early periods can determine the subsequent course of
plot changes. A case in point is the significant effect that pin cherry (Prunus
pennsylvanica) has on early successional
nutrient dynamics. The pin cherry accelerates canopy closure and, by serendipity,
this protects the soil from nutrient loss
(Bormann and Likens, 1979; Marks, 1974).

Finally, the stochastic phenomenon of
the timing of disturbance can alter the
migration process. Say that an environmental disturbance occurred in the fall of
what happened to be a good cone crop year
for spruce or fir. The success of these
two species at more rapidly occupying a
disturbed site might be greater with more
seeds available than if the disturbance had
occurred in a low seed crop year, or even
earlier in the year before the crop was
mature, and other species could preempt the
plot before the tree propagules were mature.
Such site preemption can involve allelo-
chemics and shading out (Turner and Quarterman, 1975).

Ecesis and biotic interactions work
simultaneously, but they are separated here
for emphasis. Ecesis, as Clements (1916)

said is the "...adjustment of a plant to a new home." That is, as in the case of a vascular plant seed, an organism that reaches a particular plot must be able to germinate and grow before it can greatly influence the plot. Generally this is a matter of enduring the physical environment, though biotic factors such as the presence of a species' required symbiont are also requisites. Simultaneous, and of increasing importance through the time an individual grows, are its interactions with other individuals. This interaction can take any of the many forms of a species-species interaction, ranging from predator-prey interactions to mutualism. Clements' term, and major emphasis for this process, was competition. Obviously, biotic interactions other than competition are important.

The net result is that a particular species will occur on the disturbed plot until such time as the nature of the plot violates one or more of its tolerance axes. The plot itself is constantly changing-- even if the biota is the same, seldom does the physical milieu remain the same. There is also a constant barrage of propagules reaching the plot that may change the biotic character of the associations. Of course, each of these migrants cycles through the same test of persistence.

The process of reaction, in which the occupying species change the nature of the plots--classically to a state where they themselves cannot survive--may or may not be true. McCormick's (1968) experiment where removal of annuals had little effect on perennials suggests a lack of important reaction effects. At the other extreme, the importance of reaction was probably most forcefully presented by Phillips (1934, 1935a,b) and is shown for classic sand dune succession by Olson (1958). Undoubtedly, this is a case of "it all depends" reflecting the nature of the disturbance and the particular species and environment involved. This position is similar to the one arrived at by Van Hulst (1978), who emphasizes species adaptive strategies.

The model I present uses Clements' basic processes (Table 3), but its intellectual base is clearly in the Gleasonian tradition. Thus, processes are undoubtedly, with some alteration, as Clements outlined them, but they are really working on the biota in a highly individualistic way. The superorganism approach is not necessary nor even appropriate in my view, regardless of various eloquent protestations (Williams et al., 1969; Morrison and Yarranton, 1974).

My model does not include the mathematics to describe the form of the functions involved for particular vegetation. A number of existing models attempt to do this by using various quantitative methods. Interestingly, the forester's stand yield models are a form of successional prediction model, usually limited to a few commercial species. Most extant models consider hardwood forest succession; exceptions are those examining the wet sclerophyll forests of Tasmania (Noble and Slatyer, 1978) and redwoods (Bosch, 1971; Namkoong and Roberds, 1974). Frequently such models deal with single stand predictions, although Shugart and others (1973) discuss larger regions. The most detailed model appears to be that of Ek and Monserud (1974) which includes mixed age, mixed species assemblages as well as spatial variation. Some of the models track tree-by-tree replacements as a function of Markovian processes (Horn, 1976; Waggoner and Stephens, 1970), while others use a continuous approach (Shugart et al., 1973). One recent approach even considers multiple pathways of succession (Cattelino et al., 1970).

Most of these models have fair predictive power for trees in specific forest types. What is proposed here is a general framework that should work for various vegetations in a variety of geographic areas. The model, as I envision it, does not require convergence of vegetation during succession to a single end point. In fact, its structure was designed to permit great variability since I believe convergence is partially an illusion (see a detailed example in Matthews, 1979).

An important aspect of this model is the constant possibility of additional disturbance causing a recycling of the processes. Such disturbances, if they are of moderate intensity and spatial extent, are important in maintaining diversity. This effect of disturbance has often been noted (Loucks, 1970; Mellinger and McNaughton, 1975) but recently has been the topic of increased theoretical interest (Huston, 1979; Whittaker and Levin, 1977).

Changes on Other Time Scales

The time scale of succession depends on the particular site involved. It is determined by the nature, intensity, and extent of the disturbance, the specific environment, and other factors. In any case, the time axis involved is moderately long, i.e., tens to a few hundreds of years. Superimposed on this process is a series of minor (micro) successions where seasonal changes occur in plant composition or phenological aspectation. Some animals closely track such plant changes (for example, see the microsuccession described for insects by Price, 1975). Thus, if we extend out observation to animals and microbes, we literally find successions within succession all at different time scales (Levandowsky and White, 1977). Frequently, this involves a group of coadapted species--a group similar to what Root (1973) termed "component communities." Additionally, some changes in species composition occur over a very few years. Examples are the cyclic replacement of hardwoods, apparently related to contrasting reproductive strategies (Forcier, 1975), the cases of alternation described for forests by Fox (1977), and even cases known for desert species such as cacti (Opuntia) and shrubs (Larrea) (Yeaton, 1978).

Some species turnovers presently appear to be caused by chance (Holland, 1978). Other causes of turnovers include the loss of a particular species due to pathogens or a critical environmental factor. Such "disturbances" are currently thought to provide the landscape mosaics of patches of varying sizes, which contribute to the diversity and stability of regional vegetation (Loucks, 1970; Pickett, 1976; Vitousek and Reiners, 1975; Whittaker and Levin, 1977). In some cases, replacement of the lost species is accomplished by the expansion of one or more existing species into the "gap." The replacement of chestnut (Castanea dentata) by oak (Quercus borealis) after chestnut extirpation by chestnut blight (Endothia parasitica) is an example (Karban, 1978) which typifies a one-for-one replacement, while on other sites several mesic species seem to replace chestnut (Good, 1968; Mackey and Sevic, 1973, and references therein).

All of these changes can be superimposed on the same model offered for succession (Fig. 20). Thus, for some reason a species is lost or at least its populations are reduced. Its physical or biotic environments may no longer be suitable. It is replaced wholly or in part by a species which, if it is a recent arrival, starts at the beginning of the model, i.e., can get there and survive in that milieu. The species itself may alter the environment such that other species will be replaced, but the whole process may be cycled in a roughly predictable fashion. Species already resident on the plot may simply increase in abundance. Regionally, the biotic components may appear to be in equilibrium yet changes, qualitatively the same as those ascribed to succession, are taking place constantly on a smaller scale. As Gleason (1927) said, succession does not end, it just becomes too slow to measure or observe.

His comments best fit regional patterns; a small plot analysis would, I believe, invariably show significant dynamic changes in all but the most persistent and resilient forms. Trees are often exactly such forms.

Another scale of ecosystem-time change covers hundreds to thousands of years and is what we refer to as ecosystem evolution. Whittaker and Woodwell (1972) in a previous colloquium and more recently Whittaker (1977) and Whittaker and Levin (1977) point out that all species evolve in the context of the community and that the community is the result of a history of species additions and subtractions (extinctions for that site) as well as gene pool changes for resident species, in the context of the total environment. This is qualitatively no different from the kind of model I have been discussing. If a particular species can get to a plot, survive, and reproduce there, it will persist as part of that ecosystem. If the species cannot survive on that plot under those specific conditions, it must either go extinct on the plot or produce differently adapted individuals.

Many associations we see repeated across the landscape today are composed of individual species which have formed associations relatively recently, after being parts of quite different ecosystems during the Pleistocene. Excellent examples of this come from the data of Davis (1969, 1976, 1978) for forest tree species which now form the very associations used as the data base for much of successional theory. These species have become associated by a process similar to succession. In the past their distributions were altered by various events. Former associates had slightly different tolerances. As there was remixing of species, different combinations could get to particular areas and survive there in moderate perpetuity, and therefore currently form the "climax" vegetation type. None of this denies that certain species assemblages are more stable, less vulnerable to change than others (Robinson, manuscript).

As a form of summary I will use an adaptation (Fig. 21) of Grime's model (Figs. 17 and 18). Every group of organisms exists in the milieu composed of biotic and abiotic factors. It cannot exist in a situation where any of its axes of biotic or abiotic tolerances are consistently violated. Each place on the surface of the earth, for any time interval, has a characteristic environment. This immediately places a constraint on what organisms could possibly survive there, regardless of their ability to get there. Figure 21A shows such a hypothetical limit. Many organisms may end up on a site, some not capable of

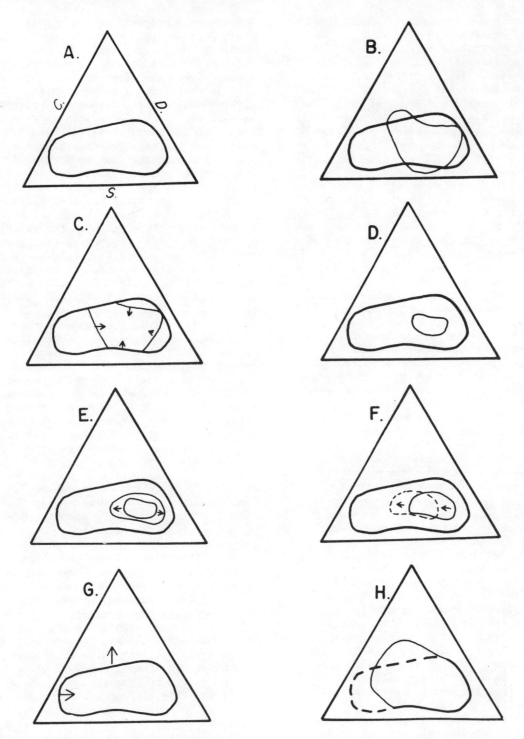

Figure 21. A depiction of several aspects of an ecosystem over time, using the life history strategy approach of Grime (1977). Axes of triangles are the same as in Figure 17. The sequence A-D represents succession where each environment can only be occupied by species exhibiting certain life history strategies (A). Since many species with various life history strategies, including those which cannot persist in a given environment, can get there, a time exists where the spectrum of species' life histories exceeds the environmental constraints (B). The nonadapted species cannot persist (C) and through time the species may interact to further reduce the spectrum of viable life history alternatives (D). E and F show that over short times, various life history strategies may become established, as long as they do not exceed environmental limits (ecosystem fluctuation). G and H show a change in life history strategies which can exist, one type of ecosystem evolution.

of existing there. Figure 21B show a hypothetical group of such organisms (the
lighter line) imposed on the limits of the
hypothetical environment. Only those organism who can get to a place and survive
there can continue to exist there. Thus the
non-survivors are eliminated (Fig. 21C). In
some cases not all members of a species can
survive the competition, or other biotic
interactions, or even the results of the
reaction process. Thus, over time perhaps a
smaller species mix persists in that plot
(Fig. 21D). This is essentially succession
via the model (Fig. 20). That some sites
are so harsh that the same group of species
are the only ones capable of replacing themselves is an extreme case of the same process; it is just one where the original
environmental constraints are so severe,
succession seems not to occur. A global
example of the possible cause and effect relationship between the unpredictability of
precipitation in low precipitation systems,
regardless of temperature, was presented
earlier.

During short time intervals there can
be changes in species composition of plots
(Figs. 21E and F). These changes, often
caused by minor biotic or abiotic changes in
the plot, are still within the overall
physical environmental constraints. Cyclic
or even stochastic composition changes are
frequently of this type.

Finally, the major climatic or other
abiotic variables may change over time
intervals, changing the very nature of a
plot, and now new species mixes might be
selected for, or extant species may adapt.
This is essentially one form of ecosystem
evolution. For all of these situations we
can conceive of biotic changes also affecting these ultimate plot characteristics; it
is merely easier to visualize the abiotic
variables over time by use of weather
records.

All ecosystem composition changes are
qualitatively similar, and can be envisioned, mechanistically, as being driven by the
same processes--equally well understood long
ago by two intellectual opponents--Gleason
and Clements. Such modern ecological
theories as island biogeography (MacArthur
and Wilson, 1967) can be considered as being
qualitatively similar to the old "conventional wisdom" couched in a modern context.
For example, the island distance from the
sources of a biota, its area, and the dispersal characteristics of various species
determine, in part, the "migration" phase.
These early species establish a biota which
may change the environment of the island,
a reaction process. This can include altering the invadability of that island. Such
ideas have even been formalized into

assembly rules (Diamond, 1975) which fit
well into the general model proposed here
(Fig. 20), though in many cases they represent specific instances of what I term
biotic interactions.

Let me conclude with an analogy.
While speaking about the universe recently,
Dr. Philip Morrison reminded me that in
physics there is a dichotomy between Newton's deterministic and Gibbs' stochastic
approach to the universe.

We regularly predict with great precision the exact timing of the orbits of
some celestial bodies (a high degree of
apparent determinism). On the contrary, we
cannot predict the movement of a particular
gas molecule in a room, even though the
same rules of motion and gravity apply to
both because, in a sense, the molecule is
affected by every event in the universe
(stochasticity). Nonetheless, we can describe the average behavior of that species
of molecule in that particular room, under
those specific conditions.

Succession and other ecosystem changes
seem of the same type. On a regional basis
we can predict with fair accuracy the average change in the biota under certain conditions, but it is difficult, nearly impossible, to predict the exact behavior of any
one very small plot for a short time period,
and even harder for a longer time period
where very many unpredictable changes might
occur.

As with entities in the universe,
different species in a plot are reacting
with their own characteristic "periods"
(Levandowsky and White, 1977). Additionally, while there is determinism involved
in the system, the stochastic properties of
such systems force us to offer "average"
answers--correct when we generalize, but
often incorrect when we attempt to be too
specific. A goal of ecologists must be to
learn where between these two extremes we
need to focus our estimates of potential
ecosystem behavior, so that man, the ecosystem manipulator, can trust our science.

ACKNOWLEDGMENTS

The members of the succession project
at Utah State University were most helpful
and unselfish in sharing their data with
me. These include: Douglas Andersen, Jan
Henderson, George Innis, David Schimpf,
Michael Schwartz, Kimberly Smith, Gary
Reese, and Neil West.

Robert Whittaker and Neil West kindly
read and commented on an early draft of the
manuscript. My alter consciences Doug
Andersen, Dave Schimpf, and Kim Smith beat

their way through several manuscript drafts.
Linda Finchum and Bette Peitersen helped
prepare all drafts. Bob Bayn executed all
figures and reduced data ad nauseum. Of
course, all of us could do this because the
National Science Foundation provided the
necessary funds.

LITERATURE CITED

Andersen, D. C., J. A. MacMahon, and M. L.
    Wolfe. 1980. Herbivorous mammals
    along a montane sere: community struc-
    ture and energetics. J. Mamm. (in
    press).

Archibold, O. W. 1979. Buried viable pro-
    pagules as a factor in postfire regen-
    eration in northern Saskatchewan.
    Can. J. Bot. 57:54-58.

Auclair, A. N., and F. G. Goff. 1971. Di-
    versity relations of upland forests in
    the western Great Lake area. Amer.
    Natur. 105:499-528.

Baker, H. G. 1972. Seed weight in relation
    to environmental conditions in Califor-
    nia. Ecology 53:997-1110.

Bazzaz, F. A. 1975. Plant species diver-
    sity in old-field successional eco-
    systems in southern Illinois. Ecology
    56:485-488.

Beatley, J. C. 1976. Vascular plants of
    the Nevada Test Site and Central-
    Southern Nevada: ecological and geo-
    graphic distributions. U.S. Dept.
    Commerce, TID-26881, Springfield, Va.

Blum, J. L. 1956. Application of the
    climax concept to algal communities of
    streams. Ecology 37:603-604.

Bonner, J. T. 1965. Size and Cycle. An
    Essay on the Structure of Biology.
    Princeton, N.J.: Princeton University
    Press.

Bormann, F. H., and G. E. Likens. 1979.
    Pattern and Process in a Forested Eco-
    system. New York: Springer-Verlag.

Bosch, C. A. 1971. Redwoods: a population
    model. Science 172:345-349.

Botkin, D. B., J. G. Janak, and J. R.
    Wallis. 1972. Some ecological con-
    sequences of a computer model of
    forest growth. J. Ecol. 60:849-872.

Burbanck, M. P., and R. B. Platt. 1964.
    Granite outcrop communities of the
    Piedmont Plateau in Georgia. Ecology
    45:292-306.

Cates, R. G., and G. H. Orians. 1975. Suc-
    cessional status and the palatability
    of plants to generalized herbivores.
    Ecology 56:410-418.

Cattelino, P. J., I. R. Noble, R. O.
    Slatyer, and S. R. Kessell. 1979.
    Predicting the multiple pathways of
    plant succession. Environ. Management
    3:41-50.

Clayton, H. H. 1944. World weather
    records. Smithsonian Misc. Coll. 79:
    1-1199.

Clayton, H. H., and F. L. Clayton. 1947.
    World weather records 1931-1940.
    Smithsonian Misc. Coll. 105:1-646.

Clements, F. E. 1916. Plant Succession:
    An Analysis of the Development of
    Vegetation. Carnegie Inst. Wash. Publ.
    No. 242, pp. 1-512.

Clements, F. E. 1928. Plant Succession
    and Indicators: A Definitive Edition
    of Plant Succession and Plant Indi-
    cators. New York: H. W. Wilson Co.

Clements, F. E. 1936. Nature and struc-
    ture of the climax. J. Ecol. 24:252-
    284.

Colinvaux, P. 1973. Introduction to Eco-
    logy. New York: John Wiley and Sons,
    Inc.

Connell, J. H. 1972. Community inter-
    actions on marine rocky intertidal
    shores. Ann. Rev. Ecol. Syst. 3:169-
    192.

Connell, J. H. 1975. Some mechanisms pro-
    ducing structure in natural communi-
    ties: a model and evidence from field
    experiments. In Ecology and Evolution
    of Communities, edited by M. L. Cody
    and J. M. Diamond, pp. 460-490.
    Cambridge, Mass.: Harvard University
    Press.

Connell, J. H., and R. O. Slatyer. 1977.
    Mechanisms of succession in natural
    communities and their role in community
    stability and organization. Amer.
    Natur. 111:1119-1144.

Cooper, W. S. 1926. The fundamentals of vegetational change. Ecology 7:391-413.

Cowles, H. C. 1899. The ecological relations of the vegetation on the sand dunes of Lake Michigan. Bot. Gaz. 27: 95-117, 167-202, 281-308, 361-391.

Dansereau, P., and K. Lems. 1957. The grading of dispersal types in plant communities and their ecological significance. Universite de Montreal Institut Botanique Contr. No. 71.

Daubenmire, R. 1975. An analysis of structural and functional characters along a steppe-forest catena. Northwest Sci. 49:122-140.

Davis, M. B. 1969. Palynology and environmental history during the quaternary period. Amer. Sci. 57:317-332.

Davis, M. B. 1976. Pleistocene biogeography of temperate deciduous forests. Geoscience and Man 13:13-26.

Davis, M. B. 1978. Climatic interpretation of pollen in quaternary sediments. In Biology and Quaternary Evnironments, edited by D. Walker and J. C. Gappy, pp. 35-51, Canberra: Australian Academy of Science.

Davis, W. M. 1899. Complications of the geographical cycle. Eighth International Geographical Congress, pp. 150-163.

Davis, W. M. 1909. Geographical Essays. Boston: Ginn and Co.

Diamond, J. M. 1975. Assembly of species communities. In Ecology and Evolution of Communities, edited by M. L. Cody and J. M. Diamond, pp. 342-444. Cambridge, Mass.: Harvard University Press.

Drury, W. H., and I. C. T. Nisbet. 1973. Succession. J. Arnold Arboretum 54: 331-368.

Duffey, E. 1978. Ecological strategies in spiders including some characteristics of species in pioneer and mature habitats. Symp. Zool. Soc. (London) 42:109-123.

Dureau de la Malle, A. J. C. A. 1825. Memoire sur l'alternance ou sur ce probleme: la succession alternative dans la reproduction des especes vegetales vivant en societe, est- elle une loi generale de la nature? Ann. Sci. Nat. (Paris) 15:353-381.

Egler, F. E. 1954. Vegetation science concepts. 1. Initial floristic composition--a factor in old-field vegetation development. Vegetatio 4:412-417.

Ek, A. R., and R. A. Monserud. 1974. FOREST: a computer model for simulating the growth and reproduction of mixed forest stands. Univ. of Wisconsin, Coll. Agric. and Life Sci. Res. Rep. A2635.

Forcier, L. K. 1975. Reproductive strategies and the co-occurrence of climax tree species. Science 189:808-810.

Fox, J. F. 1977. Alternation and coexistence of tree species. Amer. Natur. 111:69-89.

Gleason, H. A. 1917. The structure and development of the plant association. Bull. Torrey Bot. Club 44:468-481.

Gleason, H. A. 1926. The individualistic concept of the plant association. Bull. Torrey Bot. Club 53:7-26.

Gleason, H. A. 1927. Further views on the succession concept. Ecology 8:299-326.

Gleason, H. A. 1939. The individualistic concept of the plant association. Amer. Midl. Natur. 21:92-110.

Golley, F. B., ed. 1977. Ecological Succession. Benchmark Papers in Ecology, Vol. 5. Stroudsburg, Penn.: Dowden, Hutchinson and Ross, Inc.

Good, N. F. 1968. A study of natural replacement of chestnut in six stands in the highlands of New Jersey. Bull. Torrey Bot. Club 95:240-253.

Gorham, E. 1957. Development of peatlands. Quart. Rev. Biol. 32:145-166.

Goudie, A., and J. Wilkinson. 1977. The Warm Desert Environment. Cambridge: Cambridge University Press.

Grime, J. P. 1977. Evidence for the existence of three primary strategies in plants and its relevance to ecological and evolutionary theory. Amer. Natur. 111:1169-1194.

Grime, J. P. 1979. Plant Strategies and Vegetation Processes. Chichester, England: Wiley-Interscience.

Hammond, A. L. 1972. Ecosystem analysis: biome approach to environmental science. Science 175:46–48.

Harper, J. L., P. H. Lovell, and K. G. Moore. 1970. The shapes and sizes of seeds. Ann. Rev. Ecol. Syst. 1:327–356.

Holdridge, L. R. 1967. Life Zone Ecology, rev. ed. San Jose, Costa Rica: Tropical Science Center.

Holland, P. G. 1978. Species turnover in deciduous forest vegetation. Vegetatio 38:113–118.

Horn, H. S. 1971 The Adaptive Geometry of Trees. Princeton, N.J.: Princeton University Press.

Horn, H. S. 1974. The ecology of secondary succession. In Annual Review of Ecology and Systematics, Vol. 5, edited by R. F. Johnston, P. W. Frank, and C. C. Michener, pp. 25–37. Palo Alto, Calif. Annual Reviews, Inc.

Horn, H. S. 1975. Markovian properties of forest succession. In Ecology and Evolution of Communities, edited by M. L. Cody and J. M. Diamond, pp. 196–211. Cambridge, Mass.: Harvard University Press.

Horn, H. S. 1976. Succession. In Theoretical Ecology, edited by R. M. May, pp. 187–204. Philadelphia, Penn.: W. B. Saunders Co.

Hubbell, S. P. 1979. Tree dispersion, abundance, and diversity in a tropical dry forest. Science 203:1299–1309.

Hurd, L. E., M. V. Mellinger, L. L. Wolf, and S. J. McNaughton. 1971. Stability and diversity of three trophic levels in terrestrial successional ecosystems. Science 173:1134–1136.

Huston, M. 1979. A general hypothesis of species diversity. Amer. Natur. 113:81–101.

Hutchinson, G. E. 1978. An Introduction to Population Ecology. London: Yale University Press.

Innis, G. S., and J. A. Wiens. 1977. BIRD model: Version II description and documentation. Utah State Univ. Wildlife Sci. Dept. Rep. Ser. No. 3.

Johnson, E. A. 1979. Succession, an unfinished revolution. Ecology 60:238–240.

Karban, R. 1978. Changes in an oak-chestnut forest since the chestnut blight. Castanea 43:221–228.

King, W. 1685. Of the bogs and loughs of Ireland. Royal Society (London) Philos. Trans. 15:948–960.

Leak, W. B. 1970. Successional change in northern hardwoods predicted by birth and death simulation. Ecology 51: 794–801.

Levandowsky, M., and B. S. White. 1977. Randomness, time scales, and the evolution of biological communities. In Evolutionary Biology, Vol. 10, edited by M. K. Hecht, W. C. Steere, and B. Wallace, pp. 69–161. New York: Plenum Press.

Levin, D. A. 1974. The oil content of seeds: an ecological perspective. Amer. Natur. 108:193–206.

Lewontin, R. C. 1966. On the measurement of relative variability. Syst. Zool. 15:141–142.

Loucks, O. L. 1970. Evolution of diversity, efficiency, and community stability. Amer. Zool. 10:17–25.

MacArthur, R. H. 1958. A note on stationary age distributions in single-species populations and stationary species populations in a community. Ecology 39:146–147.

MacArthur, R. H., and E. O. Wilson. 1967. The Theory of Island Biogeography. Princeton, N.J.: Princeton University Press.

Mackey, H. E., and N. Sivec. 1973. The present composition of a former oak-chestnut forest in the Allegheny Mountains of western Pennsylvania. Ecology 54:915–919.

MacMahon, J. A. 1976. Species and guild similarity of North American desert mammal fauna: a functional analysis of communities. In Evolution of Desert Biota, edited by D. W. Goodall, pp. 133–148. Austin: University of Texas Press.

MacMahon, J. A. 1979. North American deserts: their floral and faunal components. In Arid-land Ecosystems: Structure, Functioning and Management, Vol. 1, edited by R. A. Perry and D. W. Goodall, pp. 21-82. Cambridge: Cambridge University Press.

MacMahon, J. A., D. L. Phillips, J. V. Robinson, and D. J. Schimpf. 1978. Levels of biological organization: An organism-centered approach. BioScience 28:700-704.

MacMahon, J. A., and T. F. Wieboldt. 1978. Applying biogeographic principles to resource management: A case study evaluating Holdridge's life zone model. In Intermountain Biogeography: A Symposium, Great Basin Naturalist Mem. No. 2, pp. 245-257. Provo, Utah: Brigham Young University Press.

MacMahon, J. A., and F. H. Wagner. 1979. The Mojave, Chihuahuan, and Sonoran deserts of North America. In Warm Desert Ecosystems, Vol. 12 of Ecosystems of the World, edited by I. Noy-Meier. Elsevier Publ. (in press).

MacMahon, J. A., and D. J. Schimpf. 1980. Water as a factor in the biology of North American desert plants. In Water in Desert Ecosystems, US/IBP Synthesis Series No. 12, edited by D. Evans and J. Thames. Stroudsburg, Penn.: Dowden, Hutchinson and Ross, Inc. (in press).

Major, J. 1974. Kinds and rates of changes in vegetation and chronofunctions. In Vegetation Dynamics, edited by R. Knapp, pp. 7-18. The Hague: Junk.

Margalef, R. 1963a. Successions of populations. Adv. Frontiers of Plant Sci. (Instit. Adv. Sci. and Culture, New Delhi, India) 2:137-188.

Margalef, R. 1963b. On certain unifying principles in ecology. Amer. Natur. 97:357-374.

Margalef, R. 1968. Perspectives in Ecological Theory. Chicago, Ill.: University of Chicago Press.

Marks, P. L. 1974. The role of pin cherry (Prunus pensylvanica L.) in the maintenance of stability in northern hardwood ecosystems. Ecol. Monogr. 44:73-88.

Marks, P. L. 1975. On the relation between extension growth and successional status of deciduous trees of the northeastern United States. Bull. Torrey Bot. Club 102:172-177.

Matthews, J. A. 1979a. A study of the variability of some successional and climax plant assemblage-types using multiple discriminant analysis. J. Ecology 67:255-271.

Matthews, J. A. 1979b. Refutation of convergence in a vegetation succession. Naturwissenschaften 66:47-49.

May, R. 1976. Patterns in multi-species communities. In Theoretical Ecology: Principles and Applications, edited by R. M. May, pp. 142-162. London: Blackwell.

McCormick, J. 1968. Succession. Student publication of graduate school of fine arts. University of Pennsylvania, Philadelphia.

McIntosh, R. P. 1975. H. A. Gleason-- "Individualistic Ecologist" 1882-1975: His contributions to ecological theory. Bull. Torrey Bot. Club 102:253-273.

McNaughton, S. J. 1974. The role of diversity in the energetics of plant communities. Ohio J. Sci. 74:351-358.

McNaughton, S. J., and L. L. Wolf. 1979. General Ecology, 2nd ed. New York: Holt, Rinehart and Winston.

Mellinger, M. V., and S. J. McNaughton. 1975. Structure and function of successional vascular plant communities in central New York. Ecol. Monogr. 45:161-182.

Moldenke, A. R. 1976. California pollination ecology and vegetation types. Phytologia 34:305-361.

del Moral, R., and L. A. Standley. 1979. Pollination of angiosperms in contrasting coniferous forests. Amer. J. Bot. 66:26-35.

Morrison, R. G., and G. A. Yarranton. 1974. Vegetational heterogeneity during a primary sand dune succession. Can. J. Bot. 52:397-410.

Muller, C. H. 1940. Plant succession in the Larrea-Flourensia climax. Ecology 21:206-212.

Muller, G. H. 1952. Plant succession in arctic heath and tundra in northern Scandinavia. Bull. Torrey Bot. Club 79:296-309.

Namkoong, G., and J. H. Roberds. 1974. Extinction probabilities and the changing age structure of redwood forests. Amer. Natur. 108:355-368.

Newell, S. J., and E. J. Tramer. 1978. Reproductive strategies in herbaceous plant communities during succession. Ecology 59:228-234.

Niering, W. A., and B. H. Goodwin. 1974. Creation of relatively stable shrublands with herbicides: arresting "succession" on rights-of-way and pastureland. Ecology 55:784-795.

Noble, I. R., and R. O. Slatyer. 1977. Post-fire succession of plants in Mediterranean ecosystems. In Proc. Symp. on the Environmental Consequences of Fire and Fuel Management in Mediterranean Climate Ecosystems, pp. 27-36. USDA Forest Service Gen. Tech. Rep. WO-3.

Odum, E. P. 1969. The strategy of ecosystem development. Science 164:262-270.

Olson, J. S. 1958. Rates of succession and soil changes on southern Lake Michigan sand dunes. Bot. Gaz. 119:125-170.

Ostler, W. K., and K. T. Harper. 1978. Floral ecology in relation to plant species diversity in the Wasatch Mountains of Utah and Idaho. Ecology 59:848-861.

Otte, D. 1975. Plant preference and plant succession: a consideration of evolution of plant preference in Schistocerca. Oecologia 18:129-144.

Peterson, K. M. 1978. Vegetational successions and other ecosystemic changes in two arctic tundras. Ph.D. dissertation, Duke University, Durham, N.C.

Phillips, J. F. V. 1934. Succession, development, the climax, and the complex organism: an analysis of concepts. Part I. J. Ecol. 22:554-571.

Phillips, J. F. V. 1935a. Succession, development, the climax, and the complex organism: An analysis of concepts. Part II. Development and the climax. J. Ecol. 23:210-246.

Phillips, J. F. V. 1935b. Succession, development, the climax, and the complex organism: An analysis of concepts. Part III. The complex organism: Conclusions. J. Ecol. 23:488-508.

Pickett, S. T. A. 1976. Succession: an evolutionary interpretation. Amer. Natur. 110:107-119.

Pielou, E. C. 1966. Species-diversity and pattern-diversity in the study of ecological succession. J. Theoret. Biol. 10:370-383.

Price, P. W. 1975. Insect Ecology. New York: John Wiley and Sons, Inc.

Rabotnov, T. A. 1974. Differences between fluctuations and successions. In Vegetation Dynamics, edited by R. Knapp, pp. 19-24. The Hague: Junk.

Ricklefs, R. E. 1977. Environmental heterogeneity and plant species diversity: a hypothesis. Amer. Natur. 111:376-381.

Robinson, J. V. 1979. An assortative model of island biogeography. (in manuscript).

Root, R. B. 1973. Organization of a plant-arthropod association in simple and diverse habitats: the fauna of collards (Brassica oleracea). Ecol. Monogr. 43:95-124.

Salt, G. W. 1979. A comment on the use of the term emergent properties. Amer. Midl. Natur. 113:145-148.

Schimpf, D. J., J. A. Henderson, and J. A. MacMahon. 1980. Aspects of succession in spruce-fir forests of northern Utah. Great Basin Natur. (in press).

Sears, P. B. 1956. Some notes on the ecology of ecologists. Scien. Monthly 83:22-27.

Shafi, M. I., and G. A. Yarranton. 1973. Diversity, floristic richness, and species evenness during a secondary (post-fire) succession. Ecology 54:895-902.

Shelford, V. E. 1912. Ecological succession. IV. Vegetation and the control of land animal communities. Biol. Bull. 23:59-99.

Shields, L. M., and P. V. Wells. 1962. Effects of nuclear testing on desert vegetation. Science 135:38-40.

Shreve, F., and A. L. Hinckley. 1937. Thirty years of change in desert vegetation. Ecology 18:463-478.

Shugart, H. H., Jr., T. R. Crow, and J. M. Hett. 1973. Forest succession models: A rationale and methodology for modeling forest succession over large regions. Forest Sci. 19:203-212.

Smith, K. G., and J. A. MacMahon. Bird communities along a montane sere: community structure and energetics (mans. submitted).

Spurr, S. H. 1952. Origin of the concept of forest succession. Ecology 33: 426-427.

Theophrastus. ca. 300 B.C. An Enquiry into Plants. Book IV: "Of the trees and plants special to particular districts and positions." Sir Arthur Hort Edition, 1916. London: Heinemann.

Thompson, K. 1978. The occurrence of buried viable seeds in relation to environmental gradients. J. Biogeography 5:425-430.

Thoreau, H. D. 1860. Succession of forest trees. Mass. Board Agric. Rep. VIII.

Tramer, E. J. 1975. The regulation of plant species diversity on an early successional old-field. Ecology 56: 905-914.

Turner, B. H., and E. Quarterman. 1975. Allelochemic effects of Petalostemon gattingeri on the distribution of Arenaria patula in cedar glades. Ecology 56:924-932.

Van Hulst, R. 1978. On the dynamics of vegetation: patterns of environmental and vegetational change. Vegetatio 38: 65-75.

Vitousek, P. M., and W. A. Reiners. 1975. Ecosystem succession and nutrient retention: a hypothesis. BioScience 25:376-381.

Waggoner, P. E., and G. R. Stephens. 1970. Transition probabilities for a forest. Nature 255:1160-1161.

Waring, R. H., and J. F. Franklin. 1979. Evergreen coniferous forests of the Pacific Northwest. Science 204:1380-1386.

Warming, E. 1909. Oecology of Plants: An Introduction to the Study of Plant Communities, trans. by P. Groom and I. B. Balfour. Oxford: Oxford University Press.

Wautier, J. 1951. A propos de la dynamique des biocoenoses limniques: La notion de climax en biocoenotique dulcaquicole. Verh. Internat. Verein. Theor. Angew. Limnol. 11:446-448.

Wells, P. V. 1961. Succession in desert vegetation on streets of a Nevada ghost town. Science 134:670-671.

Whittaker, R. H. 1951. A criticism of the plant association and climatic climax concepts. Northwest Sci. 25:17-31.

Whittaker, R. H. 1953. A consideration of the climax theory: The climax as a population and pattern. Ecol. Monogr. 23:41-78.

Whittaker, R. H. 1957. Recent evolution of ecological concepts in relation to the eastern forests of North America. Amer. J. Bot. 44:197-206.

Whittaker, R. H. 1962. Classification of natural communities. Bot. Rev. 28:1-239.

Whittaker, R. H. 1974. Climax concepts and recognition. In Handbook of Vegetation Science: Vegetation Dynamics, Part 8, edited by R. Knapp, pp. 139-154. The Hague: Junk.

Whittaker, R. H. 1975a. Communities and Ecosystems, 2nd ed. New York: Macmillan.

Whittaker, R. H. 1975b. Functional aspects of succession in deciduous forests. In Sukzessionsforschung, Berlin Symp. Internat. Verh. Vegetationskunde (Rinteln, 1973), pp. 377-405.

Whittaker, R. H. 1977. Evolution of species diversity in land communities. In Evolutionary Biology, Vol. 10, edited by M. K. Hecht, W. C. Steere, and B. Wallace, pp. 1-67. New York: Plenum Press.

Whittaker, R. H., and D. Goodman. 1979.
    Classifying species according to their
    demographic strategy. I. Population
    fluctuations and environmental hetero-
    geneity. Amer. Natur. 113:185-200.

Whittaker, R. H., and S. A. Levin. 1977.
    The role of mosaic phenomena in
    natural communities. Theor. Pop. Biol.
    12:117-139.

Whittaker, R. H., and G. M. Woodwell. 1972.
    Evolution of natural communities. In
    Ecosystem Structure and Function,
    edited by J. A. Wiens, pp. 137-159.
    Corvallis: Oregon State University
    Press.

Wiens, J. A., and G. S. Innis. 1974. Esti-
    mation of energy flow in bird communi-
    ties: A population bioenergetics
    model. Ecology 55:730-746.

Wilbur, H. M., D. W. Tinkle, and J. P.
    Collins. 1974. Environmental cer-
    tainty, trophic level, and resource
    availability in life history evolution.
    Amer. Natur. 108:805-817.

Williams, W. T., G. N. Lance, L. J. Webb,
    J. G. Tracey, and M. B. Dale. 1969.
    Studies in the numerical analysis of
    complex rain-forest communities. III.
    The analysis of successional data.
    J. Ecol. 57:515-535.

Woodwell, G. M. 1970. Effects of pollution
    on the structure and physiology of eco-
    systems. Science 168:429-433.

Yeaton, R. I. 1978. A cyclical relation-
    ship between Larrea tridentata and
    Opuntia leptocaulis in the northern
    Chihuahuan Desert. J. Ecol. 66:651-
    656.

Distinctive Features of the Northwestern Coniferous Forest: Development, Structure, and Function

Jerry F. Franklin and Richard H. Waring

INTRODUCTION

The coniferous forests of the Pacific Northwest, those found on the slopes of the Cascade and Coastal ranges of Oregon, Washington, northern California, and British Columbia, are known throughout the world. This is the region renowned for Douglas-fir (Pseudotsuga menziesii) stands and western red cedar/western hemlock (Thuja plicata/ Tsuga heterophylla) climaxes. Surely these forests, observed by foresters and botanists since the time of von Humboldt and Douglas, are well understood and can hold few surprises. Indeed, when the Coniferous Forest Biome Project of the U.S. International Biological Program (US/IBP) started more than 10 years ago, we thought we knew about all we needed to know about the natural forests of this region. The U.S. Forest Service had already reduced their studies of older forests in order to concentrate on younger stands. Biome program designers seriously debated the wisdom of studying natural, older forests when major questions seemed to revolve around managed stands.

During the last 10 years, however, we have made gigantic advances in our knowledge of these forest ecosystems. We have learned how they are structured, their functional behavior, and controlling factors. Research on these systems has evolved into tests of specific hypotheses as relevant questions have become apparent. Many results presented in this and other Colloquim papers are from these first- and second-generation ecosystem studies--i.e., biomes and sons and daughters of biomes!

Increasing knowledge has brought continual surprises--counterintuitive finds that make clear how little we really know about these coniferous forests. The high productivity and rapid turnover found belowground in forests, for example, is outlined by Harris and Santantonio (this volume),

and the extent and importance of coarse woody debris in terrestrial and stream ecosystems is outlined by Triska and Cromack (this volume). The nitrogen cycle has been the source of one unexpected discovery after another. Ten years ago no clear idea existed of nitrogen sources in these forests; fixation by nonleguminous woody plants such as red alder has been widely known only since the mid-1950's. Textbooks hypothesized that free-living blue-green algae might be a source of nitrogen inputs along with precipitation. In the last decade at least two major sources of nitrogen have been identified: (1) the crown and ground dwelling lichens with a blue-green algal symbiont and (2) microbial activity in some types of organic matter such as coarse woody debris (logs). Almost certainly the nitrogen cycle will be the source of many further surprises.

Our objective in this paper is to highlight some findings on the structure and function of these coniferous forests. We also hope to transmit some sense of the progress and exciting directions of current research and stimulate you to reexamine what you think you already know about these forests. We will cover: (1) biomass and productivity; (2) factors responsible for evergreen dominance and massiveness; (3) successionally oriented studies of age structure and coarse woody debris; and (4) aspects of the old-growth systems.

Several topics highlighted in this paper are discussed more thoroughly elsewhere in this volume (see Waring, Triska, and Cromack on coarse woody debris, Swanson on erosion, Carroll on tree canopy ecosystems, and Cummins on stream ecosystems).

BIOMASS AND PRODUCTIVITY

Over the last decade scientists have documented what we have always suspected about northwestern forests--they contain the largest biomass accumulations in the world and are very productive. Trees have been dissected and equations developed and applied, and the results have shattered many theories about forest maxima which were based upon studies of temperate forests in other regions of the world.

Biomass

Biomass accumulates to record levels in large, long-lived species from dense coniferous forests. Maximal values in the Pacific Northwest contrast most strongly with maximal biomass values from other regions of the world (Table 1). The analysis of a coast redwood (Sequoia sempervirens) stand in Humboldt State Park in California provides the greatest accumulation ever recorded, with a basal area of 343 m^2/ha and a stem biomass of 3,461 ton/ha (Fujimori, 1977). Addition of branch, leaf, and, particularly, root biomass would increase the estimate of standing crop to well in excess of 4,000 ton/ha--very close to Fujimori's (1972) earlier estimate of 4,525 ton/ha for a coast redwood grove. These figures are larger but are consistent with the biomass of 3,200 ton/ha reported by Westman and Whittaker (1975) for three redwood stands on alluvial flats. Superlative stands are not confined to coast redwood, however (Table 1); maximum values

Table 1. *Maximal biomass values for three coniferous forest types in the Pacific Northwest and comparable data for different forest formations elsewhere in the world.*

Formation, type, and stand location	Stem volume	Basal area	Total biomass
	m^3/ha	m^2/ha	mt/ha
Coniferous forests, Pacific Northwest			
Sequoia sempervirens[1] (> 1,000 years old)	10,817	338	3,461[4]
Pseudotsuga menziesii-[2] Tsuga heterophylla (450 years old)	3,600	127	1,590[4]
Abies procera[2] (325 years old)	4,106	147	1,562[4]
Evergreen hardwood[3] (Quercus cinnamomum in Nepal)	n.a.	n.a.	575
Deciduous hardwood[3] (Quercus prinus in USA)	n.a.	n.a.	422
Temperate conifer[3] (Tsuga sieboldii in Japan)	n.a.	n.a.	730
Conifer plantation[3] (Cryptomeria japonica in Japan)	n.a.	n.a.	1,200

[1] Fujimori, 1977.

[2] Fujimori et al., 1976.

[3] Art and Marks, 1971.

[4] Stem mass only.

for noble fir (<u>Abies procera</u>) and Douglas-fir are about half those for redwood, but they still greatly exceed maxima for temperate and tropical forests in other parts of the world. The contrast is further emphasized by the fact that biomass figures for the Pacific Northwest (Table 1) include stem biomass only, while those from other regions are for total biomass.

Current studies in the Pacific Northwest continue to gather evidence that large biomass accumulations are the rule rather than the exception. Average values contrast as greatly with those for other regions as the maximal values (Table 2). High values are characteristic of young (100 to 150 years old) as well as old Douglas-fir stands and of subalpine forests (noble fir) as well as temperate forests. Coastal stands of young-growth Sitka spruce (<u>Picea sitchensis</u>) and western hemlock (<u>Tsuga heterophylla</u>) tend to be particularly high (Table 2). One of the more extensive analyses available is for a 10-ha watershed in the Cascade Mountains of western Oregon (Grier and Logan, 1978):

Item	Biomass (ton/ha)
Foliage	12.4
Aboveground in living plants	718.0
Total in living plants	870.0
In logs and standing dead trees	215.0
Total ecosystem organic matter	1,249.0

The amount of biomass in living trees is quite remarkable, given the apparent decadence of the stand as evidenced by the large weight of dead trees and logs.

One noteworthy biomass component is foliage. Leaf biomass and surface area in the Pacific Northwest develop slowly, taking 30 years or more to reach a maximum (Long and Turner, 1975); in the eastern United States and other temperate regions of the world, equilibrium is achieved much earlier, reportedly in as little as 4 years (Marks and Bormann, 1972). Projected canopy surface areas in the Pacific Northwest typically reach 10 m^2/m^2 and may reach as much as 20 m^2/m^2, which is very close to the theoretical maximum (Gholz, 1979).

Table 2. *Biomass values in representative stands of various types.*

Type and age class[1]	Number of stands	Aboveground biomass	
		Average	Range
		mt/ha	
Douglas-fir 70 to 170 years	10	604	422–792
Douglas-fir/western hemlock 250 to 1,000 years	19	868	317–1,423
Sitka spruce/western hemlock 121 to 130 years	3	1,163	916–1,492
Noble fir 130 years	1	880	---
Temperate deciduous forest Mature	19	243	87–422
Tropical rain forest Mature	9	318	67–415

[1]See appendix for data sources for stands from the Pacific Northwest which include aboveground tree biomass only; source for temperate deciduous and tropical rain forests is Art and Marks (1971) and includes shrubs and herbs.

Leaf mass values are also very high, with an average of nearly 20 tons/ha (Table 3). These leaf mass and projected area values are much higher than those in temperate deciduous hardwood and evergreen hardwood stands. Values for temperate conifer stands in other parts of the world range near the low values for coniferous forests in the Pacific Northwest (Table 3). Interestingly, the values for leaf area and mass in northwestern coniferous forests also far exceed leaf areas developed by red alder (Alnus rubra), one of the most common and productive of the northwestern deciduous hardwoods; values in red alder stands, converted from biomass values, represent less than 10 m^2/m^2 (which is very high for a deciduous hardwood stand).

Productivity

Productivity of the northwestern American temperate forests is generally comparable to forest stands in other temperate regions. Biomass in young stands probably accumulates at 15 to 25 tons/ha annually in fully stocked stands on better than average sites. Mature or old-growth stands have lower net productivities (Table 4).

Annual net productivity can be very great on the best sites. Fujimori (1971) reported a net production of 36.2 ton/ha in a 26-year-old coastal stand of western hemlock. Young forests of coast redwood also have high early productivities on good sites (Fujimori, 1972, 1977). Maximum values are substantially lower for temperate deciduous forests (24.1 ton/ha for tulip poplar, Liriodendron tulipifera) and temperate evergreen hardwood forests (28.0 ton/ha) (Art and Marks, 1971). Conifer plantations, with a reported maximum of 29.1 ton/ha for Cryptomeria japonica, approach the higher productivity values for northwestern stands.

In many other mesic temperate forests, however, annual productivity in early years typically equals or exceeds that in the Pacific Northwest. The key to the larger biomass accumulations in the Pacific Northwest is clearly the sustained height growth and longevity of the dominants, not the differences in productivity rates. This growth is aided by the trees' ability to accumulate and maintain a large amount of foliage. Northwestern tree species continue

Table 3. Leaf biomass and projected leaf areas for four forest types in the Pacific Northwest, three forest formations in Japan, and tropical rain forest.

Type[1]	Number of stands	Leaf mass	Projected leaf area
		mt/ha	m^2/m^2
Douglas-fir (young)	10	19	9.7
Douglas-fir/western hemlock (old)	19	23	11.7
Sitka spruce/western hemlock	4	21	13.2
Noble fir	1	18	10
Deciduous hardwood forest (Japan)	14	3.1	3 to 7
Evergreen hardwood forest (Japan)	40	8.6	5 to 9
Conifer (Japan)[2]	66	16.9	6 to 10
Tropical rain forest	6	9.4	7 to 12

[1]Data sources: Pacific Northwest, see appendix; Japan, Tadaki, 1977; tropical rain forest, Art and Marks, 1971.

[2]No stands of pine or Cumpressaceae included.

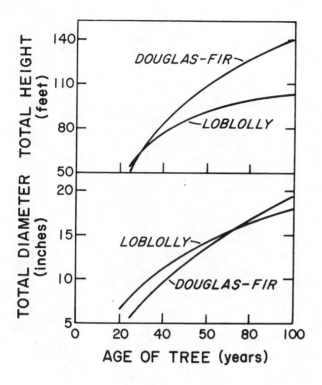

Figure 1. Comparison of the growth rates of Douglas-fir and loblolly pine. Pine has a faster earlier growth rate, but the sustained growth of the Douglas-fir results in the latter eventually overtaking the former.

to grow substantially in diameter and height, and stands in biomass, long after those in other temperate regions have reached equilibrium. This is well illustrated by comparing growth of loblolly pine (<u>Pinus</u> <u>taeda</u>) in the southeast and Douglas-fir in the Pacific Northwest (Worthington, 1954). Initially, the pine outgrows the Douglas-fir, being 100 percent taller at 10 years; however, Douglas-fir overtakes the pine in diameter growth at 25 years and in height growth at 30 years (Figure 1). Wood production from a single (100-year) rotation of Douglas-fir is about 22 percent greater than yields from two 50-year rotations of pine. Recent studies of height growth patterns for higher elevation Douglas-fir, noble fir, and mountain hemlock have further documented sustained height growth of northwestern species into their second and third centuries (Curtis et al., 1974; Herman et al., 1979; Herman and Franklin, 1977).

Table 4. Aboveground net primary production estimates for coniferous forests in the Pacific Northwest (west of the crest of the Cascade Range)

Community type	Stand age	Biomass	Net primary productivity	Source
	years	mt/ha	mt/ha/yr	
Coast redwood	"old"	3,200	14.3	Westman and Whittaker, 1975
Western hemlock	26	192	36.2	Fujimori, 1971
Western hemlock/Sitka spruce	110	871	10.3	Fujimori et al., 1976
Sitka spruce/western hemlock	130	1,080	14.7	Gholz, 1979
Western hemlock/Sitka spruce	130	1,492	12.3	Gholz, 1979
Douglas-fir	150	865	10.5	Gholz, 1979
Douglas-fir	125	449	6.6	Gholz, 1979
Douglas-fir/western hemlock	100	661	12.7	Fujimori et al., 1976
Douglas-fir/western hemlock	150	527	9.3	Gholz, 1979
Noble fir/Douglas-fir	115	880	13.0	Fujimori et al., 1976
Douglas-fir/western hemlock	450	718	10.8	Grier and Logan, 1977

Gross productivity rates are probably greater in many tropical rain forests and in warm-temperate evergreen broadleaf forests, but lower respiration rates in the Pacific Northwest result in greater net productivity. However, total autotrophic respiration appears much higher in northwestern coniferous forests than in temperate deciduous forests. Grier and Logan (1978) estimated respiration by a 450-year-old Douglas-fir stand at 150 ton/ha/year; estimates for a mixed oak and pine forest in New York and a tulip poplar forest in Tennessee were 15.2 and 15.9 ton/ha (Woodwell and Botkin, 1970; Sollins et al., 1973). The large respiration cost reflects the much larger foliar biomasses and the presence of respiring foliage during the relatively warm winters. The net effect of the high levels of autotrophic respiration is to accentuate differences in productivity between northwestern conifer and temperate deciduous hardwood forests, making the contrast in gross production even greater than that in net primary production.

In summary, the coastal regions of the Pacific Northwest are dominated by coniferous forest stands having biomass accumulations far exceeding forests in other northern temperate forest regions. Leaf masses and projected leaf areas greatly exceed those found in temperate deciduous hardwood forests. The large biomass values result from sustained growth of tree species with long lifespans rather than from greatly superior net annual productivities.

EVERGREEN CONIFER DOMINANCE

Another outstanding feature of the forests of the Pacific Northwest is their dominance by evergreen coniferous trees. Typically, forests in moderate environments in north temperate regions are dominated by deciduous hardwoods or by a mixture of hardwoods and conifers. This is true of natural forests in Asia, Europe, and the eastern United States. Yet, in the Pacific Northwest the ratio of conifers to hardwoods is more than 1,000:1 (Kuchler, 1946), a unique phenomenon. Furthermore, the few hardwoods that are present tend to occur as pioneer species (e.g., red alder) or occupy environmentally marginal or severe habitats (e.g., oaks), while in other temperate regions conifers tend to pioneer or be pushed toward more severe environments (see e.g., Regal, 1977).

What factors have been responsible for the evolution of these temperate forests in which conifers so completely dominate hardwoods? Scientists have speculated about this since the time of von Humboldt in the

mid-1800's. Some suggest that many hardwood genera were eliminated by cold temperatures during glacial epochs (Kuchler, 1946; Gray and Hooker, 1882). Most hardwood extinctions actually occurred during the Pliocene, however, eliminating glaciation as a factor. Furthermore, some scientists (Silen, 1962) feel that favorable Pleistocene environments in the Pacific Northwest, including the availability of migration routes, were factors contributing to the survival of the outstanding conifer gene pool.

Moisture and temperate deficiencies have also been proposed as important factors in eliminating hardwoods. Chaney and others (1944) suggest that arid periods were responsible for hardwood losses. Daubenmire (1975, 1976) identifies the annual distribution of the heat budget, i.e., summer heat deficiencies coupled with an inability to utilize the frequent warm days in the spring and fall. Regal (1977) proposes that gymnosperms survive as dominants only in environments that are, in some way, harsh or rigorous, but he concedes uncertainty as to how the coniferous forests of the Pacific Northwest conform to this hypothesis.

Research conducted under the auspices of the Coniferous Forest Biome clearly indicates that existing forests are very well adapted to the current climatic regime. In a variety of ways, the evergreen coniferous habit appears superior to that of a deciduous hardwood within the macroclimatic regime of warm, relatively dry summers and mild, wet winters. Since comparable climatic regimes have existed for several epochs, we propose that these were also key factors in the evolution of the northwestern coniferous forests and the competitive elimination of much of the original hardwood flora.

Climate

The climatic regime in the Pacific Northwest has striking contrasts to the climate in other temperate forest regions. Salient elements shown in Figures 2, 3, and 4 illustrate the temperature regime, precipitation pattern, and vapor pressure deficits for several stations in the Pacific Northwest and in temperate forest regions of the eastern United States and Europe.

Climatically, the region experiences wet, mild winters and warm, relatively dry summers. The dormant season, when shoot growth is inactive, is characterized by heavy precipitation with daytime temperatures usually above freezing. The growing season has warm temperatures associated with clear days, relatively little precipitation, and frequent vapor pressure deficits, except directly on the Pacific Coast (i.e., in the _Picea sitchensis_ Zone of Franklin and Dyrness, 1973). Water storage in snowpack, soils, and vegetation, as well as pulses of fog, clouds, or cool maritime air which reduce evaporation, are obviously important during the summer drought period experienced in the Pacific Northwest.

Climate in the region varies consider-

ably because of interactions between maritime and continental air masses and mountain ranges. Along the coast, where the maritime influence is strongest, mild temperatures are associated with prolonged cloudiness and narrow diurnal and seasonal fluctuations in temperature (6 to 10°C). Winters are extremely wet and freezing temperatures are rare. Summers are cool and relatively dry, but extended periods of cloudiness and fog greatly reduce evaporation. Valleys located in the lee of the Coast Ranges are drier and subject to greater temperature extremes and evaporative demand. For example, Eureka on the California coast contrasts with Roseburg in Oregon's Umpqua Valley, which is located between the Cascade and Coastal ranges (Figures 2, 3, and 4). On the western slopes of the Cascade Range, percipitation again increases and temperature regimes moderate until subalpine environments, with their cooler temperatures and deep winter snowpacks, are encountered. Similar patterns occur elsewhere in the

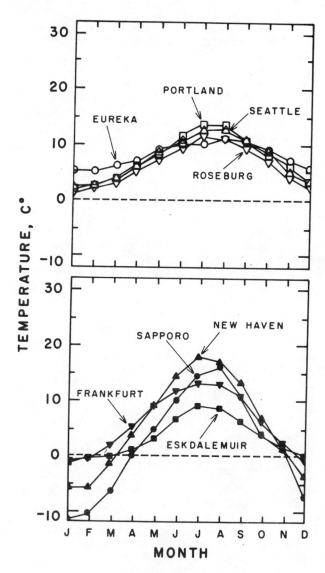

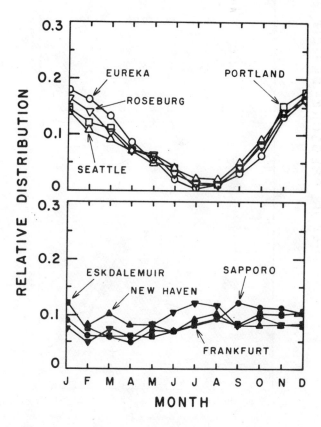

Figure 2. _Temperature patterns that illustrate the contrast between the Pacific Northwest and other temperate forest regions of the world. Four stations in the Pacific Northwest are illustrated in section A, including one (Eureka) on the immediate coast. Stations from the eastern United States (New Haven), Japan (Sapporo), Scotland (Eskdalemuir), and Europe (Frankfurt) are illustrated in section B. Note the higher winter temperatures in the Pacific Northwest._

Figure 3. _Relative distribution of precipitation in the Pacific Northwest (section A) and other temperate forest regions throughout the world (section B). Note the relatively dry summer period in section A and the equitable distribution of precipitation in section B._

region, although areas to the south are, of course, warmer and drier while those to the north are cooler and moister.

The climatic contrasts with other temperate forest regions are striking (Figures 2, 3, and 4). Major forest regions in the eastern United States, eastern Asia, and Europe have precipitation more evenly distributed with no reduction during the growing season (Figure 3). Throughout most of the Pacific Northwest, less than 10 per-

cent of the total precipitation falls during the growing season. In other temperate forest regions, summers are typically hotter and more humid, and winters are colder. Night temperatures during the growing season in the Pacific Northwest generally remain below 12°C. Near the coast, or along cold air drainages in the mountain valleys, nights often experience 10°C. Cool nights may create dew, but this quickly evaporates on clear warm days and evaporative demands are ultimately much higher than those experienced at similar temperatures in other temperate forest regions. Past regional comparisons have underestimated evaporative differences by failing to consider differences in humidity. This method underestimates evaporation in the Pacific Northwest by 25 to 60 percent for July and August, as seen by comparing maximum temperatures (Figure 2) with maximum vapor pressure deficits (Figure 4).

How Environment Favors Evergreen Conifers

Almost all structural features of the northwestern forests are functionally advantageous under the moisture, temperature, and nutrient regimes of the Pacific Northwest--massiveness, evergreenness, conifer wood structure, and needle leaves. Factors favoring these habits can be aggregated into three categories:
   (1) Possibility of nongrowing season assimilation,
   (2) Constraint of photosynthesis by unfavorable moisture regimes in the summer, and
   (3) Peculiarities of the nutrient regime.

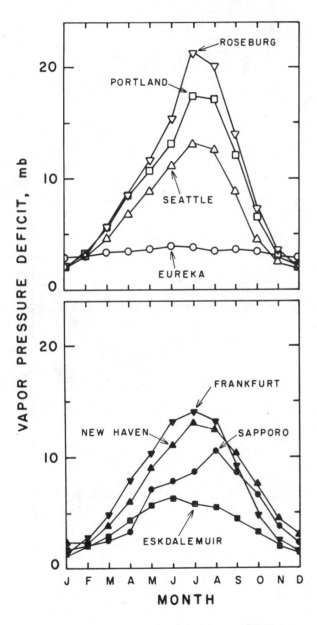

Figure 4. Monthly vapor pressure deficits for selected stations in the Pacific Northwest (section A) and other temperate forest regions of the world (section B). Summer deficits are generally much higher in the Pacific Northwest; the Eureka station is located on the immediate Pacific Coast.

Nongrowing Season Assimilation. Mild temperatures permit substantial photosynthesis during the so-called dormant season of fall, winter, and spring. Conifers can assimilate over a broad temperature range. Considerable carbon uptake is possible below freezing (Ungerson and Scherdin, 1968) even by coastal species such as Sitka spruce (Neilson et al., 1972). Significant winter accumulations of dry matter by conifers have been documented in climates as diverse as those of western Norway and Great Britain (Hagem, 1947, 1962) (Rutter, 1957; Pollard and Wareing, 1968). Sitka spruce seedlings in Scotland actually doubled their dry weight between late September and mid-April (Bradbury and Malcom, 1979).

Substantial net photosynthesis occurs over a wide range of environments during the dormant season in the Pacific Northwest. Winter temperatures are mild and subfreezing day temperatures uncommon, even in montane environments. This is equally true of soil and air temperature; frozen soils are extremely uncommon even in subalpine environments, so water uptake is not a major problem. Model simulations indicate that as much as half of the annual net carbon assimilation by Douglas-fir occurs between October and May (Emmingham and Waring, 1977) (Figure 5). This long period of favorable temperature (and moisture conditions, as will be seen) is entirely lost to the deciduous hardwoods. The winter photosynthetic opportunity of the evergreen conifers is further enhanced by their long, conical crowns that intercept greater amounts of light during the low angles of the winter sun.

Unfavorable Summer Moisture Regimes. Now we can consider the second of the factors--constraint of summer or growing season photosynthesis by unfavorable moisture regimes. Extended periods of vapor pressure deficits during the summers force stomata on leaf surfaces to close, reducing water loss and subsequent carbon dioxide uptake. Effects of summer drought are particularly evident on dry sites, where nearly 70 percent of the annual net photosynthesis probably occurs outside of the growing season. Such site-to-site variations are apparent in Figure 5, where the effects of summer drought are compared in such contrasting sites as the coastal Sitka spruce zone environment and a hot, dry habitat type in the Cascade Mountains where Douglas-fir is the climax species.

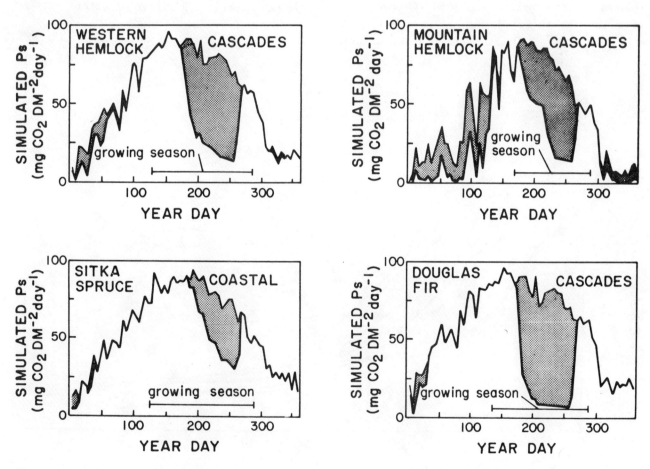

Figure 5. Simulated photosynthetic rates for Douglas-fir growth (1 to 2 m tall) in different forest environments characteristic of the Pacific Northwest. Maximal (upper) line shows potential photosynthesis without constraints due to moisture stress, frost, or low soil temperature; lower line incorporates these constraints, with the difference between the two projections shaded. A high proportion of the yearly photosynthesis occurs outside the "growing season" on all of these sites. "Western Hemlock Cascades" is for a moderate forest site, "Mountain Hemlock Cascades" for a very cold and snowy subalpine forest site, "Sitka Spruce Coastal" for a very favorable coastal site, and "Douglas-fir Cascades" for a very dry site.

Stomatal closure results from both soil moisture deficiencies and high evaporative demand (Hallgren, 1977; Running et al., 1975). Seasonal reductions in available soil water cause plant water deficits in many locations and will limit the degree to which stomata may open (Running et al., 1975). Increasing evaporative demand, measured by the water vapor deficit of the atmosphere, can also bring about stomatal closure, even in the presence of adequate soil water (Figure 6). Hundreds of field measurements reveal that both conifers and hardwoods are affected.

Evergreen conifers still have significant advantages over hardwoods during periods of moisture deficiency even though stomatal closure reduces photosynthesis in both groups. Heat exchange is less inhibited in needle-shaped than broad leaves, maintaining closer to ambient temperatures (Gates, 1968), particularly when stomata

are completely closed. Because evaporative demand usually exceeds critical limits during the growing season over much of the Pacific Northwest, the environment is obviously less than optimum for plants dependent upon this season for carbon uptake. Cool temperatures at night during the summer months also mean that evergreens are not penalized as severely by respiration losses as might be the case in temperate regions with warm summer nights.

Large volumes of sapwood are a structural feature of conifer forests that also helps dampen the effect of dry summer days. Both hardwoods and conifers utilize some water from conducting tissues to help meet daily transpiration requirements (Gibbs, 1958). However, the conifers have cells that are easier to recharge and that, because the trees grow larger, store much more water (Figure 7). A single 80-m Douglas-fir tree may store 4,000 liters of water

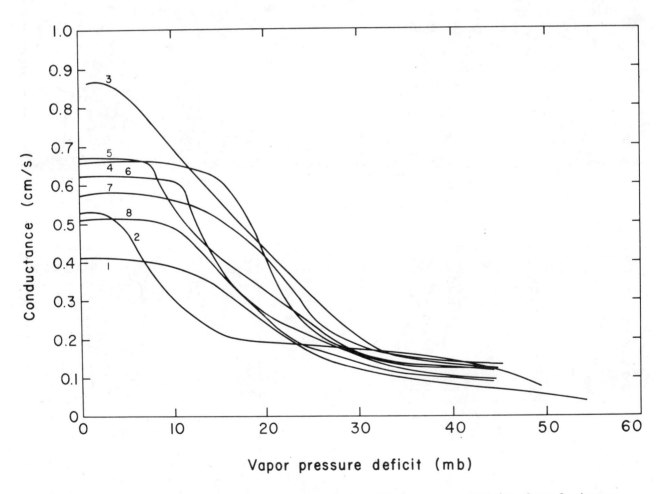

Figure 6. Maximum stomatal conductances recorded at different evaporative demands (vapor pressure deficits) for a variety of native species growing under conditions with adequate soil water. Conifers: 1 is Douglas-fir (n = 312), 2 is western hemlock (n = 404). Deciduous trees: 3 is Pacific dogwood (n = 402), 4 is bigleaf maple (n = 68). Evergreen broadleaf trees: 5 is golden chinkapin (n = 159). Deciduous shrub: 6 is vine maple (n = 429). Evergreen broadleaf shrubs: 7 is Pacific rhododendron (n = 451), 8 is salal (n = 435).

(Running et al., 1975). A forest stand can have more than 250 m^3/ha of water available, enough to supply up to half the daily water budget (Waring and Running, 1978). Therefore, the sapwood represents a significant buffer against extremes in transpiration demand and helps offset the disadvantage of lifting water to great heights. Furthermore, although full hydration occurs during the winter, conifers may partially recharge sapwood after summer rain showers. Many hardwoods have no mechanism for effectively refilling the larger evacuated vessels until the next spring.

Large leaf areas may provide additional structural advantages for evergreen conifers in the dry summer climate of the Pacific Northwest. Water is sorted on and in the foliage in proportion to its area. The large needle mass also serves as a condensing surface for fog or dew, thus supplementing summer precipitation.

Summarizing contrasts in conifer-hardwood response to summer moisture deficiencies, both groups suffer stomatal closure and reduction in photosynthesis. Conifers have excellent control of water loss without increasing their leaf temperatures, however. They also can develop greater water storage capacities than hardwoods and utilize these adaptations to reduce the impact of stress common during the growing season.

Adaptations to Nutrient Regime. We can now consider the last of the three environmental influences—the distinctive nutrient regime of the Pacific Northwest. Nutrients clearly rank below temperature and moisture in their influence on the evolution of these forests, but they are still an important factor. The region has a nutrient regime that contrasts with that characteristic of other temperate forest regions, partially because of the winter-wet, summer-dry climate.

Decomposition and subsequent nutrient release from the organic layer occurs mostly during the cool, wet "dormant" season in the Pacific Northwest and may essentially cease during the relatively dry summer (Figure 8). Slow summer decomposition has been reported from such diverse sites as Douglas-fir and western hemlock forests at low to middle elevations and subalpine fir forests at high elevations in the Cascade Range (Fogel and Cromack, 1979; Turner and Singer, 1976). In the western Oregon Cascade Range almost no measurable decomposition occurs in July and August (Fogel and Cromack, 1979).

The massiveness of the forests also contributes to the uniqueness of the nutrient regime by binding large amounts of nutrients into standing crops. Over the long

sequences between disturbances organic matter accumulates on the forest floor, particularly as slowly decomposed coarse woody debris—large logs and branches. Ultimately, this creates conditions for large episodic losses of nitrogen and other nutrients as a result of wildfires.[1]

The pecularities of these nutrient regimes combine to favor plants that have relatively low nutrient requirements, conservatively use acquired nutrients, and can accumulate nutrients during the wet season when decomposition is most active. Evergreen conifers appear to have advantages over deciduous hardwoods on all scores.

Conifers generally have lower nutrient requirements and use nutrients more efficiently than most hardwoods. Foliage retention for several years is obviously advantageous in reducing annual nutrient requirements; current foliage may be only 15 to 16 percent of the total in Douglas-fir forests (Overton et al., 1973; Pike et al., 1977). The relatively low levels of nutrients found in foliage are also evidence of lower conifer requirements. Nitrogen in healthy foliage of 450-year-old Douglas-fir rarely exceeds 0.8 percent (dry weight basis), less than half the level of most hardwoods (Rodin and Bazilevich, 1967). Similar contrasts have been demonstrated with calcium.

Northwestern conifers also meet increasing proportions of their total nutrient requirements by redistribution from older tissue, especially senescent needles. Half of the nitrogen required by a 100-year-old stand of Douglas-fir (down to 30 kg/ha/yr from a high of 50) is met by translocation

_____

[1] There are a large array of organisms associated with nitrogen fixation in the Pacific Northwest. Successional pioneers in the genera of Alnus and Ceanothus, as well as other higher plants, have nitrogen-fixing microbial associates. Large amounts of nitrogen—50 to 300 kg/ha/yr—can be fixed by such plants during early stages of forest development, partially or completely balancing losses associated with catastrophic fires. Foliose lichens endemic to the old-growth forests provide further, continuing nitrogen inputs of 3 to 5 kg/ha/yr. Finally, large boles which, as snags and down logs, survive major disturbances, are a source of slowly available nitrogen as well as the site for substantial microbial fixation. All of these pathways for fixation and retention of nitrogen may represent adaptations to catastrophic wildfires and related nitrogen deficiencies in a region otherwise favorable to vegetative growth.

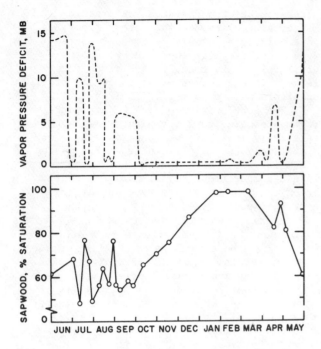

Figure 7. Seasonal variation in sapwood water storage of old-growth Douglas-fir (section B) in relation to evaporative demand (section A). Periodic summer storms totaling less than 10 cm precipitation reduced the evaporative demand, but clear weather following the storms encouraged a partial recharge before depletion began again. With the onset of fall precipitation, the evaporative demand remained below 2 ml and sapwood recharged at a constant rate until January when filled. In April 1976 the average evaporative demand exceeded 5 ml; some water columns in the sapwood were broken and the water was utilized for transpiration. Recharge is still possible after April, but only under abnormally low evaporative demand.

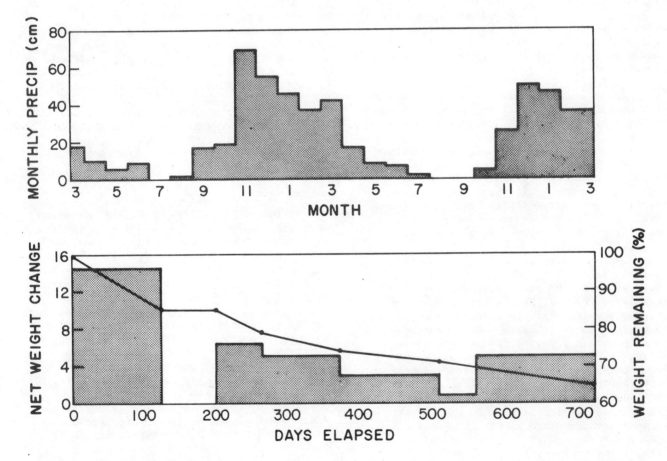

Figure 8. Decomposition rate for leaf litter stored in litter bags for two years, illustrating the highly seasonal nature of decomposition in the Pacific Northwest and its relation to precipitation (courtesy Kermit Cromack, Jr.)

(Cole et al., 1975). Other northwestern conifers behave similarly and may be even more conservative.

Deciduous hardwoods also redistribute substantial amounts of nutrients from foliage prior to leaf fall, but their total requirements are higher. Mature hardwoods reportedly require 70 kg/ha of nitrogen to develop their canopy each year, and less than one-third of this can be met by trans-location from storage sites within the tree (Bormann et al., 1977).

Nutrient cycles also tigten during succession accentuating problems for a deciduous hardwood. Trees are increasingly dependent upon the forest floor, rather than the soil, for nutrients (Cole et al., 1975). Yet litter quality declines and litter decay slows, making this a poorer source of nutrients.

Hence, nutrient regimes in the Pacific Northwest again appear to be penalizing hardwoods. Total nutrient requirements are higher for hardwoods than evergreen conifers. Requirements must be largely met by absorption from soil and forest floor since hardwoods cannot provide as much of their nutrient requirements by internal redistribution. Yet decomposition and nutrient release are lowest during summer months when hardwood nutrient demand is high; the large pulses of nutrients during the wet fall and winter seasons is of less value for deciduous trees since they are less capable than evergreens of absorbing nutrients during the dormant season (Mooney and Rundel, 1979).

In summary evergreen coniferous trees are well adapted to the existing moisture, temperature, and nutrient regimes in the Pacific Northwest. Deciduous hardwood species have, on the other hand, numerous disadvantages in competing with conifers. First, they cannot utilize the "dormant" season for photosynthesis. Second, they are dependent upon assimilation during the growing season, a time when photosynthesis is frequently constrained by atmospheric and soil moisture deficiencies. Third, hardwoods have higher nutrient requirements and a higher proportion must be met by uptake from the soil and litter layers; again, this must be done during the growing season when decomposition and nutrient release are at minimal levels due to reduced soil moisture. Dominance by evergreen conifers appears to be an evolutionary response to a climate with cool, wet winters and warm, dry summers.

FOREST MASSIVENESS

The advantages of being massive are not as clear as those of being evergreen. Massiveness is, to a degree, related to some of the same environmental factors that favor evergreenness, however.

Size or massiveness results from the sustained growth and longevity of the tree species that occur in the Pacific Northwest. The fact that many species sustain their height and diameter growth for more than two or three centuries has already been mentioned. It is also important to recognize that every coniferous genus represented in the Pacific Northwest (save only Juniperus) has its largest and often longest-lived representative here--and often its second and third largest as well (Table 5).

Such a circumstance requires at least two conditions. First, there must be species' gene pools that favor persistent growth and long life. Second, there must be environmental conditions that allow the expression of this genetic potential--or at least do not select against such genotypes. Such environments are not necessarily pervasive in the temperate zone of the world. Periodic storms with high winds (hurricanes and typhoons) are, in fact, characteristic of most temperate forest regions. Indeed, Fujimori (1971) suggests that infrequent strong winds, such as those that disturb or weaken forest communities, are a key factor in the development of massive, long-lived forests in the Pacific Northwest. Less favorable conditions for development of pathogens is one of several alternative hypotheses. Neither explanation seems completely satisfactory.

Large size and longevity have adaptive advantages. Competitively, they obviously allow a species to overtop one of smaller structure or out-persist a species of short lifespan, or both. Long-lived species classed as pioneers or shade-intolerant are able to span the long periods between destructive episodes. Forest sites in the Pacific Northwest can go for many centuries between disturbances sufficient to allow regeneration of shade-intolerant species. For example, Hemstrom (1979) calculated the average fire-return period for Mount Rainier National Park, a site typical of much of the Cascade and Coastal ranges, to be more than 400 years. A short-lived, shade-intolerant species is clearly at a disadvantage under such disturbance regimes.

As with many organisms large size allows for buffering against adverse environmental conditions and stresses of various types. The value of the large sapwood storage areas in conifers in reducing

Table 5.   Typical and maximum ages and dimensions attained by selected species of forest trees on better sites in the Pacific Northwest[1]

Species	Typical			Maximum	
	Age	Diameter	Height	Age	Diameter
	years	cm	m	years	cm
Silver fir (Abies amabilis)	400+	90–110	44–55	590	206
Noble fir (Abies procera)	400+	100–150	45–70	>600	270
Port-Orford-cedar (Chamaecyparis lawsoniana)	500+	120–180	60	--	359
Alaska yellow-cedar (Chamaecyparis nootkatenis)	1,000+	100–150	30–40	3,500	297
Western larch (Larix occidentalis)	700+	140	50	915	233
Incense-cedar (Libocedrus decurrens)	500+	90	120	>542	368
Engelmann spruce (Picea engelmannii)	400+	100+	45–50	>500	231
Sitka spruce (Picea sitchensis)	500	180–230	70–75	>750	525
Sugar pine (Pinus lambertiana)	400	100–125	45–55	--	306
Western white pine (Pinus monticola)	400+	110	60	615	197
Ponderosa pine (Pinus ponderosa)	600+	75–125	30–50	726	267
Douglas-fir (Pseudotsuga menziesii)	750+	150–220	70–80	1,200	434
Coast redwood (Sequoia sempervirens)	1,250+	150–380	75–100	2,200	501
Western redcedar (Thuja plicata)	1,000+	150–300	60+	>1,200	631
Western hemlock (Tsuga heterophylla)	400+	90–120	50–65	>500	260
Mountain hemlock (Tsuga mertensiana)	400+	75–100	35+	>800	221

[1]Typical values mainly from Franklin and Dyrness, 1973; maximum diameters from American Forestry Association, 1973; maximum ages from Fowells, 1965; or personal observations by the authors.

effects of high moisture deficiencies has already been pointed out. The large mass of various organs, such as leaves, are also valuable for storage of nutrients and carbohydrates for use during times of high demand (the growing season) or stress.

SUCCESSIONAL ASPECTS OF NORTHWESTERN FORESTS

The lack of quantitative data on various aspects of forest succession in the Pacific Northwest is astounding. Foresters and botanists have been observing these forests for nearly a century, yet most successional analyses are either anecdotal (e.g., Munger, 1930, 1940) or based upon inferences drawn from current size class distributions (e.g., Franklin, 1966). Quantitative data have been especially scarce for older forests. Some data have been collected on compositional and structural changes in recently logged or burned areas (Dyrness, 1973).

This situation is rapidly changing and there are many interesting new findings in regard to changes in diversity, leaf and biomass development, and nitrogen budgets during forest succession (Long and Turner, 1975). Another interesting development is the increased recognition of multiple pathways in the development of stands on a given site, i.e., several possible species series as contrasted with a single sequence of pioneer and climax species.

We will consider briefly two aspects of forest succession which have been explored in recent studies: (1) age structures in old-growth Douglas-fir/western hemlock forests and (2) dynamics of coarse woody debris in a Douglas-fir forest chronosequence.

Age Structures in Old-Growth Douglas-fir Stands

Foresters and ecologists have always assumed that the old-growth forests dominated by Douglas-fir are even-aged. The Douglas-firs in these stands presumably were established over short time periods following major fires or other disturbances. In part, these assumptions were based upon observations of forest development and Douglas-fir regeneration following the extensive fires in the mid and late 1800's as well as in the Yacholt and Tillamook Burns of the twentieth century (Munger, 1930, 1940). For a time it was even believed that new Douglas-fir forests sprang almost instantly from seed stored in the litter layers (Hofmann, 1971), a hypothesis later disproved by Isaac (1943). No one bothered to analyze age structures of any old-growth stands, however, to test their hypothesized even-aged nature.

In 1975, an age structure analysis was conducted in an old-growth Douglas-fir stand at H. J. Andrews Experimental Forest in the western Cascades of Oregon. Experimental Watershed No. 10, a 10-hectare drainage, was clearcut. Previously, all of the trees in this drainage more than 15 cm diameter at breast height (dbh) had been stem mapped, recorded by dbh and species, and tagged at stump level. Following clearcutting, rings were counted on stumps of more than 600 of the 2,700 inventoried stems, including a large proportion of the dominant Douglas-firs.

The age distribution of the counted Douglas-fir trees on Watershed No. 10 is shown in Figure 9A. A disturbance in about 1800 is obvious from a wave of younger Douglas-firs; this partial burn is also apparent in the age distribution of hemlocks, most of which date from 1800. The surprising result is the very wide range in ages of dominant, old-growth Douglas-firs in this stand--from 275 to 540 years of age. Furthermore, there is no evidence of multiple peaks or waves of establishment-- just a gradually increasing number of individuals followed by a broad-crested peak and gradually declining period of establishment (Figure 9B). Analysis of separate habitat segments on this diverse watershed (Hawk, 1979), such as the moist lower slope and dry ridgetop situations, provided no explanation for the forest age pattern; a similar age distribution was found on all habitats.

Watershed No. 10 might be considered an aberrant situation, especially in view of the overall decadence of the stand (Grier and Logan, 1977) and relatively low site quality. Subsequent age structure analyses, however, have revealed similar patterns elsewhere. Joseph Means (pers. comm., 1979) analyzed a dense, thrifty Douglas-fir stand at about 1,000 m on a cool, moist habitat type. The same pattern, with a 125-year age range in the dominant Douglas-firs, is present (Figure 10). Ring counts on several clearcuts surrounding Thornton T. Munger Research Natural Area in the Wind River drainage of the southern Washington Cascade Range reveal an even more extended age range (200 years) in the dominant Douglas-firs (Figure 11); this stand is at around 500 m. The Douglas-fir age structures reported by Boyce and Bruce-Wagg (1953) are further evidence for wide ranges of age in old-growth stands; the implications of these early data were apparently overlooked.

The conclusion from all of these analyses is that many of the old-growth Douglas-fir forests are not even-aged. For some reason, many of these stands did not close up rapidly following the disturbance or series of disturbances that destroyed the previous stands. Douglas-fir has apparently taken a long period (100 to 200 years) to fully reoccupy many of these sites. There are several possible explanations. The disturbance or disturbances that gave rise to these stands, many of which are 400 to 500 years of age, may have been so extensive as to eliminate seed source; gradual re-colonization of the area would have been required, with a few individuals becoming established and eventually providing the seed source for development of a closed stand. The age structure patterns fit Harper's (1978) hypothesized sequence of this type. Competing vegetation may have delayed establishment of trees. Multiple disturbances subsequent to the first one may have wiped out portions of young stands, creating open spaces for establishment of even younger cohorts; reburns of young Douglas-fir stands occur, with survival of individual and small patches of trees.

In any case, the assumed pattern of forest succession with early establishment of even-aged Douglas-fir stands does not appear to be the pattern followed by many of the old-growth stands. Successional studies during coming years should provide evidence of additional patterns and the responsible factors. Indeed, a recent study of tree ages in the Cowlitz River drainage of Mount Rainier National Park shows that establishment of shade-intolerance tree species, such as Douglas-fir and western white pine, is still taking place more than 80 years after the last wildfire (Figure 12) (Hemstrom, 1979).

Coarse Woody Debris in a Forest Chronosequence

Structural changes associated with suc-cessional development of forest stands in the Douglas-fir region are currently under study. These studies were stimulated, in part, by an analysis of old-growth forests (Franklin et al., 1979) that revealed precious little knowledge of northwestern forest structure beyond measurements of wood volumes and production. A series of nine Cascade Range stands have been studied thus far, ranging in age from about 100 years to more than 1,000 years. A major structural feature is the amount and distri-bution of coarse woody debris as standing dead (snags) and down (logs and chunks) (Table 6).

One of the most surprising findings from this survey was the large amount of dead wood in young stands. Much wood is being carried from the old into the new stand. Wildfire or windthrow may kill the previous stand but consumes very little of the wood; indeed, one or, more probably, several subsequent fires would be required to eliminate the large snags and down logs. Consequently, large amounts of woody debris bridge the disturbance and remain important structural features of the young stand for several centuries because of their slow rate of decomposition. By the time the woody debris carried over has largely dis-appeared, stems in the young stand are sufficiently large to provide an input of large woody debris. As a result, there seems to be a rather high level of woody debris found at all stages in forest suc-cession. The large amount of coarse woody debris provides a major structural con-trast between the natural "second-growth" stands and the managed forests created after logging.

A second interesting feature is the suggestion of greater amounts of woody debris with stand age. There is a trend toward greater absolute amounts as well as a higher ratio of dead/live organic matter in the stands more than 750 years of age (Figure 13). Amounts of coarse woody debris

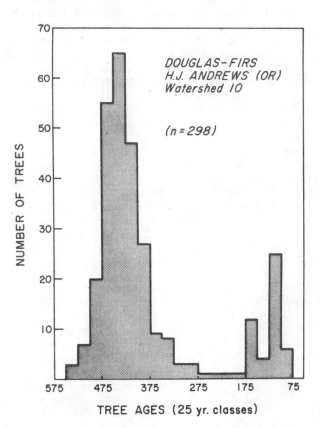

Figure 9A. Age class distribution of Douglas-fir trees on Watershed No. 10 at the H. J. Andrews Experimental Forest in the western Oregon Cascade Range. Tabulation of all counts by 25-year age classes.

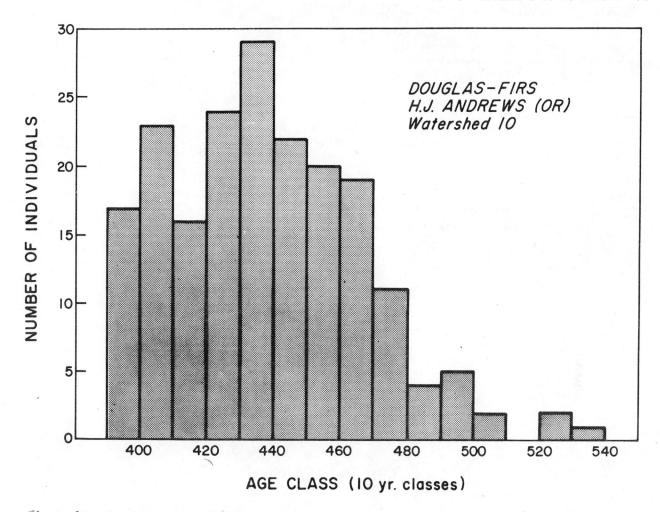

Figure 9B.   *Age class distribution of Douglas-fir trees on Watershed No. 10 at the H. J. Andrews Experimental Forest in the western Oregon Cascade Range.   Tally of old-growth trees by 10-year age classes.*

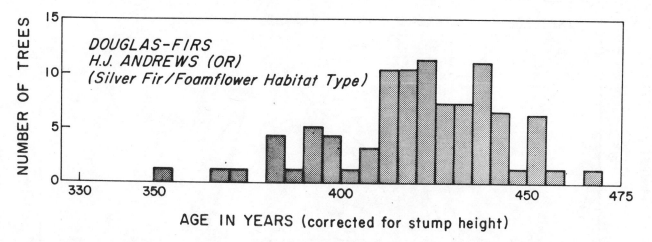

Figure 10.   *Age-class distribution of Douglas-fir trees in an old-growth stand located at about 900 m in the H. J. Andrews Experimental Forest on the Oregon Cascade Range.*

at a given age vary widely, almost certainly because of peculiarities in development of individual stands.   This variability makes it difficult to substantiate any statistical trends associated with stand age.   There is, however, some corollary evidence from an analysis of old-growth stands at Mount Rainier National Park that suggests reduced amounts of live biomass in very old stands (Table 6).   A current hypotheses is that live organic biomass in a stand may peak at around 300 to 400 years, total biomass (live and dead) at around 750 years, and dead (coarse woody debris) at 800 to 1,000 or more years.   Many more stand analyses are required, however, given the variability in patterns of stand development.

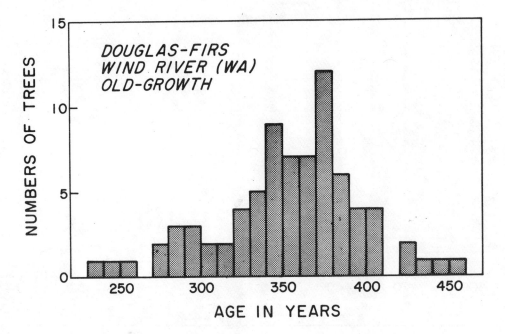

Figure 11.   *Age-class distribution of Douglas-fir trees in old-growth stands located around the periphery of the Thornton T. Munger Research Natural Area in the Wind River valley of the southern Washington Cascade Range.*

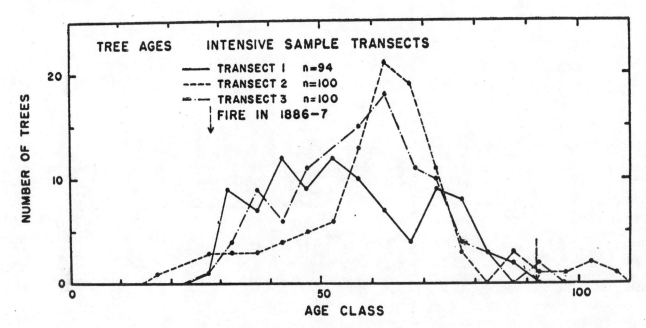

Figure 12.   *Age-class distribution of trees in stands developed following wildfires in the later 1800's in the Cowlitz River drainage, Mount Rainier National Park, Washington (from Hemstrom, 1979).*

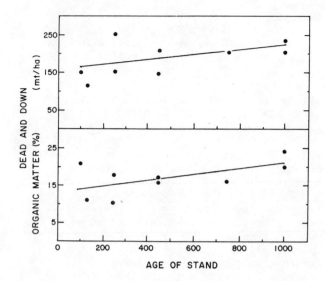

Figure 13. *Total amounts (mt/ha) and percent of the total organic matter provided by coarse woody debris (standing dead trees and down logs) in a chronosequence of Douglas-fir/western hemlock forests located in the Cascade Range of Oregon and Washington; only a weak relationship with age is apparent in this preliminary data set.*

Table 6. *Coarse woody debris in a chronosequence of stands from mid-elevations in the northern Oregon and southern Washington Cascade Range[1]*

Stand[2]	Age	Live biomass[3]	Coarse woody debris			Dead/total biomass
			Snags	Logs	Total	
	yrs	mt/ha		mt/ha		%
HJA RS 24	100	564	37	113	150	21
HJA RS 26	130	934	48	70	118	11
MR 1	250	1,318	67	85	152	10
Bagby	250	1,069	122	129	251	19
HJA RS 2	450	1,189	58	90	148	11
HJA RS 3	450	991	79	131	210	17
Squaw	750	1,094	85	119	204	16
MR 2	1,000+	638	48	156	204	24
MR 3	1,000+	931	120	112	232	20

[1] Unpublished data on file at the Forestry Sciences Laboratory, Corvallis, Oregon.

[2] "HJA RS" refers to hectare "reference stands" or permanent sample plots at H.J. Andrews Experimental Forest in the western Cascades of Oregon. "MR" stands are similar plots in Mount Rainier National Park, Washington. Bagby and Squaw are located in the northern Oregon Cascade Range.

[3] Including 20 percent of live aboveground biomass as estimate of live belowground biomass.

OLD-GROWTH FOREST ECOSYSTEMS

Old-growth forests are distinctive ecosystems that have not been well understood
by either foresters or the lay public. Indeed, no one was really very interested in
them until recently. Some viewed these forests as biological deserts although, insofar
as biologic diversity is concerned, that
description is most applicable to the dense,
productive young forest. Others viewed them
solely in aesthetic or religious terms. In
any case, with their broadened sense of land
stewardship, foresters are thinking increasingly in terms of maintaining and re-
creating such systems in order to provide a
diversity of habitats and organisms.
Questions have arisen as to the essential
features of old-growth forests, however.
What are their key characteristics and how
do they differ from managed stands or from
the natural second-growth forests that
follow wildfire?

General features of old-growth (>200
years old) forest stands in the Douglas-fir
region now have been described (Franklin
et al., 1979). We have extracted a few
highlights from that characterization and
will briefly examine the compositional
(what is there), functional (how it runs),
and structural (how it's put together) features of old-growth forests. The emphasis
will be on structure, since this provides a
major key to the distinctiveness of old-
growth stands.

Composition

The composition of old-growth forests
is obviously different from that of young
stands. Changes in composition--the array
of plant and animal species--is, after all,
a keystone of ecological succession. Many
species, including some saprophytic plants,
some epiphytic lichens, and several vertebrates, find optimum habitat conditions in
old-growth forests. There are relatively
few species of plants or animals that are
found only in old-growth forests, however.
Some organisms may require old-growth for
maintenance of viable populations, although
that is not yet clear. Currently, verte-
brate/old-growth relationships are best
understood, and a list of 14 birds and nine
mammals finding their optimum habitat in
old-growth Douglas-fir forests has been
compiled (Franklin et al., 1979). Several
of these, such as the northern spotted owl
(Strix occidentalis) and the red tree vole
(Arborimus longicaudus), may be examples of
species that require a reservoir of their
optimum habitat in old-growth forest to
survive.

Function

Functional aspects of forests include
primary production and the cycling of
nutrients and energy. Productivity in old-
growth forests is typically high, despite
statements to the contrary. The large leaf
areas and masses found in northwestern forests were mentioned earlier, and there is
no indication that levels decline significantly in older stands. A single long-
crowned old-growth Douglas-fir tree may
have as many as 66 million needles and
2,800 m^2 of needle surface area. With such
large and intact photosynthetic factories,
production values are maintained at comparable levels over many centuries. However, respiration costs are high in old-
growth stands because of their large live
biomasses, greatly reducing the amount of
net production.

On the more practical level, little
accumulation of additional live biomass or
board feet occurs in most old-growth stands.
Substantial wood increment is taking place
on individual trees, including associated
western hemlock and other shade-tolerant
species. Typically, this wood growth is
largely offset by mortality and decay
losses in living trees. In a 250-year-old
Douglas-fir stand in the Mount Hood National
Forest annual wood increment over 10 years
was 15.8 m^3/ha; an episode of heavy mortality (14.1 m^3/ha/yr) caused by bark
beetles and windthrow nearly offset this
large growth. In the Thornton T. Munger
Research Natural Area in the Gifford Pinchot
National Forest a 450-year-old Douglas-fir/
western hemlock stand grew 7.4 m^3/ha/yr
over 12 years; the average annual mortality
was 6.7 m^3/ha/yr. Hence, both stands
registered small net gains. Over the long
run, living biomass in stands in old stands
probably fluctuates around a plateau in
response to episodes of heavy and light
mortality.

Old-growth forests are known to be
highly retentive of nutrients. Complex
detrital pathways exist in such stands and
the release of energy and nutrients from
dead organic matter is slow. This is reflected in the low levels of nutrients and
other dissolved and suspended materials in
streams from old-growth forests (see
Fredriksen, 1970, 1972). Mechanisms for
fixation of atmospheric nitrogen are also
well developed in old-growth forests, providing for substantial increments by foliose
lichens in tree crowns and by microbial
fixation in coarse woody debris (see Carroll,
this volume; Triska and Cromack, this
volume).

Structure

Structural diversity is characteristic of old-growth forests. There is, for example, a large range in tree sizes, a more varied canopy, and greater patchiness in the understory.

There are, however, three structural components of overwhelming importance--the individual, large, old-growth tree, the large, standing dead tree or snag, and the large, dead, down trunks or logs. These structural components are, in large measure, unique to an old-growth forest ecosystem, setting it apart from young growth and, especially, managed stands. These components are all related (Figure 14), with the tree playing a progression of roles from the time it is alive through its routing to an unrecognizable component of the forest floor. Further, most of the unique (or at least distinctive) compositional and functional features of old-growth forests can be related to these structures (Table 7); that is, these structural components make possible much of the uniqueness of old-growth forests in terms of flora and fauna and the way in which energy and nutrients are cycled. Finally, logs are at least as important (and possibly more so) to the stream component as they are to the terrestrial component of the ecosystem (see Triska and Cromack; Swanson; and Cummins, all this volume).

The most conspicuous structural component is probably the live, old-growth Douglas-fir tree. Diameters of 1 to 2 m and heights of 50 to 90 m are typical. The trees are highly individualistic, having been shaped over the centuries by a wide range in forces. The large, deep, irregular crown is an important ecological feature (Figure 15). Live branch systems often extend two-thirds of the length of the bole. Flattened, fan-shaped branch arrays are characteristic and provide extensive horizontal surfaces for the development of epiphytic communities and wildlife habitat. Carroll (this volume) discusses the role of such canopies in nutrient cycling and the importance of canopy lichens (especially Lobaria oregana) in nitrogen fixation.

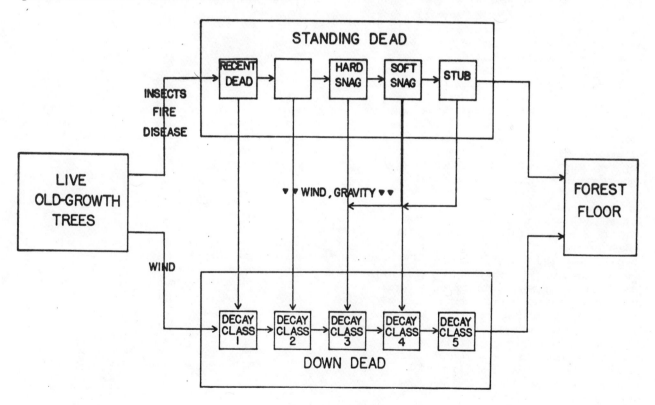

ROUTING OF FOREST TREES FROM LIVE THROUGH
VARIOUS DEAD ORGANIC COMPARTMENTS

Figure 14. Diagrammatic illustration of the relationships between the key structural features (live trees, snags, and down logs) of old-growth forest stands.

Standing dead trees or snags are well known for the fire and safety hazards they represent and, more recently, as critical habitat for wildlife (Cline et al., 1979). Thomas and others (1979) have thoroughly analyzed the role of snags as sites for nesting, food sources, and other uses by wildlife. In the Blue Mountains of Oregon, snags are the primary location for 39 birds and 24 mammals species that utilize the cavities. Furthermore, a direct correlation is indicated between numbers of snags and related wildlife populations. Snags undergo a steady process of decay and disintegration, and a variety of standing dead size and decay classes are necessary to meet differing animal requirements. Snags also play the same functional roles as down logs.

Down dead trees, also known as logs or coarse woody debris, are nearly as conspicuous as the large live trees. Large masses of logs constitute an important component of old-growth forests (Table 6). In addition to their volume and weight, these logs can occupy 10 to 20 percent of the ground surface area. Logs provide several important habitat and functional roles (Table 7). Many animals utilize logs as food sources, protection, and living sites. The logs provide important pathways for small mammals that may be important in providing for the spread of mycorrhizal-forming fungi (Maser et al., 1978). Down logs also serve as habitat for reproduction of some tree species, especially western hemlock. In natural stands this is important in providing seedlings and saplings for potential canopy replacements. Logs, of course, represent large storehouses of energy and nutrients and, as pointed out by Triska and Cromack (this volume), are sites where significant bacterial fixation of nitrogen takes place.

These structural features of old-growth forests provide one handle for foresters to use in perpetuating or mimicking natural processes. Silvicultural methods can be developed for creating stands with these characteristics as well as individual structural (and, hence, compositional and functional features) of the virgin forests. It will be a challenge for foresters to see if they can learn to manage dead wood as imaginatively as they do live! Or, to put it another way, to manage for decadence as well as board feet! There certainly is evidence that they can--for example, in the new snag management policies.

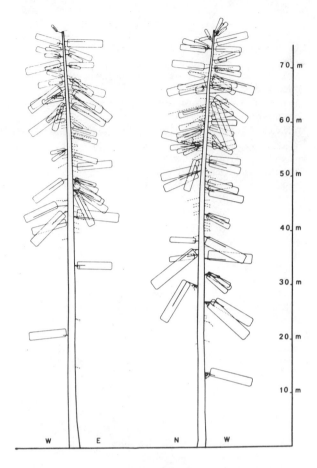

Figure 15. *Schematic illustration of the branch systems of an old-growth Douglas-fir tree, illustrating the deep crown characteristic of many of the trees (courtesy Wm. Denison and G. Carroll).*

CONCLUSIONS

Studies of our forest ecosystems during the last decade have produced many significant new insights into the structure and functioning of forests in the Pacific Northwest. We have much improved understandings of how forests are adapted to their environment and how they respond to various natural and man-created disturbances. These findings contribute to improved management of forest lands, and the development of applicable results can be expected to accelerate as we enter our third generation of ecosystem-level studies. I strongly suspect that, however much we currently think we know, we are going to be in for many more surprises.

Table 7. *Relationship of the key structural components of old-growth Douglas-fir forests to compositional and functional attributes of these forests*

Compositional role	Structural element	Functional role
	Individual, large old-growth tree	
Distinctive epiphytes Distinctive vertebrates Distinctive invertebrates		Site of N-fixation Ionic storage Interception of H_2O nutrients, light
	Large standing dead	

Utilized by cavity
  dwellers and other
  vertebrates
		Energy and nutrient
		  source

	Large down dead on land	

Distinctive animal
  communities
Seedbed or nursery
  for seedlings
		Site of N-fixation
		Energy and nutrient
		  source

	Large down dead on stream	

Distinctive animal
  communities
Creates habitat
  diversity
		Site of N-fixation
		Energy and nutrient
		  source
		Maintains physical
		  stability of stream
		Retains high-quality
		  energy materials for
		  processing

ACKNOWLEDGEMENTS

This work is aggregated from that of many others. The discussion of evergreen conifer dominance is taken largely from Waring and Franklin (1979) and that on the old-growth forest from Franklin and others (1979), which includes contributions by K. Cromack, Jr., W. Denison, A. McKee, C. Maser, J. Sedell, F. Swanson, and G. Juday. W. Moir has been a contributor to these ideas and directed studies at Mount Rainier which provided data utilized here. The dissertation research of H. Gholz and M. Hemstrom provided data and ideas. J. Means provided data and assistance on the age structure analyses, and S. Lewis provided data from her analysis of the Wind River stand. T. Thomas and M. James collected the data on dead and down coarse woody debris in the chronosequence stands. Additional input has been provided by P. Sollins, G. Carroll, G. Hawk, W. Emmingham, and R. Lambert.

LITERATURE CITED

American Forestry Association. 1973. AFA's social register of big trees. Amer. Forests 79(4):21-47.

Art, H. W., and P. L. Marks. 1971. A summary table of biomass and net annual primary production in forest ecosystems of the world. In Forest Biomass Studies, Univ. of Maine Life Sci. and Agric. Expt. Sta. Misc. Publ. 132.

Bormann, F. H., G. E. Likens, and J. M. Melillo. 1977. Nitrogen budget for an aggrading northern hardwood forest ecosystem. Science 196:981-983.

Boyce, J. S., and J. W. Bruce Wagg. 1953. Conk rot of old-growth Douglas-fir in western Oregon. Oregon State Forestry Dept. Res. Div. Bull. 4.

Bradbury, I. K., and D. C. Malcolm. 1979 Dry matter accumulation by Picea sitchensis seedlings during winter. Can. J. Forest Res. 8:207-213.

Chaney, R. W., C. Condit, and D. I. Axelrod. 1944. Pliocene Floras of California and Oregon. Carnegie Inst. Wash. Publ. 533.

Cline, S. P., A. B. Berg, and H. M. Wight. 1979. Snag characteristics and dynamics in Douglas-fir forests, western Oregon. J. Wildlife Management (accepted for publication).

Cole, D. W., J. Turner, and S. P. Gessel. 1975. Elemental cycling in Douglas fir ecosystems of the Pacific Northwest: a comparative examination. Proc. Twelfth International Botanical Congress (Leningrad) (in press).

Curtis, R. O., F. R. Herman, and D. J. DeMars. 1974. Height growth and site index for Douglas-fir in high-elevation forests of the Oregon-Washington Cascades. Forest Sci. 20(4):307-315.

Daubenmire, R. 1975. Floristic plant geography of eastern Washington and northern Idaho. J. Biogeography 2:1-18.

Daubenmire, R. 1977. Derivation of the flora of the Pacific Northwest. In Terrestrial and Aquatic Ecological Studies of the Pacific Northwest. Cheney: Eastern Washington State College Press.

Dyrness, C. T. 1973. Early stages of plant succession following logging and burning in the western Cascades of Oregon. Ecology 54(1):57-69.

Emmingham, W. H., and R. H. Waring. 1972. An index of photosynthesis for comparing forest sites in western Oregon. Can. J. Forest Res. 7(1):165-174.

Fogel, R., and K. Cromack, Jr. 1977. Effect of habitat and substrate quality on Douglas-fir litter decomposition in western Oregon. Can. J. Bot. 55(12): 1632-1640.

Fowells, H. A. 1965. Silvics of Forest Trees of the United States. USDA Agric. Handbook 271.

Franklin, J. F. 1966. Vegetation and soils in the subalpine forests of the southern Washington Cascade Range. Ph.D. thesis, Washington State Univ., Pullman.

Franklin, J. F., and C. T. Dyrness. 1973. Natural vegetation of Oregon and Washington. USDA Forest Service Gen. Tech. Rep. PNW-8.

Franklin, J. F., K. Cromack, Jr., W. Denison, A. McKee, C. Maser, J. Sedell, F. Swanson, and G. Juday. 1979. Ecological characteristics of old-growth forest ecosystems in the Douglas-fir region. USDA Forest Service Gen. Tech. Rep. (in preparation).

Fredriksen, R. L. 1970. Erosion and sedimentation following road construction and timber harvest on unstable soils in three small western Oregon watersheds. USDA Forest Service Res. Paper PNW-104. Pacific Northwest Forest and Range Expt. Sta., Portland, Oregon.

Fredriksen, R. L. 1972. Nutrient budget of a Douglas-fir forest on an experimental watershed in western Oregon. In Research on Coniferous Forest Ecosystems, Proc. Symp. Northwest Scientific Assoc., edited by J. L. Franklin, L. J. Dempster, and R. H. Waring, pp. 115-131. USDA Forest Service, Pacific Northwest Forest and Range Expt. Sta., Portland, Oregon.

Fujimori, Takao. 1971. Primary productivity of a young Tsuga heterophylla stand and some speculations about biomass of forest communities on the Oregon coast. USDA Forest Service Res. Paper PNW-123. Pacific Northwest Forest and Range Expt. Sta., Portland, Oregon.

Fujimori, Takao. 1972. Discussion about the large forest biomasses on the Pacific Northwest in the United States of America. J. Japanese Forestry Soc. 54(7):230-233.

Fujimori, Takao. 1977. Stem biomass and structure of a mature Sequoia sempervirens stand on the Pacific Coast of northern California. J. Japanese Forestry Soc. 59(12):435-441.

Fujimori, Takao, Saburo Kawanabe, Hideki Sito, C. C. Grier, and Tsunahide Shidei. 1976. Biomass and primary production in forests of three major vegetation zones of the northwestern United States. J. Japanese Forestry Soc. 58(10):360-373.

Gates, D. N. 1968. Transpiration and leaf temperature. Ann. Rev. Plant Physiol. 19:211-238.

Gholz, H. L. 1979. Limits on aboveground net primary production, leaf area, and biomass in vegetation zones of the Pacific Northwest. Ph.D. thesis, Oregon State University, Corvallis.

Gholz, H. L., F. K. Fitz, and R. H. Waring. 1976. Leaf area differences associated with old-growth forest communities in the western Oregon Cascades. Can. J. Forest Res. 6(1):49-57.

Gibbs, R. D. 1958. Patterns in the seasonal water content of trees. In The Physiology of Forest Trees, edited by Kenneth V. Thimann, pp. 43-69. New York: Ronald Press.

Gray, A., and J. D. Hooker. 1882. The vegetation of the Rocky Mountain region and a comparison with that of other parts of the world. U.S. Geol. Survey Geogr. Survey Bull. 6.

Grier, C. C. 1976. Biomass, productivity, and nitrogen-phosphorus cycles in hemlock-spruce stands of the central Oregon coast. In Western Hemlock Management, pp. 71-81. Univ. of Washington, Coll. Forest Resources, Institute of Forest Products Contrib. No. 34.

Grier, C. C., and R. S. Logan. 1977. Old-growth Pseudotsuga menziesii communities of a western Oregon watershed: biomass distribution and production budgets. Ecol. Monogr. 47(4):373-400.

Grier, C. C., and R. H. Waring. 1974. Conifer foliage mass related to sapwood area. Forest Sci. 20:205-206.

Hagem, O. 1962. Additional observations on the dry matter increase of coniferous seedlings in winter. Investigations in an oceanic climate. Medd. Vestl. Forestl. Forsoeksstn. 37:253-345.

Hallgren, S. W. 1978. Plant-water relations in Douglas-fir seedlings and screening selected families for drought resistance. M.D. thesis, Oregon State University, Corvallis.

Harper, J. L. 1977. Population Biology of Plants. New York: Academic Press, Inc.

Hawk, G. M. 1979. Vegetation mapping and community description of a small western Cascade watershed. Northwest Sci. 53(3):200-212.

Hemstrom, M. A. 1979. A recent disturbance history of forest ecosystems at Mount Rainier National Park. Ph.D. thesis, Oregon State University, Corvallis.

Herman, F. R., R. O. Curtis, and D. J. DeMars. 1978. Height growth and site index estimates for noble fir in high-elevation forests of the Oregon-Washington Cascades. USDA Forest Service Res. Paper PNW-243. Pacific Northwest Forest and Range Expt. Sta., Portland, Oregon.

Herman, F. R., and J. F. Franklin. 1976. Errors from application of western hemlock site curves to mountain hemlock. USDA Forest Service Res. Note PNW-27. Pacific Northwest Forest and Range Expt. Sta., Portland, Oregon.

Hofmann, J. V. 1917. Natural reproduction from seed stored in forest floor. J. Agric. Res. 11:1-26.

Isaac, L. A. 1943. Reproductive habits of Douglas-fir. Charles Lathrop Pack Forestry Foundation, Washington, D.C.

Jarvis, P. G. 1975. Water transfer in plants. In Heat and Mass Transfer in the Environment of Vegetation. 1974 seminar of Inter. Centre for Heat and Mass Transfer (Dubrovnik, Yugoslavia). Washington, D.C.: Scripta Book Co.

Küchler, A. W. 1946. The broadleaf deciduous forests of the Pacific Northwest. Ann. Assoc. Amer. Geographers 36:122-147.

Long, J. N., and J. Turner. 1975. Aboveground biomass and understory and overstory in an age sequence of Douglas-fir stands. J. Applied Ecol. 12:179-188.

Marks, P. L., and F. H. Bormann. 1972. Revegetation following forest cutting. Science 176:914-915.

Munger, T. T. 1930. Ecological aspects of the transition from old forests to new. Science 72(1866):327-332.

Munger, T. T. 1940. The cycle from Douglas fir to hemlock. Ecology 21(4):451-459.

Maser, C., J. M. Trappe, and R. A. Nussbaum. 1978. Fungal-small mammal interrelationships with emphasis on Oregon coniferous forests. Ecology 59(4):799-809.

Neilson, R. E., M. M. Ludlow, and P. G. Jarvis. 1972. Photosynthesis in Sitka spruce (Picea sitchensis (Bong.) Carr.). II. Responses to temperature. J. Applied Ecol. 9:721-745.

Overton, W. S., D. P. Lavender, and R. K. Hermann. 1973. Estimation of biomass and nutrient capital in stands of old-growth Douglas-fir. In IUFRO Biomass Studies, S.4.01 Mensuration, Growth and Yield, pp. 91-103. Nancy, France, and Vancouver, B.C., Canada. Univ. of Maine, Coll. Life Sci. and Agric., Orono.

Pike, L. H., R. A. Rydell, and W. C. Denison. 1977. A 400-year-old Douglas-fir tree and its epiphytes:biomass, surface area, and their distributions. Can. J. Forest Res. 7(4):680-699.

Pollard, D. F. W., and P. F. Wareing. 1968. Rates of dry-matter production in forest tree seedlings. Ann. Bot. 32:573-591.

Regal, P. J. 1977. Ecology and evolution of flowering plant dominance. Science 196:622-629.

Rodin, L. E., and N. I. Bazilevich. 1967. Production and mineral cycling in terrestrial vegetation. Edinburgh: Olives and Boyd.

Running, S. W. 1976. Environmental control of leaf water conductance in conifers. Can. J. Forest Res. 6:104-112.

Running, S. W., R. H. Waring, and R. A. Rydell. 1975. Physiological control of water flux in conifers:a computer simulation model. Oecologia 18:1-16.

Rutter, A. J. 1957. Studies in the growth of young plants of Pinus sylvestris L. I. The annual cycle of assimilation and growth. Ann. Bot. 21:399-426.

Silen, R. R. 1962. A discussion of forest trees introduced into the Pacific Northwest. J. Forestry 60:407-408.

Sollins, P., W. F. Harris, and N. T. Edwards. 1976. Simulating the physiology of a temperate deciduous forest. In Systems Analysis and Simulation in Ecology, Vol. 4, edited by B. C. Patten, pp. 329-371. New York: Academic Press, Inc.

Tadaki, Y. 1977. Forest biomass. In Primary Productivity of Japanese Forests: Productivity of Terrestrial Communities, pp. 39-64. JIBP Synthesis Vol. 16. Tokyo: University of Tokyo Press.

Thomas, J. W., ed. 1979. Wildlife Habitats in Managed Forests--The Blue Mountains of Oregon and Washington. USDA Tech. Bull. 533.

Turner, J., and M. J. Singer. 1976. Nutrient distribution and cycling in a subalpine coniferous forest ecosystem. J. Applied Ecol. 13:295-301.

Ungerson, J., and G. Scherdin. 1968.
Jahresgang von Photosynthese und Atmung
unter naturlichen Bedingungen bei
Pinus silvestris L. an ihrer Nordgrenze
in der Subarktis. Flora 157:391-400.

Walker, R. B., D. R. M. Scott, S. O. Salo,
and K. L. Reed. 1972. Terrestrial
process studies in conifers--a review.
In Research on Coniferous Forest Ecosystems, Proc. Symp. Northwest Scientific Assoc., edited by J. L. Franklin,
L. J. Dempster, and R. H. Waring,
pp. 211-215. USDA Forest Service,
Pacific Northwest Forest and Range
Expt. Sta., Portland, Oregon.

Waring, R. H., and J. F. Franklin. 1979.
Evergreen coniferous forests of the
Pacific Northwest. Science 204:1380-
1386.

Waring, R. H., and S. W. Running. 1978.
Sapwood water storage: its contribution to transpiration and effect upon
water conductance through the stems of
old-growth Douglas-fir. Plant, Cell,
and Environment 1:131-140.

Westman, W. E., and R. H. Whittaker. 1975.
The pygmy forest region of northern
California: studies on biomass and
primary productivity. J. Ecol. 63(2):
493-520.

Woodwell, G. M., and D. B. Botkin. 1970.
Metabolism of terrestrial ecosystems
by gas exchange techniques: the
Brookhaven approach. In Analysis of
Temperate Forest Ecosystems, edited by
D. E. Reichle, pp. 73-85. New York:
Springer-Verlag.

Worthington, N. 1954. The loblolly pine
of the south versus the Douglas fir of
the Pacific Northwest. Pulp and Paper
28(10):34-35, 87-88, 90.

Appendix 1. Data sources for biomass and leaf area in stands in the Pacific Northwest

Dominant species	Stand age	Basal area	Aboveground biomass			Projected leaf area	Source and plot identification[2]
			Total	Wood[1]	Foliage		
	yrs	m^2/ha		mt/ha		m^2/m^2	
Douglas-fir	70	60	422	406	16	8.1	Santantonio (Dry)
Douglas-fir	110	63	661	650	11	5.6	Fujimori et al., 1976
Douglas-fir	100	56	478	466	12	6.1	Franklin (RS 24)
Douglas-fir	120	72	531	509	22	11.2	Santantonio (Wet)
Douglas-fir	125	54	449	437	12	6.1	Gholz, 1979 (III)
Douglas-fir	130	90	792	772	20	10.2	Franklin (RS 26)
Douglas-fir	150	72	527	509	18	9.2	Gholz, 1979 (IV)
Douglas-fir	150	84	865	849	16	7.4	Gholz, 1979 (II)
Douglas-fir	150	90	786	762	24	12.2	Franklin (MR 13)
Douglas-fir	170	72	532	510	22	10.2	Santantonio (Modal)
Group average		71	604	585	19	9.7	
Noble fir	130	98	880	862	18	9.9	Fujimori et al., 1976
Sitka spruce/hemlock	121	100	916	908	8	5.1	Grier, 1976 (Plot 12)
Sitka spruce/hemlock	130	118	1,080	1,057	23	14.1	Gholz, 1979 (IA)
Sitka spruce/hemlock	130	111	1,492	1,460	32	20.2	Gholz, 1979 (IB)
Group average		110	1,163	1,142	21	13.4	
Western hemlock	26	49	192	171	21	13.4	Fujimori, 1971
Douglas-fir/hemlock	250	106	1,117	1,094	23	11.7	Franklin (MR 1)
Douglas-fir/hemlock	250	99	991	968	23	11.7	Franklin (Bagby)
Douglas-fir/hemlock	450	68	715	701	14	7.1	Franklin (RS 1)
Douglas-fir/hemlock	450	84	911	893	18	9.2	Franklin (RS 2)
Douglas-fir/hemlock	450	92	826	801	25	12.7	Franklin (RS 3)
Douglas-fir/hemlock	450	99	1,223	1,203	20	10.2	Franklin (RS 28)
Douglas-fir/hemlock	450	118	1,237	1,208	29	14.7	Franklin (RS 29)
Douglas-fir/hemlock	450	116	1,137	1,107	30	15.2	Franklin (RS 30)
Douglas-fir/hemlock	450	92	1,039	1,018	21	10.7	Franklin (RS 31)
Douglas-fir/hemlock	450	129	1,423	1,392	30	15.2	Franklin (RS 27)
Douglas-fir/hemlock	500	50	317	303	14	7.1	Franklin (MR 6)
Douglas-fir/hemlock	500	81	590	567	23	11.7	Franklin (MR 5)
Douglas-fir/hemlock	500	76	585	559	26	13.2	Franklin (MR 8)
Douglas-fir/hemlock	500	65	606	586	19	9.7	Franklin (MR 4)
Douglas-fir/hemlock	500	89	957	933	24	12.2	Franklin (MR 11)
Douglas-fir/hemlock	750	79	927	908	18	9.2	Franklin (Squaw)
Douglas-fir/hemlock	1,000	69	541	520	21	10.7	Franklin (MR 2)
Douglas-fir/hemlock	1,000	98	789	760	29	14.7	Franklin (MR 3)
Douglas-fir/hemlock	1,000	74	563	539	24	12.2	Franklin (MR 14)
Group average		89	868	845	23	11.7	

[1] Bole, bark, and branches.

[2] Daniel Santantonio: personal communication; stands located on wet, modal, and dry sites in McKenzie River drainage of Oregon Cascade Range. J. F. Franklin: data on file at Forestry Sciences Laboratory, Corvallis, Oregon. "RS" plots are hectare reference stands or permanent sample plots located at elevations between 360 and 1,200 m on the H. J. Andrews Experimental Ecological Reserve in the Western Cascades of Oregon. "Bagby" is a plot in the Bagby Research Natural Area, Mount Hood National Forest, Oregon. "Squaw" is located in the Squaw Creek drainage, a tributary of the South Fork of the Santiam River, Willamette National Forest, Oregon. "MR" plots are hectare reference stands or permanent sample plots located at elevations below 1,200 m in Mount Rainier National Park, Washington.

Forest Canopies: Complex and Independent Subsystems

George C. Carroll

The growth of trees, indeed that of all vascular plants, involves the transfer of matter and energy through two critical interfaces between the organism and its environment: one between roots and the soil and a second between the canopy and the atmosphere. Studies on the root-soil interface have largely dealt with the movement of plant nutrients other than carbon, while investigations in the canopy have centered on carbon fixation and energy budgets (Monteith, 1975). Where the movement of nutrients across the canopy interface has been investigated, the canopy has been regarded as a homogeneous black box for which only total inputs from the atmosphere and forest floor and total outputs to the forest floor can be known. Thus, multiple exchanges of substances within the canopy itself and the processes which mediate such exchanges have largely been ignored.

Even the measurement of net inputs and outputs for the canopy subsystem has often proved fraught with difficulties. The collection, sorting, and chemical analysis of litterfall is a time-consuming and expensive task which has burdened ecosystems investigations since their inception. In moist climates substantial amounts of material may move from the canopy to the forest floor in solution or in suspension. While an exhaustive review of the literature on elemental cycling in stemflow and throughfall is beyond the purview of the present discussion, some mention of the problems involved is in order, if only to justify the microcosm experiments discussed in this paper. Many of the difficulties associated with throughfall/stemflow collection and analysis relate to the necessity for a cumulative sample if seasonal or annual totals are to be generated for elemental budgets. Collectors containing water are left in the field for periods varying from one day to four weeks; the integrity of such samples begins to deteriorate the moment the water is collected, with the degree of alteration in water chemistry varying with the climate, the length of the interval before the sample is processed, and the load of microbial cells and other suspended particulates in the water. Beyond this, the size of the collecting area for field samples is seldom adequate to provide a sample large enough for multiple analyses (Lewis and Grant, 1978). Use of small sampling areas generates high variability in the data and requires that large numbers of collectors be installed to provide estimates of satisfactory precision at a stand level (Kimmins, 1973; Best, 1976). Most of the throughfall studies in the literature provide insufficient information about sampling design, collector construction, and/or sample processing to allow consistent interpretation of the results.

Lewis and Grant (1978) have discussed this entire array of difficulties with admirable succinctness and have proposed an improved design for throughfall collectors. While use of such collectors will resolve certain of the problems discussed (adequate sample size, collection of snow), they do not help with the fundamental quandary of sample integrity versus cumulative collections. The only truly satisfactory method for handling throughfall involves immediate filtration of the water through microbiological filters and freezing the filtrate prior to analysis; if tared filters are used, estimates for the microparticulate fraction in throughfall can also be generated. Such an approach is labor-intensive and can only be used on an episodic basis. Because concentrations of substances in canopy wash change over short intervals during the course of single rainstorms and seasonally, from one rainstorm to the next, data from single-storm episodes or portions thereof cannot be simply extrapolated to provide annual totals.

Even if such extrapolations were legitimate and if the data reported in the literature could be regarded as an accurate reflection of real nutrient exchanges, most investigations of elemental cycling in stemflow and throughfall suffer from a fundamental debility: they are essentially descriptive and empirical, and as such they lack predictive power. The information from such studies is peculiar to the forest stands, seasons, and climatic conditions for which it was garnered. Consequently, few inferences are possible from existing studies about probable nutrient exchanges in canopy wash from different forest stands under a different climatic regime. Thus, the basic measurement of nutrient concentrations in precipitation, stemflow, and throughfall must be repeated each time a new ecosystem is studied. This will continue to be the situation as long as we regard the canopy as a black box, as long as we lack basic knowledge of the processes involved in nutrient exchanges as incident precipitation flows and trickles over canopy surfaces.

NUTRIENT EXCHANGES IN AN OLD-GROWTH CONIFEROUS CANOPY

During the last ten years, as a result of pioneering work of W. C. Denison and his colleagues, access techniques for the canopies of old-growth Douglas fir trees have been developed, and a large amount of information is available on the biomass and distribution of various canopy components (Denison et al., 1972; Denison, 1973; Pike et al., 1975; Pike et al., 1977). The availability of accessible, described canopies has permitted me and my colleagues to make a more analytical approach towards estimating annual nutrient fluxes in the canopy wash. In brief, we hope to construct simulation models of nutrient fluxes in the canopy solution, based on experiments with laboratory microcosms in which isolated canopy components are misted with rainfall and nutrient concentrations in the water are monitored before and after contact with the canopy sample. After describing our progress and comparing results with those from the pertinent literature, I will discuss the role of insects in the system briefly.

Nutrient Exchanges in the
Canopy Solution

Materials and Methods. All studies described were carried out with samples from old-growth Douglas fir (Pseudotsuga

menziesii (Mirb.) Franco) trees located at two sites within the H. J. Andrews Experimental Forest. Both sites were located in stands corresponding to the Tshe/Rhma/Bene community type (Franklin and Dyrness, 1970) and were composed predominantly of 400- to 500-year-old Douglas-fir trees. Samples were taken from the canopies of permanently rigged trees (Denison et al., 1972) and stored overnight at the laboratory at 4°C. The following day they were picked clean, placed in funnel assemblies, and misted for one hour at 16°C with previously collected incident rainwater that had been stored frozen until just prior to use. After misting, the leachates were filtered sequentially through 30 μm nylon mesh and Nuclepore filters with 0.2 μm pore size; aliquots were removed for cation, total dissolved solids, and total nitrogen determinations; the remainder of the filtrate was lyophilized, reconstituted to 10 ml, and stored at -20°C for subsequent analysis. In some cases where nitrogen concentrations were extremely low, determinations of total nitrogen were carried out on the lyophilized samples.

A flow chart is presented in Figure 1 and a synopsis of analytical methods with references is shown in Table 1. In all cases net fluxes of materials were computed by subtracting concentrations of substances in the control rainwater from those in the corresponding leachates and by correcting for the amount of water with dissolved substance retained by the components in the funnel assemblies. In order to assess the possible magnitude of nutrient transfers mediated by the canopy solution, we initiated a biweekly, and later a monthly, sampling and laboratory misting program.

We have misted Lobaria oregana, moss bolsters, 2- to 3-year-old foliage and twigs, dead twigs, and living twigs 0.5 to 2.0 cm in diameter from three heights in the canopy during each regular sampling episode. The sample has been expanded to include 1-year-old foliage, 5- to 7-year-old foliage, trunk bark, Alectoria spp., Sphaerophorus globosus, Platismatia glauca, Hypogymnia spp., and Lobaria pulmonaria on a quarterly basis. Occasionally we have misted rotting Lobaria thalli, both from the canopy and from the forest floor. This program has provided information in fluxes of cations (Na^+, K^+, Ca^{++}, Mg^{++}), total organic nitrogen, and total phosphorus both in dissolved and particulate form. Subsequently, we have carried out prolonged misting experiments with some of the dominant canopy components. Since the data for the cation fluxes have been treated differently from those for other nutrients, they are dealt with first.

Results: cations.   Information on cation fluxes was analyzed and summarized by my colleague, Dr. L. H. Pike, for the bi-weekly misting episodes from September 1976 through August 1977. A multivariate approach was taken in attempting to assess the importance of several factors which may influence cation fluxes from canopy components. Specifically, multiple regressions were carried out with cations concentration in incident rainwater, day in the water year when samples were collected, presence or absence of at least 2.0 cm rain in the three days preceding sample collection, and height of sample in the canopy as independent variables and mean net cation flux as the dependent variable. This information is summarized in Table 2. We do not ascribe great significance to the absolute numbers in the upper portion of the table, but many of the trends are highly significant, with the r^2 in the multiple regressions often greater than 0.7. Actual plots of Ca^{++} and K^+ fluxes for Lobaria oregana are provided in Pike (1978).

Reference to Table 2 reveals several general trends:

1. Uptake of Ca^{++} and Mg^{++} from the incident rainwater occurs quite commonly for the four components regularly tested. Uptake of Na^+ occurs less commonly and seems to be restricted to Lobaria and moss; uptake of K^+ occurred only once in all the samples monitored.

2. Generally, the concentration of cations in the incident rain is the most important independent variable in the multiple regressions. In virtually every case an increase in the concentration of a cation in the incident rainwater has resulted either in increased uptake or decreased leaching of that cation by the canopy component.

3. The leaching of Na^+ and K^+ from foliage and of Na^+ from twigs is strongly influenced by the day in the water year when the samples were collected, with leaching losses decreasing with increasing exposure to rain in the field during the fall and winter.

4. Loss of K^+ from the lichen Lobaria oregana is strongly affected by the occurrence of rain in the three days prior to sample collection (leaching losses decreased after rain) and by the height in

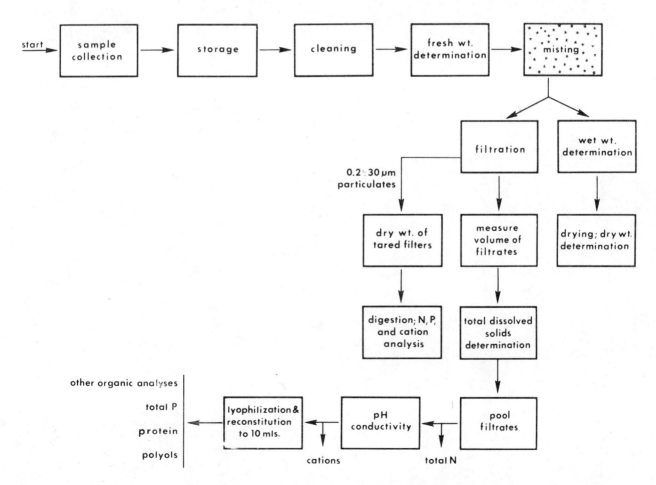

Figure 1.   Flow chart for processing and analyzing canopy samples and leachates.

Table 1. Synopsis of chemical analyses for leachates.

Analysis	Method	Nature of sample	No. of samples per sampling period
Suspended particulates, 0.2-30 μm	Serial filtration through 30μ mesh + 0.2 μm Nucleopore filters; dry weights of material on tared filters	No prior treatment	36 + 2 controls
Leachate volume	Measured in graduated cylinder	Filtered leachate	36 + 2 controls
Pigment (post-filtration optical density)	O.D. reading (λ=410 nm)	Filtered leachate	36 + 2 controls
Total dissolved solids	Evaporation of 5 ml aliquots in tin-foil boats (tared); subsequent weights of tared boats	Filtered leachate	36 + 2 controls
pH	Beckman pH meter	Filtered, samples pooled	9 + 1 control
Conductivity	Markson conductivity meter	Filtered, samples pooled	9 + 1 control
Total organic nitrogen	Perchloric acid digest of 200 μl aliquots; N determined as NH_4^+ by indophenol blue method (Jaenicke, 1974)	Filtered, samples pooled	9 + 1 control
Cations (Na^+,K^+,Ca^{++},Mg^{++})	Atomic absorption spectrophotometry	Filtered, samples pooled	9 + 1 control
Total phosphorus	Perchloric acid digest of 200 μl aliquots; P determined by molybdenum blue method (Jaenicke, 1974)	Filtered, pooled, concentrated to 10 ml	9 + 1 control
Total protein	Measurement of absorption increase at 595 nm by Coomassie Blue G-250 on binding to protein (Bradford, 1976; Sedman and Grossberg, 1977)	Filtered, pooled, concentrated to 10 ml	9 + 1 control
Total polyols	Periodate oxidation followed by spectrophotometric determination of formaldehyde formed using chromotrophic acid (λ=570 nm) (Tibbling, 1968)	Filtered, pooled, concentrated to 10 ml	9 + 1 control

the canopy where the sample was collected (leaching losses less for samples collected high in the canopy). Pike (1978) has provided a chart of these trends.

Similar trends have already been reported or can be inferred from other reports in the literature. For instance, studies by Lang, Reiners, and Heier (1976) have documented uptake of NH_4^+ and losses of K^+ from thalli of Platismatia glauca, a chlorophycophilous lichen. Throughfall studies of Abee and Lavender (1972) have shown that concentrations of K^+ in the throughfall decrease greatly during the course of a rainy season in the Pacific Northwest.

Particulate matter >0.2μm <30μm collected from these misting episodes has not been analyzed for cations. Where concentrations in solution are low (e.g., Mg^{++}), fluxes in particulate form may completely overshadow the effects reported here. If such material is derived from microepiphytes, it may be extraordinarily efficient in cation uptake; this has been well demonstrated by Odum et al. (1970) and Witkamp (1970) for microepiphylls in a tropical rain forest in Puerto Rico. In any case, as Table 2 makes clear, the multiple exchanges of cations in a canopy can be affected by a number of factors, and any predictive models for cation fluxes in real canopies will be necessarily complex.

Results: nitrogen. The canopies of the stands studied here contain large populations of cyanophycophilous lichens which are capable of fixing nitrogen (Pike et al., 1977; Caldwell et al., 1979). Because such stands are frequently nitrogen-limited, the flow of fixed nitrogen through the canopy has been a focus for our laboratory and field studies and related modeling efforts. Total organic nitrogen in solution has been analyzed by an extremely sensitive micromethod which involves block digestion of 0.2 ml samples with 25 μl of perchloric acid and which can reliably detect as little as 0.03 μg of nitrogen (Jaenicke, 1974). The colorimetric reagents are added to the same tube in which the digestion is carried out. The analysis is simpler, faster, and far more sensitive than the conventional micro-Kjeldahl digestion followed by ammonia distillation; it deserves to be widely adopted by laboratories where organic nitrogen and ammonia are of interest. Nitrate concentrations in throughfall have been found to be very low in the Pacific Northwest, so nitrate was not analyzed in this study. Organic nitrogen in particulate matter was determined by digesting with a conventional Kjeldahl procedure tared Nuclepore filters on which microparticulates had been collected and by measuring the nitrogen in the digest spectrophotometrically as described above.

In our initial consideration of data from our biweekly and monthly misting program we discovered that the meteorological history of the samples prior to collection greatly affected fluxes of particulate and dissolved nitrogen from canopy components. To assess the susceptibility of various components in canopy leaching, misting episodes were designated "Wet" (>0.5 cm rain in three days preceding sample collection) or "Dry" (<0.5 cm rain in same period), and the data for biweekly (9/20/76 - 12/27/76) and monthly (1/10/77 - 2/12/78) episodes were lumped accordingly. Figures 2 through 5 show these data in summary form. Although the standard errors are high for some components, several striking trends are evident:

1. Net fluxes of both dissolved and particulate nitrogen are high for cyanophycophilous lichens and relatively low for tree components. Nitrogen content for filterable solids = microparticulates varies from 3 to 4 percent.

2. Chlorophycophilous lichens and moss bolsters take up dissolved nitrogen from the incident rain.

3. Fluxes of dissolved nitrogen are higher for "dry" episodes than for "wet" episodes; for particulate nitrogen this pattern is reversed. These trends are particularly striking for cyanophycophilous lichens.

4. Older foliage tends to leach more dissolved nitrogen than younger foliage.

The differences in leaching patterns between wet and dry episodes suggest that important changes in the leaching potential of canopy components occur during the transition from a dry to a wet canopy. We investigated this transition by monitoring nutrient fluxes during prolonged (6-48 hr) laboratory misting experiments. Our results for one such experiment with Alectoria (a chlorophycophilous lichen) and Lobaria (a cyanophycophilous lichen) have been discussed by Pike (1978). For Alectoria, dissolved nitrogen is taken up from the incident rainwater almost from the start of the experiment, while particulate nitrogen is released. For Lobaria, an initial pulse of leaching releases nitrogen to the incident rain; after 2 to 3 hours (1-1.5 cm rain), uptake from the incident rain commences, and when cumulative net flux for a prolonged experiment is plotted, the Lobaria is also found to be a net sink for dissolved nitrogen (Figs. 9-10). While cumulative nitrogen output in particulates only partially compensates for uptake of dissolved nitrogen in Alectoria, the two quantities are roughly equivalent in Lobaria. More recent misting experiments have shown similar patterns for other canopy surfaces, notably 2- to 4-year-old

Table 2. *Trends in net cation fluxes from four canopy components as influenced by several independent factors*[1]

	Lobaria				Moss				Foliage (2-3 yrs)				Dead twigs (0.5-2.0 cm diam.)			
	Ca	Mg	Na	K	Ca	Mg	Na	K	Ca	Mg	Na	K	Ca	Mg	Na	K
Data from misting episodes																
Mean net flux $\pm S\overline{X}$ (ng g^{-1} ml^{-1})	-10.1 ±1.7	-1.5 ±0.39	10.0 ±3.9	131.5 ±13.6	11.5 ±4.1	1.7 ±0.65	16.8 ±5.1	95.7 ±18.1	-5.1 ±2.1	0.60 ±0.23	10.2 ±1.5	52.7 ±3.4	2.8 ±1.9	1.23 ±0.21	9.75 ±1.4	52.2 ±5.5
Mean control rainwater concentration (ppm)	.90	.19	1.56	.66	.88	.19	1.60	.58	.93	.18	1.53	.57	.92	.19	1.69	.55
No. of samples showing: Output	4	11	31	42	28	25	33	35	16	28	36	36	27	29	32	36
Uptake	38	31	11	0	8	11	9	1	20	8	0	0	9	7	4	0
Factors affecting net fluxes																
Cation concentration in incident rainwater	−(1)	−(1)	−(1)		−(1)	−(1)	−(1)		−(1)	−(1)		−(3)	−(1)	−(1)	+(2)	
Day in water year (Sept. 1 = Day 1)			−(2)			−(4)	−(2)				−(1)	−(1)		−(2)	−(1)	
Wet or dry period (Dry = 0, Wet = 1)	+	+	+(3)	−(1)	+(3)	+(3)	+(3)		+	−(2)			+(3)			
Height in canopy			−(4)	−(2)	−(2)	−(2)						−(2)				
Maximum r^2 in multiple regression with above variables	.79	.78	.81	.26	.61	.76	.76		.89	.40	.39	.60	.85	.34	.50	

[1] + and − indicate the direction of change in flux with increasing values of the variable listed. Numbers in parentheses indicate order of entry into multiple stepwise regression and, by extension, relative importance in influencing cation fluxes. Blank spaces indicate no significant effect. Samples from "wet" periods were exposed to 2.0 cm or more precipitation in the field during three days prior to collection; samples from dry periods were exposed to 0.3 cm or less precipitation.

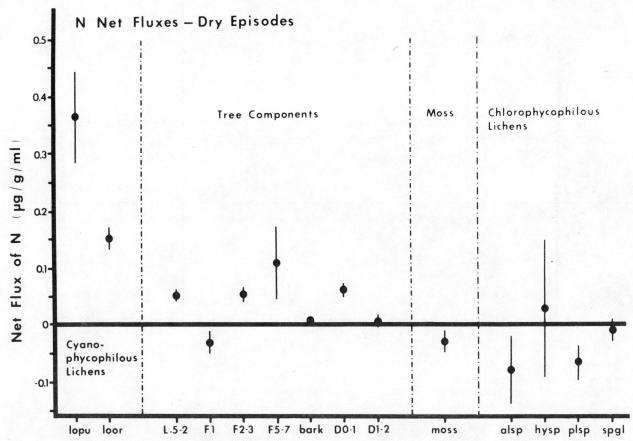

Figure 2. *Mean net fluxes of dissolved nitrogen from canopy components collected during dry periods. Less than 0.3 cm of rain fell in the three days preceding collections. Bars indicate one standard error above and below the mean. lopu = Lobaria pulmonaria; loor = Lobaria oregana; roor = rotten Lobaria oregana; L.5-2.0 = living twigs 0.5-2.0 cm in diameter; Fl = age class 1 foliage, 0-1 yr old; F2-3 = age classes 2-3 foliage; F5-7 = age classes 5-7 foliage; D0-1 = dead twigs 0-1 cm in diameter; D1-2 = dead twigs 1-2 cm in diameter; alsp = Alectoria spp.; hysp = Hypogymnia spp.; plsp = Platismatia spp.; spgl = Sphaerophoros globosus.*

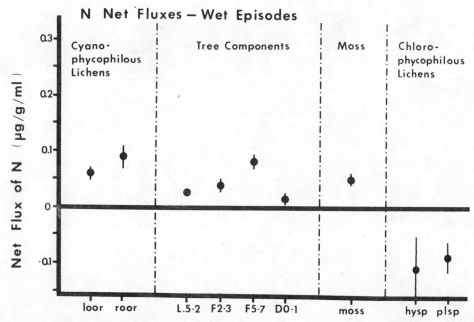

Figure 3. *Mean net fluxes of dissolved nitrogen from canopy components collected during wet periods. More than 2.0 cm of rain fell in the three days preceding collections. Bars indicate one standard error above and below the mean. Code names for canopy components are the same as in Figure 2.*

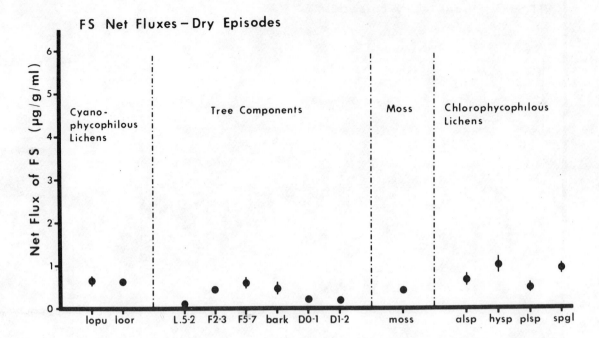

Figure 4. Mean net fluxes of filterable solids <30 μm >0.2 μm from canopy components collected during dry periods. Less than 0.3 cm of rain fell in the three days preceding collections. Bars indicate one standard error above and below the mean. FS = filterable solids. Code names for canopy components are the same as in Figure 2.

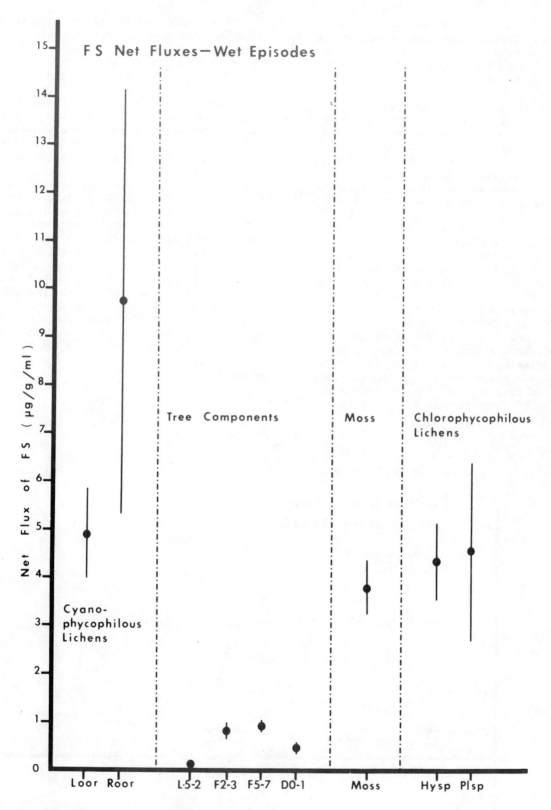

Figure 5. *Mean net fluxes of filterable solids <30 μm >0.2 μm from canopy components collected during wet periods. More than 2.0 cm of rain fell in the three days preceding collections. Bars indicate one standard error above and below the mean. FS = filterable solids. Code names for canopy components are the same as in Figure 2.*

foliage (Fig. 6), living twigs, and moss bolsters. For the tree components the net fluxes per unit weight are lower than for the epiphytes, and longer periods of misting are required before uptake of dissolved nitrogen begins.

The behavior of canopy surfaces in regard to their interactions with dissolved nitrogen becomes more explicable when the nature of the released particulates is examined. Particulates washed from the surface of Lobaria and other cyanophycophilous lichens consist almost exclusively of rod-shaped bacteria (Fig. 7); inspection of the surface of a Lobaria oregana thallus with the scanning electron microscope after a misting episode reveals dense populations of similar bacteria (Fig. 8). Caldwell et al. (1979) have isolated and identified bacteria from this substrate. They report 5-10 x 10^5 colony-forming units (CFU)/g from Lobaria collected during dry periods and 100-200 x 10^5 CFU/g during wet periods, observations consistent with data on outputs of microparticulates during dry and wet misting episodes in the laboratory. Pseudomonas fluorescens, Arthrobacter-like rods, and Gram-negative aerobic rods were found to be dominant bacterial taxa on Lobaria thalli.

Examination of the microparticulate fraction from misting episodes with foliage reveals a large number of fungal and algal cells, microorganisms which are also predominant on needle and twig surfaces (Bernstein et al., 1973; Bernstein and Carroll, 1977; Carroll, 1979; Carroll et al., 1980). In fact the observed differences between cyanophycophilous lichens and other canopy components in efficiency of dissolved nitrogen uptake can be largely ascribed to the prevalence of bacteria on lichen surfaces and of eukaryotic microorganisms on other canopy surfaces: the response time and doubling times for bacterial cells are much faster than those for eukaryotic microorganisms. In summary, all canopy surfaces examined during leaching time-course experiments have proved ultimately to be net sinks for dissolved nitrogen. For some components (chlorophycophilous lichens) this involves nitrogen uptake by the sample itself; for most other leaching substrates nitrogen uptake is mediated by epiphytic microorganisms whose cells are released into the rainwater as the populations grow.

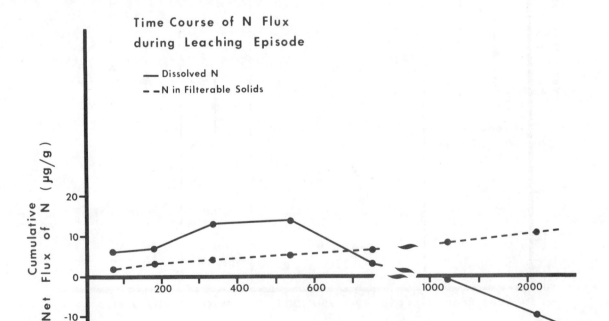

Figure 6. Cumulative net flux of dissolved nitrogen from foliage age classes 2-4 yr during a prolonged misting episode.

These results are consistent with the data of Lang et al. (1976), who showed nitrogen uptake as NH_4^+ for <u>Platismatia glauca</u>, and with numerous throughfall studies showing coniferous canopies to be net sinks for dissolved nitrogen in incident rainfall (Tamm, 1951; Voigt, 1960; Nihlgaard, 1970; Foster, 1974; Miller et al., 1976; Feller, 1977; Cronan, 1980). This effect is particularly pronounced where glass wool plugs have been inserted in the necks of the collecting funnels to partially block the entrance of microparticulate matter into the collecting funnel.

Given this consistency, one may ask how far the patterns of nitrogen uptake and loss observed for individual components in microcosm rainstorms can be extended to actual canopies in the field, where multiple layers of intermingled components are stacked to a depth of 40 to 50 m. Loading the funnels with multiple layers of a single canopy component prior to misting represents a first approximation to the field situation. Figures 9 and 10 show results from a prolonged misting of <u>Lobaria oregana</u> in which different amounts of lichen were put into the funnels. In Figure 9 a mean dry weight of 1.8 g per funnel was used; in Figure 10, 16.8 g per funnel was used. The

trend is clear: as multiple layers of lichen are added to the microcosm, less and less nitrogen escapes in dissolved form and more and more is released in particulate form, as bacterial cell mass. Similar experiments with other canopy components revealed the same trend.

In addition to laboratory time-course experiments, we attempted to monitor the fluxes of nitrogen in the field during a single rainstorm in February 1979. Samples were taken from six 0.3 m^2 throughfall collection troughs placed at random beneath a single old-growth tree (MINERVA) at one of our collection sites in the H. J. Andrews Experimental Forest. Incident rainfall was collected in a single sampler located in an adjacent clearcut. Water samples beneath the tree were taken at 1, 2, 3, and 4 hours, those in the clearcut at 2 and 4 hours. Samples were filtered in the field and were stored on ice prior to analysis. Although samples for the control rainwater were not replicated in this preliminary experiment, the trends in nitrogen fluxes are readily apparent in Figure 11: nitrogen was taken up from the incident rain throughout the portion of the storm that was monitored, a result that might have been predicted on the basis of our

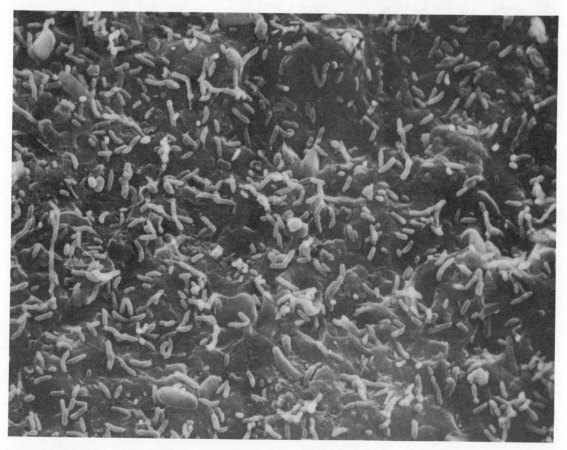

Figure 7. Bacteria from a thallus of <u>Lobaria oregana</u> collected on a Nucleopore filter as seen under the scanning electron microsopce (x 2,500).

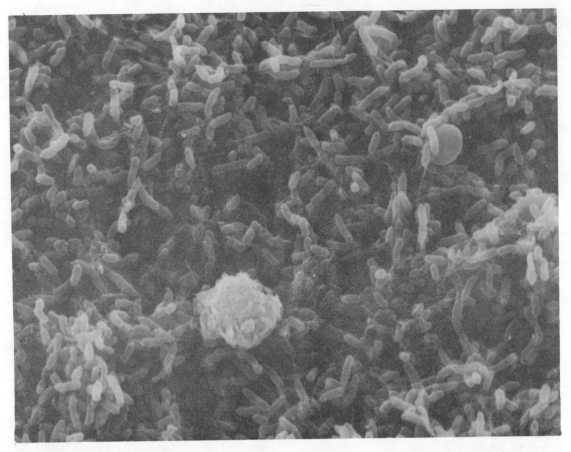

Figure 8. Bacteria on the surface of a _Lobaria_ thallus as seen under the scanning electron microscope (x 1,800).

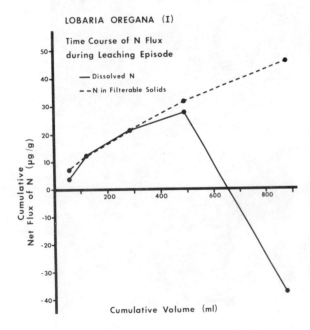

Figure 9. Cumulative net flux of nitrogen from _Lobaria oregana_ during a prolonged misting episode; 1.8 g dry weight of _Lobaria_ were placed in each funnel.

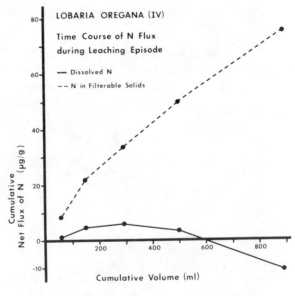

Figure 10. Cumulative net flux of nitrogen from _Lobaria oregana_ during a prolonged misting episode; 16.8 g dry weight of _Lobaria_ were placed in each funnel.

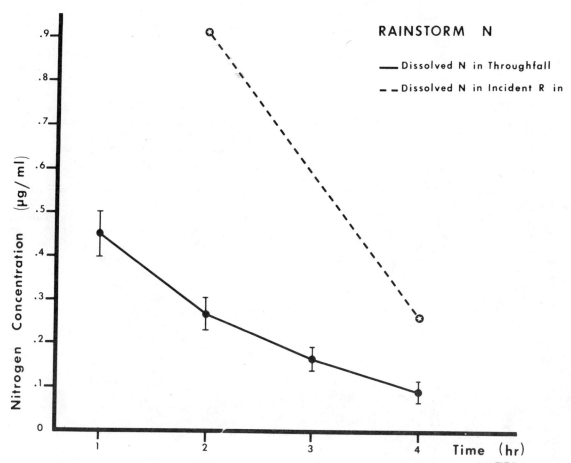

Figure 11. Concentrations of dissolved nitrogen in incident precipitation and throughfall during the course of a single rainstorm in the field.

microcosm experiments. However, when patterns of particulate output from the canopy are considered, the extrapolation fails. Analysis of filter weights from the field experiment reveals an initial flux of particulates out of the canopy during the first hour of the storm and low levels of suspended particulates in the throughfall thereafter. An entire canopy is, of course, more complex than a funnel with several layers of Lobaria.

In an attempt to deal with this complexity and to resolve discrepancies between laboratory and field observations, we have resorted to computer simulation models. My colleague, Dr. W. J. Massman, has developed a preliminary model of canopy nitrogen fluxes in which the paramount role of surface microorganisms in regulating nitrogen uptake and release is explicitly recognized. The model is based on chemostat theory, but has been generalized such that neither a constant dilution rate nor a constant volume must be assumed. Further, the model allows for luxury nitrogen consumption by microbes. Certain simplifying assumptions have, however, been made.

These include: (1) nitrogen is the only limiting nutrient; (2) grazing of microbial cell mass does not occur; (3) microbial growth is non-colonial; (4) the canopy strata are homogeneous; (5) nitrogen is not lost from the system in gaseous form; and (6) the flow of nitrogen into microbial cells is unidirectional; i.e., losses of nitrogen from microbial cells do not occur. Although certain of these assumptions are blatantly incorrect (no. 4 above), most of them are reasonable, at least over the time span of a single storm event. Currently the model deals with the behavior of stacked strata of only one component, Lobaria oregana.

Considering the assumptions and limitations of this model, the degree of qualitative agreement between the predictions of the simulation runs and the observed patterns of nitrogen flux in both laboratory and field is encouraging. Specifically, runs of the model for just a single stratum show a rough agreement with time-course experiments in the laboratory; most notably, dissolved nitrogen is released initially, but is taken up later as bacterial growth and release of particulate nitrogen commences. When several strata are stacked, such that the output from one becomes the input for the next lower one, the model predicts that efficiency of uptake will increase, but that the output of particulates will be delayed. With five strata in the model, this delay amounts to four or five hours. Thus, for our field experiment (Fig. 11) we might well have seen a pulse of particulates from the bottom of the canopy if the storm had been monitored for several more hours. During storms of short duration the microparticulate fraction may never be flushed from the canopy. Instead it may be left as a particulate residue as water evaporates from the tree, only to be washed from the canopy during the initial phases of the next storm. This process could well account for the observed flush of microparticulates at the beginning of the single storm we monitored.

Results: phosphorus and organic matter. Concentrations of phosphorus and certain organic substances have also been measured during laboratory misting experiments. In general, much lower levels of phosphorus than nitrogen are present in the canopy solution; patterns of leaching and uptake resemble those for nitrogen. The occurrence of higher levels of phosphorus in throughfall than in incident precipitation in coniferous stands has been widely reported in the literature (Attiwill, 1966; Nihlgaard, 1970; Abee and Lavender, 1972; Foster, 1974; Hart and Parent, 1974; Henderson et al., 1977). Although phosphorus concentrations were so low in both incident rain and throughfall during the storm sequence mentioned earlier that no consistent trends were evident, data from earlier studies at the same site in which throughfall and incident rain were field-filtered indicate net losses of phosphorus from the canopy. Thus, while microbial uptake of phosphorus certainly occurs, phosphorus is probably not a limiting element for microbial growth in most canopies.

Fluxes of organic matter in the canopy have been little investigated here or in conventional throughfall studies. Where total organic matter or concentrations of specific organic molecules have been determined in throughfall and stemflow, they have been found to be high and to account for a significant return of fixed carbon to the forest floor (Tamm, 1951; Carlisle, 1965; Carlisle et al., 1966; Gersper and Holowaychuck, 1971; Eaton et al., 1973). Concentrations of ammonia and nitrate are low in throughfall from coniferous stands in the Pacific Northwest and the bulk of nitrogen in solution is in organic form; this also appears to be the case for phosphorus.

If the specific nitrogenous compounds leached from Lobaria were identified, radio-isotopes could be employed to follow their fate in subsequent transformations within the canopy. Cooper and Carroll (1978) attempted to isolate and identify dominant organic nitrogenous compounds in Lobaria leachates. They found that simple preliminary fractionation of the leachates by means of dialysis and extraction in acetone did not result in nitrogen enrichment in any fraction; they concluded that a number of different nitrogen-containing molecules were present. Ribitol, a five-carbon sugar-alcohol, was, however, identified as a major component of these leachates. Subsequent studies have shown that ribitol accumulates in the thalli during dry periods and leaches very rapidly in subsequent rainstorms.

The chemistry of organic molecular transformations in the canopy is undoubtedly extremely complex. A great deal of further investigation is required before these transformations can be understood, even in broad outline.

Insects and Canopy Processes

In the last ten years the role of canopy arthropods in regulating growth of trees in forest ecosystems has been investigated by a number of workers. Such studies have largely focused on the activities of defoliating insects, particularly their effects on primary production (Franklin, 1970; Rafes, 1970; Reichle et al., 1973), and on elemental cycling (Kimmins, 1972; Nilsson, 1978; Schroeder, 1978). Defoliating and sucking insects appear to be of little importance in old-growth canopies. However, in collaboration with an entomologist, Dr. David Voegtlin, we have noted subtle and pervasive effects of the fauna on nutrient exchanges within the canopy.

Materials and methods. Census work on canopy consumers was carried out over a 3-year period. Initially, we implemented a biweekly sampling program in which important and distinctive canopy habitats were sampled on a cumulative or episodic basis. More recently, intensive sampling of arthropod communities on needles and twigs has been carried out. The habitats sampled and techniques used are summarized in Table 3.

Results: canopy arthropods. The data from the arthropod census suggest that the canopy fauna partitions the tree very finely, both with regard to habitat type and phenology. To date, 1,200 to 1,500 taxa have been collected, from 50 to 70 percent of them more than once. Only about 150 of these taxa can be considered common. In many cases they are abundant only in one habitat or during one particular season.

Table 3. *Biweekly sampling techniques, Douglas-fir canopy arthropod survey (Sept. 1976 – Sept. 1977)*

Sampling technique	Technique description	Number of samples taken and location	Duration of sampling period	Information produced
Sticky screens	20 cm² screens of ¼" hardware cloth coated with stikem special	12 screens, 4 on each of 3 halyards run into the lower, middle, and upper canopy	Cumulative; screens left up 2 weeks	Qualitative information on the movement and phenology of flying insects provides evidence for intercanopy movement by wingless arthropods, such as ballooning by spiders
Tullgren	A series of funnels which use heat and light above to drive arthropods into a collecting vessel	9 samples (3 per branch system); one branch system in lower, middle, and upper canopy	Episodic; taken every 2 weeks	Quantitative information on microarthropods inhabiting epiphyte-lodged litter-perched soil habitat
Vacuum	A backpack blower with the intake adapted for sucking	3 samples, foliage surface area of branch systems used for tullgren and filtration vacuumed	Episodic; taken every 2 weeks	Semi-quantitative information (surface area vacuumed is estimated) on arthropods found on the needles and twigs. Collects rapidly moving arthropods not collected by other techniques.
Filtration	Branchlets washed vigorously and the wash filtered through a series of nested sieves	6 samples, 3 living and 3 dead branchlets chosen from branch systems used for tullgren and vacuum	Episodic; taken every 2 weeks	Quantitative information on slower moving organisms associated with foliage and dead branchlet material

Table 3 continued on next page

Table 3. Biweekly sampling techniques, Douglas-fir canopy arthropod survey (Sept. 1976 – Sept. 1977)

Sampling technique	Technique description	Number of samples taken and location	Duration of sampling period	Information produced
Pitfall	Plastic containers hung in cavities on trunk, contain water-alcohol-ethylene-glycol mixture to trap arthropods	4 samples, located from lower to upper canopy	Cumulative; fluid in containers changed every 2 weeks	Qualitative information on movement of arthropods on the trunk
Trunk stickies	Screens of same size as hung from halyards, held approximately 1 cm away from trunk	4 samples, located near the four pitfalls	Cumulative; screens left in place 2 weeks	Qualitative information on movement of arthropods on the trunk and also landing on trunk of flying insects
Blacklight	A large funnel trap run into canopy on halyard	1 sample, trap run one night every 2 weeks	Episodic; 8-12 hours	Qualitative information on night-flying insects in the canopy. Funnels fixed so that only insects flying above it, 42 m, can see the light
Emergence traps	Tent-shaped traps set on forest floor	6 samples, traps located in vicinity of tree with halyards and sticky screens	Cumulative; traps left in place 2 weeks	Qualitative information used as a means of determining which insects collected in the canopy come from the soil
Cookie cutter	Equal sized samples 1 dm^2 taken from a uniform habitat	4 samples, taken from large moss bolsters in lower to middle canopy	Episodic; once every month	Quantiative information on microarthropods in a fairly uniform habitat

Distribution throughout the canopy is often highly aggregated. The major groups of arthropods and the techniques used to collect them are listed in Table 4.

In terms of abundance, microarthropods associated with needles and twigs were the dominant group in the canopy. Mites, in particular a new species of Camisia, Camisia carrollii Andre, were very numerous on needles and small twigs. Microscopic observations of both frass and gut contents revealed that these organisms feed almost exclusively on epiphytic microbial cells. Fungivorous psocids and collembolans were also prevalent in the foliage. Numerous small invertebrates, including tardigrades, rotifers, and testate amoebae were present on various canopy surfaces. We did not study this truly microfaunal community, but these organisms presumably graze on populations of epiphytic bacteria.

While we have no data on the intensity with which canopy microorganisms are grazed, indirect evidence suggests that the canopy microfauna may significantly affect standing crops of microepiphytes and thus indirectly affect patterns of nutrient exchange within the canopy. Bernstein and Carroll (1977) and Carroll (1979) made visual estimates of microbial standing crops for various age-classes of needles at several heights in the canopy, where mites are most abundant (Voegtlin, unpub.). When microbial standing crops are considered with regard to needle age, a striking pattern frequently emerges. Percent cover and cell volume per needle rise steadily from year 1 through year 3 and then drop precipitously on year 4 needles. The microbial populations then return to peak abundance at year 8. More recently these patterns have been confirmed (Carroll, unpub.) using the method of Swisher and Carroll (1980), in which the hydrolysis of fluorescein diacetate and release of fluorescein dye is used as an index of microbial standing crop. A plausible explanation for such patterns invokes grazing by foliar microarthropods, which feed selectively on needles 4 to 6 years old. Andre and Voegtlin (in press) have noted that populations of the twig-dwelling mite Camisia carrollii are concentrated on twigs 4 to 10 years old. Thus,

Table 4. *Sampling techniques used during biweekly sampling and major categories of arthropods collected by each method*

| Techniques | Arthropods | |
	Commonly collected	Infrequently collected
Sticky screens	Diptera, Neuroptera, Hymenoptera, Homoptera, Hemiptera, Coleoptera	Trichoptera, Plecoptera, Acarina, Collembola, Thysanoptera
Tullgren and cookie cutter	Acarina, Collembola, Coleoptera larvae and adults	Diptera larvae, Araneae, Pseudococcidae, Hymenoptera
Vacuum	Acarina, Collembola, Thysanoptera, Diptera larvae, Lepidoptera larvae Homoptera	Coleoptera, Psocoptera
Filtration	Acarina, Collembola, Thysanoptera, Diptera larvae, Lepidoptera larvae, Homoptera	Araneae, Hymenoptera
Pitfall	Collembola, Araneae, Phalangida, Coleoptera, Diptera, Psocoptera	Acarina, Hymenoptera, Lepidoptera
Trunk stickies	Araneae, Diptera, Phalangida, Coleoptera, Psocoptera	Acarina, Collembola
Blacklight	Lepidoptera (moths), Trichoptera, Plecoptera, Diptera, Coleoptera, Hymenoptera, Hemiptera	Ephemeroptera, Homoptera
Emergence	Diptera, Collembola	Hymenoptera

there is precedent for such precise partitioning of habitats among foliage- and twig-
dwelling microarthropods.

Census studies by Voegtlin have shown
a relative paucity of defoliators and sucking insects. Measurement of frass-fall
during periods of peak needle consumption
in the summer suggests that less than 1 percent of the new foliage is consumed by
caterpillars each year. Voegtlin (unpub.)
considers this striking aspect of old-growth
canopy insect communities to be a result of
the large numbers of spiders, other predators, and parasitoids found in the canopy.
During the winter months large numbers of
mycetophilid flies and adults of aquatic
insects are trapped on sticky screens.
Studies with emergence traps reveal that
these insects originate in the forest floor
or streams, where they feed as larvae.
This input of adult insects from the forest
floor may provide a food source for spiders
and other canopy predators during the winter
and early spring and serve to maintain their
populations at high levels throughout the
year. Thus, herbivorous insects in these
forests never experience a season in which
to develop relatively free from predation

pressure and, as a consequence, their populations never build to levels which significantly affect the trees.

CONCLUSIONS

Studies in the canopy of an old-growth
coniferous forest have revealed biological
communities whose diversity and trophic
structure resemble those found in the soil
and streams. Primary producer, decomposer,
and consumer populations are all prominent
and appear to function in elemental cycling
within the canopy in a fashion parallel to
that in the soil and aquatic systems. We
now have evidence for the operation of
mechanisms for the conservation of nutrients
within the canopy. With regard to nitrogen
these mechanisms involve the fixation of
atmospheric nitrogen by cyanophycophilous
lichens, the loss of organic nitrogen from
such lichens through leaching, the uptake
of leached organics from dilute canopy
solution by microorganisms and other epiphytes, and the consumption of a portion of
the resulting microbial production by canopy microarthropods. Thus, leached

SCHEME OF CANOPY NITROGEN FLOW

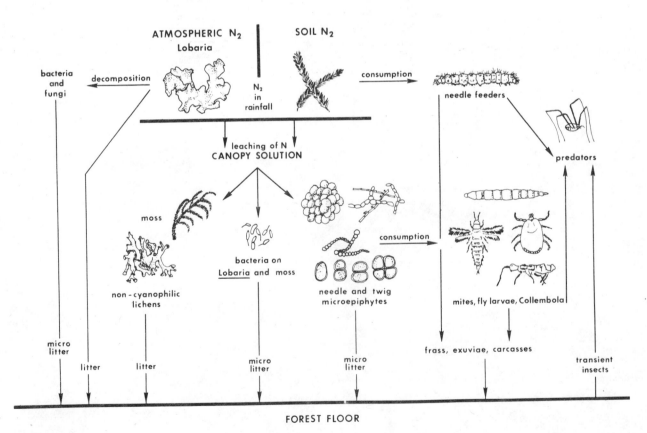

Figure 12. Scheme of nitrogen fluxes in canopy.

organics serve indirectly as a base for many canopy food chains. Conservation of nutrients within the canopy operates continually against the force of gravity; in old-growth stands canopy production must be balanced ultimately by a return of materials to the forest floor (see Fig. 12).

Microorganisms and epiphytes play a key role in regulating fluxes of nutrients from the bottom of the tree. These processes are probably not of universal occurrence in forest stands, and therefore it is of interest to consider the climatic and biological factors which enhance development of these canopy populations. A primary requirement for any system in which leaching plays a role is the input of atmospheric moisture in the form of rain or fog. Leaching is a solution process. In addition, poikilohydric organisms such as lichens, mosses, and microepiphytes require periodic additions of liquid water in order to survive. As a result, the processes described above will not be of much importance in desert environments with low precipitation or in subarctic and subalpine stands where much of the annual precipitation is recieved as snow that falls from the canopy before melting. Beyond this, conditions which lead to the availability of fixed carbon and nitrogen in the canopy solution will foster growth of heterotrophic microepiphytes. These conditions include the prevalence of readily leached surfaces such as those of older evergreen leaves and cyanophycophilous lichens. Evergreen foliage persists for a number of years, providing additional surface area for the buildup of perennial colonies of microepiphytes. Conversely, deciduous canopies in which the leaves are shed annually should show less evidence of nutrient uptake and release by microbial cells. Other situations where concentrations of macroelements in the canopy solution may be high involve: (1) aphid infestations, which are widely reported to encourage the growth of yeasts and sooty molds on canopy surfaces coated with honeydew (Fraser, 1937; Reynolds, 1975); (2) outbreaks of defoliating insects (Kimmins, 1972; Nilsson, 1978; Schroeder, 1978); (3) foliar fertilization; and (4) atmospheric pollution. In this final instance, the extent of nutrient enrichment in precipitation from pollution is attested to by the enhanced growth of pigmented fungi on painted surfaces in cities and by the necessity for adding microbicides to paint to prevent such growth.

In view of the above considerations, canopies of moist evergreen forests in temperate and tropical regions should prove to be microbiologically active, whatever the specific identities of the trees and the canopy inhabitants, wherever they occur within that climatic zone. Indeed, microepiphytes are abundant on the leaves of broadleaved tropical evergreens (Odum et al., 1970; Reynolds, 1975), and several studies suggest that they function in uptake of canopy nutrients just as those studied in the Andrews Forest do (Odum et al., 1970; Witkamp, 1970). If the canopy nitrogen model developed for the old-growth Douglas-fir trees in the Andrews Forest were to be tested in functionally similar forests elsewhere, evergreen broadleaved forests throughout the tropics and the gymnosperm forests of New Zealand and South America should provide appropriate stands. Closer to home, the model could be tested by experimental manipulation of the canopy nutrient regime with fertilization or insect defoliation programs. Such an approach deserves serious consideration.

ACKNOWLEDGMENTS

The original work cited in this review has been a collaborative effort. In particular I should like to acknowledge the contributions of Drs. William Denison, William Massman, Lawrence Pike, and David Voegtlin. Bill Hopper, Terry Montlick, and Robert Rydell have dealt with computer programming and data analysis. Fanny Carroll, Judi Horstmann, and Jan Wroncy have been responsible for the laboratory misting experiments and water analyses. Undergraduate work-study students have put in hundreds of hours in routine laboratory work and analyses; our program would not have been possible without their continuing contributions. This work has been supported with funds from NSF grants BMS 7514003 and DEB 78-03583.

LITERATURE CITED

Abee, A., and D. Lavender. 1972. Nutrient cycling in throughfall and litterfall in 450-yr-old Douglas-fir stands. In Research on Coniferous Forest Ecosystems, Proc. Symp. Northwest Scientific Assn., edited by J. F. Franklin, L. J. Dempster, and R. H. Waring, pp. 133-144. USDA Forest Service, Pacific Northwest Forest and Range Expt. Sta., Portland, Oregon.

Andre, H., and D. Voegtlin. 1980. Some observations on the biology of Camissia carrollii Andre. Acarologia (in press).

Attiwill, P. M. 1966. The chemical composition of rainwater in relation to recycling of nutrients in mature Eucalyptus forest. Pl. Soil 24:390-406.

Bernstein, M. E., and G. C. Carroll. 1977. Microbial populations on Douglas fir needle surfaces. Microbial Ecol. 4:41-52.

Bernstein, M. E., H. M. Howard, and G. C. Carroll. 1973. Fluorescence microscopy of Douglas fir foliage. Can. J. Microbiol. 19:1129-1130.

Best, G. R. 1976. Treatment and Biota of an Ecosystem Affect Nutrient Cycling, Ph.D. thesis, University of Georgia, Athens.

Bradford, M. M. 1976. A rapid and sensitive method for the quantification of microgram quantities of protein utilizing the principle of protein-dye binding. Analyt. Biochem. 72:248-254.

Caldwell, B. A., C. Hagedorn, and W. C. Denison. 1979. Bacterial ecology of an old-growth Douglas fir canopy. Microbial Ecol. 5:91-103.

Carlisle, A. 1965. Carbohydrates in the precipitation beneath sessile oak, Quercus petraea (Mattushna) Liebl. Pl. Soil 22:399-400.

Carlisle, A., A. H. F. Brown, and E. J. White. 1966. The organic matter and nutrient elements in the precipitation beneath a sessile oak canopy. J. Ecol. 54:87-98.

Carroll, G. C. 1979. Needle microepiphytes in a Douglas fir canopy: biomass and distribution patterns. Can. J. Bot. 57:1000-1007.

Carroll, G. C., L. H. Pike, J. R. Perkins, and M. A. Sherwood. 1980. Biomass and distribution patterns of conifer twig microepiphytes in a Douglas fir forest. Can. J. Bot. (in press).

Cronan, C. S. 1980. Solution chemistry of a New Hampshire subalpine ecosystem: a biogeochemical analysis. Oikos (in press).

Cooper, G., and G. C. Carroll. 1978. Ribitol as a major component of water soluble leachates from Lobaria oregana. The Bryologist 8:568-572.

Denison, W. C. 1973. Life in tall trees. Sci. American 228:74-80.

Denison, W. C., D. M. Tracy, F. M. Rhoades, and M. Sherwood. 1972. Direct, nondestructive measurement of biomass and structure in living old-growth Douglas-fir. In Research on Coniferous Forest Ecosystems, Proc. of Symp. of Northwest Scientific Assoc., edited by J. F. Franklin, L. J. Dempster, and R. H. Waring, pp. 147-158. USDA Forest Service, Pacific Northwest Expt. Sta., Portland, Oregon.

Eaton, J. S., G. E. Likens, and F. H. Bormann. 1973. Throughfall and stemflow chemistry in a northern hardwood forest. J. Ecol. 61:495-508.

Feller, M. C. 1977. Nutrient movement through western hemlock-western red cedar ecosystems in southwestern British Columbia. Ecology 58:1269-1283.

Foster, N. W. 1974. Annual macroelement transfer from Pinus banksiana Lamb. forest to soil. Can. J. Forest Res. 4:470-476.

Franklin, R. T. 1970. Insect influences on the forest canopy. In Analysis of Temperate Forest Ecosystems, edited by D. E. Reichle, pp. 86-99. New York: Springer-Verlag.

Fraser, L. M. 1937. Distribution of sooty mold fungi and its relation to certain aspects of their physiology. Proc. Linn. Soc. New South Wales 62:35-56.

Gersper, P. L., and H. Holowaychuk. 1971. Some effects of stemflow from forest canopy trees on chemical properties of soils. Ecology 52:691-702.

Hart, G. E., and D. R. Parent. 1974. Chemistry of throughfall under Douglas fir and Rocky Mountain juniper. Amer. Mid. Natur. 92:191-201.

Henderson, G. S., W. F. Harris, D. E. Todd, and T. Grizzard. 1977. Quantity and chemistry of throughfall as influenced by forest-type and season. J. Ecol. 65:365-374.

Jaenicke, L. 1974. A rapid micromethod for the determination of nitrogen and phosphate in biological material. Analyt. Biochem. 61:623-627.

Kimmins, J. P. 1972. Relative contributions of leaching, litterfall, and defoliation by Neodiprion sertifer (Hymenoptera) to the removal of Cesium-134. Oikos 23:226-234.

Kimmins, J. P. 1973. Some statistical aspects of sampling throughfall precipitation in nutrient cycling studies in British Columbia coastal forests. Ecology 54:1008-1019.

Lang, C. E., W. A. Reiners, and R. K. Heier. 1976. Potential alteration of precipitation chemistry by epiphytic lichens. Oecologia 25:229-241.

Lewis, W. M., Jr., and M. C. Grant. 1978. Sampling and chemical interpretation of precipitation for mass balance studies. Water Resources Res. 14:1098-1104.

Miller, H. G., J. M. Cooper, and J. D. Miller. 1976. Effect of nitrogen supply on nutrients in litter fall and crown leaching in a stand of Corsican pine. J. Applied Ecol. 13:233-248.

Monteith, J. L., ed. 1975. Vegetation and the Atmosphere, Vols. I and II. New York: Academic Press, Inc.

Nihlgaard, B. 1970. Precipitation, its chemical composition and effect on soil water in a beech and a spruce forest in south Sweden. Oikos 21:208-217.

Nilsson, I. 1978. The influence of Dasychira pudibunda (Lepidoptera) on plant nutrient transports and tree growth in a beech Fagus sylvatica forest in southern Sweden. Oikos 30: 133-148.

Odum, H. T., G. A. Briscoe, and C. B. Briscoe. 1970. Fallout radioactivity and epiphytes. In A Tropical Rain Forest, edited by H. T. Odum and R. F. Pigeon, pp. H-167-H-176. USAEC Technical Information Center, Oak Ridge, Tenn.

Pike, L. H. 1978. The importance of epiphytic lichens in mineral cycling. The Bryologist 81:247-257.

Pike, L. H., W. C. Denison, D. M. Tracy, M. A. Sherwood, and F. M. Rhoades. 1975. Floristic survey of epiphytic lichens and bryophytes growing on old-growth conifers in western Oregon. The Bryologist 78:389-402.

Pike, L. H., R. A. Rydell, and W. C. Denison. 1977. A 400-year-old Douglas fir tree and its epiphytes: biomass, surface area, and their distributions. Can. J. Forest Res. 7:680-699.

Rafes, P. M. 1970. Estimation of the effects of phytophagous insects on forest production. In Analysis of Temperate Forest Ecosystems, edited by D. E. Reichle, pp. 100-106. New York: Springer-Verlag.

Reichle, D. E., R. A. Goldstein, R. I. Van Hook, Jr., and G. J. Dodson. 1973. Analysis of insect consumption in a forest canopy. Ecology 54:1076-1084.

Reynolds, D. R. 1972. Stratification of tropical epiphylls. Kalikasan, Philipp. J. Biol. 1:7-10.

Reynolds, D. R. 1975. Observations on growth forms of sooty mold fungi. Nova Hedwigia 26:179-193.

Schroeder, L. A. 1978. Consumption of black cherry leaves by phytophagous insects. Amer. Midl. Natur. 100:294-306.

Sedmake, J. J., and S. Grossberg. 1977. A rapid, sensitive, and versatile assay for protein using Coomassie Brilliant Blue G-250. Analyt. Biochem. 79:544-552.

Swisher, R., and G. C. Carroll. 1980. Fluorescein diacetate as an estimator of microbial biomass on coniferous needle surfaces. Microbial. Ecol. (in press).

Tamm, C. O. 1951. Removal of plant nutrients from tree crowns by rain. Physiol. Plant 4:184-188.

Tibbling, G. 1968. A routine method for microdetermination of mannitol in serum. Scand. J. Clin. Lab. Invest. 22:7-10.

Voigt, C. K. 1960. Alteration of the composition of rainwater by trees. Amer. Midl. Natur. 63:321-326.

Witkamp, M. 1970. Mineral retention by epiphyllic organisms. In A Tropical Rain Forest, edited by H. T. Odum and R. F. Pigeon, pp. H-177-H-179. USAEC Technical Information Center, Oak Ridge, Tenn.

Aspects of the Microbial Ecology of Forest Ecosystems

Dennis Parkinson

INTRODUCTION

Since the 1950's there have been regular and, at times, detailed studies of the microbial ecology of forest soils in which most detailed attention was given to microorganisms in the organic horizon. In the initial studies a great deal of attention was paid to the microorganisms isolated from the different layers of the organic horizon. The fungi were, and in fact still are, the group of microorganisms most studied, and attempts have been made to elucidate "successional patterns" of these organisms and their roles in decomposing leaf litter on the forest floor (Hayes, 1979).

Subsequently, interest became more directed to the general phenomenon of organic matter decomposition in forest soils. Through detailed studies, mainly using litter bag methods, information was gathered on rates of organic matter decomposition on a range of sites. From such studies a number of generalizations have been postulated (and have become part of the lore of decomposition!). Quality of the substrate(s) undergoing decomposition has been shown to be a major factor governing decomposition rates; there being a negative correlation of such rates with initial lignin content and C:N of the substrates, and a positive correlation with soluble carbohydrate and (to a lesser extent) N and P contents. Climatic factors of temperature and moisture were found to be important governing factors. Thus, in dry exposed sites decomposition rates were severely restricted in standing dead material, but tended to increase within the soil profile. Whereas in wet climates, decomposition rates of standing dead and surface litter were high but might decline with profile depth. Of course, freeze-thaw and drying-re-wetting events over short periods of time play a very important role in nutrient release from decomposing leaf litter. In general, there is an increase in decomposition rates in the temperature "transect" from pole to equator. Finally, the availability of suitable decomposer organisms is essential. It is well known that following an initial weathering period, during which time leaching of soluble nutrients from freshly fallen litter occurs, the decomposition process is effected by microorganisms and litter and soil invertebrates. Therefore, interest has been re-directed to the roles of decomposer organisms in litter decomposition and consequent nutrient cycling.

Whilst the range of interactions between invertebrate fauna and microflora has been known for a considerable period of time, only relatively recently have detailed studies been made in attempt to quantify these interactions and to assess their possible consequences in the cycling of nutrients in forest ecosystems.

In this presentation attention will be centered on two aspects of forest microbial ecology that have received considerable attention over the past few years. Firstly, to microbial biomass determinations in decomposing litter on the forest floor. This may appear to be a "perennial topic"; however, new methods of obtaining reliable data are being developed to allow better quantitative assessment of nutrient tie-up (and release) in the microorganisms. Secondly, some comments will be made on recent work on specific fungus-fauna interactions which may affect the pattern of fungal colonization and decomposition of organic matter.

A considerable body of excellent publications is available in both these areas, but this presentation will deal specifically with two case studies involving the author. References to the research will be minimized.

STUDIES ON MICROBIAL BIOMASS
OF FOREST LITTER LAYERS

One of the factors impeding the development of studies on the participation of microorganisms in forest ecosystems has been the lack of suitable methods for rapidly assessing total microbial biomass in soils and organic matter, fluctuations of that biomass, and the relative contributions of fungi and bacteria to this biomass. Direct observation methods have been used in several studies of fungi in leaf litter decomposing on the forest floor, but the techniques used (Frankland, 1975; Visser and Parkinson, 1975) are time consuming and probably underestimate total lengths of fungal hyphae associated with the leaf debris. Furthermore, in many cases, it is difficult to distinguish live hyphae from dead. The use of phase-contrast microscopy partly overcomes the difficulty of distinguishing hyphae with cell contents from empty hyphae. Using this method, Frankland (1975) calculated that of the 289 µg fungi g^{-1} L layer litter (deciduous woodland) about 35 percent was "live" (possessed cell contents), whilst Visser and Parkinson (1975) calculated that the fungal standing crop of L layer leaves in a <u>Populus tremuloides</u> woodland at the time of snowmelt was about 1,421 mg dwt m^{-2} with more than 50 percent of observed hyphae containing protoplasm.

These data can be compared with those for live hyphal data obtained for oak-beech forest L and F layer litter of 79 to 82 percent and 15 to 20 percent respectively (Nagel de Boois and Jansen, 1971), and 76 to 97 percent of observed mycelium being active during initial stages of decomposition of beech leaves (Waid, Preston, and Harris, 1973). However, Soderstrom (1979), using fluorescent staining (fluorescein diacetate), has recorded much lower values for "live" hyphae in soil (2-3%).

Direct observation methods, being time consuming in operation, are difficult to apply in large comparative studies on fungal biomass changes that require very frequent sampling (replicate). Chemical techniques have been developed for specific studies (e.g., chitin determination, Swift, 1973) or for general investigations (ATP determinations). Recently Anderson and Domsch (1978) described a rapid method for total microbial biomass determinations in soil samples, and when this method is coupled with the selective inhibition method (Anderson and Domsch, 1975) determinations of bacterial and fungal biomass are possible. While this total method was originally developed for studies on agricultural soils, it has been valuable for detailed investigations of the organic horizon of forest soils (Parkinson et al., 1978).

This method was used in a detailed study of three spruce (<u>Picea</u> <u>abies</u>) soils in the Solling area of Germany, but only one site (a 95-year-old spruce site) will be discussed here. Firstly, tests showed that measurements on composite organic horizon samples could give an accurate index of the microbial biomass in the organic horizon (L, F, and H layers). Then the Anderson and Domsch (1978) method was used on regularly taken samples (at least once per month over 10 months) from the field, and the effects of moisture content and temperature of the organic horizon were investigated under laboratory conditions. From these studies the following major points emerged:

1. Maximum total microbial biomass developed at about 15°C and in the 60 to 80 percent moisture range. These data allowed simple predictions for the spruce forest site which were testable against actual determinations on field samples. March samples were taken at field conditions where the temperature of the organic layer was + 1.5°C with 65 percent moisture, and from these data the predicted total microbial biomass was 180.0 to 190.0 mg C 100 gdwt^{-1}. In May the organic horizon temperature and moisture conditions were + 14.0°C and 65 percent, the predicted microbial biomass was 320.0 to 330.0 mg C 100 gdwt^{-1}, and the observed value was 304.0 ± 8.4 mg C 100 gdwt^{-1}.

2. Seasonal microbial biomass changes ranged between 194 mg C 100 gdwt^{-1} (late autumn-winter) and 310 mg C 100 gdwt^{-1} (late spring-summer). However, particularly in autumn and spring when more marked diurnal variations in temperature would be expected, considerable microbial biomass variations would be expected and in fact were observed. In autumn, between 6 and 20 September total microbial biomass increased by 48 percent, whereas in the next 10 days (20-30 Sept.) it fell by 7 percent and by late October it had fallen by a further 32 percent. In the spring, between 9-17 March there was a 43 percent increase in microbial biomass which was followed (17 March - 4 April) by a 27 percent fall. These periods would be expected to be ones of a drastic changes in nutrient tie-up and release. Gross calculations of C "tie-up" and release during the year (not taking into account any "internal recycling" of C within the decomposer complex) would indicate an overall release of 105 mg C 100 gdwt^{-1} organic horizon between 20 September and 9 March; while, between 9 March and 6 June there was a C tie-up of 116 mg C 100 gdwt^{-1}.

3. Considering the annual mean temperature (and the absence of limiting moisture conditions at the experimental site during the study period), an annual mean microbial biomass of about 212 mg C 100 gdwt^{-1} (or about 9.6 g microbial C m^{-2}) could be expected. Selective inhibition experiments indicated the average partitioning of the total microbial biomass was 77 percent fungi and 23 percent bacteria.

4. In view of the comments made regarding the calculation of bacterial maintenance requirements and substrate available for microbial growth in forest soils (Gray and Williams, 1971; Hissett and Gray, 1976), an attempt was made to assess the implications of the annual microbial biomass in the organic horizon of the spruce forest. The following summary carbon balance sheet could be made up:

Input of above
   ground litter : 230 g C m^{-2} yr^{-1}
Estimated input of
   root exudates
   and dead roots : 70 g C m^{-2} yr^{-1}
Output of leachates
   from the H layer
   (data from Ulrich,
   pers. comm.) : 34 g C m^{-2} yr^{-1}

i.e., in a 'steady state' condition (no accumulation, no depletion) 266 g C m^{-2} yr^{-1} would be available for microbial maintenance and growth.

However, in the 95-year-old spruce forest studied it was more reasonable to assume that some organic matter accumulation was still occurring. In comparing weights per square meter of organic horizons of spruce forests of different ages in the Solling area it was estimated that accumulation at the study site could be occurring at the rate of 20 g C m^{-2} yr^{-1}.

Therefore, 246 g C m^{-2} yr^{-1} would actually be available for microbial maintenance and development.

Data from selective inhibition studies indicated that the average yearly total microbial biomass of 9.6 g C m^{-2} was made up of 2.2 g bacterial C and 7.4 g fungal C. Assuming a yield coefficient of 0.5 and a maintenance constant of 0.001 hr^{-1} (Hissett and Gray, 1976), then: 56.6 g C m^{-2} yr^{-1} would be available for bacterial maintenance and turnover, of which 38.5 g C m^{-2} yr^{-1} would be required for maintenance, leaving 18.1 g C m^{-2} yr^{-1} available for 'turnover' (which would allow a mean generation time of about 45 days). 189.4 g C m^{-2} yr^{-1} would be available for fungal maintenance and growth.

Undoubtedly these calculations are primitive, as they do not take any account of the recycling of microbial carbon within the complex decomposer system. However, they do indicate the availability of resources to support the level of microbial biomass recorded.

The method of Anderson and Domsch (1978) was also applied to a study of three spruce forests of different ages (Parkinson et al., in press). In this study an attempt was made to asses direct relationships between primary production parameters and decomposer biomass and respiratory activity. Fortunately, a considerable body of data on the primary producers was available since the three chosen spruce sites were studied in the German IBP (many of these data were published by Ulrich et al., 1974, and unpublished data were provided by Dr. Heller).

The ages of the three study sites were 48, 95, and 123 years. The highest aboveground standing crop was seen in the 95-year-old site and the lowest value was at the oldest site. Aboveground productivity was highest at the youngest site; the lowest value was recorded at the oldest site.

Estimation of annual productivity per unit weight of standing crop (based on unpub. data, Heller, pers. comm.) yielded the somewhat curious data given in Table 1, with the middle-aged site showing the lowest value. Table 1 also presents similar data based on estimations of standing crop and productivity made in 1968 (Ulrich et al., 1974).

The total standing crop of roots in the organic horizon was significantly higher at the youngest site, and the proportion of mycorrhizal roots was also highest at this site.

Data on the organic horizon at each study site are given in Table 1. These indicate that the contribution of L + F$_1$ layers to the total organic horizon varied considerably from site to site (highest in the youngest site, lowest in the oldest). They also indicate variations from site to site in percent C, percent N and C/N. From the data on total weight of organic matter (m^{-2}) of the organic horizon at each site, it would appear that the weight of the organic horizon (m^{-2}) at the middle-aged site (95 years), i.e., 4,545 g m^{-2} was much less than would be expected. Given the age of the site plus the data obtained from the other sites, 9,000 to 10,000 gdwt litter m^{-2} would be expected for this site.

The data on basal respiration of the total organic horizon material (measured at 22°C) are given in Table 2. However, the mean annual temperature for all sites was 6.2°C. Laboratory experiments at this mean annual temperature indicated that the loss of carbon m^{-2} yr^{-1} at each site would be

Table 1. General data on primary producers and allied material for each of the study sites.

Site age	48 years	95 years	123 years
Aboveground standing crop 1968 (g m^{-2})	14,300	24,446	23,500
Aboveground standing crop 1977 (g m^{-2})	17,741	26,884	15,823
Aboveground productivity 1968 (g m^{-2} yr^{-1})	849	886	651
Aboveground productivity 1977 (g m^{-2} yr^{-1})	767	525	441
$\frac{\text{Productivity}}{\text{Standing crop}}$ 1968	0.059	0.036	0.029
$\frac{\text{Productivity}}{\text{Standing crop}}$ 1977	0.043	0.0195	0.028
Total weight (g m^{-2}) organic horizon	5,207	4,545	11,453
Percent contribution of L + F$_1$ to organic horizon	10.3	7.3	5.8
Percent organic matter in organic horizon (composite)	83.6	75.8	69.3
Percent C	42.5	39.2	36.6
Percent N	1.6	1.4	1.3
Roots (<5 mm diam.) standing crop (g m^{-2}) in organic horizon	216	78	146
Mycorrhizal roots (g m^{-2})	97	10	43

Table 2. Average yearly basal respiration of composite organic horizon samples from the three study sites (measurements made at 22°C)

	Average yearly value	
	ml CO$_2$ ↑ 100 g dwt^{-1} hr^{-1}	g C ↑ m^{-2} hr^{-1}
48-year-old site	3.47	0.097
95-year-old site	1.80	0.044
123-year-old site	1.36	0.084

approximately: 48-year-old site: 266 g C $m^{-2} yr^{-1}$; 95-year-old site: 114 g C $m^{-2} yr^{-1}$; 123-year-old site: 206 g C $m^{-2} yr^{-1}$.

General data on total microbial biomass at each of the three study sites are given in Table 3. Selective inhibition experiments indicated no significant variations in the percentage contribution of bacteria and fungi to this total biomass over the 10-month study (the ratio bacteria: fungi remaining constant at 20:80). The data indicate that, on the basis of 100 gdwt organic horizon samples, average total microbial biomass was highest in the youngest site and lowest at the oldest site. When calculated on a square-meter basis this order was altered, the youngest site still holding the highest microbial biomass but the middle-aged site holding the lowest. Similar relationships were observed when considering data on maximum microbial biomass change at each site over the study period -- a parameter which is at best crude because of the demonstrated short-term large fluctuations in total microbial biomass in coniferous forest organic horizons (Parkinson et al., 1978).

By any form of calculation, the organic horizon of the youngest site emerged as having both the highest activity (as indicated by basal respiration measurements in Table 2) and the highest microbial biomass (Table 3). Furthermore the variations (both positive and negative) in total microbial biomass during the study period (Nov. - July) were much greater at this site than at the other two sites. Since the important environmental factors of temperature and moisture content of the organic horizon at each site were essentially similar, other reasons must be sought for the higher microbial activity and biomass (plus fluctuations) at the youngest site.

Judging by the data in Table 1, the major differences between the three study sites were:

1. There was a higher contribution of L + F_1 layer material to the total organic horizon (10.3% at the youngest site, 7.3% at the middle-aged site, and 5.8% at the oldest site). In a detailed study of the 95-year-old site, Parkinson et al. showed the L + F_1 layer material to be the locus of highest biological activity and microbial biomass. Therefore, this greater contribution at the youngest site is probably an important phenomenon in allowing the high values.

2. The percentage carbon in the organic layer was highest at the youngest site, and the C/N was narrowest.

3. There was a higher standing crop of roots in the organic horizon of the youngest site. There were also considerably more mycorrhizal rootlets in the F_2 and H layers of the youngest site than in the other sites.

Presumably this larger root standing crop would, via exudates and sloughed-off material plus input of dead roots, enhance microbial activity and development. A proportion of the microbial biomass determined, at least in the spring and summer samples, could be mycorrhizal fungal material (hyphae growing into the organic horizon from mycorrhizal sheaths).

These factors at the youngest site are enhanced by the figures given in Table 1 on primary productivity per unit aboveground standing crop, where the youngest site gave the highest values both in 1968 and 1977 (0.059 and 0.043).

The oldest site which, on the basis of unit weight (100 gdwt) of organic horizon, had the lowest basal respiration and total microbial biomass values, was also the site with the highest amounts of F_2 and H layer

Table 3. *Summary of total microbial biomass values in composite organic horizon samples from the three study sites.*

	Average yearly total microbial biomass values		Maximum - minimum biomass values	
	mg C 100 $gdwt^{-1}$	g C m^{-2}	mg C 100 $gdwt^{-1}$	g C m^{-2}
48-year-old site	571.9	29.8	342.7	17.9
95-year-old site	260.0	11.8	116.4	5.3
123-year-old site	209.7	24.0	84.6	9.7

Table 4. Summary of microbial and primary producer (and allied) data on a comparative, proportional basis

	Microbial (decomposer) parameters			Primary producer (and allied) parameters		
	Basal respiration	Average total biomass	Max-min biomass	Productivity standing crop	Roots <5 mm	Percent contribution of L + F1
1. m^{-2}						
48-year-old site	2.2	2.53	3.38	2.2	2.77	1.78
95-year-old site	1.0	1.0	1.0	1.0	1.0	1.23
123-year-old site	1.9	2.03	1.8	1.4	1.87	1.0
2. 100 gdwt^{-1}						
48-year-old site	2.55	2.72	4.05	2.2	3.26	1.78
95-year-old site	1.32	1.24	1.38	1.0	1.35	1.23
123-year-old site	1.0	1.0	1.0	1.4	1.0	1.0

material per sample (and, naturally, per m^2). The total amount of roots at this site was not significantly different from that found at the middle-aged site, but higher amounts of mycorrhizal roots were present as compared with the middle-aged site. Data on aboveground productivity per unit standing crop (Table 1) at the oldest site changed only very slightly in the 1968-1977 period (0.0288 in 1968 and 0.0278 in 1977). However, similar data for the middle-aged site (Table 1) indicated a considerable decline in primary productivity per unit standing crop of primary producers during the same period (0.036 in 1968 and 0.0195 in 1977).

When calculating microbial biomass on a square-meter basis for each site, it is impossible to deal with the paradox of the low total weight (m^{-2}) of the organic horizon at the middle-aged site. However, weights (m^{-2}) of the organic horizon at each study site compared with similar measurements obtained in 1968 (Ulrich et al., 1974) as follows:

	Site A	Site B	Site C
1968 data (Ulrich et al., 1974)	5,200 g m^{-2}	4,900 g m^{-2}	11,100 g m^{-2}
1976-1977 data (Parkinson et al., in press)	5,207 g m^{-2}	4,545 g m^{-2}	11,453 g m^{-2}

No significant change in the mass of organic horizon has occurred over almost a decade. Does this mean there is a steady state condition in this horizon at each site?

Table 4 summarizes the comparative (proportional) relationships of several microbial (decomposer) parameters and primary producer (and allied) parameters for each site. The data are given both for unit weights (100 gdwt) of organic horizon and on a square-meter basis. These data reinforce the comments made earlier on the three study sites. It is well known that chemical quality of litter substrates and input of material from roots (live and dead) are important factors in affecting decomposer biomass and activity in any soil, and the data exemplify this fact for the three study sites. However, relationships between primary productive vigour (productivity/standing crop) and decomposer activity and biomass (per m^2) are also indicated. While the proportional relationships of basal respiratory activity and primary productivity per unit standing crop for the three sites are very similar, other relationships are not as direct as might have been expected. The situation, particularly at the middle-aged site, has been complicated by a complex history of the vegetation (probably prior to 1968). The data provided here indicate the type of parameters which should be considered in attempting to derive re-

lationships of primary producers and decomposers, and further indicate the power of the physiological method (Anderson and Domsch, 1978) for microbial biomass determinations.

The previous comments indicate some interesting approaches, given a speedy method for microbial biomass assessment. The data can be further extended to consideration of nutrient cycling if knowledge of the other nutrients held in microbial tissue is considered (Visser and Parkinson, 1975). Regrettably, too little is known on actual microbial turnover rates in forest soils, the actual ecological efficiency of the important soil bacteria and fungi, and on death and decay rates of the various components of the litter and soil microbiota.

INTERACTION BETWEEN MICROFLORA AND FAUNA IN FOREST LITTER

Efficient organic matter decomposition in the surface layers of forest soils is effected by the joint activities of the microflora and the soil fauna. Bacteria and fungi are generally considered to play by far the major role in the actual oxidation of organic carbon, although it has been demonstrated that some of the soil animals can act as agents of primary decomposition because they possess cellulolytic enzymes in their guts. Nevertheless, the major roles in organic matter decomposition attributed to the soil fauna are:

1. Transmission of microbial inoculum in organic matter.

2. Fragmentation of large pieces of organic matter, with the consequent increase in surface area exposed for microbial development.

3. Possible enhancement of microbial activity because of changes in the chemical constitution of organic material during passage through the animal gut.

4. Possible effects (stimulatory or inhibitory) on the microflora as a result of animal grazing on that microflora.

Among the fauna active in the organic layers of the forest floor are various groups which, at least during part of their life history, consume microbial tissue. A good deal of attention has been directed to the consumption of fungi by microarthropods, and when attempts have been made to assess the actual amounts of consumption of fungi by various groups of these microarthropods in field locations, the values obtained have been frequently low. Various taxa of the microarthropods that graze on fungi do not consume all species of fungi -- they selectively consume specific groups of the mycoflora in decomposing litter. The possible implications of this selective grazing will be discussed later.

Active consumption of microbial tissue by microarthropods could restrict nutrient loss (via leaching) from decomposing organic matter. Further indication of role of soil animals as stabilizers of nutrient cycling comes from the evidence that these organisms concentrate certain nutrient elements (K and Ca) in their tissues. Also the faeces of some microarthropods (particularly mites) are slowly decomposed and thus nutrients held in the faeces are only slowly released (elemental leaching is retarded).

In a cool, temperate, deciduous forest dominated by Populus tremuloides (Lousier and Parkinson, 1976, 1978 have given general decomposition and nutrient dynamics of this area), Mitchell (1976) calculated that consumption of fungi by Oribatid mites was 6 g m^{-2} yr^{-1}, a figure which represented about 2 percent of the fungal standing crop. In this particular forest, Visser and Parkinson (1975) observed a high fungal standing crop (1,421 mg dwt m^{-2}) in the litter layer at the time of snowmelt (April), and that this standing crop rapidly declined (to 786 mg dwt m^{-2}) immediately following snowmelt. This quantitative change in fungal standing crop was accompanied by a significant qualitative change in the fungal community in the L layer litter. Before snowmelt, Basidiomycetes were isolated with a frequency of about 3 percent, and after snowmelt their frequency of occurrence was about 14 percent. Before snowmelt, sterile dark hyphal forms were isolated with about 26 percent frequency, but this fell to 14 percent after snowmelt. At the same time, Collembola were observed to be numerous and active in the litter layer, suggesting that high grazing activity by these animals could be one factor responsible for this decline in fungal standing crop.

A detailed study showed that one species of the Collembola (Onychiurus subtenuis) was particularly frequent in the surface organic matter during the snowmelt period (about 4,500 animals m^{-2} in the L layer). Examination of gut contents and of faeces indicated this species was selectively grazing on fungi possessing dark

hyphae. A food preference study (Visser and Whittaker, 1977) confirmed that selective feeding by O. subtenuis on sterile dark fungi did, in fact, occur.

Following this, the effect of grazing by O. subtenuis on the two commonly recorded, potentially competitive, groups of litter fungi (Basidiomycetes and sterile dark forms) was investigated. A single common Basidiomycete species and a single common sterile dark form, which possessed similar growth rates when grown on L layer leaf litter, were chosen for study. The microcosm experiments have been described in detail (Parkinson et al., 1977; in press), so only the general conclusions will be outlined here. The selective grazing by the Collembola could have significant effects both on fungal growth in the L layer leaf litter surfaces, and on the colonization by fungi of dead leaf material on the litter surface. In essence, the selective grazing by the animals on the sterile dark fungus tilted the balance of competition in favor of the Basidiomycete. An interesting additional fact is that the Basidiomycete used in these experiments was apparently toxic to the test animals. The Basidiomycete was capable of actively utilizing cellulose whereas the sterile dark form was not, hence the selective grazing of the animals could have very marked effects on the rate and course of litter decomposition.

Thus grazing by invertebrates on fungi in forest litter is probably a much more complex phenomenon than would appear from quantitative studies on ingestion, i.e., relatively low grazing levels could have magnified effects, if selective, by reinforcing or switching competitive relationships between litter fungi.

When Collembola are allowed to move freely in microcosms containing sterile leaves or coarse sterile macerate for 5 to 10 days, it is found that when pieces of the sterile substrate are plated many of them yield bacteria and/or fungi. With respect to O. subtenuis, very few fecal pellets of this animal yielded fungi when plated onto 2 percent malt agar (only 2 of 40 plated pellets yield fungi -- in this case, a Mortierella -- even though they contained fungal hyphae). Thus it appears that the animals carry microbial "inoculum" on their external surfaces and are efficient spreaders of inoculum within organic matter. Apart from this being an interesting and potentially important phenomenon in nature, it does cause problems in studying, by respirometric methods, the positive or negative effects of animal grazing on fungal growth and activity in decomposing litter -- it has been suggested that grazing removes senescent hyphae and stimulates fungal growth.

This contribution has dealt with only two aspects of the microbiology of forest organic matter. Topics such as wood decomposition, mycorrhizal associations and the biology of mycorrhizal fungi, nitrogen transformations and a range of intermicrobe interactions are currently under detailed study. These studies will provide clearer ideas on the detailed functions of decomposer organisms in forest ecosystems.

LITERATURE CITED

Anderson, J. P. E., and K. H. Domsch. 1975. Measurement of bacterial and fungal contributions to respiration of selected agricultural and forest soils. Can. J. Microbiol. 21:314-322.

Anderson, J. P. E., and K. H. Domsch. 1978. A physiological method for the quantitative measurement of microbial biomass in soils. Soil Biol. Biochem. 10:215-221.

Frankland, J. C. 1975. Fungal decomposition of leaf litter in a deciduous woodland. In Biodegradation et Humification, edited by G. Kilbertus et al. pp. 33-44. Sarreguemines, France: Pierron Editeur.

Gray, T. R. G., and S. T. Williams. 1971. Microbial productivity in soil. In Microbes and Biological Productivity. Symp. Soc. Gen. Microbiol. 21:255-286.

Hayes, A. J. 1979. The microbiology of plant litter decomposition. Sci. Prog. (Oxford) 66:25-42.

Hissett, R., and T. R. G. Gray. 1976. Microsites and time changes in soil microbe ecology. In The Role of Terrestrial and Aquatic Organisms in Decomposition Processes, edited by J. M. Anderson and A. Macfadyen, pp. 23-29. Oxford: Blackwell Sci. Publ.

Lousier, J. D., and D. Parkinson. 1976. Litter decomposition in a cool temperate deciduous forest. Can. J. Bot. 54:419-436.

Lousier, J. D., and D. Parksinson. 1978. Chemical element dynamics in decomposing leaf litter. Can. J. Bot. 56: 2795-2812.

Mitchell, M. J. 1974. Ecology of oribatid mites in an aspen woodland soil. Ph.D. thesis, University of Calgary, Alberta, Canada.

Nagel-de Boois, H. M., and E. Jansen. 1971. The growth of fungal mycelium in forest soil layers. Rev. Ecol. Biol. Sol. 8:509-520.

Parkinson, D., S. Visser, and J. B. Whittaker. 1977. Effects of Collembolan grazing on fungal colonization of leaf litter. In Coil Organisms as Components of Ecosystems, Ecol. Bull. (Stockholm) 25:75-79.

Parkinson, D., K. H. Domsch, and J. P. E. Anderson. 1978. Die entwicklung mikrobieller Biomassen un organischen Horizont eines Fichtenstandortes. Oecol. Plant 13:355-366.

Parkinson, D., K. H. Domsch, and J. P. E. Anderson. Studies on the relationship of microbial biomass to primary production in three spruce forest soils. Bakt. Centrbl. (in press).

Parkinson, D., S. Visser, and J. B. Whittaker. Effects of Collembolan grazing on fungal colonization of leaf litter. Soil Biol. Biochem. (in press).

Soderstrom, B. 1979. Seasonal fluctuations of active fungal biomass in horizons of a podzolized pine-forest soil in central Sweden. Soil Biol. Biochem. 11: 149-154.

Swift, M. J. 1973. The estimation of mycelial biomass by determination of the hexosamine content of wood tissue decayed by fungi. Soil Biol. Biochem. 5:321-332.

Ulrich, B., R. Mayer, and H. Heller. 1974. Data analysis and data synthesis of forest ecosystems. Gottinger Bodenk. Ber. 30:1-459.

Visser, S., and D. Parkinson. 1975. Litter respiration and fungal growth under low temperature conditions. In Biodegradation et Humification, edited by G. Kilbertus et al., pp. 88-97. Sarreguemines, France: Pierron Editeur.

Visser, S., and J. B. Whittaker. 1977. Feeding preferences for certain litter fungi by Onychiurus subtenuis. Oikos 29:320-325.

Waid, J. S., K. J. Preston, and P. J. Harris. 1973. Autoradiographic techniques to detect active microbial cells in natural habitats. In Modern Methods in Microbial Ecology, Ecol. Bull. (Stockholm) 17:317-322.

The Dynamic Belowground Ecosystem[1]

W. F. Harris, Dan Santantonio, and D. McGinty

INTRODUCTION

Roots comprise the primary interface between plant and soil for uptake of water and nutrients. Much is known about the biochemistry, cell physiology, and membrane physics associated with these important processes (Devlin, 1966; Larcher, 1975; and Pitman, 1976). In this paper we discuss the role of the belowground ecosystem, especially the autotrophic root component, in the structure and function of forest ecosystems. Beyond recognizing roles of anchoring terrestrial plants and uptake of water and nutrients, this component of the forest has been largely neglected in an ecosystem context. In order to focus our discussion on the properties of the belowground ecosystem, we use the term "rhizosphere" to include roots, mycorrhizae, microbes, and rhizophagus invertebrates. Each component of the rhizosphere merits review and speculation as to its own specific roles. However, we have chosen to develop our discussion on the entire subsystem rather than individual components. Many answers to questions we pose about dynamics of belowground subsystems rely on continuing research into detailed processes at organism and community levels.

Roots comprise a substantial portion of forest ecosystems, generally accounting for 15 to 25 percent of total biomass. The range of values reported for individual stands, however, extends from 9 to 44 percent (Santantonio et al., 1977). The greatest amount of root biomass accumulates in temperate old-growth conifer forests (over 200 t/ha, e.g., Rodin and Provdvin (n.d.) in Rodin and Bazilevich, 1967). Broadleaved and subtropical forest types are characterized by a maximum of 70 to 100 t/ha dry weight of root organic matter (Bazilevich and Rodin, 1968). Regardless of the type of forest, a consistent structural relationship exists between root and shoot across a wide variety of environments inhabited by trees (Fig. 3, Santantonio et al., 1977). Researchers have used this relationship to develop regression equations to estimate the logarithm of root system biomass from the logarithm of stem diameter at breast height. Consistent structural relations have been applied widely to estimate biomass of tree components from easily measured plant dimensions by using these equations, an approach termed "dimensional analysis" by Whittaker and Woodwell (1968, 1971). The proportion of total biomass represented by roots is lowest for forests and ranges up to 90 percent for tundra and certain grasslands. This is because forests accumulate large amounts of woody material aboveground, whereas tundra and grassland communities invest heavily into their structure belowground. Studies of root biomass have been summarized in reviews by Ovington (1962), by Rodin and Bazilevich (1967), and by Santantonio and others (1977).

The most reliable methods of estimating total root biomass usually consist of a combination of excavation and soil coring techniques. Root systems of a limited number of trees are excavated to develop logarithmic regression equations to estimate large structural roots. Soil cores or soil monoliths are taken to estimate small and fine roots on a unit area basis.

[1] Research supported jointly by the National Science Foundation's Ecosystem Studies Program under Interatency Agreement No. DEB-77-26722, and the Office of Health and Environmental Research, U.S. Department of Energy, under contract W-7405-eng-26 with Union Carbide Corporation. Publication No. 1350 from the Environmental Sciences Division.

Such a large amount of organic matter, accumulated at considerable metabolic expense, clearly could serve several purposes, such as storage of plant carbohydrates and essential nutrients. The following discussion briefly reviews recent findings on the behavior of belowground ecosystems and suggests some questions yet to be resolved. In particular, seasonal production/turnover of root biomass, role of root processes in nutrient turnover, root exudation, and the significance of belowground dynamics to the energy balance of the forest ecosystems are considered.

Before proceeding further, let us note why understanding the belowground ecosystem is important. Our concept of forest root dynamics incorporates several reasonable but generally untested assumptions. For example, root production has been assumed to be related to shoot production in the same manner as biomass, i.e.,

$$\frac{\text{root production}}{\text{root biomass}} = \underline{(k)} \frac{\text{shoot production}}{\text{shoot biomass}}.$$

Lacking information, the constant $\underline{(k)}$ has been assumed to equal 1.0. Assumptions such as these have arisen primarily because of technical problems and excessive labor required for research on forest tree roots (Newbould, 1967; Lieth, 1968). Recent progress in this area of study is related to two factors. First, much work emanates from large integrated studies of forest ecosystems such as those initiated as part of the International Biological Program. These studies supported skilled and dedicated technicians necessary to obtain the requisite data. Second, as more became known about the metabolism of forest ecosystems, the potential role of roots in ecosystem function and their energy demands associated with the accumulation and turnover of carbon and other essential elements surfaced as a central link coupling physiological processes and their environmental constraints with ecosystem behavior. Some interesting findings are counter to what has been commonly assumed. A few examples follow.

SEASONAL ACCUMULATION/TURNOVER OF ROOT ORGANIC MATTER

Root biomass of forests is not static. It changes annually and represents a varying proportion of the total biomass during stand development. By far the most dynamic component of root biomass is the fraction defined as "fine roots." No standard definition exists for fine roots. The distinction between fine and large roots is usually based on an arbitrarily chosen diameter ranging from 1.0 to 10 mm. These roots are distributed in upper soil layers; generally 90 percent are in the top 30 cm. In peat soils, however, the same proportion is in the top 10 cm (Heikurainen, 1957). It has long been known that a seasonal periodicity of root growth is common in woody plants (see reviews by Lyr and Hoffman, 1967; Kozlowski, 1971; Hermann, 1977; and Santantonio et al., 1977). For example, radial growth of woody roots (with secondary xylem thickening) can closely follow the pattern of radial increment growth aboveground (Fayle, 1968). Studies concerned with seasonal periodicity of root elongation, initiation of laterals, and subsequent growth have not clarified whether periods of inactivity reflect physiological or environmentally mediated dormancy. Sutton (1969) concluded that primary growth of roots is probably dominated by environmental conditions. Control probably lies in the interaction of endogenous and environmental mechanisms, but this remains to be demonstrated satisfactorily.

While there is considerable information on the phenology of root growth, there is an insufficient basis for making estimates of root production and turnover. The earliest studies of root production are probably those of Heikurainen (1957) and Kalela (1957). Both studies involved Scots pine (Pinus sylvestris L.) in Finland and both reported a modal pattern of rapid growth to peak root biomass in the spring and a gradual decline during the summer to a low of about 50 percent of the peak level. A biomodal peak in root biomass has been reported for an oak woodland in central Minnesota, USA (Ovington et al., 1963) and a stand of European beech (Fagus sylvatica L.) in the Solling area of West Germany (Göttche, 1972). In both instances, biomass peaked in spring with a second but lower peak in the fall. Investigations by Harris and others (1978) in a 45-year-old yellow poplar (Liriodendron tulipifera L.) stand in east Tennessee also revealed a spring-fall biomodal peak, while for loblolly pine (Pinus taeda L.) in North Carolina the modality was less clear with peaks observed in late fall, late winter, and possibly late spring. The year-to-year consistency observed for yellow poplar (Harris et al., 1978) suggests a strong measure of endogenous control. As with root elongation, the correlations of periods of peak biomass with environmental patterns are inconclusive. Current studies of mature Douglas-fir in western Oregon, however, reveal changing seasonal patterns of standing crop of roots <5 mm diam. from one year (moderately dry) to the next (wet) (Santantonio, 1979).

The surprising result of recent studies on seasonal dynamics of fine roots is the large flux of organic matter which is involved -- large in an absolute sense as well as relative to other organic matter fluxes of forest ecosystem (Harris et al., 1975). Using a coring device, Harris and others (1978) sampled a yellow poplar forest stand intensively over a two-year period. The lateral root biomass of yellow poplar showed considerable variation in the smaller root size classes (Fig. 1). Small roots within this forest were characterized by a peak in late winter (1 March), a minimum in mid-May, a second peak in mid-September, and a minimum in early winter (December to January). This pattern appears to be consistent among successive years. Based on summation of positive seasonal differences between minimum and subsequent peak biomass, net root biomass production was 9.0

t/ha, with a net annual turnover (translocation and sloughing) of equal magnitude. This value of net annual small root production is 2.8 times larger than mean annual aboveground wood production determined for the study area from allometric equations and periodic (1965 to 1970) dbh inventory (Sollins et al., 1973).

Other experimental data on ecosystem carbon metabolism for the same Liriodendron forest study area corroborate the existence of a large, annual belowground allocation of carbon. Estimated net photosynthetic influx and soil-litter carbon efflux yield an amount of unaccounted carbon input to soil equivalent to 7.5 tons organic matter per hectare (Harris et al., 1975; Edwards and Harris, 1977). For temperate deciduous forests, the common assumption that belowground primary production is a fraction of aboveground primary production proportional

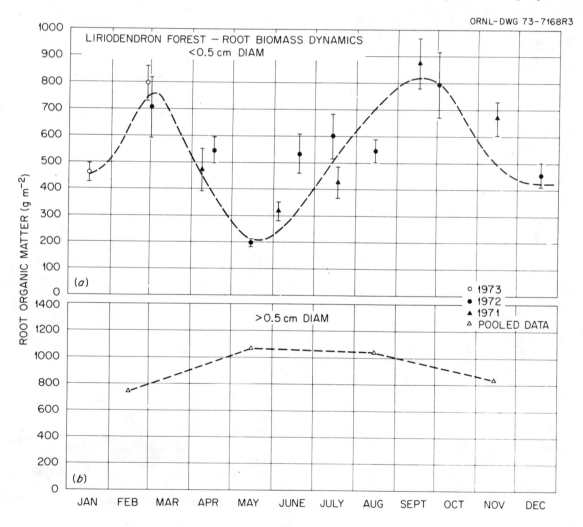

Figure 1. Seasonal distribution of lateral root biomass in a Liriodendron forest for (a) roots <5 mm diam. and (b) roots > 5 mm diam. ($\bar{x} \pm 1$ SE). Net biomass production and turnover were calculated from differences in pool size through the year. Based on monthly summary of core data, no consistent pattern of biomass dynamics could be detected for roots >5 mm diam.

to biomass pool size would lead to an underestimate of total annual root production.

The results from yellow poplar are not
an extreme example. While the number of
studies is limited, a sufficient range of
forest ecosystem types is represented to
indicate that the large flux of organic
matter belowground is a general property of
forest ecosystems. In mature (70-170 yrs),
natural stands of Douglas-fir in western
Oregon, Santantonio (1979) has found that
seasonal patterns and ratios of live-to-
dead roots (<5 mm diam.) distinctly differ
between wet and dry sites (Figs. 2 and 3).
Accounting for quantitative changes in live
and dead fine roots from one month to the
next, root growth, mortality, and decomposition from March 1977 to March 1978 were
estimated. Root growth was 8.5, 10.2, and
10.1 t/ha for wet, moderate, and dry sites,
respectively; root mortality was 10.9, 12.2,
and 13.1 t/ha, respectively; and root decomposition was 12.3, 12.5, and 18.4 t/ha,
respectively.

In another study of 40-year-old
Douglas-fir stands, Keyes (1979) found a
contrasting pattern in biomass of roots
<2 mm diameter between "good" and "poor"
sites. On the good site, no seasonal pattern was apparent (mean of 2.5 t/ha), while
on the poor site there was a modal pattern

with a late-spring peak (8.3 t/ha in June)
and a November minimum (2.1 t/ha). Keyes
did not separate live and dead roots, but
he observed rapid appearance and disappearance of root tips, suggesting rapid turnover even on the good site where no seasonal pattern was observed.

McGinty (1976) found no seasonal pattern of fine root biomass in a mixed hardwood watershed at Coweeta (western North
Carolina). McGinty suggested that the
absence of a seasonal pattern might reflect
niche differentiation belowground, but he
did not separate living and dead root components. McGinty indicated there may be a
"root capacity" for a mature forest-soil
combination -- as the forest matures, net
root production equilibrates with root
mortality. While McGinty's study did not
provide a conclusive estimate of primary
production of roots, growth into filled
trenches represented a fine root production of
6.0 t/ha/yr. Given the standing pool of
roots, <25 mm of 27 t/ha, this suggests a
turnover time of 4 to 5 years. His measured decay rates for roots would support a
turnover time at least as rapid as proposed.

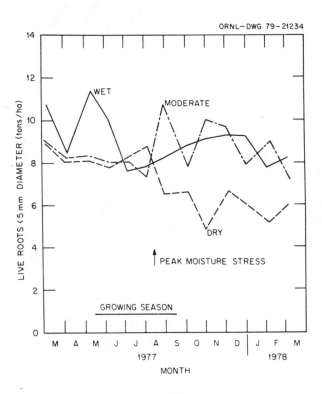

Figure 2. Seasonal fluctuations of live fine
roots of Douglas-fir on three sites. Standard errors of estimate are approximately
equal to ± 1.0 t/ha.

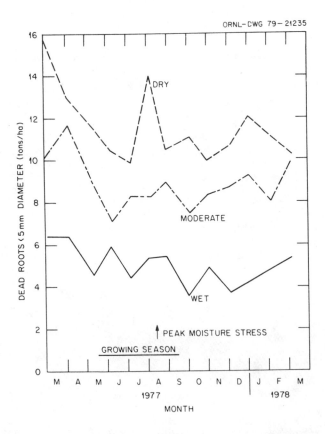

Figure 3. Seasonal fluctuations of dead fine
roots of Douglas-fir on three sites. Standard errors of estimate are approximately
equal to ± 1.0 t/ha.

McGinty's large size cut-off (25 mm) vastly underestimates the dynamics of fine roots (<5 mm) or absorbing roots (<1 mm). Thus his estimates of production and turnover should be considered conservative.

McClaugherty (1980) studied fine root production and turnover in a red pine plantation (54 yrs old) and a natural mixed hardwood stand in southern New England. Root production in the pine plantation was 4.1 t/ha; mortality was 4.3 t/ha. Based on CO_2 evolution attributable to root organic matter decay (an equivalent of 0.7 t/ha) and estimates of herbivore consumption (0.8 t/ha), 2.8 t/ha were transferred to soil organic matter. A similar pattern of fine root dynamics was observed in the natural hardwood stand. Production was 5.3 t/ha; mortality was 4.2 t/ha; CO_2 loss was only 0.9 t/ha; herbivore consumption was 0.3 t/ha; transfer to soil organic matter was 3.0 t/ha. While these results are in contrast with other studies cited here which suggest prompt ($\sim$1 yr) turnover of root organic matter, these findings are consistent with the general accumulation of organic matter in northern temperate forest soils.

Another recently completed study in Abies amabilis forests in the Pacific Northwest region (Grier et al., ms. in prep.) further strengthens the case for large throughput of organic matter belowground. Net primary production above- and belowground was studied in 23-year-old and 180-year-old stands. Total organic matter (aboveground plus belowground) in the two stands was 77 and 585 t/ha, respectively. Belowground net production was 9.9 and 11.7 t/ha, respectively, with root detritus production amounting to 8.1 and 11.0 t/ha, respectively. Aboveground production was 6.5 t/ha in the 23-year-old stands and 4.6 t/ha in the 180-year-old stands.

Recent studies in coniferous forests have shown that a significant fraction of the small root turnover is comprised of mycorrhizal roots (Fogel and Hunt, 1979; Grier et al., ms. in review). The relative contributions of mycorrhizal and non-mycorrhizal roots to root turnover in deciduous forests is presently unknown.

The large accumulation of root organic matter is a seasonal phenomenon. The net annual accumulation of structural root organic matter (not to be confused with fine root production) is much smaller and can best be described as a ratio of total aboveground and belowground biomass times the net annual aboveground production. What, then, is the fate of seasonal fluxes of organic matter belowground? Most of this material is promptly metabolized by soil heterotrophs (Edwards and Harris, 1977).

Analysis of total and proportional efflux of CO_2 from the soil surface (Edward and Harris, 1977) and experimental measurements of root decay rate (W. F. Harris, unpub. data) corroborate the prompt metabolism of root detritus. Similar findings (Kanazawa et al., 1976; McGinty, 1976; Persson, 1978, 1979; Santantonio, 1979; and Keyes, 1979) all point to prompt disappearance of fine root organic matter. We are thus left with the following generalization: the soil of temperate coniferous and deciduous forest ecosystems annually receives an input of root organic matter equal to or much greater than the input from any other source; this organic matter is promptly metabolized by heterotrophs.

Information on root biomass dynamics of tropical forests is extremely limited. However, one recent study suggests that for certain tropical forest types, production of root organic matter also may be large with turnover equally rapid, similar to the general pattern emerging from analysis of temperate forests. Jordan and Escalente (1979) observed significant root growth activity at the soil surface in "tierra forme" (never flooded) forests growing on oxisols in the Amazon Territory of Venezuela. The surface growth appeared to be in response to litterfall. Roots (<6 mm) grew around fallen litter but were subsequently sloughed as the "captured" litter decayed. This growth amounted to 117 $g/m^2/yr$, a flux equivalent to 12 percent of aboveground detritus inputs. Such a response may represent a highly developed adaptation to the lower available nutrients in highly weathered tropical soils.

Before leaving the subject of root organic matter dynamics, we should mention the dynamics of larger structural roots ($\geq$5 mm diameter). Generally, this organic matter component is much more stable, certainly not exhibiting significant seasonal or even annual dynamics. However, it would be incorrect to consider this a static pool. Again, evidence is sparse, but Kolesnikov (1968) observed that a cyclic renewal of large structural roots occurs during the development of a forest stand. One cannot pass up the speculation that a physiological balance might exist within individual forest trees, causing this main structural component to shift so that the fine root structure continually invades "new" areas of its soil habitat. Whether this speculation will withstand closer observation, and what the controlling factors and mechanisms might be, remain to be answered.

ROOT ORGANIC ACCUMULATION
DURING STAND DEVELOPMENT

During forest stand development, the amount of root organic matter increases on an absolute basis, but the proportion of the total biomass as root organic matter decreases. Patterns of root/shoot ratio between deciduous and coniferous forests vary (Rodin and Bazelivich, 1967). Generally, coniferous forests reach an equilibrium root/shoot ratio earlier in stand development (i.e., at a lower total biomass) than is the case for deciduous forests.

THE SIGNIFICANCE OF ROOT DYNAMICS
TO ELEMENT INPUTS TO SOIL
AND ELEMENT CYCLING

Much more limited than our knowledge of root organic matter dynamics is our knowledge of the role of root production/turnover (sloughing) to element cycling. Of course, some assumptions about root element content can be used to estimate the flux of elements to the soil. McGinty's (1976) work begins to place the contribution of roots in perspective. In oak-hickory and eastern white pine forests of Coweeta, North Carolina, roots comprised 28 percent of the forest biomass but contained 40 percent of plant nutrients in hardwoods and 65 percent of plant nutrients in pines. Thus, this dynamic root component is a nutrient-rich substrate. Roots can return nutrients to the soil in several ways: death and decay, exudation and leaching, and, indirectly, when consumed by grazers.

Studies of leaching and exudation from roots are likewise limited. In a northern hardwood forest ecosystem, Smith (1970) has found root exudation (during growing season) to account for 4 kg/ha of carbon, 8 Kg K/ha, and 34.2 kg Na/ha for three principal tree species (Betula alleghaniensis, Fagus grandifolia, and Acer saccharum). Although the techniques employed (modified axenic culture) risk introducing artifacts, a considerable potential for contribution of elements to the soil via exudation exists.

Direct exudation of mineral nutrients to the soil may be of minor significance, however, in comparison to the role of low molecular weight organic acids contained in root oxidation. This small loss of reduced carbon may have a major effect on pH regulation in the rhizosphere and nitrogen metabolism of the plant (Sollins et al., 1979), and the oxalate as a product of fungal metabolism as well as higher plants could have a significant effect on weathering of soil minerals, especially the availability of phosphorus to plants (Graustein et al.,

1977; Cromack et al., 1979). Results thus far implicate a complex control system in which forest trees exert a strong influence over their chemical environment suggestive of a high degree of co-adaptation.

Radiotracer studies with ^{134}Cs have shown that over 50 percent of ^{134}Cs in roots of tagged yellow poplar seedlings was transferred to culture solutions in less than 7 days (Cox, 1972). Sandberg and others (1969) estimated that during one growing season 75 percent of ^{137}Cs transfers by yellow poplar seedlings grown in sand was due to exudation-leaching. In their analysis of a cesium-tagged yellow poplar forest, Waller and Olson (1967) considered root exudation leaching processes as important pathways of cesium transfer to soil based on concentration of ^{137}Cs in soil at various depths. If in situ processes of Cs are comparable to those of the chemical analog, potassium, large quantities of K could be transferred to soil annually by leaching-exudation processes.

Very few data are available to compare return of elements to the soil via aboveground and belowground processes. Table 1 summarizes a comparison for an extensively studied yellow poplar forest at Oak Ridge, Tennessee (Cox et al., 1978). In this analysis, consumption was assumed to be 10 percent of root detritus. Root detritus turnover was estimated by the large residual CO_2 efflux from soil unaccounted for after litter decomposition and autotrophic root respiration were subtracted from total soil CO_2 efflux.

In this example (Table 1), annual return of elements to soil by root processes was three times the combined aboveground inputs (including atmospheric) for K and at least 1.5 times aboveground inputs for N. Of the total (aboveground and belowground) return to soil, root processes accounted for turnover of 70 percent of organic matter, 62 percent of N, and 86 percent of K. Some additional fraction (here assumed to be about 10 percent of the total estimated detrital flux) was transferred to soil consumer pools.

Estimates of total herbivory on roots do not exist. Root-feeding nematodes and various larval stages (e.g., cicada) might be principal consumers (Ausmus et al., 1978). Assuming consumption as 10 percent of the estimated turnover may be high for temperate forests. Schauermann (1977) reported that rhizophagous Curculionidae consumed 81×10^3 kcal/ha/yr and comprised 12 percent of the biomass of soil invertebrates. Assuming comparable consumption rates per unit weight among all soil invertebrates, total consumption might approach 800×10^3 kcal/ha/yr. In Schauermann's beech forest study, Curculionidae consumption was 0.1 percent of net primary production (presumed to be aboveground only). Edwards (in Auerbach, 1974, p. 86) estimated the total energy consumed by invertebrates to be 2 percent of total amount fixed annually. Thus, evidence to date points to a small absolute flux of energy by consumption of root (or aboveground) biomass. Despite the small absolute role of consumers, we cannot dismiss their importance to the functioning of forest ecosystems. Schauermann regarded the Curculionidae as accelerators of the mineralization processes because of physical damage to roots and effects of their feces on microbial decomposition. He found that 87 percent of energy turnover in the rhizophagous larval population occurred between August and April -- a period generally coincident with high root turnover. Waldbauer (1968) reported a similar pattern for many insect populations.

SIGNIFICANCE OF ROOT SLOUGHING TO FOREST ENERGY BALANCE

Odum (1969) suggested a strategy of increasing conservation of nutrients in element cycling during forest ecosystem development. The mechanism leading to a closed cycle for nitrogen could be root sloughing and subsequent microbial mineralization. In temperate, deciduous forests at Oak Ridge, Tennessee, biomass and nitrogen accumulate in roots during periods favorable for growth (summer) or just preceding growth (late winter); and winter growth occurs largely at the expense of stored photosynthate. During periods unfavorable for growth (fall-winter) or when aboveground energy demands are high (spring-early summer canopy development), root biomass is sloughed, thus reducing the total energy demand on the temperate forest system at a time when reserves are seasonally depleted and/or plant requirements for carbon are high elsewhere (e.g., canopy development).

Table 1. *Annual aboveground and belowground organic matter and element returns to soil in a yellow poplar (Liriodendron tulipifera L.) stand*[1]

	Biomass	Nitrogen	Potassium
	kg/ha	kg/ha	kg/ha
Aboveground[2]			
Dryfall/wetfall	...	7.2	3.6
Canopy leaching	...	2.3	29.4
Litterfall	3,310	42.2	10.0
Total aboveground return	3,310	51.7	43.0
Belowground[3]			
Root transfer processes[4]			
Death and decay	6,750	76	128
Consumption	750	9	14
Exudation-leaching	...	...	128
Total belowground return	7,500	85.0	270
Total return to soil	10,810	136.7	313

[1] From Cox et al., 1978.

[2] Aboveground data from Edwards and Shanks (unpub. data); chemical determinations were made on fallen material.

[3] Root biomass estimates from *Liriodendron* stand (>80% *Liriodendron*).

[4] Exudation-leaching data are extrapolated from seedling studies of Cox (1975), assuming equivalent behavior of Cs and K. Element losses via root sloughing are based on amount of sloughed biomass times mean root N content; element flux via consumption assumed to be 10 percent of total belowground return.

Nitrogen contained in sloughed organic matter is conserved as part of the soil detritus by those microbial processes which immobilize it.

The cyclic pattern of photosynthate accumulation in a deciduous forest and the sustained productivity, which is in part dependent on available N, are closely coupled through activities of soil microbes on a large systematically replenished substrate rich in nitrogen. In this respect, continuous maintenance of living roots in temperate forests would impose energy limitations on detritivores by reducing periodic influx of nitrogen-rich root organic matter, because this flux represents 70 percent of total detrital input. While data from other deciduous systems are scarce, we hypothesize that evolution of temperate forest species has favored mechanisms which contribute to systematic return of elements and organic matter through belowground sloughing. Sloughing, therefore, stabilizes biogeochemical cycles of potentially limiting elements in an environment typified by seasonally limited photosynthate availability. As illustrated in Table 2, carbon (energy) is rapidly metabolized within the ecosystem and lost (as CO_2). Essential elements, on the other hand, are retained effectively

because of the interactions of autotrophs and decomposers.

The energy expenditure to forest ecosystems represented by root sloughing is high. In the yellow poplar forest at Oak Ridge (Harris et al., 1975; Edwards and Harris, 1976), Edwards (in Auerbach, 1974) estimated that lateral root growth, sloughing, and maintenance respiration accounts for 44.8 percent of the total energy fixed annually in photosynthesis (1.88×10^3 $kcal/m^2$). Root sloughing, with subsequent microbial immobilization, offers a particularly attractive mechanism to explain retention of essential elements in the uptake zone. In another context, maintenance and development of a fertile soil requires significant input of energy (contained in organic matter). For the yellow poplar forest, energy requirements for maintenance of soil are on the order of 66 percent of the energy fixed annually by photosynthesis (roots + 21% allocation to leaves). Many of man's activities which reduce both energy fixed photosynthetically and/or energy input to soil are most severely manifested by degradation of the soil with respect to humified soil organic matter and fertility. The energy inputs to soil (dominated in temperate forests by root

Table 2. *Comparison of turnover times for carbon, nitrogen and calcium in temperate deciduous forests (Tennessee)*[1]

Component	Turnover time (yrs)[2]		
	Carbon	Nitrogen	Calcium
Soil	107	109	32[3]
Forest biomass[4]	155	88	8
Litter (01 + 02)	1.12	<5	<5
Total[5]	54	1,815	445
Decomposers	0.01	0.02	?

[1]From O'Neill et al., 1975.

[2]Carbon data based on carbon metabolism of yellow poplar forest (Harris et al., 1975; Reichle et al., 1973); nitrogen data based on nitrogen budget for mixed deciduous forest (Henderson and Harris, 1975); calcium data based on calcium budget from a *Liriodendron tulipifera* forest (Shugart et al., 1976).

[3]Turnover time based on available Ca and assumes all losses of Ca from soil are from the pool of available Ca.

[4]Considers aboveground biomass pool. Cyclic renewal of structural roots (Kolesnikov, 1968) would lower turnover time. Tree mortality estimated from permanent plot resurvey (3-year interval) and likely underestimates the mortality rate over the duration of a forest generation.

[5]Total calculated as sum of elements in living and dead components of the ecosystem; element loss based on sum of all losses from ecosystem.

sloughing) contribute to maintenance of soil fertility.

A number of areas require additional study. First, the pattern of belowground detritus contributions needs to be determined for additional forest types, especially forests of extreme climates. The large photosynthate requirements for maintenance respiration of forests combined with a large annual sloughing of root organic matter may limit forest growth in climates severely limiting photosynthate production. In this same vein, the influence of stresses (whether natural or of anthropogenic origin such as air pollutants) on photosynthate translocation needs to be examined in mature forests in order to evaluate forest response to perturbations. The decay of root organic matter occurs rapidly. Are there biochemical changes in sloughed roots that promote decomposability or alter the behavior of fungal symbionts generally associated with the rhizosphere? Answering these and other questions about the dynamic belowground component of forest ecosystems will provide an exciting challenge to forest ecology for the next several years.

LITERATURE CITED

Auerbach, S. I. 1974. Environmental Sciences Division Annual Report for the period ending September 30, 1973. Oak Ridge National Lab. Rep. ORNL-4935, Oak Ridge, Tenn.

Ausmus, B. S., J. M. Ferris, D. E. Reichle, and E. C. Williams. 1978. The role of belowground herbivores in mesic forest root dynamics. Pedobiologia 18:289-295.

Bazilevich, N. I., and L. E. Rodin. 1968. Reserves of organic matter in the underground sphere of terrestrial phytocoenoses, In International Symposium, USSR, Methods of Productivity Studies in Root Systems and Rhizosphere Organisms, pp. 4-8. (Reprinted for the International Biological Program by Biddles, Ltd., Guildford, U.K.).

Cox, T. L. 1972. Production, mortality and nutrient cycling in root systems of Liriodendron seedlings. Ph.D. thesis, University of Tennessee, Knoxville.

Cox, T. L. 1975. Accumulation and mobility of cesium in roots of tulip poplar seedlings. In Mineral Cycling in Southeastern Ecosystems, edited by F. G. Howell, J. B. Gentry, and M. H. Smith, pp. 482-488. ERDA Symp. Series (CONF-740513).

Cox, T. L., W. F. Harris, B. S. Ausmus, and N. T. Edwards. 1978. The role of roots in biogeochemical cycles in an eastern deciduous forest. Pedobiologia 18:264-271.

Cromack, K., Jr., P. Sollins, W. Graustein, K. Speidel, A. Todd, G. Spycher, C. Li, and R. Todd. 1979. Calcium oxalate accumulation and soil weathering in mats of the hypogeous fungus (Hysterangium crassum). Soil Biol. and Biochem. (in press).

Devlin, R. M. 1966. Plant Physiology. New York: Reinhold Publishing Corp.

Edwards, N. T., and W. F. Harris. 1977. Carbon cycling in a mixed deciduous forest floor. Ecology 58:431-437.

Fayle, D. C. F. 1968. Radial growth in tree roots. Univ. of Toronto, Fac. For. Tech. Rep. No. 9

Göttsche, D. 1972. Verteilung von Feinwurzeln und Mykorrhizen in Bodenprofileines Buchen- und Fichtenbestandes in Solling. Hamburg: Kommissionsverlag Buchhandlung Max Wiedebusch.

Graustein, W. C., K. Cromack, Jr., and P. Sollins. 1977. Calcium oxalate: Occurrence in soils and effect on nutrient and geochemical cycles. Science 198:1252-1254.

Grier, C. C., K. Vogt, M. Keyes, and R. Edmonds. Above- and belowground production in subalpine (Abies amabilis) stands: Changes with ecosystem development. (Mans. in preparation).

Harris, W. F., R. A. Goldstein, and G. S. Henderson. 1973. Analysis of forest biomass pools, annual primary production and turnover of biomass for a mixed deciduous forest watershed. In Proc. IUFRO Conference on Forest Biomass Studies, edited by H. Young, pp. 41-64. Orono: University of Maine Press.

Harris, W. F., P. Sollins, N. T. Edwards, B. E. Dinger, and H. H. Shugart. 1975. Analysis of carbon flow and productivity. In Productivity of World Ecosystems, Proc. IBP 5th General Assembly, edited by D. E. Reichle and J. F. Franklin, pp. 116-122. Washington, D. C.: National Academy of Sciences.

128 FORESTS: FRESH PERSPECTIVES FROM ECOSYSTEM ANALYSIS

Harris, W. F., R. S. Kinerson, and N. T.
Edwards. 1978. Comparisons of belowground biomass of natural deciduous
forest and loblolly pine plantations.
Pedobiologia 17:369–381.

Heikurainen, L. 1957. Über Veränderungen
in der Wurzelverhältnissen der Kiefern-
bestände auf Moorböden in Laufe des
Jahres. Act. For. Fenn. 62:1–54.

Henderson, G. S., and W. F. Harris. 1975.
An ecosystem approach to the characterization of the nitrogen cycle in a
deciduous forest watershed, In Forest
Soils and Forest Land Management,
edited by B. Bernier and C. H. Winget,
pp. 179–193. Quebec, Canada: Laval
University Press.

Hermann, R. K. 1977. Growth and production
of tree roots: A review. In The
Belowground Ecosystem: A Synthesis of
Plant-Associated Processes, edited by
J. K. Marshall, pp. 7–28. Range
Science Dept. Series No. 26, Colorado
State University, Fort Collins.

Jordan, C. L., and Gladys Escalente. 1979.
Root productivity in an Amazonian rain
forest. Ecology (mans. submitted).

Kalela, E. K. 1950. Manniköiden ja Kunsi-
koiden jurrisuhteista. I. Acta For.
Fem. 57:1–79 (English summary).

Kanazawa, S., T. Asami, and Y. Takai.
1976. Characteristics of soil organic
matter and soil respiration in subalpine, coniferous forests of Mt.
Shigayama. 3. Soil respiration under
field conditions. J. Sciences of Soil
and Manure 47(12):549–554.

Keyes, M. R. 1979. Seasonal patterns of
fine root biomass, production and turnover in two contrasting 40-year-old
Douglas-fir stands. M.S. thesis,
University of Washington, Seattle.

Kolesnikov, V. A. 1968. Cyclic renewal of
roots in fruit plants. In International
Symposium, USSR, Methods of Productivity
Studies in Root Systems and Rhizosphere
Organisms, pp. 102–106. (Reprinted for
the International Biological Program by
Biddles, Ltd., Guildford, U.K.).

Kozlowski, T. T. 1971. Growth and Development of Trees, Vol. 2. New York:
Academic Press, Inc.

Larcher, W. 1975. Physiological Plant
Ecology, trans. by M. A. Brederman-
Thorson. New York: Springer-Verlag.

Lieth, H. 1968. The determination of
plant dry-matter production with
special emphasis on the underground
parts. In Functioning of Terrestrial
Ecosystems at the Primary Production
Level, edited by F. E. Eckhardt, pp.
179–186. Proc. of Copenhagen Symp.,
Vol. 5. Paris: UNESCO.

Lyr, H., and G. Hoffmann. 1967. Growth
rates and growth periodicity of tree
roots. In International Review of
Forestry Research, Vol. 2, edited by
Romberger and Mikola, pp. 181–236.
New York: Academic Press, Inc.

McClaugherty, C. A. 1980. The role of fine
roots in the organic matter and nitrogen budgets of forest ecosystem.
Unpub. M.S. thesis, University of
Virginia, Charlottesville.

McGinty, D. T. 1976. Comparative root and
soil dynamics on a white pine watershed and in the hardwood forest in the
Coweeta basin. Ph.D. dissertation,
University of Georgia, Athens.

Newbould, D. J. 1967. Methods for Estimating the Primary Production of Forests, IBP Handbook No. 2. Oxford:
Blackwell Scientific Pub.

Odum, E. P. 1969. The strategy of ecosystem development. Science 164:262–
270.

O'Neill, R. V., W. F. Harris, B. S. Ausmus,
and D. E. Reichle. 1975. A theoretical basis for ecosystem analysis with
particular reference to element cycling. In Mineral Cycling in Southeastern Ecosystems, edited by F. G.
Howell, J. B. Gentry, and M. H. Smith,
pp. 28–40. ERDA Symp. Series (CONF-
740513).

Ovington, J. D. 1962. Quantitative ecology
and the woodland ecosystem concept.
Adv. Ecol. Res. 1:103–192.

Ovington, J. D., D. Heitkamp, and D. B.
Lawrence. 1963. Plant biomass of
prairie, savanna, oakwood and maize
field eocsystems in central Minnesota.
Ecology 44:52–63.

Persson, H. 1978. Root dynamics in a
young Scots pine stand in Central
Sweden. Oikos 30:508–519.

Persson, H. 1979. Spatial distribution of
fine-root growth, mortality and decomposition in a young Scots pine
stand in Central Sweden. Oikos (in
press).

Pitman, M. G. 1976. Nutrient uptake by roots and transport to the xylem. In Transport and Transfer Processes in Plants, edited by I. F. Wardlaw and J. B. Passioura, pp. 85–100. New York: Academic Press, Inc.

Reichle, D. E., B. E. Dinger, N. T. Edwards, W. F. Harris, and P. Sollins. 1973. Carbon flow and storage in a forest ecosystem. In Carbon and the Biosphere, Proc. 24th Brookhaven Symp. on Biology (AEC-CONF-720510), edited by G. M. Woodwell and E. V. Pecan, pp. 345–365. Springfield, Va.: National Technical Information Service.

Rodin, L. E., and N. I. Bazilevich. 1967. Production and Mineral Cycling in Terrestrial Vegetation, trans. by G. E. Fogg. London: Oliver and Boyd.

Sandberg, G. R., J. S. Olson, and E. E. C. Clebsch. 1969. Internal distribution and loss from roots by leaching of cesium-137 inoculater into Liriodendron tulipifera L. seedlings grown in sand culture. Oak Ridge National Lab. Rep. ORNL/TM-2660, Oak Ridge, Tenn.

Santantonio, D., R. K. Hermann, and W. S. Overton. 1977. Root biomass studies in forest ecosystems. Pedobiologia 17:1–31.

Santantonio, D. 1979. Seasonal dynamics of fine roots in mature stands of Douglas-fir of different water regimes -- a preliminary report. In Root Physiology and Symbiosis, Proc. of IUFRO, Sept. 11-15, 1978, Nancy, France (in press).

Schauermann, J. 1977. Energy metabolism of rhizophagous insects and their role in ecosystems. In Soil Organisms as Components of Ecosystems, Ecol. Bull. NFR 25, edited by U. Lohm and T. Persson, pp. 310–319. Stockholm: Swedish Natural Research Council.

Shugart, H. H., D. E. Reichle, N. T. Edwards, and J. R. Kercher. 1976. A model of calcium cycling in an East Tennessee Liriodendron forest: model structure, parameters, and frequency response analysis. Ecology 57:99–109.

Smith, W. H. 1970. Technique for collection of root exudated from mature trees. Plant and Soil 32:238–241.

Sollins, P., K. Cromack, Jr., R. Fogel, and C. Y. Li. 1979. Role of low molecular weight organic acids in the inorganic nutrition of fungi and higher plants. In The Fungal Community, edited by D. T. Wicklow and G. Carroll. New York: Marcel Dekker, Inc. (in press).

Sollins, P., D. E. Reichle, and J. S. Olson. 1973. Organic matter budget and model for a southern Appalachian Liriodendron forest. USAEC Rep. EDFB-IBP-73-2, Oak Ridge National Lab., Oak Ridge, Tenn.

Sutton, R. F. 1969. Form and development of conifer root systems. Commonwealth For. Bull., Tech. Commun. 7, Oxford, England.

Waldbauer, G. 1968. The consumption and utilization of food by insects. Adv. Insect Physiol. 5:229–288.

Waller, H. D., and J. S. Olson. 1967. Prompt transfers of cesium-137 to the soils of a tagged Liriodendron forest. Ecology 48:15–25.

Whittaker, R. H., and G. M. Woodwell. 1968. Dimension and production relations of trees and shrubs in the Brookhaven Forest, New York. J. Ecol. 56:1–25.

Whittaker, R. H. 1971. Measurement of net primary production of forests. In Productivity of Forest Ecosystems, edited by P. Duvigneaud, pp. 159–175. Paris: UNESCO.

Vital Signs of Forest Ecosystems

R. H. Waring

INTRODUCTION

Forest ecosystems, like the human body, are composed of many parts carrying on functions essential to the well-being of the whole. Given sufficient fresh air, liquids, and balanced nutrition, most forest ecosystems lead long, productive lives.

There are times, however, when inflictions of old age, environmental stress, or unwelcomed visitors produce unhealthy ecosystems. In many cases, part of the system dies and is replaced -- a sad but normal expectation. We should be concerned, however, when critical functions become impaired. In recognizing that forests and other ecological systems provide irreplaceable services, when these systems are threatened, we must administer aid.

DIAGNOSTIC AIDS

Diagnosing sick systems is a new science in which practitioners have learned much from autopsies but, so far, saved few patients. Some scientists who have observed healthy ecosystems have charted probable forest responses under a variety of environments. Comparing predicted carbon dioxide uptake for healthy Douglas-fir needles growing in a maritime climate with that expected in a more continental environment (Fig. 1), we find that a maritime forest breathes more deeply. These predictions of leaf activity correlate well with those of forest growth (Fig. 2). Thus, an observed departure from predicted growth patterns is casue for concern.

Similarly, the rate at which organic wastes decompose on the forest floor is expected to differ with climate and the quality of material (Fogel and Cromack, 1977; Bunnell et al., 1977a,b). We can measure and compare the weight loss, after a year, of litter packaged in porous bags with that predicted. Where decomposition is unexpectedly suppressed, further analyses may show toxic pollutants are accumulating (O'Neill et al., 1977).

Table 1. *Redistribution of nitrogen (N,g m^{-2}) in leaves indicates the level of available nutrients on infertile and fertile sites[1]*

Species	Infertile			Fertile		
	Fresh	Fallen	Δ%	Fresh	Fallen	Δ%
Alder	---	---	---	8.26	7.88	- 5
Hornbeam	1.57	0.56	-64	1.76	1.11	-37
Oak	2.65	0.99	-63	1.14	0.63	-45
Pine	2.32	0.54	-77	---	---	---

[1]After Stachurski and Zimka, 1975.

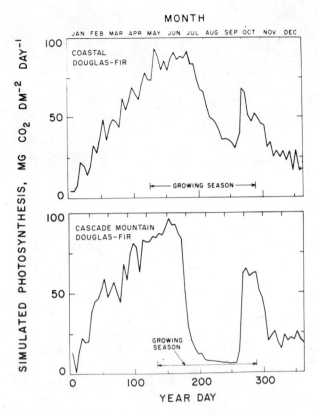

Figure 1. *The yearly predicted pattern of photosynthesis for Douglas-fir growing in the Oregon Coast Range and the more continental Cascade Mountains (after Emmingham and Waring, 1977).*

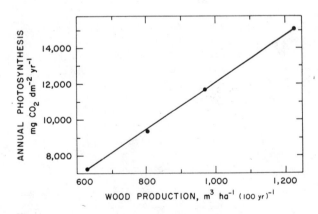

Figure 2. *A comparison of annual predicted photosynthesis and Douglas-fir wood production for a 100-year period for four sites in western Oregon (after Emmingham and Waring, 1977).*

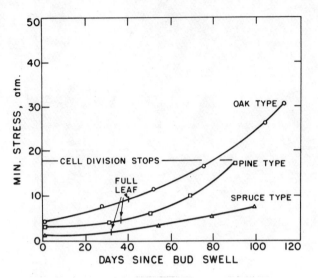

Figure 3. *Seasonal patterns of plant moisture stress in Douglas-fir saplings growing on progressively drier habitats (after Waring et al., 1972).*

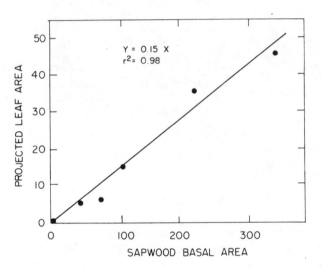

Figure 4. *Projected leaf area of lodgepole pine linearly related to sapwood cross-sectional area at 1.3 m height (Waring, unpub.).*

To tell whether plants are receiving a balanced mineral diet, compare the nutrient content of fresh with fallen foliage (Table 1). Well-nourished leaves generally store and pass on more nutrients as they die. As a mineral becomes more scarce, plants expend more energy translocating it before leaves are shed. Because the total weight of leaves varies seasonally, mobilization of nutrients is best perceived in analyses as weight per unit of leaf area.

To see whether plants are receiving sufficient liquid, measure the tension in water columns by sampling twigs in a pressure chamber (Waring and Cleary, 1967; Ritchie and Hinckley, 1975). When water stress exceeds 40 to 50 atmospheres, notify the next of kin. Predictably different patterns of water stress are expected in different environments (Fig. 3), but when plants depart from expected patterns, some infirmity or adverse condition has surely set in.

The general vigor of forest ecosystems is reflected by how efficiently they accumulate carbohydrate reserves. Unfortunately, keeping track of how much carbon dioxide is assimilated by a forest and used to sustain life is a very complicated task. We know that healthy forests generally grow larger and develop denser canopies than forests in more stressful situations (Waring et al., 1978). We also recognize that all forests must allocate resources so that a balance is maintained between the energy-capturing foliage and the mineral- and water-extracting roots (Gordon and Larson, 1968; Thornley, 1972; Rangekar and Forward, 1973; Harris et al., 1978). Carbohydrate reserves are available for making wood only after all essential needs are met.

Because large trees generally grow more wood each year than small ones, we need a means of comparing how efficiently wood is being accumulated. Because leaves are the factories which produce carbohydrates, one measure of efficiency is the rate of wood accumulation per unit of leaf area (Waring et al., 1980). However, determining how many leaves a tree has is not simple. Fortunately, a balance exists--not only between leaves and roots, but also between the cross-sectional area of vascular tissue conducting water and nutrients through the stem and the amount of foliage (Fig. 4) (Dixon, 1971; Grier and Waring, 1974; Waring et al., 1977; Whitehead, 1978). Such a balance in symmetry often indicates additional relationships between functions still undiscovered. Growth in volume or biomass is directly related to annual growth in basal area; leaf area is directly related to sapwood basal area which, if not immediately obvious, can be identified by stains (Kutscha and Sachs, 1962). Thus, extracting a small core of wood from the stem may provide an estimate of the increment in both biomass and leaf area.

In a particular forest, if the amount of light reaching the leaves can be controlled by modifying the density of the canopy, tree vigor (the efficiency with which wood is accumulated per unit of leaf area) decreases linearly as the adjacent canopy becomes more dense (Fig. 5). In this example, the number of layers of

leaves was estimated by summing the sapwood basal area in all the trees in a sampled area.

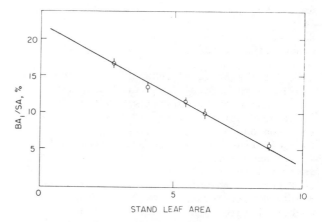

Figure 5. *Mean tree vigor of Douglas-fir, indicated by the ratio of basal area increment (BA₁) to total cross-sectional area (SA) of sapwood, decreases linearly as the canopy density increases (after Newman, 1979). Values represent means of 30 trees with standard error bars.*

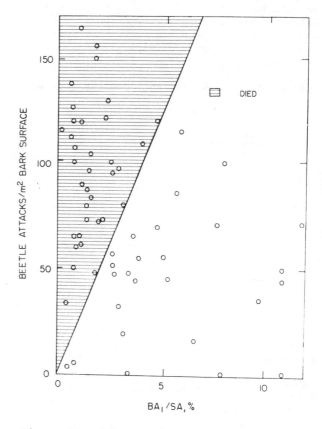

Figure 6. *Trees growing more than 8 percent of their sapwood basal area (BA₁) in one year are unlikely to be killed, whereas less vigorous trees are killed by mountain pine beetles attacking above critical levels (Waring and Pitman, 1980).*

At times, the vigor of individual trees within a stand dramatically differs. For example, in an old lodgepole pine forest being attacked by mountain pine beetles, only those trees with low vigor are attacked, and only those attacked by a sufficient number of beetles are actually killed (Fig. 6).

Yet the death of less efficient individuals in a forest bequeaths additional resources to those surviving. Often, the total productivity of the system increases (Mattson and Addy, 1975; Wickman, 1978). By monitoring both growth and mortality, we can assess the effect of thinning, whether brought about by nature or by man. In Figure 7, thinning a forest to different densities accelerated growth, although the number of trees was reduced to a quarter of that in the original stand.

How large a forest may grow is ultimately determined by the amount of foliage it can support (Fig. 8). In harsh environments, the canopy remains open; in favorable environments, cathedral groves of giant trees capture almost all the light. In diagnosing the health of forest ecosystems, we need to know whether a young stand is a potential dwarf or giant. Environmental analyses provide such estimates (Grier and Running, 1978; Waring et al., 1978).

The company trees keep in a forest often is a good indicator of the kind of environment in which they grew up (Franklin and Dyrness, 1973; Arno and Pfister, 1977). Trees associated with juniper and sagebrush are individualists that have struggled to survive in harsh surroundings; they grow slowly and tolerate little crowding.

Wrapped in soft clouds, the pampered trees in the protected valleys of the Oregon Coast Range are surrounded by companions from birth. Not surprisingly, such intimacy fosters many communicable diseases. Though conifers, once established, reach for the sky, a host of former playmates--salmonberry, sword fern, and the like--continue to survive in their shadow, often attending the funerals of the giants. Recognizing these associates may aid us in selecting seed for re-establishing a well-adapted forest (Arno and Pfister, 1977).

Forest ecosystems, like the human body, are complex. We are only now discovering how to take their pulses and listen to their heartbeats. With the concern of a general practitioner for his patients, we are beginning to make "field calls" to check the development of young and the malaise of old forests. We have a small bag of instruments but a growing confidence that the care of forests is a rewarding and essential endeavor.

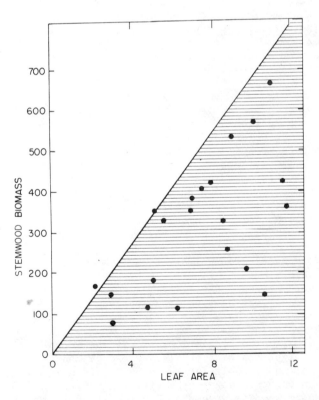

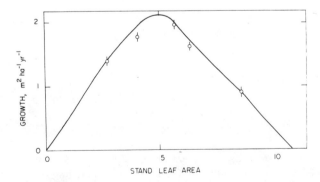

Figure 7. Stand growth in basal area follows a parabolic function as the canopy density increases (after Newman, 1979).

Figure 8. Maximum accumulation of stemwood biomass is ultimately limited by the forest canopy that can be supported (Waring, unpub.).

LITERATURE CITED

Arno, S. F., and R. D. Pfister. 1977. Habitat types: an improved system for classifying Montana's forests. Western Wildlands 4:6-11.

Bunnell, F. L., D. E. N. Tart, P. W. Flanagan, and K. Van Cleve. 1977a. Microbial respiration and substrate weight loss. I. Soil Biol. and Biochem. 9:33-40.

Bunnell, F. L., D. E. N. Tart, P. W. Flanagan, and K. Van Cleve. 1977b. Microbial respiration and substrate weight loss. II. Soil Biol. and Biochem. 9:41-47.

Dixon, A. F. G. 1971. The role of aphids in wood formation. I. The effect of the sycamore aphid, Drepanosiphum platanoides (Schr.) (Aphidae), on the growth of sycamore, Acer pseudoplatanus (L.). J. Applied Ecol. 8:165-179.

Emmingham, W. H., and R. H. Waring. 1977. An index of photosynthesis for comparing forest sites in western Oregon. Can. J. Forest Res. 7:165-175.

Fogel, R., and K. Cromack, Jr. 1977. Effect of habitat and substrate quality on Douglas-fir litter decomposition in western Oregon. Can. J. Bot. 55:1632-1640.

Gordon, J. C., and P. R. Larson. 1968. Seasonal course of photosynthesis, respiration, and distribution of ^{14}C in young Pinus resinosa trees as related to wood formation. Plant Physiol. 43:1617-1624.

Franklin, J. F., and C. T. Dyrness. 1973. Natural vegetation of Oregon and Washington. USDA Forest Service Gen. Tech. Rep. PNW-8, Pacific Northwest Forest and Range Expt. Sta., Portland, Oregon.

Grier, C. C., and S. W. Running. 1978. Leaf area of mature northwestern coniferous forests: relation to a site water balance. Ecology 58:893-899.

Grier, C. C., and R. H. Waring. 1974. Conifer foliage mass related to sapwood area. Forest Sci. 30:205-206.

Harris, W. F., R. S. Kinerson, and N. T. Edwards. 1978. Comparison of belowground biomass of natural deciduous forest and loblolly pine plantations. Pedobiologia 17:369-381.

Kutscha, N. P., and I. B. Sachs. 1962. Color tests for differentiating heartwood and sapwood in certain softwood tree species. USDA Forest Service Publ. No. 2246, Madison, Wisconsin.

Mattson, W. H., and N. D. Addy. 1975. Phytophagous insects as regulators of forest primary production. Science 190:515-522.

Newman, K. 1979. Sapwood basal area as an estimator of individual tree growth. M.S. thesis, Oregon State University, Corvallis.

O'Neill, R. V., B. S. Ausmus, D. R. Jackson, R. I. Van Hook, P. Van Voris, C. Washburne, and A. P. Watson. 1977. Monitoring terrestrial ecosystems by analysis of nutrient export. Water, Air, and Soil Pollution 8:271-277.

Rangnekar, P. V., and D. F. Forward. 1973. Foliar nutrition and wood growth in red pine: effects of darkening and defoliation on the distribution of ^{14}C-photosynthate in young trees. Can. J. Bot. 51:103-108.

Ritchie, G. A., and T. M. Hinckley. 1975. The pressure chamber as an instrument for ecological research. In Advances in Ecological Research, Vol. 9, edited by A. Macfayden, pp. 165-254. London: Academic Press, Inc.

Stachurski, A., and J. R. Zimka. 1975. Methods of studying forest ecosystems: leaf area, leaf production, and withdrawal of nutrients from leaves of trees. Ekologia Polska 23:637-648.

Thornley, J. H. M. 1972. A balanced quantitative model for root:shoot ratios in vegetative plants. Ann. Bot. 36:431-441.

Waring, R. H., and B. D. Cleary. 1967. Plant moisture stress: evaluation by pressure bomb. Science 155:1248-1254.

Waring, R. H., W. H. Emmingham, H. L. Gholz, and C. C. Grier. 1978. Variation in maximum leaf area of coniferous forests in Oregon and its ecological significance. Forest Sci. 24:131-140.

Waring, R. H., H. L. Gholz, C. C. Grier, and M. L. Plummer. 1977. Evaluating stem conducting tissue as an estimator of leaf area in four woody angiosperms. Can. J. Bot. 55:1474-1477.

Waring, R. H., and G. B. Pitman. 1980. A
    simple model of host resistance to bark
    beetle attack. Forest Research Labora-
    tory Res. Note 65, Oregon State Uni-
    versity, Corvallis.

Waring, R. H., K. L. Reed, and W. H. Emming-
    ham. 1972. An environmental grid for
    classifying coniferous forest eco-
    systems. In Research on Coniferous
    Forest Ecosystems, Proc. Symp. North-
    west Scientific Assoc., edited by J. L.
    Franklin, L. J. Dempster, and R. H.
    Waring, pp. 79-91. USDA Forest Service,
    Pacific Northwest Forest and Range
    Expt. Sta., Portland, Oregon.

Waring, R. H., W. G. Thies, and D. Muscato.
    1980. Stem growth per unit of leaf
    area: a measure of tree vigor. Forest
    Sci. (in press).

Whitehead, D. 1978. The estimation of
    foliage area from sapwood basal area
    in Scots pine. Forestry 51:137-149.

Wickman, B. E. 1978. A case study of a
    Douglas-fir tussock moth outbreak and
    stand conditions 10 years later. USDA
    Forest Service PNW-244, Pacific North-
    west Forest and Range Expt. Sta.,
    Portland, Oregon.

Interpretation of Nutrient Cycling Research in a Management Context: Evaluating Potential Effects of Alternative Management Strategies on Site Productivity

Wayne T. Swank and Jack B. Waide

INTRODUCTION

One of the fresh perspectives alluded to in the title of this volume is the increased emphasis on understanding the biogeochemistry of forest ecosystems (Bormann and Likens, 1967; Jorgensen et al., 1975; Waide and Swank, 1976). Understanding nutrient cycling processes in forests is needed not only to explain forest eocsystem dynamics in space and time, but also for the wise husbandry of forest resources. The circulation of essential elements in forest ecosystems integrates biological populations with a variety of physicochemical processes (Hutchinson, 1948). Thus, nutrient cycling research is amenable to holistic interpretation and provides an essential means of evaluating the environmental consequences of resource management.

Our research program in forest biogeochemistry at the Coweeta Hydrologic Laboratory, North Carolina, was initiated in 1968 with a cooperative study between the Institute of Ecology, University of Georgia, and the U.S. Forest Service. This research program has descriptive, predictive, and conceptual objectives (Monk et al., 1977). We are trying to describe the biogeochemical behavior of forested watersheds in the southern Appalachians. By measuring net nutrient budgets of experimental watersheds, we can hypothesize mechanisms of nutrient recycling and conservation internal to the systems. Our watershed-level measurements indicate responses that can be related to mechanistic process studies.

Our research results also permit development of both a conceptual framework and specific methods for evaluating the environmental consequences of alternative land management practices. We have been concerned with effects on both water quality and sustainable productivity of forests.

This objective is strongly guided by our underlying philosophy that resource management is synonymous with ecosystem management.

In this paper we evaluate the effects of various harvesting practices and alternative levels of wood fiber utilization on the sustainable productivity of forests. Such evaluations are now mandated by the Forest and Rangeland Renewable Resources Planning Act of 1974 and by the National Forest Management Act of 1975. The latter Act specifically requires demonstration that management systems used on land administered by the Forest Service "will not produce substantial and permanent impairment of the productivity of the land. . . ." Accelerated demands for wood products and derivations have led to such intensified forest management practices as site preparation (Balmer and Little, 1978), short rotation forestry (Ribe, 1974) and whole-tree utilization (Koch and McKenzie, 1975). The economic benefits of these practices will be much reduced if soil fertility and productivity decline because of altered nutrient cycles (Waide and Swank, 1976). Thus, there is urgent need for information and analytical tools which can be used to address these difficult questions. Answers now are tentative because we still have much to learn about forest ecosystems, but we must attempt to provide relevant answers. Wood has been viewed as eventually supplying up to 20 percent of our current energy needs (Ripley and Doub, 1978), and the Forest Service has initiated a program to increase the use of wood for energy fourfold within 10 years (Wahlgren, 1978).

In this paper, our analysis includes three steps or phases: 1) characterization of ecosystem budgets (input minus output) of selected nutrients for several contrasting forest ecosystems located in different physiographic regions of the United States;

137

2) examination of nutrient pools contained within ecosystem compartments, and annual transfer rates among compartments for these same ecosystems; and 3) elaboration of the conceptual framework which has guided ecosystem research at Coweeta, and illustration of how specific data sets can be used to determine important management needs. Proceeding from a general to a more detailed, complex analysis, we will attempt to integrate theory, data, and modeling in a management context.

NUTRIENT BUDGETS OF
FOREST ECOSYSTEMS

Nutrient budgets of forest ecosystems are an integrated measure of biogeochemical behavior and are thus useful in characterizing the net result of many interacting physical, chemical, and biological processes. Input-output data taken at ecosystem boundaries are valuable for characterizing undisturbed ecosystems (Likens et al., 1967), for generalizing across ecosystems located in diverse physiographic or climatic regions (Henderson et al., 1978), and for documenting changes produced by human activities (Likens et al., 1970; Johnson and Swank, 1973; Swank and Douglass, 1975, 1977). Budgets are derived by monitoring quantities of precipitation and streamflow, as well as concentrations of elements in water entering and leaving catchments (Bormann and Likens, 1967). The elements nitrogen (N), calcium (Ca), and potassium (K) have been selected for discussion here based on their importance in tree nutrition, their origin, and their contrasting mobility in biogeochemical cycles.

Average annual inputs and outputs of N, Ca, and K for four contrasting baseline ecosystems representing different physiographic regions of the United States are shown in Table 1. These four systems provide major contrasts in vegetation, bedrock geology, soils, and hydrology (Likens et al., 1977; Henderson et al., 1978). The three eastern sites contain deciduous forests (oak-hickory or northern hardwoods), while the western site is characterized by an old-growth coniferous forest. Soils and bedrock underlying these forests vary widely among sites, ranging from typic paleudults derived from dolomite bedrock at Oak Ridge, soils derived from volcanic tuff overlying andesitic bedrock at H. J. Andrews, typic hapludults derived from granodiorite, gneiss, and schist at Coweeta, to spodosols overlying highly metamorphosed mudstones and sandstones at Hubbard Brook. The amount, form, and seasonal distribution of annual precipitation are also variable,

ranging from 130 to 233 cm with both wet and dry growing seasons and the absence or dominance of a snowpack.

Although N inputs to these systems differ by a factor of 10 and outputs by a factor of 2, net budgets are similar, with all systems showing an accumulation of N (Table 1). Organic N is an important component of input at all sites where this form of N has been measured. The N budget is most nearly balanced for the old-growth conifer forest at H. J. Andrews, largely because of small inputs in bulk precipitation. The remoteness of Andrews from industrial sources may account for the lower deposition of N than at eastern sites, which are in the vicinity of heavy industrial or agricultural activity. This comparison of N budgets includes only hydrologic constitutents; large gains and losses which occur in gaseous form will be discussed later.

In contrast to N budgets, those for Ca and K show net losses for all ecosystems (Table 1). The wide range of values for Ca discharge reflects differences in bedrock mineralogy and solubility (Henderson et al., 1978). The dolomitic bedrock at Walker Branch and the andesitic bedrock at Andrews contribute to especially large stream losses of Ca. Gains and losses of K, a relatively mobile cation, are small. Net budgets reflect the combined effects of weathering rates and conservation mechanisms retaining K within ecosystems. Smaller losses of this ion from Andrews and Hubbard Brook may reflect lower rates of K release from bedrock.

These baseline data are useful in evaluating impacts of management activities on nutrient cycling only when compared with similar data for manipulated catchments. Data in Table 2 were derived by measuring nutrient inputs and outputs for several altered, young, successional forest ecosystems at Coweeta and comparing them with budget data for adjacent undisturbed hardwood-covered watersheds. Both white pine and hardwood coppice forests at this site show small losses of nitrate nitrogen (NO_3-N), no change in ammonium nitrogen (NH_4-N), and either no change or small accumulations of K and Ca, relative to undisturbed forests. Thus, except for NO_3-N, biogeochemical cycles during developmental stages of successional forests at Coweeta appear as conservative as cycles for more mature hardwoods. This conclusion agrees with predictions of Vitousek and Reiners (1975). These results suggest that increased losses of nutrients in stream discharge from regrowing stands are not sufficient to deplete site productivity, at least for the time period covered in Table 2.

Table 1. *Comparison of nitrogen (organic and inorganic), calcium, and potassium inputs in precipitation and outputs in streamflow for four watershed ecosystems in different physiographic regions of the United States*

Site and vegetation type	Nutrient											
	Organic N			Inorganic N			Ca			K		
	Input	Output	Net budget	Input	Output	Net budget	Input	Output	Net budget	Input	Output	Net budget
	---------------------------------- kg/ha/yr ----------------------------------											
Walker Branch, Tennessee[1] Oak-Hickory	3.7	1.6	+2.1	9.3	1.5	+7.8	12.0	148.0	-136.0	3.0	7.0	-4.0
Hubbard Brook, New Hampshire[2] Northern Hardwoods	---	---	---	6.5	3.9	+2.6	2.2	13.7	-11.5	0.9	1.9	-1.0
Coweeta, North Carolina[3] Oak-Hickory	4.3	3.1	+1.2	4.5	0.1	+4.4	4.8	7.7	-2.9	2.1	5.6	-3.5
H. J. Andrews, Oregon[4] Douglas-fir	1.5	1.8	-0.3	0.7	0.1	+0.6	2.3	50.3	-48.0	0.1	2.2	-2.1

[1]Henderson and Harris, 1975; Henderson et al., 1978
[2]Likens et al., 1977; data not available for organic N
[3]Swank and Douglas, 1975; unpublished data for organic N
[4]Fredriksen, 1975; Grier et al., 1974

Table 2. *Net loss (-) or gain (+) of selected nutrients in treated watersheds at Coweeta as compared with adjacent hardwood-covered watersheds*[1]

Treated vegetation, type and age	Nutrient			
	NO_3-N	NH_4-N	Ca	K
	kg/ha/yr			
Eastern white pine (ages 14 through 20 yrs)	-0.6	0.0	+2.3	+1.7
Hardwood coppice regrowth (ages 7 through 13 yrs)	-2.2	0.0	+0.1	-0.3

[1]Each value in this table represents the net budget for the treated watershed minus the associated net budget for an adjacent control watershed.

Table 3. *Annual change in net nitrogen budget in the first 2 years after road construction and clearcutting on WS 7 at Coweeta*[1]

Nutrient	Years after treatment	
	1	2
	kg/ha/yr	
NO_3-N	-0.01	-0.60
NH_4-N	-0.08	-0.11
Dissolved organic N	-0.18	-1.31
Particulate organic N[2]	-6.16	-1.55
Totals	-6.43	-3.57

[1]Each value in this table is calculated as the net budget for the treated watershed (WS 7) minus the net budget for the adjacent control watershed (WS 2).

[2]Suspended solids plus weir pond sediments.

Before this conclusion can be accepted, however, nutrient losses immediately following logging must be considered.

As demonstrated in a recent experiment at Coweeta (Table 3), elevated losses of N can be expected during and immediately following logging activity. Following the construction of roads on an experimental watershed, which disturbed only 5 percent of the area, the mixed oak-hickory forest was clearcut and cable logged. Response in the first year of treatment was primarily influenced by the construction and use of logging roads. Insignificant changes were observed in inorganic and dissolved organic N discharges; however, a net loss of 6.2 kg/ha was observed for organic N associated with the elevated discharge of suspended particulates and sediments. This large loss of particulate organic N was associated with two large storms (precipitation amounts of 25 and 15 cm) during the period of road construction. During the second year of treatment and following road stabilization, altered N dynamics due to cutting were evident in the measured ecosystem response.

Increased losses of NO_3-N and dissolved organic N were observed and, when combined with a reduction in losses of particulate organic N, resulted in a total net loss of 3.6 kg/ha in the second year. Taken collectively, budget data at Coweeta indicate that annual N losses attributable to clear-cutting and natural regrowth via hydrologic vectors are rather small, but may persist for at least 20 years (Swank and Douglass, 1975, 1977). The cumulative net N loss is approximately 55 kg/ha.

Effects of cutting and harvest activities on nutrient discharge have also been documented at the other sites shown in Table 1, except for Walker Branch. Modest increases in losses of NO_3-N have been observed following clearcutting and slash burning in conifer forests of the Cascades and Coast Range of Oregon (Fredriksen, 1975). Responses appear to be only slightly greater than at Coweeta. On the other hand, in northern hardwood stands hydrologic losses of N have been substantially greater, both at Hubbard Brook following clearcutting and herbicide treatment (Likens et al., 1970) and elsewhere in New Hampshire following clearcutting alone (Pierce et al., 1972). However, stream concentrations of NO_3-N at Hubbard Brook appear to return to baseline levels in only 4 to 6 years, perhaps due to the depletion of readily mineralizable forms of N in litter and soil horizons (Likens et al., 1978).

Hence, it appears that increased hydrologic losses of nutrients may persist for varying periods following cutting, but that such losses are not of sufficient magnitude alone to cause significant reductions in site productivity. This conclusion seems justified, despite the tremendous range in nutrient losses after cutting (especially for NO_3-N), and in the underlying mechanisms regulating nutrient loss, among forest ecosystems in the United States (Vitousek et al., 1979). For northern hardwood forests, hydrologic losses of N approach the amount of N removed in wood products (Likens et al., 1978). But when hydrologic losses from these systems are averaged over normal rotation lengths of 110 to 120 years, they do not appear to be severe (approx. 2 kg N/ha/yr). Thus, if we are searching for sources of potential major reductions in site quality following forest cutting, we must look beyond increased losses of nutrients (especially N) in streamwater. In particular, we must examine in detail processes of nutrient recycling and conservation internal to experimental forested watersheds.

NUTRIENT DISTRIBUTION AND CYCLING WITHIN FOREST ECOSYSTEMS

A more detailed analysis of potential impacts of forest management strategies on biogeochemistry and sustainable productivity may be obtained by examining processes of nutrient recycling and conservation internal to forest ecosystems. Such an analysis will reveal the major pools of nutrient storage in forests, significant pathways for nutrient transfer among storage pools, and mechanisms that regulate biogeochemical responses to forest alteration. Table 4 summarizes information on nutrient distribution and cycling for the same ecosystems considered in analyses of nutrient budgets. Values again are given for N, Ca, and K.

For all ecosystems, the majority of N is found in the soil organic matter fraction. Values for the four sites are comparable, with the amount of N stored in this compartment at Coweeta being slightly higher than at the other three locations. The second largest N storage pool for the two oak-hickory forests is in vegetation. Again, the Coweeta value is higher than those for the other sites, largely due to higher concentrations of N in the roots (McGinty, 1976; Henderson et al., 1978). Vegetation pools at all four sites contain between 8 and 12 percent of the total N in the forest. In contrast with the oak-hickory forests, ecosystems at Andrews and Hubbard Brook have the second largest N storage in the forest floor compartment. Such a large accumulation of N in litter at these sites is related to slower decomposition rates (e.g., Gosz et al., 1973; Cromack and Monk, 1975; Fogel and Cromack, 1977) due to climatic differences (dry summer at Andrews, cold winter with snow at Hubbard Brook). Stone (1973) has suggested that enhanced microenvironmental conditions following clearcutting of northern hardwoods greatly accelerate decay rates for these large litter pools, and that such increased decay rates may explain why these forest ecosystems lose so much N in streamwater after forest removal. Soil exchangeable N (i.e., inorganic mineral N) is the smallest pool in all four forests. Amounts of N in this pool are highest at Coweeta and Walker Branch, perhaps due to more rapid microbial turnover and mineralization at these sites.

Table 4 also reveals that litterfall is the major aboveground transfer pathway in the N cycle. Values for this N transfer are highest at Hubbard Brook, intermediate in the two oak-hickory forests, and lowest at Andrews. Woody increment and uptake (aboveground only) values for the three hardwood forests are fairly similar, and are

Table 4. Summary and comparison of compartment sizes and transfer rates for the cycles of nitrogen, calcium, and potassium in four forest ecosystems in contrasting physiographic regions of the United States[1]

	Nitrogen				Calcium				Potassium			
	WB	HB	CHL	HJA	WB	HB	CHL	HJA	WB	HB	CHL	HJA
Compartment sizes (kg/ha)												
Vegetation (aboveground and belowground)	470	532	995	560	980	484	830	750	340	218	400	360
Forest floor	310	1,256	140	740	430	372	130	570	20	66	20	90
Mineral soil												
Exchangeable	75	26	117	5	710	510	940	4,450	170	---	510	860
Total[3]	4,700	4,890	6,800	4,500	3,800	9,600	2,500	---	38,000	---	124,000	---
Percent of system total in vegetation	8.4	8.0	12.4	9.6	16.6	4.4	18.9	---	0.9	---	0.3	---
Transfer rates (kg/ha/yr)												
Litterfall	39	54	33	21	55	41	44	41	19	18	18	9
Canopy leaching	3	3	4	4	14	4	8	8	19	29	31	15
Woody increment	15	9	13	-2	31	8	23	-4	8	6	13	-1
Uptake[4]	57	66	50	23	100	53	75	45	46	53	62	23

[1]Data from Bormann et al., 1977; Likens et al., 1977; and Henderson et al., 1978.

[2]Site codes as follows: WB, Walker Branch, Tennessee; HB, Hubbard Brook, New Hampshire; CHL, Coweeta Hydrologic Laboratory, North Carolina; HJA, H. J. Andrews, Oregon.

[3]Values to 94.5 cm depth at Hubbard Brook, to 60 cm depth at other sites.

[4]Hubbard Brook values exclude uptake that is recycled in root litter/root exudates.

considerably higher than for the old-growth conifer forest, where mortality exceeds growth. Nitrogen leaching is uniformly low at all four sites.

For the Ca cycle, the dominant storage pool is in the soil, either in bound mineral form for the three deciduous forests or in exchangeable form for the conifer stand. The high total Ca pool at Hubbard Brook may reflect the fact that the glaciated soils there are developmentally younger. The high exchangeable Ca value for Andrews is associated with the high cation exchange capacity of soils there (Henderson et al., 1978). Storage of Ca in vegetation is lowest at Hubbard Brook, and higher and quite similar at the other sites. These vegetation pools represent 4 to 19 percent of the total Ca found in these forests. Litter pools of calcium are again lowest at Coweeta, where decay rates are rapid and immobilization of Ca in litter is low. Indeed, water passing through the litter layer at Coweeta becomes enriched in Ca (Best and Monk, 1975).

Litterfall is also the major mechanism for transfer of Ca. Values for this pathway are quite similar across all sites. The aboveground uptake of Ca, and its incorporation as annual woody increment, are highest for the two oak-hickory forests and lowest for Hubbard Brook and Andrews. The latter site shows a negative increment value for Ca as it did for N.

For the K cycle, the overwhelmingly dominant storage pool is in bound form in the soil. Exchangeable K pools are also quite high and vary across sites in relation to soil cation exchange capacities, being especially high at Andrews (Henderson et al., 1978). Vegetation pools are comparable and appear to represent less than 1 percent of the system total. Storage of K in litter is quite low, reflecting differences in decay rates among sites.

In contrast to the cycles of N and Ca, transfers of K via canopy leaching are large. Values for K increment and uptake are reasonably similar for the deciduous forests and are much higher than comparable values for the old-growth Douglas-fir forest.

Analyses presented so far have excluded two additional mechanisms important in recycling nutrients within forest ecosystems --root mortality and internal redistribution. Root mortality may be more important than litterfall in returning elements to soil pools at both Walker Branch (Henderson and Harris, 1975) and Coweeta (Mitchell et al., 1975; McGinty, 1976). Such a transfer mechanism must also be important at the other two sites, although comparative data are currently lacking. Additionally, the importance of retranslocation of N from

leaves to woody tissues has been noted at all four sites (Henderson and Harris, 1975; Mitchell et al., 1975; Bormann et al., 1977; Waring and Franklin, 1979; Franklin, this volume). Such internal redistribution of N may account for more than 50 percent of annual requirements at all sites and may be even more important in the Douglas-fir stand than in the three deciduous forests. A similar redistribution of K, about one-third as large as for N, occurs at Coweeta, although not for the less mobile element Ca (Waide and Swank, unpub. data).

Several tentative conclusions emerge from these analyses of nutrient distribution and cycling in the four forest ecosystems relative to potential management impacts. First, much greater amounts of all three nutrients are stored and recycled within these forests than are lost annually in drainage waters. This is especially true for N, the cycle of which is more strongly biologically regulated, than for the cations Ca and K, for which cycles and especially losses are more strongly regulated by geochemical factors (Henderson et al., 1978). This result reinforces the importance of examining internal recycling mechanisms. Second, quantities of N, Ca, and K stored in vegetation and removed in wood fiber from the site do not appear sufficient to cause major reductions in site quality. This is especially true if nutrient removals are expressed as rates (e.g., kg/ha/yr) averaged over reasonable rotation lengths. Third, of the pools considered here, the most susceptible to management disruptions appears to be the exchangeable soil pool, as compared to annual uptake requirements of vegetation. This relationship appears to be more important for N than for Ca or K. For the latter two ions, exchangeable soil pools represent 400 percent to 10,000 percent of annual uptake. Comparable values for N range from 20 percent to 200 percent. Thus, the amount of N mineralized annually, relative to nutritional requirements of vegetation, may be the key to a forest ecosystem's response to management actions.

Two components of the N cycle not yet considered may also be especially susceptible to cutting disturbance. These are the microbially mediated gaseous transformations --N fixation and denitrification. Data presented in Table 5 for Coweeta and Andrews show that for undisturbed forests these gaseous inputs and outputs of N are much larger than hydrologic components of ecosystem budgets (Todd et al., 1975; Todd et al., 1978). Moreover, because these processes are mediated by microbial populations, they may change drastically following forest cutting. Microbial populations have extremely high growth rates and can respond rapidly to changes in forest microenvironments, availability of requisite substrates, and energy sources.

Thus, our analyses suggest that understanding the following three processes in the N cycle is central to evaluating the effects of forest management alternatives on site productivity: mineralization, inputs via biological fixation, and outputs via denitrification. Changes in these three processes may, in large measure, regulate the response of the forest ecosystem to forest cutting and removal.

EVALUATION OF IMPACTS OF MANAGEMENT ALTERNATIVES ON SITE PRODUCTIVITY

We have attempted to use specific data both on forest ecosystem nutrient budgets and on nutrient distribution and recycling within forests to identify possible causes of reductions in productivity on intensively managed forests. We have demonstrated points at which nutrient cycles, especially the nitrogen cycle, may be sensitive to management disruptions. These results are specific to the sites considered here, and generalization to a wide variety of management situations becomes tenuous. Similar empirical data are unavailable for a variety of forest types because costs and manpower requirements are high for large ecosystem studies.

How can we best utilize such data on undisturbed ecosystems to predict environmental consequences of man's resource management activities? In a management context, it is both impractical and unreasonable to expect precise, quantitative predictions over millions of hectares of forest land. Instead, a methodology is needed to rank or scale one ecosystem relative to another based on theoretical and known behavior. Our approach in attempting to couple ecosystem theory and nutrient cycling research with management needs has proceeded within the framework of a conceptual model of ecosystem relative stability. Stability is an important concept in scientific ecology as well as an intuitive concept in human experience that can be related to solving resource management problems. The incorporation of stability concepts into ecosystem analysis has been discussed by many investigators (Child and Shugart, 1972; Waide et al., 1974; Patten, 1974; Botkin and Sobel, 1975; O'Neill et al., 1975; Waide and Webster, 1975; Webster et al., 1975; Van Voris, 1976; Botkin, this volume). We have previously detailed extensions of stability analysis to questions of forest management (Waide and Swank, 1976, 1977).

Table 5. *Estimated rates of nitrogen fixation and denitrification for an undisturbed oak-hickory forest at Coweeta, and of nitrogen fixation in several components of an old-growth conifer forest at H. J. Andrews*

Process	Ecosystem component	Site Coweeta[1]	Site H. J. Andrews
		--------- kg/ha/yr ------------	
Nitrogen fixation	Phyllosphere	0.22	5.0[2]
	Bole	1.00	
	Woody litter	1.66	2.6[3]
	Leaf litter	0.63	
	Soil	8.55	
	Total	12.04	
Denitrification	Soil	10.70	

[1]Todd et al., 1975; Todd et al., 1978; Waide and Swank, 1976.

[2]W. C. Dennison, pers. comm.

[3]Larson et al., 1978.

Conceptual Model of Resistance and Resilience

We begin by considering the general nature of an ecosystem's response to disturbance. Illustrated in Figure 1 are several hypothetical responses to an ecosystem disturbance such as clearcutting, fire, or major windstorm. The vertical axis in this diagram represents the deviation of some (unspecified) functional property or measure of the state of the ecosystem from a nominal or pre-disturbance level. The horizontal axis represents time, in any appropriate units. Such curves are meant to be quite general and could represent, for example, changes in streamflow volumes, NO_3-N concentrations in streamwater, or total losses of K following forest cutting. If the curves were inverted (i.e., were mirrored across the horizontal axis in Fig. 1), they might represent total forest biomass or productivity over the period of post-disturbance succession. A similar conceptual approach was taken by Trudgill (1977) in his analyses of terrestrial nutrient cycling.

As illustrated in Figure 1, two components of ecosystem disturbance and recovery may be recognized (Table 6). The first is the maximum extent of system displacement from a pre-disturbance functional level, or the resistance of the ecosystem. The smaller the deviation from a nominal functional level for a given amount or type of disturbance, or the greater the disturbance required to produce a given maximum deviation, the greater the resistance of the ecosystem.

The second component of response to disturbance is the resilience of the ecosystem--i.e., the rate at which the ecosystem recovers or returns to within a definable range of pre-disturbance function. The faster the system recovers, or the shorter the time required to return to a previous level of function, the more resilient the ecosystem. The several curves depicted in Figure 1 were chosen to illustrate different possible combinations of resistance (extent of displacement) and resilience (rate of recovery).

The curve forms shown in the graphical model of ecosystem disturbance and recovery (Fig. 1), as well as many other similar curves, may be generated by the following equation for a second-order damped oscillator (i.e., a pendulum):

$$\ddot{y} + 2\zeta\omega_n\dot{y} + \omega_n^2 y = \omega_n^2 z.$$

In this equation, y and z represent outputs and inputs of the system of interest, the dot and double-dot notations indicate first and second derivatives with respect to time, ω_n is the undamped natural frequency of the system, and ζ is the damping coefficient. This second-order equation is used only as an analogy to an ecosystem's response to disturbance, and as a means of quantifying the concepts of resistance and resilience. As will be shown below, we associate quantitative indices of resistance and resilience with the magnitudes of ω_n and ζ.

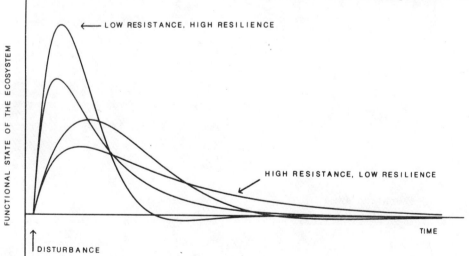

Figure 1. *Hypothetical response of an ecosystem following a specific disturbance (fire, windstorm, clearcutting). The vertical axis represents the deviation of some unspecified functional property or measure of the state of the ecosystem from its nominal or pre-disturbance level. The horizontal axis represents time, in unspecified units. Several possible responses to disturbance are shown, each differing in the magnitude of deviation from the pre-disturbance level of function (resistance) and in the rate of recovery or return to the previous state (resilience).*

Previous analyses of hypothetical models of ecosystem nutrient cycles (Webster et al., 1975) indicated that ecosystem resistance is related to the presence of organic components having large standing stocks with slow turnover. However, resilience is high when biotic components have low mass but high turnover or metabolic rates. These general conclusions agree well with current understandings of functional properties of forest ecosystems. For example, Waring and Franklin (1979) and Franklin (this volume) suggest that the large size of dominant trees in coniferous forests of the Pacific Northwest "provides a buffer against environmental stress (especially for nutrients and moisture)" (Waring and Franklin, 1979, p. 1380). By storing large amounts of water and nutrients (especially N) internally, conifers are buffered against extremes of water and nutrient availability in the climate typical of the region. This is certainly directly related to the concept of ecosystem resistence--massive trees storing large quantities of water and N, thereby reducing variability in functional processes during times of environmental stress. Also related to ecosystem resistance is the concept of a "big-slow" component in terrestrial ecosystems (O'Neill et al., 1975; O'Neill and Reichle, this volume). The term big-slow refers to large storage pools of organic matter and elements which turn over slowly. Such big-slow components are believed to buffer ecosystems against environmental extremes and serve as an alternate energy base during times of stress. Again, such a functional component contributes to the resistance property of ecosystems.

Similarly, we interpret the functional role of pin cherry in disturbed forests at Hubbard Brook (Marks, 1974) in terms of resilience. The high rate of growth and elemental uptake by pin cherry, and its rapid accretion of biomass and leaf area, contribute to the recovery of northern hardwood forests following severe disturbance. Webster and others (1975) suggested that successional species regulate the resilience of ecosystems following disturbance.

Table 6. *Definition of resistance and resilience as two complementary components of ecosystem relative stability*[1]

Component	Analogous terms	Meaning
Resistance	Inertia Rigidity	1. Inversely proportional to the amount by which some functional property or measure of the state of the ecosystem deviates from a nominal level in response to a specific disturbance. 2. Directly proportional to the extent of disturbance required to produce a certain magnitude of deviation in some ecosystem functional property.
Resilience	Elasticity Restoration time Classical stability	1. Directly proportional to the rate at which some functional measure of the state of the ecosystem recovers or returns to a predisturbance or nominal level. 2. Inversely proportional to the time required for ecosystem recovery following disturbance.

[1]See Figure 1 for diagrammatic illustrations of these concepts.

Because this conceptual model of ecosystem disturbance and recovery is central to our analyses in the remainder of the paper, and because it has been criticized both generally (Botkin and Sobel, 1975; Botkin, this volume) and specifically (Harwell et al., 1977), several additional points must be made about the sense in which we are using the model. First, we are in no way suggesting that an ecosystem behaves like a pendulum. We are using the equation of a second-order damped oscillator, and specifically the curve forms it generates, as an analogy or general model of ecosystem responses following some man-induced or natural environmental disturbance. We are taking advantage of the well-accepted engineering approach (Shinners, 1972) of using a second-order model to approximate the behavior of a higher-order system. This approach allows us to quantify or derive indices for the concepts of ecosystem resistance and resilience. But these indices are of value only in a comparative sense, and only in the context of specific theoretical or applied questions.

Second, we are not considering forest disturbances severe enough to cause a new ecosystem to appear on site. For example, following the clearcutting of WS 2 at Hubbard Brook, WS 7 at Coweeta, or WS 10 at H. J. Andrews, one would expect the regrowth of northern hardwoods, oak-hickory, and Douglas-fir forests to be similar in all quantifiable functional properties to the pre-cut forests, differing mainly in details of species composition.

Third, in these analyses we are measuring the state of the ecosystem in terms of functional variables, not in structural terms. Species composition is not used as a measure of the state of the ecosystem. Within this context, the curve forms depicted in Figure 1 correspond well to responses documented in a variety of watershed manipulation experiments throughout this country, for many types of functional variables: total streamflow, total evapotranspiration, net production, total forest biomass, litterfall, stream nutrient concentrations. Thus, our approach is based upon a reasonable general model of ecosystem disturbance and recovery.

Finally, rather than using this conceptual approach to analyze the static stability (Botkin, this volume) of ecosystems, we argue that the context in which this model is used is consistent with a stochastic view of both ecosystems and environments. The apparent resistance and resilience of forest ecosystems following cutting results from the evolution of biotic components of forests within continuously variable environments. Thus, biotically

regulated mechanisms of ecosystem homeostasis exist in response to environmental oscillations acting at a wide variety of frequencies (Schindler et al., in press).

Therefore, the concepts of resistance and resilience are appropriate at two quite different levels of analysis. At one level of analysis, the concepts of resistance and resilience relate to the persistence of ecosystems within temporally variable environments. The physicochemical environment impinging on any natural ecosystem varies, often substantially, over time. In this sense, resistance and resilience relate to the integrated sets of responses of the biotic components of ecosystems for persisting in the face of environmental oscillations (Webster et al., 1975). At quite another level of analysis, ecosystems exhibit functional responses to specific disturbances, both natural disturbances and those induced by man. The nature of the response to a specific disturbance allows us to recognize the ecosystem as being highly resistant or not (extent of displacement from previous level of function) and highly resilient or not (rate of recovery to previous level of function).

It is at the first, more theoretical level of analysis identified above that the concepts of resistance and resilience were first defined explicitly (Webster et al., 1975). It is also at this level that Watson and Loucks (1979) recently analyzed the turnover times of organic matter, N, and P in Lake Wingra. However, it is at the second, more applied level of analysis that the concepts of resistance and resilience have been previously applied to problems of forest management (Waide and Swank, 1976, 1977; Huff et al., 1978) and in which they will be employed here.

Resistance, Resilience, and the Nitrogen Cycle

The concepts of resistance and resilience will now be quantified for models of the N cycle for two forest ecosystem types important in the southeastern United States, a natural oak-hickory forest and a loblolly pine plantation. Details of parameter estimation for the second-order model are given elsewhere (Waide and Webster, 1975; Webster et al., 1975; Waide and Swank, 1976).

Figure 2 depicts a compartment model of the N cycle in an undisturbed hardwood forest at Coweeta (see Mitchell et al., 1975, for details of model construction). The model provides estimates of pool sizes (kg N/ha), vegetation increments (kg N/ha/yr), and transfers of N among compartment (kg N/ha/yr). For comparison, a compartmental model for the N cycle in a 16-year-old loblolly pine plantation in the Duke Forest, North Carolina, is shown in Figure 3. Values shown are from studies by Wells and Jorgensen (1975) and by Wells and others (1975). Inspection of these figures shows that both forests are dominanted by large storage pools of N which turn over slowly. The loblolly stand, in comparison with the oak-hickory forest, has a smaller proportion of the total N in the system contained in vegetation pools, with nearly twice as much N in the litter and only about half as much soil N.

The most dynamic portion of the N cycle for the oak-hickory forest at Coweeta (Fig. 2) is in the soil, with high rates of transfer between microbial and mineral N pools. Similar data were unavailable for the loblolly plantation; thus, the two nitrogen models are conceptualized at grossly different levels of resolution. The importance of level of resolution to systems analyses has previously been documented for these two models (Waide and

Swank, 1976, 1977). Hence, direct comparison of results for the two systems is difficult.

Results of relative stability analyses for these two nitrogen models are shown in Table 7. Resistance of the ecosystem models is inversely related to the natural frequency, ω_n (Webster et al., 1975). In fact, for these systems, it can be shown analytically (Waide, unpub.) that resistance is directly proportional to ω_n^{-2}. Values in Table 7 thus suggest that the oak-hickory N cycle is more resistant to displacement than the loblolly cycle.

Interpretations of resilience values depend on whether one is interested in a relative (Webster et al., 1975) or an absolute (Harwell et al., 1977) index. Given two ecosystems, the value of ζ alone provides a good measure of resilience if values of the natural frequency (ω_n) for the two systems are within one order of magnitude: the closer ζ is to 1.0, the more resilient the system. However, if values of ω_n for the two systems differ by at least an order of magnitude, resilience

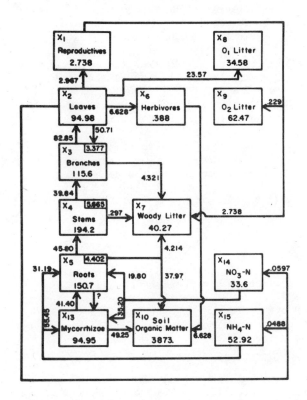
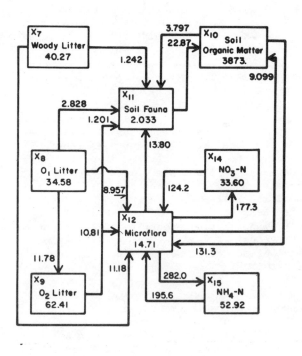

Figure 2. Compartment model of the nitrogen cycle in an undisturbed oak-hickory forest at Coweeta. Shown in the left half of the diagram are storage pools and flows associated with N uptake from and return to soil pools. Compartments and flows associated with decomposition and N mineralization are depicted in the right portion. Values in boxes represent the magnitudes of nitrogen storage pools (kg/ha). Numbers within rectangles in vegetation compartments represent annual increments (kg/ha/yr). Rates of nitrogen transfer among storage pools are shown on arrows, in units of kg/ha/yr (see Mitchell and others, 1975, for details of model construction; figure modified from Mitchell and others, 1975).

is proportional to $\zeta\omega_n$. The absolute time required for recovery (the inverse of absolute resilience) is proportional to $1/\zeta\omega_n$. Thus, relative and absolute indices of resilience provide different interpretations in this case (Table 7), suggesting that the oak-hickory nitrogen cycle is more resilient (relative) or less resilient (absolute) than the loblolly pine cycle. However, from a practical standpoint, the absolute index ($1/\zeta\omega_n$) is useful only if the allowable recovery times (i.e., the rotation lengths) of the two systems are

nearly identical. Clearly, this is not the case for the two forest types considered here. Thus, the relative index of resilience is more appropriate for our analyses. Also, we are largely concerned here with questions of forest resistance to various management strategies, for which the analyses (Table 7) give unambiguous results. Finally, we again emphasize that the N cycle in the two forests is conceptualized at different levels of resolution, complicating interpretations of results.

Nonetheless, relative stability analyses indicate that management impacts on the N cycle would be greater in the loblolly pine plantation than in the oak-hickory forest. This conclusion will be examined in light of specific simulation predictions below.

Simulations of Alternative
Management Strategies

The previous discussion provides an operational framework for predicting comparative biogeochemical responses of different forest ecosystems to manipulation. In this section, we consider specific management alternatives and use the compartmental models (Figs. 2, 3) to simulate changes in N pools and associated impacts on productivity. In related papers, we have discussed a wider variety of simulations (Waide and Swank, 1976) and have predicted changes in several compartments of the N cycle (Waide and Swank, 1977). Here, for illustrative purposes, we discuss only a few representative forest alterations and their simulated effects on the soil N pool. Details of simulation models may be found in our earlier papers.

Management practices simulated for oak-hickory and loblolly pine forests are shown in Table 8. These alternatives focus on rotation length and degree of tree utilization, two practical decisions faced by managers today. Changes in soil N for

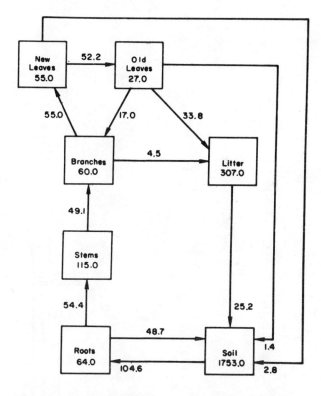

Figure 3. Compartment model of the nitrogen cycle in a loblolly pine plantation in the Duke Forest. Labeling terms same as in Figure 2 (see Waide and Swank, 1976, for details of model construction; figure modified from Waide and Swank, 1977).

Table 7. Comparison of relative stability indices for the nitrogen cycle in southeastern oak-hickory and loblolly pine forest ecosystems

Ecosystem type	Indices of Resistance		Indices of Resilience	
	ω_n	$1/\omega_n^2$	ζ	$1/\zeta\omega_n$
Oak-hickory	0.106	89.0	0.906	10.4
loblolly pine	0.167	35.9	0.850	7.0

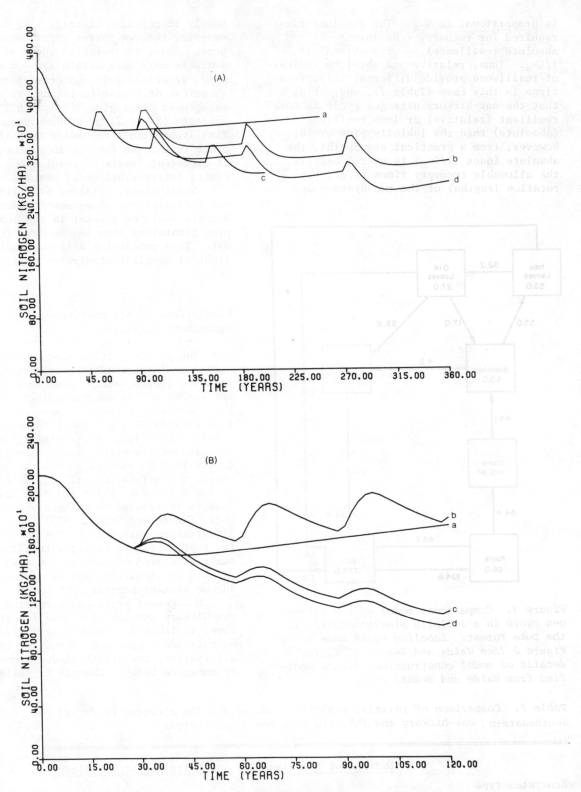

Figure 4. Simulated changes in total soil nitrogen (kg/ha) for (A) oak-hickory and (B) loblolly pine forest ecosystems following several types of forest alteration. All simulations begin at time = 0 with a recently cut, regrowing forest. Cutting alternatives in part (A) are: a. uncut forest; b. merchantable harvest, 90-yr rotation; c. merchantable harvest, 50-yr rotation; d. complete-tree harvest, 90-yr rotation. Cutting alternatives in part (B) are: a. uncut forest; b. merchantable harvest, 30-yr rotation; c. merchantable harvest with residue removal, 30-yr rotation; d. complete-tree harvest with residue removal, 30-yr rotation.

each management alternative (Table 8) are compared with values for an uncut oak-hickory forest over four successive rotations in Figure 4(A). For all simulated alternatives, depletion of soil N increases with each succeeding harvest. The merchantable harvest with 90-year rotation length produced the least impact, with a 405 kg/ha (11%) depletion in soil N at the end of the first rotation. Shortening the rotation length to 50 years produced large additional decreases in soil N, as did the simulated complete-tree harvest with a 90-year rotation.

Simulation results from the loblolly pine model are shown in Figure 4(B). The merchantable tree harvest with no residue removal showed little difference from the uncut forest, but increased removal of plant material associated with the other alternatives produced substantial reductions in soil N. As suggested previously (Waide and Swank, 1976, 1977), if sufficient soil dynamics data were available to provide an expanded pine model, simulated changes in soil N might be even larger.

We are interested not only in changes in soil N for these two forests, but also in changes in yield of forest products associated with any reductions in soil N. Data for all management alternatives considered here (Table 9) are based on assumptions that yield of wood fiber is directly proportional to standing crops of nitrogen in vegetation compartments (Figs. 2, 3). If the merchantable stem harvest, without residue removal and for a "standard" rotation length (90 yrs for hardwood, 30 yrs for pine) is con-

sidered typical for each site, it is clear from values in Table 9 that increased levels of wood fiber utilization are predicted to have a greater impact on the loblolly pine than on the oak-hickory forest. This result is consistent with the relative stability comparisons of the two sites, specifically the resistance component (Table 7). However, even for the oak-hickory forest, increased levels of wood utilization from a merchantable to a complete-tree harvest nearly doubled the predicted reduction in yield in subsequent rotations. Hence, increasing the frequency or the level (or both) of wood fiber harvest may lead to significant reductions in productivity. Such reductions may be quite severe, especially for the pine site.

These simulated reductions in yield are consistent with experimental evidence from other areas such as Australia (Keeves, 1966), New Zealand (Whyte, 1973), and Europe (Troup, 1928), where reduced productivity of conifer plantations has been documented over several successive rotations. With specific reference to N, Weber (1978) concluded that fertilization would be needed to sustain productivity of Pinus radiata in New Zealand under intensified management practices such as shorter rotations, closer utilization, and slash burning. Nutrient cycling studies in a variety of forest ecosystems in North America have similarly led investigators to express concern about impacts of intensified management on nutrient removals, soil impoverishment, and site degradation (Boyle et al., 1973; Kimins, 1977; Patric and Smith, 1975; Pritchett and Wells, 1978;

Table 8. *Summary of management alternatives considered in model simulations of the nitrogen cycle in oak-hickory and loblolly pine forest ecosystems[1]*

Ecosystem type	Type of cut	Residue removal	Rotation length (years)
Oak-hickory	Merchantable	No	90
	Merchantable	No	50
	Complete-tree	No	90
Loblolly pine	Merchantable	No	30
	Merchantable	Yes	30
	Complete-tree	Yes	30

[1]See Figures 2 and 3.

Aber et al., 1979). Based on findings at
Hubbard Brook, Likens and others (1978)
concluded that conventional rotation lengths
(110-120 years) for even-aged hardwood in
the White Mountains of New Hampshire would
not seriously affect nutrient replenishment and long-term productivity. However,
these authors pointed out that such questions must be reexamined for intensified
management practices. Indeed, other
analyses (Hornbeck, 1977; Aber et al.,
1978) indicate that replenishment of available N in such ecosystems could be a problem following whole-tree utilization or
shortened rotations. Simulated changes in
available N pools (NO_3-N and NH_4-N) in oak-
hickory forests at Coweeta (Fig. 2) parallel
changes shown in total soil N in Figure
4(A). Hence, a consistent conclusion is
drawn from our simulation predictions, from
our earlier analyses of storage pools and
transfer rates in the N cycle for several
forest ecosystems, and from the results of
Aber and others (1978). Mineralization of
N may be insufficient to meet uptake
requirements of successional vegetation
following intensive forest management in
the Southern Appalachians.

It is important to recognize limitations in our simulation results. The models
of N cycling (Figs. 2,3) are incomplete;
improved information is needed for certain
processes, particularly belowground N
dynamics. Also, our results are site

specific, and both ecosystems analyzed here
are of average or better quality. Therefore it is not unreasonable to expect even
greater impacts on sites which are less
fertile initially. We feel that the
strength of our analyses lies in the overall approach taken, and we submit that the
qualitative, comparative aspects of our
predictions are useful. Refined stability
analyses and simulation models incorporat-
ing improved data might be utilized to rank
expected responses of specific ecosystems,
areas, or entire regions to intensified
management. Energy plantations, more complete fiber utilization, or shorter rotations might be evaluated in this manner.
Another appealing aspect of the modeling
approach is that data from many sources can
be used in a framework that is consistent
with theoretical treatments of ecosystem
dynamics. With the need to provide
immediate answers to problems that may
evolve over long periods of time, this general approach appears to be the only viable
recourse.

We have also used our modeling approach
to identify specific research needs. For
example, the partitioning of N losses and
accretions for the hardwood simulations
(Table 10) provides a basis for placing
priorities on future studies. In terms of
losses, increasing levels of fiber removal
can double the N loss rate in wood products,
but denitrification still appears to be the

*Table 9. Predicted changes in yield of forest products after three simulated
rotations for several forest management alternatives for southeastern oak-hickory
and loblolly pine forest ecosystems*

Ecosystem type	Type of cut	Predicted change in yield (%)
Oak-hickory	Merchantable, 90-year rotation	−10.3
	Merchantable, 50-year rotation	−12.7
	Complete-tree, 90-year rotation	−16.8
Loblolly pine	Merchantable, 30-year rotation	+6.9
	Merchantable with residue removal, 30-year rotation	−24.9
	Complete-tree with residue removal, 30-year rotation	−29.5

dominant reason for simulated reductions in soil fertility and fiber yield. Thus, large errors in estimating losses via fiber removal and stream discharge are greatly overshadowed by minor inaccuracies in denitrification estimates. Yet, we know little about denitrification in forest ecosystems. Improved field techniques are urgently needed to provide estimates of rates of denitrification in forest soils.

Similarly, biological fixation of N is viewed as the primary mechanism of accretion, but quantitative information for a variety of forest ecosystems is lacking. At Coweeta, rates of N fixation have increased roughly sevenfold in the first 18 months after cable logging (Todd and Waide, unpub. data), but the duration of such elevated N inputs is unknown. In the southern Appalachians, black locust (Robinia pseudo-acacia L.), a legume, is a ubiquitous early successional tree species on disturbed sites. Ike and Stone (1958) estimated an accumulated N increase of nearly 700 kg/ha in the soil of a 16- to 20-year-old black locust plantation. In the Pacific Northwest, snowbrush (Ceanothus velutinus) is an early successional, nonleguminous plant;

Youngberg and Wollum (1976) estimated fixation by this species to be about 1,000 kg/ha over a 10-year period. Significant N fixation by other woody species in forest ecosystems in Oregon has also been documented (Dyrness and Youngberg, 1966; Dalton and Zobel, 1977; Newton et al., 1968). Lichens are another important biological symbiont; Pike and others (1972) found large accretions of nitrogen in the phyllosphere of older Douglas-fir stands by Lorbaria oregana. Major research is needed to quantify gaseous nitrogen transformations in undisturbed and managed forest ecosystems.

CONCLUSIONS

At Coweeta we plan to continue studying the problems discussed in this paper by improving our current techniques of measurement, and by more intensified sampling of N fixation, immobilization, mineralization, denitrification, and N availability associated with forest management practices involving traditional and increased levels of wood utilization. Recently initiated research in this area is part of a coopera-

Table 10. Simulated components of total gains and losses for the nitrogen cycle in a southeastern oak-hickory forest ecosystem subjected to alternative management strategies[1]

Component of loss or gain	Merchantable harvest, 90-yr rotation	Merchantable harvest, 50-yr rotation	Complete-tree harvest, 90-yr rotation	Uncut forest
	---------------------------- kg/ha/yr ----------------------------			
Nitrogen losses				
Fiber removal	2.0	3.4	5.3	0.0
Stream discharge	0.5	0.7	0.5	0.3
Denitrification	16.1	18.8	15.5	11.2
Total	18.6	22.9	21.3	11.5
Nitrogen gains				
Fixation	- - - - - - - - - - - - - 10.9 - - - - - - - - - - - - - -			
Precipitation	- - - - - - - - - - - - - 3.4 - - - - - - - - - - - - - -			
Total	- - - - - - - - - - - - - 14.3 - - - - - - - - - - - - - -			

[1]Values shown are averaged over the indicated rotation length.

tive project that includes similar studies at H. J. Andrews, Hubbard Brook, Oak Ridge, Clemson University in the South Carolina Piedmont, and the University of Washington. Our goal is to couple extensive nutrient cycling data with specific process-level research for the purpose of filling gaps in our ability to evaluate alternative management practices. We also intend to improve the nitrogen simulation models described here and to test or validate our approach with experimental data on yield and productivity for pine plantations with various rotation lengths.

Specific simulation studies within the context of our conceptual model of ecosystem resistance-resilience will remain an integral component of our total research effort. Modeling activities serve to focus research initiatives and to integrate process-level information in the context of system-level hypotheses. Such activities, however, become disoriented and inefficient unless an overall conceptual model is retained. Thus, both conceptual and simulation models serve as evolving hypotheses about the dynamical behavior of forest ecosystems, useful at any instant to make specific predictions, but also malleable as new data or interpretations become available.

We submit that the integration of empirical research and modeling in the context of a general theory is the only viable method of answering the serious questions concerning sustainable productivity facing managers of forest resources. The only alternatives are piecemeal studies or wait-and-see attitudes. Neither will suffice in the multi-demand environment within which resource management decisions must currently be made.

LITERATURE CITED

Aber, J. D., D. B. Botkin, and J. M. Melillo. 1978. Predicting the effects of different harvesting regimes on forest floor dynamics in northern hardwoods. Can. J. Forest Res. 8:306-315.

Aber, J. D., D. B. Botkin, and J. M. Melillo. 1979. Predicting the effects of different harvesting regimes on productivity and yield in northern hardwoods. Can. J. Forest Res. 9:10-14.

Balmer, W. E., and N. G. Little. 1978. Site preparation methods. In Proceedings: A Symposium on Principles of Maintaining Productivity on Prepared Sites, edited by T. Tippen, pp. 60-64. Starkville: Mississippi State University Press.

Best, G. R., and C. D. Monk. 1975. Cation flux in a hardwood forest watershed and an eastern white pine watershed at Coweeta Hydrologic Laboratory. In Mineral Cycling in Southeastern Ecosystems, edited by F. G. Howell, J. B. Gentry, and M. H. Smith, pp. 847-861. ERDA Symp. Series (CONF-740513).

Bormann, F. H., and G. E. Likens. 1967. Nutrient cycling. Science 155:424-49.

Bormann, F. H., G. E. Likens, and J. M. Melillo. 1977. Nitrogen budget for an aggrading northern hardwood forest ecosystem. Science 196:981-983.

Botkin, D. B. 1980. Perturbation frequency and ecosystem stability. In this volume.

Botkin, D. B., and M. J. Sobel. 1975. Stability in time-varying ecosystems. Amer. Natur. 109:625-646.

Boyle, J. R., J. J. Phillips, and A. R. Ek. 1973. "Whole tree" harvesting: nutrient budget evaluation. J. For. 71: 760-762.

Child, G. I., and H. H. Shugart, Jr. 1972. Frequency response analysis of magnesium cycling in a tropical forest ecosystem. In Systems Analysis and Simulation in Ecology, Vol. 2, edited by B. C. Patten, pp. 103-135. New York: Academic Press, Inc.

Cromack, K., Jr., and C. D. Monk. 1975. Litter production, decomposition, and nutrient cycling in a mixed hardwood watershed and a white pine watershed. In Mineral Cycling in Southeastern Ecosystems, edited by F. G. Howell, J. B. Gentry, and M. H. Smith, pp. 609-624. ERDA Symp. Series (CONF-740513).

Dalton, D. A., and D. B. Zobel. 1977. Ecological effects of nitrogen fixation by Purshia tridentata. Plant Soil 48: 57-80.

Dyrness, C. T., and C. T. Youngberg. 1966. Soil-vegetation relationships within the ponderosa pine type in the central Oregon pumice region. Ecology 47: 122-138.

Fogel, R., and K. Cromack, Jr. 1977. Effect of habitat and substrate quality on Douglas-fir litter decomposition in western Oregon. Can. J. Bot. 55: 1632-1640.

Franklin, J. F., and R. H. Waring. 1980. Distinctive features of the northwestern coniferous forest: Development, structure, and function. In this volume.

Fredriksen, R. L. 1975. Nitrogen, phosphorous, and particulate matter budgets of five coniferous forest ecosystems in the Western Cascades Range, Oregon. Ph.D. thesis, Oregon State University, Corvallis.

Gosz, J. R., G. E. Likens, and F. H. Bormann. 1973. Nutrient release from decomposing leaf and branch litter in the Hubbard Brook Forest, New Hampshire. Ecol. Monogr. 43:173-191.

Grier, C. C., D. W. Cole, C. T. Dyrness, and R. L. Frederiksen. 1974. Nutrient cycling in 37 and 450-year-old Douglas-fir ecosystems. In Integrated Research in the Coniferous Forest Biome, edited by R. H. Waring and R.L. Edmonds, pp. 21-34. Univ. of Washington, Coll. Forest Resources, Conif. For. Biome Bull. 5.

Harwell, M. A., W. P. Cropper, Jr., and H. L. Ragsdale. 1977. Nutrient cycling and stability: A reevaluation. Ecology 58:660-666.

Henderson, G. S., and W. F. Harris. 1975. An ecosystem approach to the characterization of the nitrogen cycle in a deciduous forest watershed. In Forest Soils and Forest Land Management, edited by B. Bernier and C. H. Winget, pp. 179-193. Quebec: Laval University Press.

Henderson, G. S., W. T. Swank, J. B. Waide, and C. C. Grier. 1978. Nutrient budgets of Appalachian and Cascade region watersheds: A comparison. Forest Sci. 24:385-397.

Hornbeck, J. W. 1977. Nutrients: A major consideration in intensive forest management. In Proc. Symp. on Intensive Culture of Northern Forest Types, pp. 241-250. USDA Forest Service Gen. Tech. Rep. NE-29.

Huff, D. D., W. T. Swank, C. A. Troendle, G. S. Henderson, J. B. Waide, and T. Haynes. 1978. Element cycles and water budget analyses applied to forest management in the eastern United States. Soc. Amer. For. Proc. 1978: 77-89.

Hutchinson, G. E. 1948. Circular causal systems in ecology. Ann. N. Y. Acad. Sci. 50:221-246.

Ike, A. F., Jr., and E. L. Stone. 1958. Soil nitrogen accumulation under black locust. Soil Sci. Soc. Amer. Proc. 22:346-349.

Johnson, P. L., and W. T. Swank. 1973. Studies on cation budgets in the southern Appalachians on four experimental watersheds with contrasting vegetation. Ecology 54:70-80.

Jorgensen, J. R., C. G. Wells, and L. J. Metz. 1975. The nutrient cycle: key to continuous forest production. J. For. 73:400-403.

Keeves, A. 1966. Some evidence of loss of productivity with successive rotations of Pinus radiata in the South-East of South Australia. Austr. For. 30:51-63.

Kimmins, J. P. 1977. Evaluation of the consequences for future tree productivity of the loss of nutrients in whole-tree harvesting. Forest Ecol. Management 1:169-183.

Koch, P., and D. W. McKenzie. 1976. Machine to harvest slush, brush, and thinnings for fuel and fiber--a concept. J. For. 74:809-812.

Larson, M. J., M. F. Jurgensen, and A. E. Harvey. 1978. N_2 fixation associated with wood decayed by some common fungi in western Montana. Can. J. Forest Res. 8:341-345.

Likens, G. E., F. H. Bormann, N. M. Johnson, and R. S. Pierce. 1967. The calcium, magnesium, potassium, and sodium budgets in a small forested ecosystem. Ecology 48:772-785.

Likens, G. E., F. H. Bormann, N. M. Johnson, D. W. Fisher, and R. S. Pierce. 1970. Effects of forest cutting and herbicide treatment on nutrient budgets in the Hubbard Brook watershed-ecosystem. Ecol. Monogr. 40:23-47.

Likens, G. E., F. H. Bormann, R. S. Pierce, J. S. Eaton, and N. M. Johnson. 1977. Biogeochemistry of a Forested Ecosystem. New York: Springer-Verlag.

Likens, G. E., F. H. Bormann, R. S. Pierce, and W. A. Reiners. 1978. Recovery of a deforested ecosystem. Science 199: 492-496.

Marks, P. L. 1974. The role of pin cherry (*Prunus pennsylvanica* L.) in the maintenance of stability in northern hardwood ecosystems. Ecol. Monogr. 44:73-88.

McGinty, D. T. 1976. Comparative root and soil dynamics on a white pine watershed and in the hardwood forest in the Coweeta Basin. Ph.D. thesis, University of Georgia, Athens.

Mitchell, J. E., J. B. Waide, and R. L. Todd. 1975. A preliminary compartment model of the nitrogen cycle in a deciduous forest ecosystem. In Mineral Cycling in Southeastern Ecosystems, edited by F. G. Howell, J. B. Gentry, and M. H. Smith, pp. 41-57. ERDA Symp. Series (CONF-740513).

Monk, C. D., D. A. Crossley, Jr., R. L. Todd, W. T. Swank, J. B. Waide, and J. R. Webster. 1977. An overview of nutrient cycling research at Coweeta Hydrologic Laboratory. In Watershed Research in Eastern North America, edited by D. L. Correll, pp. 35-50. Washington, D. C.: Smithsonian Institution.

Newton, M., B. A. El-Hassan, and J. Zavitkovski. 1968. Role of red alder in western Oregon forest succession. In Biology of Alder, edited by J. B. Trappe, J. F. Franklin, R. F. Tarrant, and G. H. Hansen, pp. 73-84, USDA Forest Service, Pacific Northwest Forest and Range Expt. Sta., Portland, Oregon.

O'Neill, R. V., and D. E. Reichle. 1980. Limits to ecological theory in light of recent ecosystem research. In this volume.

O'Neill, R. V., W. F. Harris, B. S. Ausmus, and D. E. Reichle. 1975. A theoretical basis for ecosystem analysis with particular reference to element cycling. In Mineral Cycling in Southeastern Ecosystems, edited by F. G. Howell, J. B. Gentry, and M. H. Smith, pp. 28-40. ERDA Symp. Series (CONF-740513).

Patric, J. H., and D. W. Smith. 1975. Forest management and nutrient cycling in eastern hardwoods. USDA Forest Service Res. Paper NE-324.

Patten, B. C. 1974. The zero state and ecosystem stability. Proc. First Internat. Congress of Ecology, The Hague, The Netherlands, Sept. 8-14, 1974 (Suppl.)

Pierce, R. S., C. W. Martin, C. C. Reeves, G. E. Likens, and F. H. Bormann. 1972. Nutrient loss from clear-cutting in New Hampshire. In Proc. Symp. Watersheds in Transition, pp. 285-295. Ft. Collins, Colo.

Pike, L. H., D. M. Tracey, M. A. Sherwood, and D. Nielsen. 1972. Estimates of biomass and fixed nitrogen of epiphytes from old-growth Douglas-fir. In Research on Coniferous Forest Ecosystems, Proc. Symp. Northwest Scientific Assoc., edited by J. F. Franklin, L. J. Demster, and R. H. Waring, pp. 177-187. USDA Forest Service, Pacific Northwest Forest and Range Expt. Sta., Portland, Oregon.

Pritchett, W. L., and C. G. Wells. 1978. Harvesting and site preparation increase nutrient mobilization. In Proceedings: A Symposium on Principles of Maintaining Productivity on Prepared Sites, edited by T. Tippen, pp. 98-110. Starkville: Mississippi State University Press.

Ribe, J. H. 1974. A review of short rotation forestry. Univ. of Maine Life Sci. and Agric. Expt. Sta., Misc. Rep. No. 160.

Ripley, T. H., and R. L. Doub. 1978. Wood energy: An overview. Amer. Forests 84:16.

Schindler, J. E., J. B. Waide, M. C. Waldron, J. J. Hains, S. P. Schreiner, M. L. Freedman, S. L. Benz, D. R. Pettigrew, L. A. Schissel, and P. J. Clarke. 1980. A microcosm approach to the study of biogeochemical systems: 1. Theoretical rationale. In Microcosms in Ecological Research, edited by J. P. Giesy. DOE Symp. Series (in press).

Shinners, S. M. 1972. Modern Control System Theory and Application. Reading, Mass.: Addison-Wesley.

Stone, E. L. 1973. The impact of timber harvest on soils and water. In Report of the President's Advisory Panel on Timber and the Environment, pp. 427-463. Washington, D.C.: U.S. Govt. Printing Office.

Swank, W. T., and J. E. Douglass. 1975. Nutrient flux in undisturbed and manipulated forest ecosystems in the southern Appalachian Mountains. Publication no. 117 des l'Association Internationale des Sciences Hydrologiques, Symposium de Tokyo (Decembre 1975).

Swank, W. T., and J. E. Douglass. 1977. A comparison of nutrient budgets for undisturbed and manipulated hardwood forest ecosystems in the mountains of North Carolina. In Watershed Research in Eastern North America, edited by D. L. Correll, pp. 343–364. Washington, D.C.: Smithsonian Institution.

Todd, R. L., J. B. Waide, and B. W. Cornaby. 1975. Significance of biological nitrogen fixation and denitrification in a deciduous forest ecosystem. In Mineral Cycling in Southeastern Ecosystems, edited by F. G. Howell, J. B. Gentry, and M. H. Smith, pp. 729–735. ERDA Symp. Series (CONF-740513).

Todd, R. L., R. D. Meyer, and J. B. Waide. 1978. Nitrogen fixation in a deciduous forest in the southeastern United States. Ecol. Bull. (Stockholm) 26:172–177.

Troup, R. S. 1928. Silvicultural Systems, 2nd ed. (1955, edited by E. W. Jones). Oxford: Clarendon Press.

Trudgill, S. T. 1977. Soil and Vegetation Systems. Oxford: Clarendon Press.

Van Voris, P. 1976. Ecological stability: An ecosystem perspective. Classical and current thoughts. A review of selected literature. Oak Ridge National Lab. Rep. ORNL/TM-5517, Oak Ridge, Tenn.

Vitousek, P. M., and W. A. Reiners. 1975. Ecosystem succession and nutrient retention: A hypothesis. BioScience 25:376–381.

Vitousek, P. M., J. R. Gosz, C. C. Grier, J. M. Melillo, W. A. Reiners, and R. L. Todd. 1979. Nitrate losses from disturbed ecosystems. Science 204:469–474.

Wahlgren, H. G. 1978. Tapping the forest resource. Amer. Forests 84:24.

Waide, J. B., and W. T. Swank. 1976. Nutrient recycling and the stability of ecosystems: Implications for forest management in the southeastern U.S. Soc. Amer. For. Proc. 1975:404–424.

Waide, J. B., and W. T. Swank. 1977. Simulation of potential effects of forest utilization on the nitrogen cycle in different southeastern ecosystems. In Watershed Research in Eastern North America, edited by D. L. Correll, pp. 767–789. Washington, D.C.: Smithsonian Institution.

Waide, J. B., and J. R. Webster. 1975. Engineering systems analysis: Applicability to ecosystems. In Systems Analysis and Simulation in Ecology, Vol. 4, edited by B. C. Patten, pp. 329–371. New York: Academic Press, Inc.

Waide, J. B., J. E. Kreb, S. P. Clarkson, and E. M. Setzler. 1977. A linear systems analysis of the calcium in a forested watershed ecosystem. In Progress in Theoretical Biology, Vol. 3, edited by R. Rosen and F. M. Snell, pp. 261–345. New York: Academic Press, Inc.

Waring, R. H., and J. F. Franklin. 1979. Evergreen coniferous forests of the Pacific Northwest. Science 204:1380–1386.

Watson, V., and O. L. Loucks. 1979. An analysis of turnover times in a lake eocystem and some implications for system properties. In Theoretical Systems Ecology: Advances and Case Studies, edited by E. Halfon, pp. 355–383. New York: Academic Press, Inc.

Webber, B. 1978. Potential increase in nutrient requirements of Pinus radiata under intensified management. N.Z. J. For. Sci. 8:146–159.

Webster, J. R., J. B. Waide, and B. C. Patten. 1975. Nutrient recycling and the stability of ecosystems. In Mineral Cycling in Southeastern Ecosystems, edited by F. G. Howell, J. B. Gentry and M. H. Smith, pp. 1–27. ERDA Symp. Series (CONF-740513).

Wells, C. G., and J. R. Jorgensen. 1975.
    Nutrient cycling in loblolly pine
    plantations. In Forest Soils and For-
    est Land Management, edited by B.
    Bernier and C. H. Winget, pp. 137-158.
    Quebec: Laval University Press.

Wells, C. G., J. R. Jorgensen, and C. E.
    Burnette. 1975. Biomass and mineral
    elements in a thinned loblolly pine
    plantation at age 16, USDA Forest
    Service Res. Paper SE-126.

Whyte, A. G. D. 1973. Productivity of
    first and second crops of Pinus radiata
    on the Moutere gravel soils of Nelson.
    N.Z. J. For. 18:87-103.

Youngberg, C. T., and A. T. Wollum. 1976.
    Nitrogen accretion in developing
    Ceanothus velutinus stands. Soil Sci.
    Soc. Amer. J. 40:109-112.

Geomorphology and Ecosystems

Frederick J. Swanson

INTRODUCTION

Natural ecosystems develop through the interplay of physical and biological factors. Biological factors have traditionally been emphasized because most ecologists have life science backgrounds. The purpose of this paper is to explore the significance of earth science perspectives in understanding ecosystems. Particularly in mountain landscapes and along streams and rivers, geomorphic processes and landforms have important roles in the development and geographic distribution of plant and animal communities. Geomorphologists and ecologists working in these dynamic landscapes have long relied on insights from each other's discipline to interpret causes and patterns of ecologic and geomorphic change. The full richness of geomorphic-biologic interactions really emerges from programs of ecosystem analysis where earth and life scientists work closely together on common topics, sites, and time frames.

In the pre-twentieth century era of naturalists, the mixing of earth and life science perspectives was common. In this century, there has been parallelism and interchange in the evolution of general models in geomorphology, plant ecology, and animal ecology (Drury and Nisbet, 1971). William Morris Davis' cyclical model of long-term (10^7-10^8 years) landform development set the stage for the views of vegetation development put forth by Clements (1936) and Braun (1950). The interpreted vegetation and landforms as progressing together toward a common end point--the peneplain with deep mature soils and "climax" vegetation on a nearly level landscape. Gilbert (1880), Gleason (1926), and Hack and Goodlett (1960) put forth alternative concepts of landform-vegetation relations based on dynamic short-term (immediate) interactions among vegetation, soils, water, and landforms in an open

system and on a variety of time scales. Hack and Goodlett (1960) argue that the landscape and vegetation development models of Davis and Clements are incorrect in their application to the Appalachian Mountains where they were initially developed. A model involving steady state in an open system has greater explanatory power and heuristic value in Hack and Goodlett's view. A system may be shifted from steady state by a variety of disturbances ranging from short-term events such as flash floods to long-term changes in climate or relief. Those components of the system, whose rate of response is fast relative to disturbance frequency, react to produce a new steady state.

This view of a dynamic landscape-ecosystem with the potential for biotic-geomorphic interaction over a broad range of time scales is the subject of this paper. First, I will discuss time scales of geomorphic and ecosystem variation and consider the importance of a broad time perspective in analyzing landscape and ecosystem development. From this perspective, I will briefly examine an array of interactions among fauna, flora, landforms, and geomorphic processes, concluding with a more detailed analysis of soil and sediment movement through forest watersheds and the role of vegetation in regulating material transfer and storage.

TEMPORAL PERSPECTIVES

How one perceives interactions between geomorphic and ecosystem factors depends not only on the particular landscape and ecosystem in question, but also on the time scale used for viewing the system. Types and intensities of interactions between plants and landforms, for example, on the long-time frame of landform development and biologic evolution contrast with the short-term interaction of daily operation of geomorphic processes and growth response of individual plants. Thus, in order to examine physical-biotic relationships in natural ecosystems, it is useful to recognize the full range of temporal scales of variation in both physical and biological parts of the system and then compare system behavior at appropriate time scales.

To help clarify this point, let us look at an example from the Douglas-fir/western hemlock forest ecosystem in the Cascade Mountains of Oregon (Table 1). This charting of temporal scales of landscape-ecosystem change is an outgrowth of the process of earth scientists and biologists learning to work together in an interdisciplinary research team, the Coniferous Forest Biome (CFB) of the U.S./International Biological Program. In early 1970, I began working with CFB as a geologist mapping bedrock in the H. J. Andrews Experimental Forest, a primary CFB study site. Although working side by side with terrestrial and aquatic ecologists, we had little in common, because our time frames were disjunct. I was mapping formations no younger than 3.5 million years old; the time period of major concern to the ecologists was the annual scale of nutrient budgets and physiological behavior of plants and animals. These differences in time perspective raised questions about the sorts of geomorphology-ecosystem interactions that occur over the full range of time scales from days to millions of years. Where is the common ground for interaction between geomorphologists and ecologists?

Major exogenous events affect ecosystems and landscapes over a broad range of frequencies of occurrence (Table 1). These events include climatic and geologic processes as well as major disturbances of vegetation such as fire for which ignition may be considered exogenous, but intensity and areal extent of burns may be controlled by endogenous vegetation and landscape factors. Some of these events are regular and cyclical in occurrence, while others are episodic and their frequency would be considered here in terms of average return period.

Geomorphic factors vary over this time scale, ranging from relatively frequent changes in rates of geomorphic processes to the long-term development of the physiographic province as a whole. Development of progressively larger landforms occurs on progressively longer time scales. Geomorphic response to the most frequent exogenous events listed does not lead to development of landforms attributable to an individual event. At intermediate time

scales, landforms of intermediate spatial scale, such as terraces, fans, and moraines, form in response to exogenous events. On still longer time frames, landform elements of greater geographic extent develop as the sum of all higher frequency geomorphic responses to exogenous events.

Vegetation also responds in various ways across this broad time range. Individual plants have physiological response to daily and seasonal fluctuation of moisture and temperature regimes. On the scale of centuries, vegetation (secondary) succession occurs following major ecosystem disturbances such as fire, landslides, and extensive blowdown events. Primary succession, shifts in the range of species and plant communities, and microevolution occur, in part, in response to and on the time scale of major climatic change. Most significant macroevolution takes place over still longer time periods.

To some extent, Table 1 is arranged in a hierarchical structure. Geomorphic and vegetative changes on each time scale involve response to exogenous events at that time scale as well as to the sum of all higher frequency variation in that system. For example, formation of terraces and alluvial fans may be facilitated by climate change and glaciation on the scale of 10^3 to 10^4 years, but the actual constructional processes occur as more frequent "base flow" erosion and pulses of accelerated sedimentation at the scales of decades and centuries.

One aspect of hierarchially organized systems is that system behaviors are "nearly decomposable," such that system behavior at one level or frequency may be isolated from scales of variation of higher and lower frequencies (Simon, 1973; Monk et al., 1977). Many studies of natural systems focus on one organizational level, assuming that lower frequency variations of the system are so slow that they can be considered constant and higher frequency behaviors are so rapid "that only their steady state properties appear in the system description" (Monk et al., 1977). However, CFB research in natural systems has revealed many problems with this common assumption. A notable example arose when aquatic ecologists began to compile an annual carbon budget for a small stream ecosystem. After sampling two successive years and finding two very different budgets, they quickly realized that the annual scale of behavior of this system depended strongly on streamflow characteristics for the sample period. Inputs exceeded output by about 40% in a dry year, but were nearly balanced in the wetter year, although no major peak flows occurred (Triska et al., in press).

Table 1. *Geomorphic and vegetative variation and exogenous events affecting ecosystems and landscapes on an array of time scales (example from Douglas-fir/western hemlock forests in Cascade Mountains, Oregon)*

Event frequency (yrs)	Exogenous events	Geomorphic variation	Vegetation variation
10^{-2} to 10^{-1}	Precipitation-discharge event		
10^0 to 10^1	Annual water budget, moderate storms	"Base-flow" erosion by noncatastrophic processes	Physiologic response of individual plants
10^2	Extreme storms, major disturbances of vegetation (e.g., fire)	Periods of accelerated erosion—slide scars, channel changes, etc.	Secondary succession
10^3 to 10^4	Climate change, glaciation	Intermediate-scale landforms; terraces, fans, moraines, etc.	
10^6	Episodes of volcanism	Gross morphology of major drainage and constructional (volcanic) landforms	Primary succession, migration, microevolution
10^7 to 10^8	- - - - - -	Development of physiographic province as a whole	Macroevolution

Furthermore, the system had a good memory for detrital input and channel flushing events in earlier years. It is necessary to place annual budgets in the context of broader temporal variability of the system (the 10^2 yr scale of Table 1).

Geomorphology-ecosystem interactions are most dramatic on intermediate time scales--decades and centuries (Table 1). On longer and especially shorter time frames, geomorphic setting is commonly viewed as a passive, invariant stage on which evolution and plant physiologic behavior take place. But on the intermediate scale of secondary succession, change in plant community composition, vigor, and structure can profoundly affect rates of geomorphic processes. Geomorphic events may, in turn, set the stage for succession by creating fresh substrates and may determine to some extent the rate and type of plant community development that follows a major ecosystem disturbance.

The detailed character of geomorphology-ecosystem interactions vary from one landscape-ecosystem type to another. This interaction is particularly dynamic in the coniferous forest ecosystems of the steep Cascade terrain, where vegetation is important in regulating soil and sediment movement down slopes and streams. Historically, these forests and landscapes experienced widespread wildfire, floods, landslides, and windstorms, which caused profound fluctuations in sedimentation. Today, the major process of stand and landscape disturbance is clearcut logging and associated road construction and slash disposal.

Over the course of CFB and subsequent research projects, earth scientists and biologists in our group have developed a common focus on questions at the intermediate time scale of system behavior such as ecosystem response to disturbances like logging, wildfire, and geomorphic events. The overriding concern is to understand how nature has "managed" forests, streams, and landscapes on a variety of time scales to set a basis for evaluating and directing man's management programs.

GEOMORPHIC-BIOTIC INTERACTIONS

Interactions between physical and biological realms of ecosystems offer many unexplored but interesting and fruitful research topics that tend to fall between disciplines (Fig. 1). Much of geomorphology concerns the long-term effects of geomorphic processes in sculpting landforms and the ways that landforms determine spatial distribution of geomorphic processes in the short term. Many studies in geo-

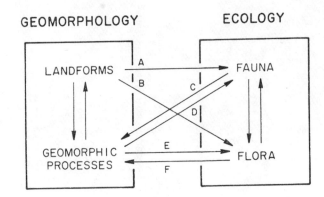

Figure 1. Relationships among landforms, geomorphic processes, fauna, and flora. A. Define habitat, range. Effects through flora. B. Define habitat. Determine disturbance potential by fire, wind. C. Affect soil movement by surface and mass erosion. Affect fluvial processes by damming, trampling. D. Sedimentation processes affect aquatic organisms. Effects through flora. E. Destroy vegetation. Disrupt growth by tipping, splitting, stoning. Create new sites for establishment and distinctive habitats. Transfer nutrients. F. Regulate soil and sediment transfer and storage.

morphology benefit from biological information derived by methods such as dendrochronology that have been exploited to only a limited extent. Fields of ecology center on relations between fauna and flora, including herbivore, habitat structuring, and the like. Ecologists have a long tradition of using information on the physical environment to interpret biological factors, but there are still many instances where ecological understanding would be enhanced by improved appreciation for the role of physical factors in ecosystems.

Linkages among geomorphic processes, landforms, fauna, and flora are manifold. Figure 1 shows interactions of major importance in forest and stream ecosystems in geomorphically active landscapes. Many of the following examples of these interactions have emerged as a result of interdisciplinary ecosystem research. We begin with landform effects on flora and fauna, then move to flora and fauna interactions with geomorphic processes, ending with regulation of geomorphic processes by vegetation, the latter probably having greatest significance to land managers.

Effects of Landforms on Flora

On the time scale of secondary succession and related major disturbances of vegetation, landforms are relatively invariant templates on which mosaics of vegetation develop. Actual patterns of vegetation types and age classes over landscapes are determined by the interplay of landforms and flora. Effects of landforms on vegetation development at a site are generally mediated by microclimatic, edaphic, and hydrologic factors. Elevation slope, and aspect, for example, are elements of landform whose main effects on vegetation are through microclimate. Slope steepness, the product of long-term landform development, influences erosion potential of soil and soil texture and nutrient capital. Narrower ridge tops and steeper slopes generally experience greater soil turnover and nutrient depletion by physical processes than more gentle topography. These effects can often be recognized in chlorotic condition of young conifer stands on these physiograph sites. Both slope steepness and soil texture determine drainage characteristics of a soil.

Soil properties are profoundly influenced by geologic factors, mainly bedrock type, and geomorphic factors that control accumulation, redistribution, and mixing of soil. In the Pacific Northwest, volcanic ash falling from the sky is an important, widespread type of soil parent material that can blanket diverse landscapes from distant sources. More typical depositional soils (alluvial, colluvial, and aeolian) commonly form the deepest, most fertile soils.

Landforms also influence vegetation by affecting the potential for disturbance of vegetation at a site. This vegetation-physical process-landform set of relationships is obvious where recurrences of the physical process have shaped the landform as well as the vegetation community. An example is the role played by floodwater in inundation and sediment deposition, which form floodplain features and associated vegetation patterns. Both the magnitude of flood impact on channel form and time for recovery of channel form depend strongly on the character of streamside vegetation (Wolman and Gerson, 1978).

Landforms play a more subtle role in determining vegetation conditions where the vegetation disturbance mechanisms are wind and fire rather than geomorphic processes. Slope position and valley configuration are important variables affecting windthrow potential of a site (Ruth and Yoder, 1953). Topography can channel and funnel winds and create intense turbulence on the lee side of ridges. Since windthrow potential is a function of tree size and shape and stand structure, topography and wind may conspire at some sites to repeatedly blow down stands as they reach a certain stage of development.

Frequency and intensity of fire at a site is also regulated by landforms in several ways (Swanson, in press). In many landscapes and storm types, topography influences geographic distribution of lightning strikes. Once ignition has occurred, type and rate of fire spread are determined by fuel conditions, wind, and topography (Brown and Davis, 1973). Faster, more intense burning occurs on steeper slopes in response to convective winds and preheating of fuels uphill of a fire front. Steep, sunny slopes have dryer fuels than flatter slopes or slopes of other aspect. The role of topography in channeling winds also affects the geographic patterns of fire regime.

Landforms also influence fire pattern by creating natural firebreaks. Completely forested but sharp ridges may be effective firebreaks where upslope mountain winds prevent fire from moving down lee slopes. Lakes, streams, talus fields, snow avalanche, and landslide tracks form more conspicuous firebreaks. Effectiveness of these landscape elements as firebreaks depends on fire intensity and direction of fire spread relative to the "grain" of topography (Swanson, in press). Landforms are more effective as firebreaks during lower intensity fires burning perpendicular to drainage pattern or other potential firebreaks.

The net effects of landforms on soil formation, geomorphic processes, vegetation disturbance regime, and light, water, and nutrient availability at a site result in systematic variation in vegetation with respect to topographic position, slope, and aspect. These effects are most pronounced in steep terrain where topographic shading and ridgetop to channel soil moisture gradients are important. Resulting vegetation patterns include more mesic communities along streams, more xeric types on ridges, and greater extent of mesic types on slopes facing away from the afternoon sun. Hack and Goodlett (1960) interpret this pattern at a site in the central Appalachians principally in terms of variation in soil water-holding capability as determined by soil texture and soil-forming geomorphic processes. A similar vegetation pattern in the Cascade Range of Oregon has been interpreted more in terms of microclimate and topographic shading (Hawk, 1979).

Effects of Landforms on Fauna

Landforms affect fauna by determining the geographic distribution of habitats and by forming special habitats. The major

influence of landform on fauna is a result
of landform effects on vegetation patterns,
since vegetation structure and distribution
determine habitat and range for most forest-
dwelling animals. Many examples come to
mind, especially with respect to migratory
large mammals whose annual ranges cover
diverse vegetation types. Distribution of
this vegetation, associated snow conditions,
and other habitat factors are commonly
strongly influenced by landforms. Floodplains and valley bottom vegetation, for
example, provide winter range, connectors
between diverse terrestrial habitat types,
and corridors for migration (Thomas et al.,
1979). Vegetation analysis of the type done
by Whittaker (1956) in the Smokies and elsewhere illustrate strongly the multiple
effects of landform on community pattern.

In a more special sense, distinctive
landforms provide special habitat opportunities, termed "geomorphic habitats" by
Maser and others (in press). Caves, talus,
and cliff faces may be utilized by animals
of a great variety of sizes and habits depending on size, stability, and accessibility
of nesting, denning, perching, and other
types of sites (Maser et al., 1979). In the
Basin and Range physiographic province
cliffs and associated talus slopes formed
along river canyons, glaciated valley walls,
and fault scarps support rich fauna in
terrain with little other large-scale
habitat density. The character of these
geomorphic habitats is determined in part
by rock type, overall topography, and mode
of origin. Type of bedrock influences the
size of talus blocks shed from a cliff and
shape and size of cavities in cliffs.
Cliff height, shape, and aspect affect
localized wind currents and utilization by
birds, particularly raptors (Craighead and
Craighead, 1969). Canyon walls cut by
rivers provide less talus and more cliff
types of habitats, because the river carries
away many of the talus blocks. Proportion
of talus to cliff habitat is higher on
fault scarps and walls of U-shaped glaciated
valleys where talus accumulates for long
periods of time.

These examples of rather obvious influences of landforms on flora and fauna
suggest an infinite complex of more subtle
physical-biological interactions running
through all large-scale natural ecosystems.
At successional and higher frequency time
scales most landforms can be viewed as the
stage or template on which geomorphic-
biologic process interactions occur.

Effects of Fauna on Geomorphic Processes

Animal activities increase the rate of
geomorphic processes by directly moving
soil or by altering soil properties, hydrology, or vegetation with the result of
accelerating subsequent erosion at a site.
Soil that is moved by burrowing animals
ranging in size from earthworms to small
mammals can be a significant component of
soil creep (Carson and Kirkby, 1972). Excavation of burrows usually involves downslope soil movement, as does subsequent
burrow collapse and erosion of bare soil on
burrow mounds (Imeson, 1976; Imeson and
Kwaad, 1976). Charles Darwin (1881) observed in detail downslope movement of
earthworm castings during dry, rainy, and
windy periods and attempted to quantify the
role of earthworms in overall landscape
denudation. Few studies since have carefully documented rates of soil movement by
animals, but qualitative observations are
common. Evidence of downslope soil movement by large mammals, particularly elk, is
conspicuous where population densities are
high. Grazing livestock accelerates erosion especially where stock concentrate in
streams and riparian zones, trampling banks
and stirring up sediment. Fluvial geomorphic processes are also affected by dam
construction, harvest of riparian vegetation, and bank burrowing by beaver.

Many impacts of animals on geomorphic
processes are the result of indirect effects
of altered vegetation, soil properties, and
hydrology. Reduced litter due to browsing
and increased compaction as a result of
trampling can cause accelerated surface
erosion, but these effects are not likely
to occur in forest ecosystems where grazing
intensities are low. Other subtle effects
of animal activity may occur. Pierson
(1977) suggested that mountain beaver
(Aplodontia rufa) burrows in areas of the
Oregon Coast Ranges may pipe water rapidly
into mass movement prone areas, thereby
increasing the potential for soil mantle
failure. Kelsey (1978) and others have
discussed the possibility that introduction
with livestock of short-rooted, annual
grasses to prairies and oak savanna, earthflow areas of northwestern California may
have led to accelerated earthflow movement
since the late 1880's. They hypothesize
that earthflow activity was less when
native deep-rooted, perennial species provided greater evapotranspiration and root
strength.

Although these examples are of a very
anecdotal nature, collectively they indicate that effects of fauna on geomorphic

processes are probably significant in many forest ecosystems.

Effects of Geomorphic Processes on Fauna

Most effects of geomorphic processes on fauna occur indirectly as a result of influences of geomorphic processes on flora and landforms, discussed in other sections. Direct effects in terrestrial environments are minimized in part by the mobility of animals. In stream ecosystems, on the other hand, sedimentation processes can have immediate and direct impacts on aquatic organisms. Microenvironments within a stream reach are shaped by the interplay of hydraulic processes, sediment characteristics, organic debris, and bedrock. Resulting channel geometry at the scales of gravel fabric, pool-riffle sequences, and downstream decreases in gradient provide a great variety of microhabitats. The many species and functional groups (Cummins, 1974) of aquatic organism are precisely distributed over this physically defined array of microhabitats (Hynes, 1970).

Stream water velocity, for example, is a critical factor in determining distribution of organisms (Hynes, 1970). Leaf and needle processing organisms such as caddis flies reside in the relatively quiet water of eddies behind boulders and logs and in pools where organic detritus collects. Many collector organisms (Cummins, 1974) build their tiny nets on stable substrates like large pieces of wood or in interstices between rocks where the current carries sufficient organic detritus to support the organisms, but does not flow at such high velocity that it destroys the nets.

Increased sediment availability, transport, and deposition causes a variety of disruptions of aquatic organisms in these habitats. A thin film of clay and silt-sized sediment deposited over organic detritus can render this food and case-building material unusable by clogging mouths and gills of shredder organisms. The nets of organisms collecting fine organic detritus from the water column may become filled with inorganic sediment. Accumulation of fine sediment in interstitial areas of spawning sites restricts flow of oxygenated water to eggs and decreases the opportunity for alevins to move through the gravel to open stream water once they have hatched.

Extremely high streamflow events can reshape stream channels and change the distribution of aquatic microhabitats. Major abrupt geomorphic disruptions commonly have a surprisingly small, short-lived impact on aquatic organisms (Hoopes, 1974). Organisms survive major floods by finding protected sites in gravel, behind logs, amongst roots and flooded vegetation, and in the lower portions of low gradient tributary streams. Many insects have life cycles with terrestrial phases during periods of high potential for major flooding. Streams are rapidly recolonized following a major flood by organisms from these terrestrial and aquatic refugia.

Thus, the mobility of animals is a cause of weaker linkage between geomorphic processes and fauna than between geomorphic processes and flora, the latter being very important.

Effects of Geomorphic Processes on Flora

Geomorphic processes affect vegetation in all stages of development. In the context of succession on bare mineral soil, geomorphic processes may initially "filter" the species of plants established on a site. Surface erosion processes may move seeds of some species off the site, while species with other seed characteristics or reproductive strategies may become established. Established seedlings may be lifted out of the soil by frost heaving and growth of needle ice. Geomorphic processes disrupt growth of established trees by tipping, splitting, and moving soil and stones against them. Disrupted growth of trees that form regular annual rings commonly provides excellent records of geomorphic activity at a site (e.g., Potter, 1969; Schroder, 1978; Carrara, 1979).

These disturbances to individual plants alter overall stand composition and structure. On an earthflow in a coniferous forest (Swanson and Swanston, 1977), for example, areas of open ground cracks indicative of differential ground movement have complex stands with numerous holes in the canopy where many of the heavily leaning trees have been blown down. Opening of the canopy has resulted in extensive development of understory vegetation and a multilayered forest. Adjacent stands not subject to recent earth movement have complete, single-level canopies and no significant understory due to heavy shading.

Geomorphic processes such as streambank cutting and landslides completely remove vegetation, but in the process create fresh sites for establishment of new plant communities. Less destructive events such as overbank deposition of fine sediment may suppress herbs for a period of time, but also allow establishment of species which root on disturbed bare mineral soil. Geomorphic disturbances can selectively affect specific components of a plant community like other disturbance processes such as fire and harvest.

At the whole ecosystem level physical processes have important roles in nutrient cycling regimes. This is most clearly recognized in the case of stream eocsystems where the biota resides in flowing water--the principal sediment transport medium. The analogous transience and mobility of the physical environment of terrestrial ecosystems are not so easily recognized because soil movement is accomplished by a mix of slow and episodic processes. But on a broad time perspective and in steep terrain the soil mantle and its accompanying terrestrial ecosystem are moving inexorably downslope. Consequently, nutrient capital of a site reflects the long-term balance of nutrient input and output processes. Physical transport of nutrients in steep terrain is an important factor in nutrient cycling and may limit accumulation of nutrients in an ecosystem (Sollins et al., in press).

The importance of geomorphic processes as nutrient transfer vectors needs further consideration in analysis and comparison of nutrient cycling regimes of diverse ecosystems. Nutrient cycling studies typically assess storage sites and transfers for only

a few years or less. Such studies run the risk of failing to account for episodic events with return periods of many years, but which accomplish in a few minutes or days the results of many "average" years (Swanson et al., in press). Debris avalanches and windthrow are two potentially dominant processes that are readily overlooked in short-term studies.

Effects of Flora on Geomorphic Processes

Vegetation regulates the movement and temporary storage of soil and sediment on hillslopes and in small to intermediate-sized streams. To appreciate the importance and variety of vegetation effects it is useful to first describe a soil/sediment routing system typical of forested mountainous terrain (Fig. 2). This model is simplified from systems defined by Dietrich and Dunne (1978) and Swanson and others (in press).

Soil moves down hillslopes by a variety of mass movement and surface erosion processes. Once in the channel, this material, now termed sediment, is moved downstream by another set of transfer processes. A single particle of material moves through a watershed from one temporary storage site to another in a series of steps by different transfer processes, and it may move by several processes simultaneously.

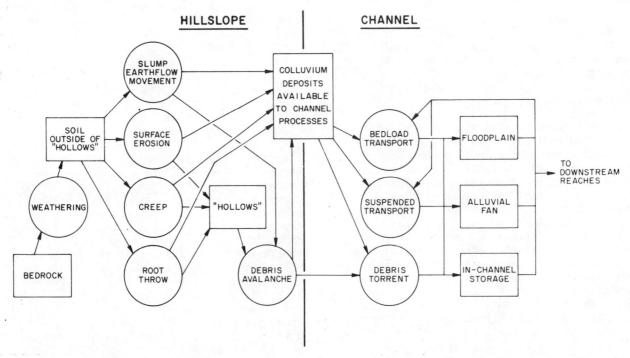

HILLSLOPE   **CHANNEL**

Figure 2. A model of soil and sediment movement through steep, forested watersheds. Transfer processes are circled. Storage areas are denoted by rectangles.

The soil mantle, for example, has several components subject to different sets of processes. All the soil surface is susceptible to surface erosion processes, and the entire soil mantle moves by the subtle group of processes termed "creep," including rheological soil deformation and root throw. Portions of a landscape subject to slump and earthflow movement also experience creep and surface erosion. These processes move soil directly to streams, where it may reside temporarily in deposits of colluvium until it is eroded during high streamflow events. Surface erosion, root throw, and creep also move soil into "hollows," linear depressions in the bedrock surface oriented downslope (Dietrich and Dunne, 1978). Periodically during conditions of extremely high soil moisture, soil stored in hollows fails and moves rapidly downslope as debris avalanches. Debris avalanches that enter small steep channels may maintain their momentum and continue to move rapidly downstream, picking up alluvium, colluvium, and organic material along the way.

Bedload and suspended sediment transport processes move particulate matter through channels. Sediment is stored in floodplains, alluvial fans, and a variety of in-channel sites, including point bars and deposits associated with large organic debris, such as logjams. Storage behind large organic debris is most important in headwater channels, whereas floodplain and non-debris-related storage sites are progressively more significant in larger channels (Swanson and Lienkaemper, 1978).

Forest vegetation strongly influences nearly all elements of the soil/sediment routing system on slopes and in small streams (Swanson et al., in press). Organic litter protects the soil surface by dissipating the energy of throughfall and raindrops and increasing the infiltration rate, thus decreasing the potential for overland flow. Evapotranspiration functions of vegetation reduce soil moisture which may significantly affect seasonal rates of creep and slump-earthflow movement (Gray, 1970). At many sites root throw associated with blowdown of trees is the major mechanism of soil movement. Roots increase soil strength, thereby decreasing the potential for shallow rapid soil mass movements (Swanston, 1969, 1970; O'Loughlin, 1974). Root systems contribute up to 40% of soil shear strength in some key landslide-prone areas (Dietrich and Dunne, 1978). Removal of material in solution in ground and stream waters is regulated in part by rate of nutrient uptake by vegetation (Likens et al., 1977). Sediment storage capacity of small channels is greatly influenced by the presence of large organic debris.

As a result of these and other effects of vegetation on geomorphic processes, sediment yield from small steep watersheds typically increases dramatically, but temporarily, following severe disturbance of vegetation by processes such as wildfire and clearcutting. Accelerated sedimentation commonly results more from increased availability of sediment for transport than from increased availability of water to transport sediment. Clearcut logging, for example, can trigger increased sediment yield by (1) input of soil and organic detritus to channels during timber felling, bucking, and yarding operations, (2) release of sediment stored in channels by removing large organic debris that trapped sediment prior to logging, and (3) reduction of ground cover, nutrient uptake, evapotranspiration, and root strength, all of which accelerate soil erosion following logging.

Erosion rates from disturbed sites recover to pre-disturbance levels partly as a result of revegetation and re-establishment of the various controls of vegetation on geomorphic processes. Because each erosion process is regulated by a different set of vegetation factors, recovery rates differ from process to process (Swanson et al., in press). On many sites, for example, invading herbs and residual vegetation rapidly reduce nutrient losses in solution, but redevelopment of a substantial network of woody roots may take a decade or more.

Consequently, erosion, sediment yield, and soil/sediment routing in steep forest land must be viewed in terms of succession and stand history, since the relative importance and absolute rates of geomorphic processes vary significantly on this time scale. In evaluating the geomorphic effects of man's activities in forest ecosystems, it is essential to contrast the frequency and erosion consequences of major vegetation disturbances in natural and managed systems.

SUMMARY AND CONCLUSIONS

Geomorphic factors, both processes and landforms, play important active and passive roles in forest ecosystems. Many influences of geomorphic processes and landforms on vegetation are mediated by physical, nutritional, and hydrologic properties of soils. Landforms principally determine the geographic distributions of fauna and flora. Landform effects on terrestrial fauna are mainly the result of landform-flora interactions. Geomorphic processes and flora interact strongly in steep terrain and along streams and rivers.

Live and dead vegetation regulates rates of geomorphic processes, which, in turn, destroy vegetation, create new opportunities for establishment, and influence the development of plant communities.

In considering the evolution of concepts of ecosystem development, a major contribution of geomorphology has been to provide time limits and temporal perspectives on ecosystem change. Clearly, forest ecosystem development on many time scales involves the interplay of physical and biological factors, particularly in mountainous regions. The physical sciences should be well represented in any major ecosystem study.

LITERATURE CITED

Braun, E. L. 1950. Deciduous Forests of Eastern North America. Philadelphia, Pa.: Blackiston.

Brown, A. A., and K. P. Davis. 1973. Forest Fire Control and Use, 2nd ed. New York: McGraw-Hill Co.

Carrara, P. E. 1979. The determination of snow avalanche frequency through tree-ring analysis and historical records at Ophir, Colorado. Geol. Soc. Amer. Bull., Pt. 1, 90:773-780.

Carson, M. A., and M. J. Kirkby. 1972. Hillsope Form and Process. London: Cmabridge University Press.

Clements, F. E. 1936. Nature and structure of the climax. J. Ecol. 24:252-284.

Craighead, J. J., and F. C. Craighead. 1969. Hawks, Owls, and Wildlife. New York: Dover Publ., Inc.

Cummins, K. W. 1974. Structure and function of stream ecosystems. BioScience 24:631-641.

Darwin, Charles. 1881. The formation of vegetable mould through the action of worms with observations on their habits, reprint (1945). London: Faber and Faber, Ltd.

Dietrich, W. E., and T. Dunne. 1978. Sediment budget for a small catchment in mountainous terrain. Zeit. für Geomorphol. Suppl. Bd. 29:191-206.

Drury, W. H., and I. C. T. Nisbet. 1971. Inter-relations between developmental models in geomorphology, plant ecology, and animal ecology. In Yearbook, Soc. Gen. Syst. Res., edited by L. von Bertalannfy and A. Rapoport, pp. 57-68.

Gilbert, G. K. 1880 (2nd ed.) Report on the geology of the Henry Mountains, U.S. Dept. Interior, Geographical and Geological Survey of the Rocky Mountain Region. Washington, D.C.: U.S. Govt. Printing Office.

Gleason, H. A. 1926. The individualistic concept of the plant association. Bull. Torrey Bot. Club 53:7-26.

Gray, D. H. 1970. Effects of forest clear-cutting on the stability of natural slopes. Bull. Assoc. Eng. Geol. 7: 45-66.

Hack, J. T., and J. C. Goodlett. 1960. Geomorphology and forest ecology of a mountain region in the central Appalachians. U.S. Geol. Surv. Prof. Paper 347.

Hawk, G. M. 1979. Vegetation mapping and community description of a small western Cascade watershed. Northwest Sci. 53:200-212.

Hoopes, L. 1974. Flooding as a result of hurricane Agnes and its effect on a macroinvertebrate community in an infertile headwater stream in central Pennsylvania. Limnol. Oceanogr. 19: 853-857.

Hynes, H. B. N. 1970. The Ecology of Running Waters. Ontario: University of Toronto Press.

Imeson, A. C. 1976. Some effects of burrowing animals on slope processes in the Luxemborg Ardennes, Part 1: The excavation of animal mounds in experimental plots. Geografiska Ann. 58A:115-125.

Imeson, A. C., and F. J. P. M. Kwaad. 1976. Some effects of burrowing animals on slope processes in the Luxembourg Ardennes, Part 2: The erosion of animal mounds by splash under forest. Geografiska Ann. 58A:317-328.

Kelsey, H. M. 1978. Earthflows in Franciscan melange, Van Duzen River basin, California. Geology 6:361-364.

Likens, G. E., F. H. Bormann, R. S. Pierce, J. S. Eaton, and N. M. Johnson. 1977. Biogeochemistry of a Forested Ecosystem. New York: Springer-Verlag.

Maser, C., J. M. Geist, D. M. Concannon, R. Anderson, and B. Lovell. Geomorphic and edaphic habitats in managed rangelands--their importance to wildlife. In Wildlife Habitats in Managed Rangelands--The Great Basin of Southeastern Oregon, edited by J. W. Thomas and C. Maser. USDA Forest Service (in press).

Maser, C., J. E. Rodick, and J. W. Thomas. 1979. Cliffs, talus, and caves. In Wildlife Habitats in Managed Forests--the Blue Mountains of Oregon and Washington, edited by J. W. Thomas, pp. 96-103. USDA Handbook 533.

Monk, C. D., D. A. Crossley, Jr., R. L. Todd, W. T. Swank, J. B. Waide, and J. R. Webster. 1977. An overview of nutrient cycling research at Coweeta Hydrologic Laboratory. In Watershed Research in Eastern North America, edited by D. L. Correll, pp. 35-50. Washington, D. C.: Smithsonian Institution.

O'Loughlin, C. L. 1974. A study of tree root strength deterioration following clearfelling. Can. J. Forest Res. 4:107-113.

Pierson, T. C. 1977. Factors containing debris flow initiation on forested hillslopes in the Oregon Coast Range. Ph.D. thesis, University of Washington, Seattle.

Potter, N., Jr. 1969. Tree-ring dating of snow avalanche tracks and the geomorphic activity of avalanches, northern Absaroka Mountains, Wyoming. In United States Contributions to Quaternary Research, edited by S. A. Schumm and W. C. Bradley, pp. 141-165. Geol. Soc. Amer. Spec. Paper 123.

Ruth, R. H., and R. A. Yoder. 1953. Reducing wind damage in the forests of the Oregon Coast Range. USDA Forest Service Paper No. 7. Pacific Northwest Forest and Range Expt. Sta., Portland, Oregon.

Schroder, J. F. 1978. Dendrogeomorphological analysis of mass movement on Table Cliffs Plateau, Utah. Quat. Res. 9: 168-185.

Simon, H. A. 1973. The organization of complex systems. In Hierarchy Theory, edited by H. D. Pattee, pp. 3-27. New York: George Braziller.

Sollins, P., C. C. Grier, F. M. McCorison, K. Cromack, Jr., R. Fogel, and R. L. Fredriksen. The internal element cycles of an old-growth Douglas-fir stand in western Oregon. Ecol. Monogr. (in press).

Swanson, F. J. Fire and geomorphic processes. In Fire Regime and Ecosystem Properties, edited by H. A. Mooney, T. M. Bonnicksen, N. L. Christensen, J. E. Lotan, and W. A. Reiners. USDA Forest Service Gen. Tech. Rep. (in press).

Swanson, F. J., R. L. Fredriksen, and F. M. McCorison. Material transfer in a western Oregon forest ecosystem. In The Natural Behavior and Response to Stress of Western Coniferous Forests, edited by R. L. Edmonds. Stroudsburg, Pa.: Dowden, Hutchinson, and Ross, Inc.

Swanson, F. J., and G. W. Lienkaemper. 1978. Physical consequences of large organic debris in Pacific Northwest streams. USDA Forest Service Gen. Tech. Rep. PNW-69.

Swanson, F. J., and D. N. Swanston. 1977. Complex mass-movement terrains in the western Cascade Range, Oregon. Geol. Soc. Amer. Rev. Engineering Geol., Vol. 3, pp. 113-124.

Swanston, D. N. 1969. Mass wasting in coastal Alaska. USDA Forest Service Res. Paper PNW-83. Pacific Northwest Forest and Range Expt. Sta., Portland, Oregon.

Swanston, D. N. 1970. Mechanics of debris avalanching in shallow till soils of southeast Alaska. USDA Forest Service Res. Paper PNW-103. Pacific Northwest Forest and Range Expt. Sta., Portland, Oregon.

Thomas, J. W., C. Maser, and J. E. Rodick. 1979. Riparian zones. In Wildlife Habitats in Managed Forests--the Blue Mountains of Oregon and Washington, edited by J. W. Thomas, pp. 40-47. USDA Handbook 533.

Triska, F. J., J. R. Sedell, and S. V. Gregory. Coniferous forest streams. In The Natural Behavior and Response to Stress of Western Coniferous Forests, edited by R. L. Edmonds. Stroudsburg, Pa.: Dowden, Hutchinson, and Ross, Inc. (in press).

Whittaker, R. H. 1956. Vegetation of the Great Smoky Mountains. Ecol. Monogr. 26:1-80.

Wolman, M. G., and R. Gerson. 1978. Relative scales of time and effectiveness of climate in watershed geomorphology. Earth Surface Processes 3:189-208.

The Role of Wood Debris in Forests and Streams

Frank J. Triska and Kermit Cromack, Jr.

In the Pacific Northwest, old-growth forests and their associated streams contain large quantities of coarse wood debris. To date, such debris has been considered an impediment to reforestation and stream quality. Consequently, it has been virtually ignored in ecological studies, partly because man's need for wood fiber has resulted in the removal of debris from forests throughout the world but also because the extended period necessary for wood to decay makes it difficult to study nutrient recycling from such a process. In this paper, we shall attempt to correct that omission by exploring how wood debris is utilized in forest and stream ecosystems.

Such an exploration is timely in view of the diminishing amount of pristine forest. In the Pacific Northwest, the greatest accumulation of wood debris occurs from natural mortality and blowdown in such forests. Now that forests are being cut every 80 years instead of standing 250 to 500 years (the interval between natural catastropic fires), it is crucial that we determine the role of wood debris in pristine habitats and then incorporate that knowledge into existing management strategies for our forests and watersheds.

Our exploration will begin with determining the amounts of wood debris in various forest and stream ecosystems and its rates of accumulation in each. We shall then examine how debris modifies existing habitats and creates new ones. Next, we shall determine how rapidly coarse wood debris breaks down into its component elements and how its carbon and other elements are recycled. Finally, we shall discuss what implications these data have for the managers of forested watersheds in the Pacific Northwest.

WOOD BIOMASS AND ACCUMULATION

As we have indicated, debris accumulation must be considered over a period of about 500 years. Accumulation over such a cycle of secondary succession--from a nearly bare forest floor to the debris beneath a 450-year-old stand of Douglas-fir--is depicted in Figure 1. The diagram, which is a composite of data from three sites on the H. J. Andrews Forest near Eugene, Oregon, is not intended to represent any particular site. It does, however, reflect the fact that accumulations of debris are greater in the Pacific Northwest than elsewhere because of the larger biomass of the region's tree boles (Grier and Logan, 1977). In most cases, natural catastrophes would result in greater accumulations than depicted here (Franklin and Waring, 1980), but those that would result from clearcutting followed by yarding and burning are adequately portrayed.

In Figure 1, event 1 represents an increase in wood debris as a result of natural thinning following canopy closure. The increase in wood biomass is slight because such debris is finely divided and readily susceptible to decomposition. Event 2 represents a long period of accumulation as low branches are shed and the canopy increases in height. Event 3 represents a decrease in wood debris because of a litter brush fire. If trees were killed by such a fire, however, the accumulation of woody debris would increase.

Event 4 represents windthrow in a large old-growth stand. Event 5 represents the accumulation of large individual trees on the forest floor over an extended period. Toward the end of succession, even a single tree can introduce a large amount of organic matter. For example, the biomass of a tree 100 cm in d.b.h. equals 10 metric tons.

171

As the foregoing sequence implies, wood carbon entering the detritus pool of both the forest and its stream varies in decomposition rate according to stand age and history. For example, woody debris in young stands is finely divided and highly susceptible to microbial attack, whereas an equal amount of large woody debris with its low surface-to-volume ratio may have a decomposition period of hundreds of years. Furthermore, the wood component in litterfall is less than 10 percent in young stands but 70 percent in old-growth forests (Grier and Logan, 1977).

Few estimates exist of the quantity of wood debris in forests and their watershed streams. One site where data are available from both ecosystems is Watershed 10, a 450-year-old stand of Douglas-fir in the H. J. Andrews Forest. Biomass estimates of downed logs were made for the forested watershed by Grier and Logan (1977) and for the watershed streams by Froehlich et al. (1972). Log debris for the forest was estimated at 55 to 580 metric tons per hectare, whereas that for the stream channel was estimated at 298 metric tons per hectare. Plotting of these data on a map of standing and downed vegetation on Watershed 10 indicates a general decrease in wood debris from stream channel to ridgetop.

This distribution results because the deep incisions in the basin cause trees to roll downhill toward the stream.

Quantities ranging from 55 to 580 metric tons per hectare represent a large pool of organic carbon. We now know that such pools of refractory (decomposition-resistant) carbon and other elements provide a nutrient source throughout secondary succession of ecosystems (O'Neill et al., 1975). Estimated wood debris in old Douglas-fir forests (Grier and Logan, 1977; MacMillan et al., 1977; Waring and Franklin, 1980) represents a larger aboveground pool of organic matter than the entire aboveground biomass of most current eastern deciduous forests (Day and Monk, 1974; Sollins and Anderson, 1971).

Although large wood debris (>10 cm in diameter) is more visible, fine wood debris also represents a substantial input and decomposes more rapidly both in streams and on land. Fine wood debris in Watershed 10 constituted only 13 percent of the biomass in the streams but decomposed faster, on the average, than coarse wood debris. The various litter inputs into the forest floor and streams of Watershed 10 are shown in Table 1.

Tables 2 and 3 indicate the biomass of wood debris in streams and on the forest

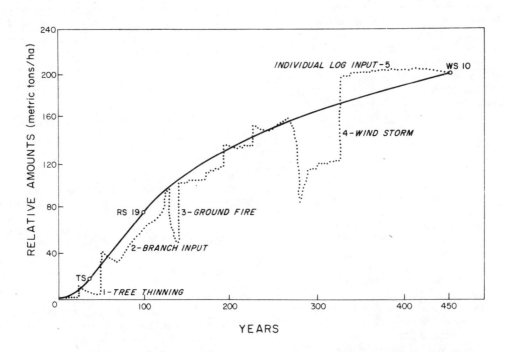

Figure 1. *Accumulation of wood debris during the life of a hypothetical stand of Douglas-fir. The solid line indicates the overall increase of wood debris over time; included as reference points are data from the Thompson Site (TS), Washington Reference Stand 19 (RS 19), and Watershed 10 (WS 10), all on the H. J. Andrews Forest near Eugene, Oregon. The dotted line depicts major events (discussed by number in text) that affect debris accumulation.*

floor of various old- and young-growth forests. By far the largest amount of wood debris occurs in streams draining old-growth redwoods and Douglas-fir/western hemlock. Even second-growth Douglas-fir/hemlock has more wood in its streams than do some old-growth sites in other parts of the country, partly because of the carryover of wood debris from the primeval forests. In old-growth forests in the Great Smoky Mountains of Tennessee, both spruce/fir and mixed hardwood stands have large quantities of wood debris in their streams.

Comparison of old- and second-growth forest types indicates that even in primeval forests, the amount of wood debris in the streams varied with species composition and environmental conditions. Regardless of these two factors, however, the quantity of such wood was probably much greater in many primeval forests than can be observed today. It follows that the biota of forested ecosystems and streams draining them evolved in a system where wood debris played a far larger role than it does today. Thus, wood debris has been removed in many parts of the world before man has fully understood its role.

One of the major difficulties in assessing the input rate of wood debris is the episodic nature of its accumulation. To date, the most successful methods have been dendrochronological, primarily the interpretation of tree scars (MacMillan et al., 1977; Swanson et al., 1976) or the assessment of dated successional sequences such as fir waves (Sprugel, 1976) in balsam fir forests (Lambert et al., in press). Permanent plots set aside for studies of tree growth and mortality afford another method of dating wood debris. While falling, trees may scrape against adjacent trees, resulting in the removal of bark and the decomposition of callus tissue in annual increments in the surviving trees. These increments or shock rings permit dating of the events (Shigo and Marx, 1977). Unfortunately, only a few trees leave such records of their deaths.

Dating the accumulation of large debris is especially difficult in third-order or larger streams. In first- and second-order streams, wood remains essentially where it falls. In the larger streams, however, it tends to be clumped by high water prior to decomposition, making it especially difficult to date the accumulations or to estimate decomposition rates or nutrient recycling. One can conclude that wood debris tends to exert a greater impact, in terms of amount, on the stream than on the surrounding forest and that this impact gradually diminishes as one proceeds downstream.

Table 1. *Leaves and coarse and fine wood debris entering the forest floor and watershed stream at Watershed 10, H. J. Andrews Forest, prior to clearcutting[1]*

Method of measurement	Leaf litter		Wood debris	
	Deciduous	Coniferous	Fine	Coarse
		$g/m^2/day$		
Litterfall	0.070	0.346	0.244	--
Lateral movement	.096	.143	.728	--
Scaling	--	--	--	0.548
Total	.166	.489	.972	.548
Percent composition	7.6	22.5	44.7	25.2

[1]Unpublished data from F. J. Triska, Dept. of Fisheries and Wildlife, Oregon State Univ., 1978.

MODIFYING AND CREATING
NEW HABITATS

On both land and in water, wood serves as more than a large pool of refractory carbon. Its very presence in large quantities modifies habitats on the forest floor and in streams and creates new ones.

As habitat, wood debris represents an alteration in the physical structure of the forest, changing the nature of light reflection to the canopy and providing new types of habitat on the forest floor. Because wood accumulates irregularly, many different states of decay are present at a particular time. In natural stands, logs may be added to the forest floor and stream channel as intact boles after catastrophes such as windthrow and localized earth movements or after bankcutting or erosion. More highly decomposed wood may enter the forest floor or stream as snags.

To differentiate various states of wood decay and their effects on habitat, we have devised a classification system based on the findings of previous researchers (Table 4). The system is based on physical characteristics such as texture, shape, color, the presence or absence of bark or twigs, and propotion of the bole in contact with the ground. Trees alive when they fell to the forest floor or stream would usually be grouped in decay class 1, while snags would probably be in decay class 2 or 3.

Table 2. *Estimated wood debris on the forest floor of selected old-growth and young-growth temperate forests.*

Location	Forest type and age (years)	Logs[1]	Branches[2]
		metric tons/hectare	
Oregon[3]	Douglas-fir > 450	218	–
New York[4]	Spruce/birch > 300	42	–
New Jersey[5]	Mixed oak > 250	21.3	2.1
New Hampshire[6]	Mixed hardwoods > 170	34	–
New Hampshire[7]	Subalpine balsam fir ~ 80	71	33
North Carolina[8]	Mixed oak/hickory > 60	11.8	.7
Great Britain[9]	Mixed oak	–	2.0
Denmark[10]	Mixed oak	5	–
Poland[11]	Mixed spruce/basswood 200–400	22	–

[1] Logs assumed to include coarse woody debris > 7.5 cm in diameter.

[2] Branches assumed to range from 2 to 7.5 cm in diameter.

[3] MacMillan et al. (1977).

[4] McFee and Stone (1966).

[5] Lang and Forman (1978).

[6] Bormann and Likens (1979).

[7] Lambert et al. (in press); peak log biomass (> 8 cm in diameter) occurs at stand age 33 years.

[8] Cromack (1973).

[9] Swift et al. (1976).

[10] Christensen (1977).

[11] Falinski (1978); assumes a density of 0.35 for 63 m^3 of logs.

The role of large wood debris as habitat depends on its decay class (Fig. 2). For example, cover and nesting sites for terrestrial vertebrates depend on such factors as shape, texture, and presence of branches and twigs. Elton (1966), Winn (1976), and Maser et al. (1979) outlined some of the important features of coarse wood debris and noted how habitat role shifts with decay class.

Other factors which affect the role of wood as habitat for wildlife include size and orientation. Obviously, large logs provide greater cover for small vertebrates than do small ones (Ruben, 1976; Maser et al., 1979). Large logs are also more persistent features of the environment because they decompose slowly as a result of a low surface-to-volume ratio (MacMillan et al., 1977). The orientation which logs take also influences their capacity to serve as habitat. Logs oriented along a contour are most likely to serve as runways for small animals (Maser et al., 1978) and to capture soil and organic debris, which slows erosion and maximizes nutrient retention.

Physical distribution is also important. Generally, the more even the overall distribution, the greater the habitat diversity and utilization (Winn, 1976; Maser et al., in press). Large blowdowns may provide excellent cover and concealment for smaller animals such as porcupines (Taylor, 1935) while interfering with the passage of larger wildlife such as deer (Lyon, 1976) and wild boar (Falinski, 1978). On the other hand, large areas devoid of wood debris lead to reduction or elimination of those species dependent on it for some stage of their life cycle.

In addition to serving as animal habitat, downed wood debris also serves an important function for the plant community. As log debris decomposes, its internal moisture and nitrogen concentration in-

Table 3. Estimated coarse wood debris in first- and second-order streams draining old- and young-growth temperate forests.

Location	Forest category	Wood[1]
	OLD-GROWTH	kg/m^2
Oregon[2]	Douglas-fir/hemlock	25–40
Idaho[2]	Spruce/lodgepole pine	7
New Hampshire[2]	Spruce/fir	4
Tennessee[3]	Spruce/fir	10
Tennessee[3]	Mixed hardwoods	13
Southeastern Alaska[4]	Spruce/hemlock	5
California[4]	Redwoods	45–80
	YOUNG-GROWTH	
Michigan[5]	Mixed hardwoods	4–8
Oregon[5]	Douglas-fir/hemlock	20–25

[1] > 10 cm in diameter

[2] Unpublished data from J. R. Sedell and F. J. Swanson, Dept. of Fisheries and Wildlife and Dept. of Forest Engineering, Oregon State Univ., 1978.

[3] Unpublished data from S. V. Gregory, Dept. of Fisheries and Wildlife, Oregon State Univ., 1978.

[4] Unpublished data of F. J. Swanson and G. W. Lienkemper, Dept. of Forest Engineering, Oregon State Univ., 1978.

[5] Unpublished data of J. R. Sedell, Dept. of Fisheries and Wildlife, Oregon State Univ., 1977.

Table 4. Decay classes of Douglas-fir, after Fogel et al. (1973), MacMillan et al. (1977), and Maser et al. (1979).

Characteristic	Class 1	2	3	4	5
Bark	Intact	Intact	Sloughing	Detached or absent	Detached or absent
Structural integrity	Sound	Sound	Heartwood sound, supports own weight	Heartwood rotten, does not support own weight, branch stubs pull out	None
Twigs < 3 cm	Present	Absent	Absent	Absent	Absent
Texture of rotten portions	Intact	Mostly intact, sapwood partly soft	Hard, large pieces	Soft, small blocky pieces	Soft, powdery when dry
Color of wood (except in portions with white rot)	Original color	Original color	Reddish brown or original color	Reddish or light brown	Red-brown to dark brown
Invading roots	Absent	Absent	Sapwood only	Throughout	Throughout
Vegetation	None	None surviving	Conifer seedlings	Tsuga < 15 cm DBH; smaller shrubs, moss	Tsuga up to 200 cm DBH: shrubs, some large; moss
Fungal fruiting	Fungal colonization, few large fruiting bodies	Cyathus, Tremella, Mycena, Collybia, Polyporus, Fomitopsis, Pseudohydnum	Polyporus, Polyporellus, Pseudohydnum, Fomitopsis	Cortinarius, Mycena, Marasmius	Cortinarius, Collybia, Cantharellus
Mycorrhizae[1]	Absent	Absent	Mycorrhizal colonization	Boletus, Corticium, Hydnotria, Lacaria, Piloderma, Rhizopogon	Boletus, Corticium, Hydnotria, Lacaria, Piloderma, Rhizopogon

[1] J. M. Trappe, USDA Forest Service, Pacific Northwest Forest and Range Experiment Station, Corvallis, Oregon, 1979.

crease (Place, 1950; Rowe, 1955). In the Pacific Northwest, decomposing logs eventually serve as nursery sites for hemlock, the climax species in moist Douglas-fir habitat (Franklin and Dyrness, 1973). Thus, by serving as plant habitat, downed logs influence forest succession (Jones, 1945; Rowe, 1955).

Besides providing habitat, wood debris also modifies the forest floor. If coverage of the forest floor is extensive, a large area may be taken out of production for extended periods. If wood is in contact with the ground, some physical and biological properties of the soil beneath may be modified significantly. Ausmus (1977) reported that soil under logs in a deciduous forest increased 4-fold in organic matter, 8-fold in adenosine triphosphate or ATP (which is a measure of microbial biomass), 18-fold in nematode density, more than 2-fold in root biomass, and 5-fold in calcium concentration. In the Pacific Northwest, preliminary data by K. Cromack, Jr., and D. H. McNabb (Dept. of Forest Science, Oregon State Univ., 1978, personal communication) indicate that Ceanothus velutinus undergoes a significant increase in nodulation (for fixation of nitrogen) in soil under old logs. B. Bormann (Dept. of Forest Science, Oregon State Univ., 1979, personal communication) has reported that nodulation of red alder occurred beneath

burned logs on a clearcut in western Washington.

In watershed streams, the accumulation of coarse wood debris also modifies the stream channel and provides specialized habitat (Figs. 3-5). The amount and relative role of wood increases dramatically as one proceeds upstream. For example, in the first-order stream called Devil's Club Creek on the H. J. Andrews Forest (Table 5), wood completely inundates the channel. In fact, at summer low-flow there is more water in the decaying wood tissue than is free-flowing in the stream channel. Under these circumstances, wood plays a strong role in directing water flow and sediment storage.

In the smallest streams, wood debris is especially valuable in creating habitat, where, because of high streambed gradients, it might not otherwise exist. Small, steep watershed streams have extensive areas of bedrock except where sediment is entrained by wood debris (Figs. 4-5). At these sites, small riffles and pools are formed behind debris, thus facilitating the establishment of a biological community. Because small streams do not have enough hydrologic force to remove debris, wood-created habitat in these streams is most often formed by individual pieces of debris or minor accumulations. The biological community in these small

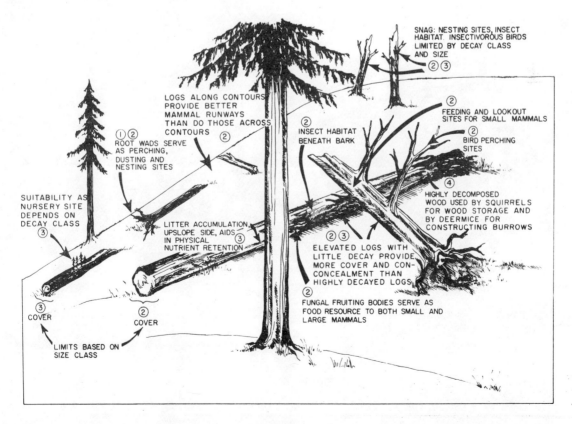

Figure 2. Role of coarse wood debris as habitat on the forest floor. Habitat role is dependent on decay class, size, amount, and orientation of debris. Circled numbers indicate decay classes.

streams, although not tremendously productive, is effective at processing particulates and even at altering certain nutrient concentrations of the water before it reaches a second-order stream (S. Gregory, Dept. of Fisheries and Wildlife, Oregon State Univ., 1978, personal communication).

First-order streams in old-growth forests are thus effective ecosystems because of the retentiveness of wood-created habitat. Time gained by slowing and directing water flow and by increasing biologically and chemically active surfaces facilitates chemical exchange with organic and mineral surfaces, as well as promoting microbial colonization and invertebrate consumption

of organic particulates. Retention is particularly important for litter processing because microbial colonization is a prerequisite to invertebrate consumption of wood and other litter (Triska, 1970; Anderson and Grafius, 1975).

Although most extensive in first-order streams, wood-created habitat is most visible in third- to fifth-order streams. In these larger streams, heavy discharges exert enough hydrologic force to clump debris. These clumps entrain large amounts of organic matter and sediment, which form areas of rich biological habitat. In streams larger than fifth-order, coarse

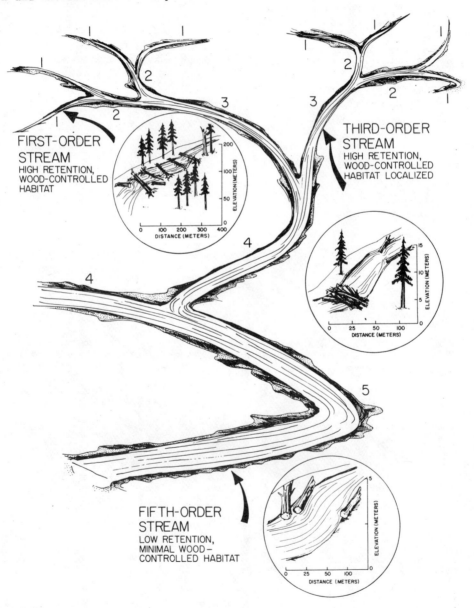

Figure 3. Role of wood in the various watershed streams of a drainage network. Note that the amount of wood-created habitat decreases as one proceeds downstream. Circled numbers indicate stream order.

FORESTED STREAM HABITATS

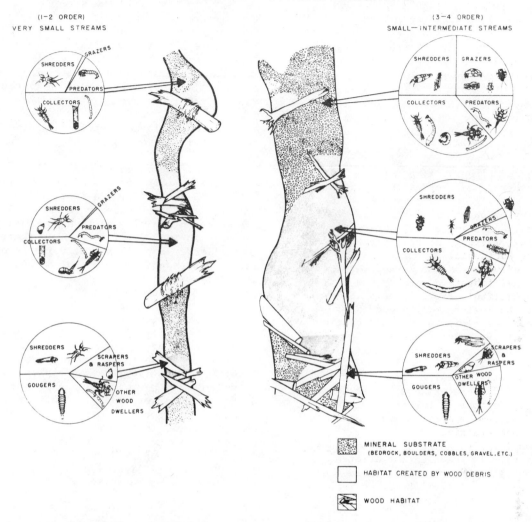

Figure 4. Formation of wood-created habitat and its influence on the invertebrate community of first- through fourth-order streams. Life functions of various invertebrate groups based on Cummins (1974) and Anderson et al. (1978). Size of segments in each chart based on proportional role of indicated functional group.

Table 5. Estimates of coarse and fine wood debris from selected streams of increasing watershed area within and adjacent to the H. J. Andrews Forest.

Stream	Stream order	Watershed area	Gradient	Coarse wood debris[1]	Fine wood debris
		km²	percent	------ kg/m² ------	
Devil's Club Creek	1	0.05	35	40.89	1.11
Mack Creek	3	5.35	20	28.50	0.61
Lookout Creek	5	60.20	12	11.65	.08
McKenzie River	7	1,642.00	9	.07	.08

[1] > 10 cm in diameter.

wood debris is found along banks or deposited in the riparian zone and thus plays a minor role in habitat formation.

Although the smallest streams have the most extensive wood-created habitat, they also have the lowest invertebrate biomass. Anderson et al. (1978) describe 38 taxa of invertebrates, mostly insects, associated with wood in Oregon streams. However, only a few of these insect species are truly xylophagous (wood-consuming): _Lara anova_ (gouging), _Heteroplectron californicum_ (boring), and _Lipsothrix_ spp. (tunneling). For the others, wood serves an incidental role--for example, as an attachment site for feeding or pupation; for oviposition; as a nursery area for early instars; or for nesting, molting, or emergence (Fig. 5).

These incidental associations can have a direct influence on the structure of the stream's invertebrate community, as evidenced by Grafius's (1977) population estimates for the leaf-consuming caddis, _Lepidostoma unicolor_, in various aquatic habitats. _L. unicolor_ consumes Douglas-fir needles after they have been conditioned by microbial colonization (Sedell et al., 1975). To test the suitability of various habitats, Grafius determined larval densities of _Lepidostoma_ in three stretches of a watershed stream--a stretch draining a clearcut, one draining an area of old-growth Douglas-fir, and one behind a debris dam (Fig. 6). In the clearcut stretch, _Lipidostoma_ larvae were scarce because of the absence of suitable litter. Larval density was higher in the stretch draining the old-growth area, where litter had been retained among pieces of coarse wood debris. There were 15 times more larvae behind the debris dam, however, because the coarse wood had captured large amounts of litter, thus facilitating microbial conditioning and expanding the amount of available habitat. Thus, wood debris sometimes plays an important role completely unrelated to its own utilization as an energy or nutrient source.

The effect of coarse wood debris on fish habitat (Fig. 5) has been summarized by Hall and Baker (1977) and Baker (1979). Overall, wood debris seems to have a direct influence on the size of fish populations but only an indirect influence on their metabolisms. Actual habitat value of debris dams is dependent on such factors as the stability of the structure and the diversity of habitat created behind it. The most important function of wood debris is to provide cover and protection from predation. For underyearling salmon and trout, debris provides not only cover but also protected rearing areas (Hartman, 1965; Coulter, 1966; Sheridan, 1969; Meehan, 1974), particularly during overwintering (Hartman, 1965; Bustard and Narver, 1975). Adult salmon often inhabit pools formed by coarse wood debris (James, 1956; Larkin et al., 1959; Sheridan, 1969). At two sites in the Oregon Coast Range, Baker (1979) found that fish biomass was significantly higher behind debris dams than either upstream or downstream.

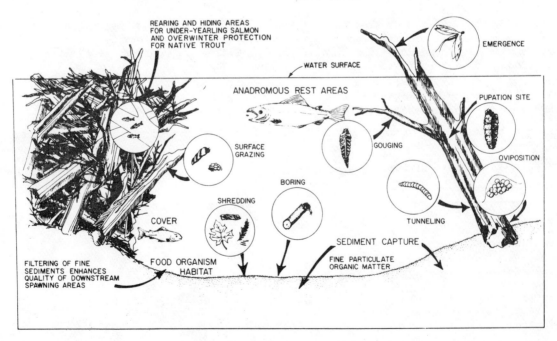

Figure 5. Role of coarse wood debris as habitat in a watershed stream. Habitat role is dependent on decay class, size, amount, and orientation of debris.

Accumulations of coarse wood debris also function as filtering devices (Hall and Baker, 1975). Bishop and Shapley (n.d.) found that the amount of fine sediments was significantly reduced and oxygen concentration was increased in gravel areas downstream from such accumulations. As pointed out previously, this filtration can increase the production of fish food organisms.

WOOD DECOMPOSITION AND NUTRIENT CYCLING

As mentioned at the outset, decomposition of coarse wood debris requires several hundred years. This persistence of debris is related to its size, shape, and nutrient composition (Fogel and Cromack, 1977; MacMillan et al., 1977; Lambert et al., in press). Because of the extended periods involved, investigators have devised broad classifications for wood decay, such as the one outlined previously in Table 4. A major problem with such schemes, however, is that a single log can contain wood in various stages of decay. This condition often arises because of (1) greater soil contact at one end than the other, (2) partial decomposition prior to contact with the forest floor, (3) distinct decay zones related to plant, animal, and microbial activity, (4) waterlogging of debris in the stream channel, and (5) significantly different diameters at the base and the tip. By later stages of log decomposition, wood texture is so soft that increased streamflow will disintegrate the softest portions and sweep them downstream as fine particles. On land, logs with advanced decay can exist for more than 500 years (MacMillan et al., 1977).

The process of water logging is depicted in Figure 7, which represents 50 years of decomposition in a single log whose length spans three distinct habitats--streams, riparian, and terrestrial. This log exhibits five stages of decay resulting from the varying environmental factors to which it has been subjected.

In streams, the decay of intact logs seems to occur primarily from the periphery of the log toward the interior, and the process is slower than on land. In small streams, for example, logs do not always have permanent contact with the water. If this contact occurs only during the rainy seasons or when the stream is at its highest, decay is likely to be retarded. And even when the log is submerged or has continuous contact with the water, waterlogging prevents oxygen diffusion deep within the woody tissue. Consequently, because most cellulolytic and lignin-decomposing fungi are aerobic, decomposition of major structural tissue is retarded.

Because decomposition of wood in streams begins on the periphery, physical processes such as scouring play a more important role than on land. Decomposition from the outside inward is also evident in the action of invertebrates within waterlogged debris. Of the 38 insect taxa reported by Anderson et al. (1978) in such debris, only two were tunneling as opposed to surface species. Of these, only _Lipsothrix_ spp. were present in substantial numbers, which were described as occurring "in tunnels in decayed alder wood that was so soft it could be broken apart by hand."

Unlike the decay process in streams, wood decay on land can occur both from the outside inward and from the center to the

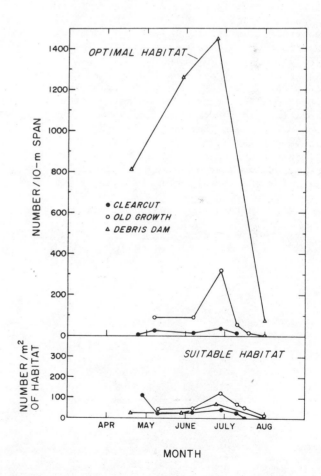

Figure 6. Density of _Lepidostoma unicolor_ larvae in three stretches of Mack Creek -- one stretch draining a clearcut, one draining an old-growth area, and one behind a debris dam--within the H. J. Andrews Forest. Upper graph depicts larval density along a 10-m span, whereas the lower graph depicts larval density per square meter of suitable habitat. (From Grafius, 1977).

outside. On land, moisture content of de-composing coarse debris increases with age (Fig. 8), but logs rarely achieve the water-logged, spongy state observed in the final stages of decomposition in water. The greater moisture content in wood debris on land in fact facilitates decomposition by preventing drying out during the warm, droughty summers characteristic of the Pacific Northwest. Thus, the terrestrial log acts as a perched water table, en-couraging not only decomposition but also invasions by burrowing mammals and tunnel-ing invertebrates. Common invertebrates such as termites, carpenter ants, and wood-boring beetles are well known for their ability to operate within the wood matrix (Elton, 1966). This activity in turn further enhances aeration.

Because wood on the forest floor re-mains permanently in place with ever-increasing soil contact as time progresses, mycorrhizal associations sometimes act as sources of nutrients to promote wood decay. Harvey et al. (1976) demonstrated the importance of decaying logs as sites for colonization by ectomycorrhizal fungi. Such fungal activity promotes carbon miner-alization and the immobilization and fixa-tion of nitrogen (Larsen et al., 1978; Silvester, 1978), thereby decreasing the carbon/nitrogen ratio of decomposing tissues and providing sources of nutrients and water for the establishment of nursery hem-locks on decaying logs. These colonizing seedlings in turn lead to further fragmenta-

tion and aeration as their roots penetrate the decomposing wood.

As log decay advances, there is a pro-gressive increase in the concentration of essential nutrients such as nitrogen and phosphorus (Fig. 8). This is due primarily to the fact that carbon is mineralized at a greater rate than most other essential elements during initial stages of decay. The net result is that other essential ele-ments are conserved for recycling within the forest ecosystem.

As log decay advances, there is a pro-gressive decrease in wood density. In a study on the H. J. Andrews Forest (MacMillan et al., 1977), Douglas-fir logs were esti-mated to lose about 75 percent of their density after about 220 years. As such logs become less dense, their habitat value for tunneling invertebrates and small mammals increases. Unfortunately, similar estimates are not available for logs in stream channels.

Although large debris is the most visible wood component on land and in streams, fine wood contributes substantially to energy flows and nutrient cycling throughout the course of secondary succes-sion. Average decomposition periods for fine wood are faster than those for coarse debris (Fogel and Cromack, 1977; MacMillan et al., 1977; Grier, 1978; Sollins et al., in press). The large nutrient pool provided by fine wood is intermediate in availability between those of leaf litter and coarse wood debris.

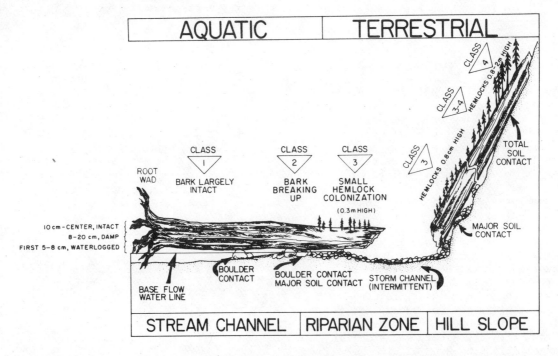

Figure 7. Decomposition over a 50-year period in a single log whose length spans three habitats. Note that five decay classes are represented within the log.

Branches and twigs also play an important role in providing habitat and a food source, particularly in aquatic environments. Anderson et al. (1978) report that the majority of invertebrate organisms they collected from seven streams in Oregon were found on wood 1 to 10 cm in diameter. Because most of the aquatic invertebrates on wood are associated with surfaces, it is reasonable that they would be associated with debris providing a large surface-to-volume ratio as well as ample sites for attachment.

The role of wood as habitat and as a

source of carbon and other nutrients varies not only be debris size but also by debris species. Tunneling invertebrates which use rotten wood as a nutrient source prefer intermediate-sized debris (1 to 10 cm in diamter) of deciduous species. When wood is intermediate in size, waterlogging in streams apparently does not cause an acute diffusion problem, as it does in large debris.

Little is known about how wood of small to intermediate size is decomposed in the terrestrial environment. Accordingly, this process is being studied at Mack Creek and on the forest floor of the H. J. Andrews Forest. Five types of fine wood substrates of Douglas-fir have been placed both on the forest floor and in the stream. Data analyzed to date indicate that fine wood debris decomposes faster in the aquatic than in the terrestrial environment (Fig. 9). The largest difference between decomposition in the two habitats was observed in chips, which have the largest surface-to-volume ratio. The next greatest difference was in twigs, which are sapwood and therefore the second most decomposable substrate. Bark and heartwood sticks, which one would expect to be the least susceptible to microbial breakdown, exhibited the smallest differences between decomposition on land and in water and also the lowest incidence of decay.

As noted previously, in large wood debris decomposition is accompanied by an increase in nitrogen concentration. The same process was observed in the fine wood substrates (Fig. 10). As with weight loss, the greatest increase in nitrogen concentration and the largest difference between reactions in the terrestrial and aquatic environments were observed in the least refractory substrates--chips and twigs. Because the data analyzed to date cover only 220 days, long-term trends, or even seasonal trends related to temperature, are not yet known.

One of the major obstacles to the decomposition of wood debris is its extremely high carbon/nitrogen ratio (322 for twigs, 357 for bark, 1,175 for heartwood chips, and 1,382 for heartwood blocks of Douglas-fir). Nitrogen fixation could play an important role in the early stages of decomposition by initially decreasing the carbon/nitrogen ratio. Therefore, acetylene reduction, as a chemical assay of nitrogen fixation (McNabb and Geist, 1979), was studied in the five substrates to determine if fixation contributes to the observed increase in nitrogen concentration. Acetylene reduction was observed at some time in all five substrates. As one might expect from previous data, acetylene reduction was

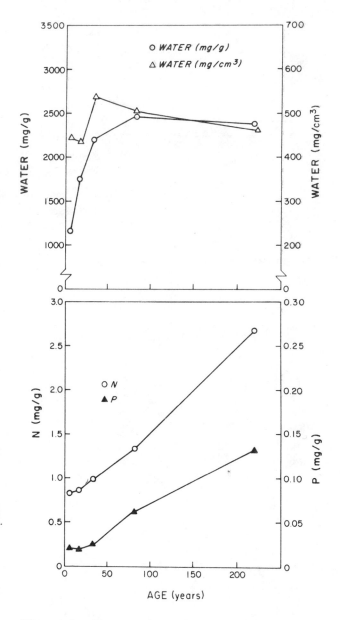

Figure 8. Water, nitrogen, and phosphorus contents in relation to age of wood debris at a mid-elevation stand of Douglas-fir in the H. J. Andrews Forest. (From MacMillan et al., 1977).

WOOD SUBSTRATE INCUBATED IN MACK CREEK   WOOD SUBSTRATE INCUBATED IN MACK CREEK

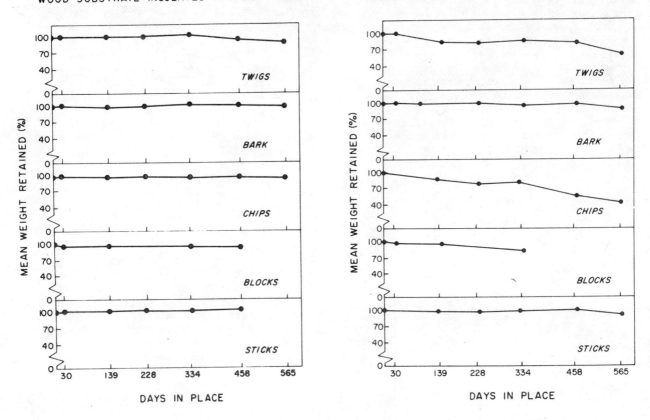

Figure 9.   Weight loss in five fine wood substrates of Douglas-fir placed on the forest floor and in Mack Creek on the H. J. Andrews Forest.   Each point is the mean of three samples.

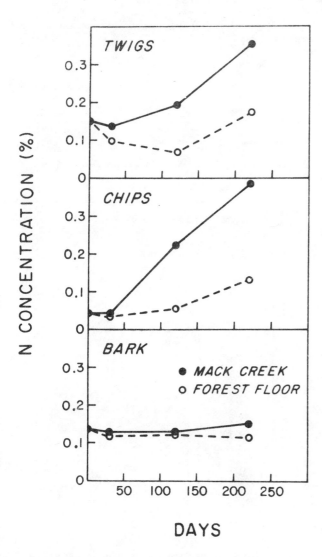

Figure 10. *Change in nitrogen concentration in three fine wood substrates placed on the forest floor and in Mack Creek on the H. J. Andrews Forest.*

greatest in the stream in the least refractory samples--chips and twigs--and lowest among samples on the forest floor (Fig. 11).

Factors such as temperature and moisture are important in influencing the nitrogen fixation rate and the rates of diffusion of nitrogen and oxygen to nitrogen-fixing bacteria. A general relationship between temperature and nitrogen fixation rates has been noted in the literature (Cromack et al., 1979; Kallio et al., 1972; Paul, 1975). Acetylene reduction has also been detected in large log debris and in small-sized wood (Cornaby and Waide, 1973; Sharp and Millbank, 1973; Sharp, 1975; Roskoski, 1977; Larsen et al., 1978). Through nitrogen fixation, logs may not only serve as an important source of habitat but may also facilitate their own decomposition and perhaps even contribute significant quantities of nitrogen to the forest floor.

MANAGEMENT IMPLICATIONS

Wood debris functions as an integral component of forest ecosystems. Concerted efforts to conserve wood debris will be needed if managed forests are to maintain the diversity of plant, animal, and microbial habitats currently present in unmanaged, primeval forests. On forest land, woody debris (slash) should be maintained over approximately 10 percent of clearcut areas (Maser et al., 1979). It would be desirable to leave several logs of decay classes 1 and 2 per hectare; these could be culled from logs of less desirable timber quality. As many logs as possible of classes 3, 4 and 5 (which have little or no commercial value) should be retained. In some instances, a portion of the woody debris could be utilized locally as firewood. Logs could be physically rearranged on the landscape to ensure optimal density and physical stability as part of the routine logging operations and site preparation (Maser et al., 1979).

The removal of natural, stable woody debris from streams can damage both the stream channel and streamside riparian habitat. Consequently, such material should be left in place when possible. In cases where massive accumulations occur, either as a result of logging or catastrophic events such as debris avalanches, significant wood removal may be necessary. In such cases, the advice of competent stream ecologists and geomorphologists should be sought before removal of massive debris jams are attempted. The general goal for wood management in streams should be to maintain well-established debris so that it can continue to function both as habitat and as a long-term nutrient source to stream organisms.

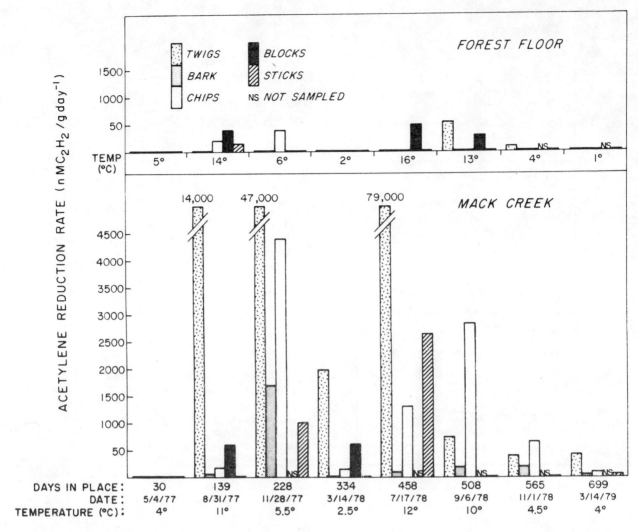

Figure 11. *Rates of acetylene reduction in five fine wood substrates placed on the forest floor and in Mack Creek on the H. J. Andrews Forest.*

ACKNOWLEDGEMENTS

We acknowledge National Science Foundation Ecosystems Grants No. DEB-76-21402 and DEB-77-06075 for support of our work. We appreciate the help of the following people from Oregon State University: for technical assistance, J. Anders, B. Buckley, G. Hawk, P. MacMillan, C. Mallonie, S. Phillip, and L. Roberts; for the use of unpublished data, C. Baker, B. Buckley, T. Dudley, R. Fogel, E. Grafius, G. Hawk, G. Lienkaemper, P. MacMillan, M. Ogawa, J. R. Sedell, F. Swanson, and J. Trappe. Additional suggestions and assistance in this work have come from P. Sollins, Oregon State University, and from J. Means and J. F. Franklin, USDA Forest Service, Pacific Northwest Forest and Range Experiment Station.

LITERATURE CITED

Anderson, N. H., and E. Grafius. 1975. Utilization and processing of allochthonous materials by stream Trichoptera. Verh. Internat. Ver. Limnol. 19:3083-3088.

Anderson, N. H., J. R. Sedell, L. M. Roberts, and F. J. Triska. 1978. Role of aquatic invertebrates in processing wood debris in coniferous forest streams. Am. Midl. Natur. 100: 64-82.

Ausmus, B. S. 1977. Regulation of wood decomposition rates by arthropod and annelid populations. In Soil Organisms as Components of Ecosystems, edited by U. Lohm and T. Persson. Proc. 6th Int. Colloq. Soil Zool., Ecol. Bull. (Stockholm) 25:180-192.

Baker, C. O. 1979. The impacts of logjam removal on fish populations and stream habitat in western Oregon. M.S. thesis, Oregon State Univ., Corvallis.

Bishop, D. M., and S. P. Shapley. n.d. Effects of log debris jams on southeastern Alaska salmon streams. Unpublished report, Inst. of Northern Forestry, Pac. Northwest Forest and Range Experiment Sta., Juneau, Alaska.

Bormann, F. H., and G. E. Likens. 1979. Patterns and Processes in a Forested Ecosystem. New York: Springer-Verlag.

Bustard, D. R., and D. W. Narver. 1975. Aspects of the winter ecology of juvenile coho salmon (Oncorhynchus kisutch) and steelhead trout (Salmo gairdneri). J. Fish. Res. Board Can. 32:667-680.

Christensen, O. 1977. Estimation of standing crop and turnover of dead wood in a Danish oak forest. Oikos 28:177-186.

Cornaby, B. W., and J. B. Waide. 1973. Nitrogen fixation in decaying chestnut logs. Plant and Soil 39:445-448.

Coulter, M. W. 1966. Ecology and management of fisheries in Maine. Ph.D. thesis, State Univ. College of Forestry at Syracuse, N.Y.

Cromack, K., Jr. 1973. Litter production and decomposition in a mixed hardwood watershed and a white pine watershed at Coweeta Hydrologic Station, North Carolina. Ph.D. thesis, Univ. of Georgia, Athens.

Cromack, K., Jr., C. C. Delwiche, and D. H. McNabb. 1979. Prospects and problems of nitrogen management using symbiotic nitrogen fixers. In Symbiotic Nitrogen Fixation in the Management of Temperate Forests, edited by J. C. Gordon, C. T. Wheeler, and D. A. Perry, pp. 210-223. Forest Res. Lab., Oregon State Univ., Corvallis.

Cummins, K. W. 1974. Structure and function of stream ecosystems. BioScience 24:631-641.

Day, F. P., Jr., and C. D. Monk. 1974. Vegetation patterns on a southern Appalachian watershed. Ecology 55: 1064-1074.

Elton, C. S. 1966. The Pattern of Animal Communities. New York: John Wiley and Sons, Inc.

Falinski, J. B. 1978. Uprooted trees, their distribution and influence in the primeval forest biotope. Vegetatio 38:175-183.

Fogel, R., and K. Cromack, Jr. 1977. Effects of habitat and substrate quality on Douglas-fir litter decomposition in western Oregon. Can. J. Bot. 55:1632-1640.

Fogel, R., M. Ogawa, and J. M. Trappe. 1973. Terrestrial decomposition: a synopsis. Conif. For. Biome Rep. 135.

Franklin, J. F., and C. T. Dyrness. 1973. Natural vegetation of Oregon and Washington. USDA Forest Service Pac. Northwest Forest & Range Experiment Stn. Gen. Tech. Rep. PNW-8.

Franklin, J. F., and R. H. Waring. 1980. Distinctive features of the northwestern coniferous forest: development, structure and function. (In this volume).

Froehlich, H. A., D. McGreer, and J. R. Sedell. 1972. Natural debris within the stream environment. Univ. of Washington, USIBP Internal Rep. 96, Conif. For. Biome.

Grafius, E. J. 1977. Bioenergetics and strategies of some Trichoptera in processing and utilizing allochthonous materials. Ph.D. thesis, Oregon State Univ., Corvallis.

Grier, C. C. 1978. A Tsuga heterophylla-Picea sitchensis ecosystem of coastal Oregon: decomposition and nutrient balances of fallen logs. Can. J. Forest Res. 8:198-206.

Grier, C. C., and R. S. Logan. 1977. Old-growth Pseudotsuga menziesii communities of a western Oregon watershed: biomass distribution and production budgets. Ecol. Monogr. 47:373-400.

Hall, J. D., and C. O. Baker. 1975. Biological impacts of organic debris in Pacific Northwest streams. In Logging Debris in Streams, Workshop II. Oregon State Univ., Corvallis.

Hartman, G. F. 1965. The role of behavior in the ecology and interaction of underyearling coho salmon (Oncorhynchus kisutch) and steelhead trout (Salmo gairdneri). J. Fish. Res. Board Can. 22:1035-1081.

Harvey, A. E., M. J. Larsen, and M. F. Jurgensen. 1976. Distribution of ectomycorrhizae in a mature Douglas-fir/larch forest soil in western Montana. Forest Sci. 22:393-398.

James, G. A. 1956. The physical effect of logging on salmon streams of southeast Alaska. USDA Forest Service, Alaska For. Res. Cent. Stn. Pap. 5.

Jones, E. W. 1945. The structure and reproduction of the virgin forests of the north temperate zone. New Phytol. 44:130-148.

Kallio, P., S. Suhonen, and H. Kallio. 1972. The ecology of nitrogen fixation in Nephroma arcticum and Solorina crocea. Rep. Kevo. Subarctic Res. Stn. 9:7-14.

Lambert, R. L., G. E. Lang, and W. A. Reiners. 1980. Weight loss and chemical change in boles of a subalpine balsam fir forest. Ecology (in press).

Lang, G. E., and R. T. Forman. 1978. Detrital dynamics in a mature oak forest: Hutcheson Memorial Forest. Ecology 59:580-595.

Larkin, P. A., and others. 1959. The effects on freshwater fisheries of man-made activities in British Columbia. Can. Fish. Cult. 25:27-59.

Larsen, M. J., M. F. Jurgensen, and A. E. Harvey. 1978. N_2 fixation associated with wood decayed by some common fungi in western Montana. Can. J. Forest Res. 8:341-345.

Lyon, L. J. 1976. Elk use as related to characteristics of clearcuts in western Montana. In Proceedings of the Elk-logging-roads Symposium, edited by S. R. Hieb, pp. 69-72. Univ. of Idaho, Moscow.

MacMillan, P. C., J. E. Means, G. M. Hawk, K. Cromack, Jr., and R. Fogel. 1977. Douglas-fir log decomposition in an old-growth Douglas-fir forest. Northwest Sci. (abstr.), p. 13.

Maser, C., J. M. Trappe, and D. C. Ure. 1978. Implications of small mammal mycophagy to the management of western coniferous forests. In Trans. 43rd North Am. Wildl. and Nat. Resour. Conf. Wildlife Manage. Inst., pp. 78-88. Washington, D. C.

Maser, C., R. G. Anderson, K. Cromack, Jr., J. T. Williams, and R. E. Martin. 1979. Dead and down woody material. In Wildlife Habitats in Managed Forests -- the Blue Mountains of Oregon and Washington, edited by J. W. Thomas, pp. 78-95. USDA Forest Serv. Agric. Handbook 553.

McFee, W. W., and E. L. Stone. 1966. The persistence of decaying wood in the humus layers of northern forests. Proc. Soil Sci. Soc. Amer. 30:512–516.

McNabb, D. H., and J. M. Geist. 1979. Acetylene reduction assay of symbiotic N_2 fixation under field conditions. Ecology 60:1070–1072.

Meehan, W. R. 1974. The forest ecosystem of southeast Alaska. 3. Fish habitats. USDA Forest Serv. Pac. Northwest Forest & Range Exp. Stn. Gen. Tech. Rep. PNW-15.

O'Neill, R. V., W. F. Harris, B. S. Ausmus, and D. E. Reichle. 1975. A theoretical basis for ecosystem analysis with particular reference to element cycling. In Mineral Cycling in Southeastern Ecosystems, edited by F. G. Howell, J. B. Gentry, and M. H. Smith, pp. 28–40. ERDA Symp. Series (CONF-740513).

Paul, E. A. 1975. Recent studies using the acetylene reduction technique as an assay for field nitrogen fixation levels. In Nitrogen Fixation by Free-living Micro-organisms, edited by W. D. P. Stewart, pp. 259–269. New York: Cambridge University Press.

Place, I. C. M. 1950. Comparative moisture regimes of humus and rotten wood. Can. Dep. Resour. & Dev., Forestry Branch, For. Res. Div., Silvicultural Leaflet 37.

Roskoski, J. 1977. Nitrogen fixation in northern hardwood forests. Ph.D. thesis, Yale Univ., New Haven, Conn.

Rowe, J. S. 1955. Factors influencing white spruce reproduction in Manitoba and Saskatchewan. Can. Dept. of Northern Affairs and Nat. Resour., Forestry Branch, For. Res. Div. Tech. Note 3.

Ruben, J. A. 1976. Reduced nocturnal heat loss associated with ground litter burrowing by the California red-sided garter snake, Thamnophis sirtalis infernalis. Herpetologica 32:323–325.

Sedell, J. R., F. J. Triska, and N. S. Triska. 1975. The processing of conifer and hardwood leaves in two coniferous forest streams. I. Weight loss in associated invertebrates. Verh. Internat. Ver. Limnol. 19:1617–1627.

Sharp, R. F. 1975. Nitrogen fixation in deteriorating wood: The incorporation of and the effect of environmental conditions on acetylene reduction. Soil Biochem. 7:9–14.

Sharp, R. F., and J. W. Millbank. 1973. Nitrogen fixation in deteriorating wood. Experientia 29:895–896.

Sheridan, W. L. 1969. Effects of log debris jams on salmon spawning riffles in Saginaw Creek. USDA Forest Service, Alaska Region.

Shigo, A. L., and H. G. Marx. 1977. Compartmentalization of decay in trees. USDA Forest Service Agric. Inf. Bull. 405.

Silvester, W. B. 1978. Nitrogen fixation and mineralization in Kauri (Agathis australis) forest in New Zealand. In Microbial Ecology: Proceedings in Life Sciences, edited by M. W. Loutit and J. A. R. Miles, pp. 138–143. Berlin: Springer-Verlag.

Sollins, P., and R. M. Anderson, eds. 1971. Dry weight and other data for trees and woody shrubs of the southeastern U.S. ORNL-IBP-71-6 Rep., Oak Ridge Natl. Lab., Oak Ridge, Tenn.

Sollins, P., C. C. Grier, F. M. McCornison, K. Cromack, Jr., R. Fogel, and R. L. Fredriksen. 1980. The internal element cycles of an old-growth Douglas-fir forest in western Oregon. Ecol. Monogr. (in press).

Sprugel, D. G. 1976. Dynamic structure of wave-generated Abies balsamea forests in the northeastern U.S. J. Ecol. 64:889–912.

Swanson, F. J., G. W. Lienkaemper, and J. R. Sedell. 1976. History, physical effects and management implications of large organic debris in western Oregon streams. USDA Forest Service Pac. Northwest Forest & Range Exp. Stn. Gen. Tech. Rep. PNW-56.

Swift, M. J., I. N. Healey, J. K. Hibberd, J. M. Sykes, V. Bampoe, and M. E. Nesbitt. 1976. The decomposition of branch-wood in the canopy and floor of a mixed deciduous woodland. Oecologia 16:139–149.

Taylor, W. P. 1935. Ecology and life
    history of the porcupine (Erethizon
    epixanthum) as related to the forests
    of Arizona and the southwestern U.S.
    Univ. of Arizona Biol. Sci. Bull.
    3,6:5-177.

Triska, F. J. 1970. Seasonal distribution
    of aquatic hyphomycetes in relation to
    disappearance of leaf litter from a
    woodland stream. Ph.D. thesis, Univ.
    of Pittsburgh, Pa.

Waring, R. H. 1980. Vital signs of forest
    ecosystems. (In this volume).

Winn, D. S. 1976. Terrestrial vertebrate
    fauna and selected coniferous forests
    habitat types on the north slope of
    the Unita Mts. USDA Forest Service
    Region 4, Wasatch Natl. Forest, Salt
    Lake City, Utah.

The Multiple Linkages of Forests to Streams

Kenneth W. Cummins

INTRODUCTION

Headwater stream ecosystems in forested watersheds are intimately related to their vegetative setting. The riparian zone, the source area of soil-forest products which enter the stream, contributes to channel stability and generates biologically active organic substrates. Large woody debris often constitutes stable geomorphic features which retain mineral sediment and finer organic material (Swanson and Lienkaemper, 1978; Swanson, Triska, this volume). Inputs of organic solutions and particulates (and inorganic nutrients) provide energy for the stream community over an annual cycle (Fisher and Likens, 1973). The stream also represents a potential source area for the riparian zone of the forest ecosystem at times of greater than bankfull discharge (Merritt and Lawson, 1979).

Thus, because of the interactive nature of forest-stream ecosystems, stream community structure and function should be studied within a watershed context (Cummins, 1974; Hynes, 1975).

BACKGROUND

Prior to the 1960's the primary emphasis in stream ecosystem investigations was on invertebrates as food organisms for game fish in specific stream reaches. In these studies a wide variety of methods was employed to sample plants and animals associated with the channel sediments (see review by Cummins, 1962), but the key role played by the watershed in supplying organic substrates utilized by stream organisms was largely neglected.

The heterotrophic nature of forested, headwater stream ecosystems and their allochthonous-based energy source was formally recognized in the early 1960's (Hynes, 1963; Ross, 1963). A major development of the 1970's has been the measurement of watershed material-balance budgets. Such studies have shown that streams are not merely conduits that export forest ecosystem products from within the boundaries of surface watersheds and subsurface source areas, but rather that they store and biologically process organic inputs (Fisher and Likens, 1973; Sedell et al., 1974). Budgets for reaches, rather than for entire watersheds, require that appropriate segments be chosen for study with all inputs adequately taken into account (Fisher, 1977). In all budget studies it is important to measure storage carefully and to relate release from (or accrual to) storage to the annual inputs. Also, the losses to and introduction from storage must be related to the seasonal and long-term flow regime (Swanson, this volume).

PERSPECTIVES

The 1970's also have involved the development of conceptual models of headwater stream ecosystem structure and function (Cummins, 1974; Minshall, 1978). Refinement of existing models and elaboration of new ones will undoubtedly continue to be a major feature of stream-watershed research in the 1980's. Examples would be evaluating and testing the "River Continuum" and "Nutrient Spiraling" hypotheses. The former depicts stream-river drainage nets as continua of biological organization that reflect geomorphic control (Cummins, 1975; Vannote et al., 1980) from low order headwater streams to higher order receiving rivers (Strahler, 1957; Leopold et al., 1964). "Nutrient Spiraling" (Webster, 1975) refers to the partially open nutrient cycles characteristic of running waters. Portions of the inputs to a given reach are stored and processed and some fraction released downstream. The incomplete efficiency of storage and processing provides energy and inorganic nutrients for downstream communities. The more efficient reaches (i.e., higher retention and processing) are considered to have the "tightest" spirals.

The River Continuum

A major distinction between lotic ecosystems can be made on the basis of the relative importance of in-stream primary production versus inputs of terrestrial origin as the major source of organic matter for community processes (Vannote et al., 1980). In forested ecosystems, small, shaded, cool headwater steams (approximately orders 1-3) may derive more than 90 percent of their organic carbon from the terrestrial surroundings (Fisher and Likens, 1973; Sedell et al., 1974). The riparian zone vegetation functions both in light attenuation and as the source of allochthonous inputs, including long-term structural (wood debris) and annual energy supplies.

The ratio of daily gross primary production (P) to total daily community respiration (R) (Odum, 1956) reflects the relative dominance of autotrophy versus heterotrophy. However, as Minshall (1978) has shown, even when primary production exceeds upstream and riparian inputs of organic matter, the in-stream derived organic substance is used primarily in a moribund state in detrital food chains. Where riparian vegetation has been removed, as in clearcut timber harvest, or is naturally sparse (high altitudes and latitudes and xeric regions), autotrophy dominates (P/R > 1). In wide shallow, generally warmer, well-lighted midsized rivers (orders 4-6), primary production is also the dominant source of organics.

In addition to increases in primary production related to higher light regimes, another significant feature of the adjustment of biological communities to changes in geomorphology, channel configuration, and vegetational setting downriver (along the "continuum") concerns the size distribution of the particulate organic matter (POM, > 0.5 µm particle size) resources. Headwater streams characteristically have greater inputs of coarse material (CPOM, > 1 mm particle size) and, therefore, greater concentrations of the microbial and macrobial biota for which coarse material is the primary nutritional resource (Cummins, 1974). With increasing stream size and reduced importance of direct riparian inputs, a larger proportion of the POM is fine particulate organic matter (FPOM, < 1 mm particle size) transported from the headwater drainage net. The greater abundance of FPOM is reflected by a change in community structure; for example, larger populations of collectors (filter feeding invertebrates) (Wallace and Merritt, 1980).

Nutrient Recyling

Present research on nutrient relationships--particulate and dissolved (DOM, < 0.5 µm) organic matter and inorganic ions--viewed as partially closed cycles, points up the need for measurements of both physical storage and biological processing. The use of radioactive tracers (Ball et al., 1963; Ball and Hooper, 1963) or stable isotope ratios--e.g., $^{13}C/^{12}C$--(Rau, 1978) can provide data for determining pathways and residence times of nutrients in stream ecosystems.

Storage pools or compartments can be defined as locations where organic matter accumulates and is processed (utilized) at rates slower than the average or exposed (oxygenated) sites in the channel. There are three general areas: the deep sediments (low oxygen), the inner core of woody debris jams (low oxygen), and the upper bank or floodplain (low moisture). When organic material buried in the sediments and within debris jams is excavated, or that on the upper bank is captured, and re-enters the aerobic stream channel processing regime, it is utilized at a faster rate (Cummins and Klug, 1979; Merritt and Lawson, 1979). Thus, the annual--and longer--hydrographic pattern is critical in determining the proportion and timing of processing and export of annual terrestrial inputs.

Along with channel and upper bank storage or retention, biological processing is the major control of quantities of material introduced and their rates of recycling. The prediction from the "River Continuum" hypothesis (Vannote et al., 1980) is that spiraling would be tighter, especially for coarse particulate organic matter (CPOM, > 1 mm particulate size), in headwater streams due to more efficient retention and processing.

ORGANIC RESOURCES AND FUNCTIONAL GROUPS

The quantities and qualities of organic resources exert a major influence on stream community structure (Cummins, 1974; Hynes, 1975; Minshall, 1978) which is expressed in the functional roles of macroinvertebrate species. Different functional groups have adapted morphologically, behaviorally, and

Table 1. Categorization of organic resources in lotic ecosystems (modified from Cummins and Klug, 1979)

Resource category	Approximate particle size range	Major sources	Ratio of carbon to nitrogen (C/N)	Macroinvertebrate functional feeding group using resource
Periphyton (microproducers)	< 500 > 10 μm	In-stream photosynthesis	5-10:1	Scrapers
Macrophytes (macroproducers)	> 1 cm (some macroalgae) < 1 cm > mm	In-stream photosynthesis	13-70:1	Shredders, scrapers
Woody detritus	> 10 cm (coarse) < 10 cm > 10 mm (fine)	Riparian zone (upstream tributaries during floods)	200-1,300:1	Shredders (gaugers)
Nonwoody detritus (particulate organic matter or POM)		Riparian zone, upstream	70-80:1; (microbial portion 10-11:1)	
Coarse (CPOM)	> 1 mm	Riparian zone	20-80:1	Shredders
Fine (FPOM)	< 1 mm > 0.5 μm	Upstream, riparian zone	7-40:1[1]	Collectors
Dissolved organic matter (DOM)	< 0.5 μm	Subsurface source areas, upstream, riparian zone	< 17 (labile portion lower)	None
Animal tissue	> 100 μm (microforms > 10 m)	In-stream	< 17	Predators

[1]A significant portion of the nitrogen may be biologically very resistant.

physiologically to utilize various components of the spectrum of available resources (Cummins, 1974, 1975; Merritt and Cummins, 1978; Cummins and Klug, 1979).

Organic Resources

The basic categories of organic resources in running waters (Table 1) differ significantly in nutritional content as defined by microbial and animal growth. In addition to animal tissue used by predators, there are three general classes of organic resources: (1) those with chlorophyll (living micro- and macroproducers), (2) detritus, ranging in size from large wood to particles less than 1 μm and all with associated microorganisms, and (3) dissolved organics (which can be taken up by microbes). If the ratio of carbon to nitrogen (C/N) is used as an index of resource nutritive value, ratios of 17 or less are generally considered in the high quality range (Russell-Hunter, 1970). However, low ratios may be misleading, as in the case of some FPOM (Table 1), because the nitrogen may be in a recalcitrant form (Ward and Cummins, 1979).

Fungi are relatively more important on CPOM where mycelia can develop, and bacteria are predominant on FPOM (Cummins and Klug, 1979). Because the microbial biomass associated with detritus is nutritionally superior (e.g., low C/N) to the organic particle substrate which is high in cellulose and lignin, it exerts the major control on the rate of detritus processing. This is mediated both through direct microbial metabolism of the detrital substrate and regulation of invertebrate feeding (Petersen and Cummins, 1974). Substrates, such as different species of leaf litter, vary in the rate at which microbial colonization and metabolism and, therefore, invertebrate feeding proceed. Thus, differences in quality of inputs are realized as differences in stream community metabolism.

The distribution of detrital size fractions in stream ecosystems is a function of the vegetative and soil characteristics of the riparian zone, hydrologic events, and biotic processing. Dissolved organic matter (DOM) generally accounts for 50 percent or more of the total annual organic flux in forested headwater streams (Fisher and Likens, 1973; Sedell et al., 1974). A significant proportion of the DOM generated is quite labile, being physically adsorbed and flocculated, and biologically incorporated by microorganisms at rates approximately equal to its production. This is exemplified by similar measured daily changes in DOM as compared

to those observed annually (Cummins et al., 1972; Manny and Wetzel, 1973). The rapid incorporation of the labile fraction of DOM onto particles and into microbes constitutes the important retention characteristic of streams because of the reduced probability of export of particles as opposed to solutions. Of the remaining annual organic flux, about one-half is fine particulate organic matter (FPOM); the greatest percent of CPOM is found in headwater streams, reflecting the close association with the riparian zone.

Annual POM input, exclusive of large woody debris, to headwater forested streams ranges from 300 to 800 g AFDW m^{-2} (Anderson and Sedell, 1979). Although annual inputs may be low, headwater streams characteristically have large standing stocks of large wood (approximately > 2 cm): from 1 to 2 kg m^{-2} in Michigan streams to 10 to 15 kg m^{-2} in western Oregon streams (Anderson et al., 1978; Swanson and Lienkaemper, 1978). The coarse woody debris undoubtedly plays a major role in retaining nonwoody POM inputs, resulting in mean annual standing stocks of approximately 200 to 500 g AFDW m^{-2}.

Macroinvertebrate Functional
Feeding Groups

Recognition of stream microinvertebrate functional groups (Fig. 1) has shown considerable promise as a tool for assessing the ecological state of a running water community (Cummins, 1974; Merritt and Cummins, 1978). The relative abundances of the groups reflect environmental conditions, particularly the quantity and quality (i.e., nutritional value) of particulate organic matter inputs and periphyton growth. Arduous and incomplete efforts at taxonomic description can be reduced or circumvented by concentrating on morphological-behavioral adaptions for food acquisition. In addition, because most species are omnivores, this method avoids the lack of resolution associated with concentration on macroinvertebrate diets. Thus, the ratios of various functional groups reflect the nature of the organic food resources available (Cummins and Klug, 1979; Wiggins and Mackay, 1979).

There are five basic macroinvertebrate functional feeding groups. Figure 1 links each group with a nutritional resource that it is morphologically and behaviorally adapted to harvest and physiologically adapted to assimilate. The highest quality nutritional resources are animal tissue, nonfilamentous periphytic algae, and the microbial biomass component of detritus (Table 1) (Anderson and Cummins, 1979).

The CPOM: fungal-bacterial:shredder association (Fig. 1), is exemplified by large invertebrates such as larvae of the cranefly Tipula, which feed on conditioned leaf litter. Conditioning involves rapid leaching of soluble organics followed by colonization and growth of aquatic fungi and bacteria. After microbial populations have softened the substrate, shredders begin actively feeding on CPOM (Cummins, 1974; Cummins and Klug, 1979). Shredders selectively feed on the CPOM with the maximum microbial biomass, and account for at least 30 percent of the total processing (conversion of CPOM to CO_2, FPOM, and consumer biomass)(Petersen and Cummins, 1974). The shredder functional group represents the closest invertebrate linkage with the riparian zone, with growth and survival dependent upon the quantity and quality of the terrestrial inputs.

The FPOM:bacterial:collector association (Fig. 1) includes macroinvertebrates that feed by filtering particles from the passing water, for example, with filtering fans (blackflies) or silt nets (net-spinning caddisflies), and those that gather particles from the stream bottom sediments (many species of midges). Although collectors require the presence of microbial biomass on ingested FPOM for adequate nutrition, they show less adaptation for selective feeding (i.e., selection for highest food quality) than shredders (Cummins and Klug, 1979). The relationship of collectors to the riparian zone is less direct because a significant portion of the FPOM is generated within the stream ecosystem (Fig. 1). Therefore, the ratio of shredders to collectors in a stream community reflects the balance between CPOM and FPOM and the relative dominance of the riparian zone.

Macroinvertebrates of the periphyton: scraper association have adaptations for removing attached algae (primarily nonfilamentous forms) from surfaces (Fig. 1). Because they frequently feed in exposed sites, scrapers are also adapted morphobehaviorally for maintaining position in the current; for example, the heavy mineral cases of scraper caddisflies or the dorsoventral flattening of heptageniid mayflies that allows them to avoid the main force of the flow. Abundance and growth of scrapers

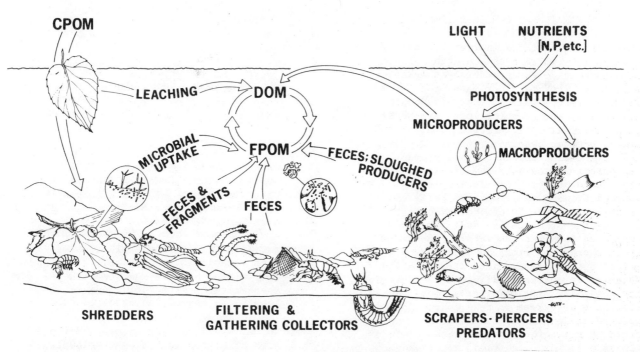

Figure 1. Diagrammatic representation of major resource inputs and partitioning among invertebrate functional groups in forested, headwater stream ecosystems. The major inputs shown, CPOM, light, and nutrients (FPOM and DOM also enter from the riparian zone, not shown), are partitioned among five general processing subsystems associated with macroinvertebrate functional feeding groups. These are the CPOM:fungal-bacterial:shredder; FPOM:bacterial:collector; algal:scraper; macrophyte:piercer; and predator:prey associations. Production of DOM from CPOM and pathways of FPOM generation are also shown. (Shredders-- amphipod, detrital stonefly, caddisfly, and cranefly; filtering collectors--blackflies and net spinning caddisfly; gathering collectors--burrowing mayfly; scrapers--tortise-shell case caddisfly, limpet, heptageniid mayfly, waterpenny beetle larva; piercers--micro- caddisflies; predators--predaceous stonefly, sulpin.)

is correlated with in-stream algal primary production, for example, P/R ratio (Anderson and Cummins, 1979). Ratios of shredders or collectors to scrapers are indicative of the importance of CPOM or FPOM relative to periphyton as nutritional resources.

The piercer:macrophyte association (Fig. 1) in streams is represented almost exclusively by microcaddisflies, which utilize filamentous macroalgae by sucking the fluids from individual cells. As primary producer communities in streams shift from diatoms to macrophytes, the ratio of piercers to scrapers increases. The piercers are a unique group in that the major utilization of macrophytes in streams is in detrital food chains (Minshall, 1978).

Predator:prey associations (Fig. 1) in stream communities appear to be relatively constant and ubiquitous. Animal tissue represents the highest quality food resource (Anderson and Cummins, 1979), but the relatively low density of prey relative to other nutritional resources means that predators are required to expend more energy in acquiring food.

MANAGEMENT CONSIDERATIONS

The multiple and intimate relationships between the riparian zone and the stream ecosystem in forested watersheds make this a critical interface for management. The riparian zone should be maintained as a suitable source area for long-term physical channel structure (e.g., wood debris) and annual organic resources. Tools are available for evaluating the stream community response to changes in the riparian source area, such as: the C/N of nutritional resources, community metabolism (P/R, and macroinvertebrate functional group ratios.

Because the quality and quantity of inputs to forested headwater stream ecosystems from the riparian zone exerts a major control on community structure and function, a number of management strategies are possible. For example, selective harvest or enhancement of tree, shrub, or herbaceous species in the riparian zone would be possible. Species such as alder generate rapidly processed litter which produces nitrogen-rich leachate that is quickly converted to FPOM, while conifer needles (e.g., Douglas-fir) are utilized at much slower rates over longer time periods.

In general, management of riparian zones is management of headwater streams, and management of headwater streams is critical for managing the larger receiving streams and rivers.

ACKNOWLEDGMENTS

Preparation of this paper was supported by Contract DE-AT06-79EV-10004 from the Division of Biomedical and Environmental Research, U.S. Department of Energy. Rosanna Mattingly and George Spengler are gratefully acknowledged for their aid in preparing the manuscript. Technical Paper No. 5341, Oregon Agricultural Experiment Station.

LITERATURE CITED

Anderson, N. H., J. R. Sedell, L. M. Roberts, and F. J. Triska. 1978. The role of aquatic invertebrates in processing wood debris in coniferous forest streams. Amer. Midl. Natur. 100:64-82.

Anderson, N. H., and J. R. Sedell. 1979. Detritus processing by macroinvertebrates in stream ecosystems. Ann. Rev. Ent. 24:351-377.

Anderson, N. H., and K. W. Cummins. 1979. Influences of diet on the life histories of aquatic insects. J. Fish Res. Bd. Can. 36:335-342.

Ball, R. C., and F. F. Hooper. 1963. Translocation of phosphorous in a trout stream ecosystem. In Radioecology, edited by V. Schultz and A. W. Klement, Jr., pp. 217-228. First Natl. Symp. Radioecol.

Ball, R. C., T. A. Wojtalik, and F. F. Hooper. 1963. Upstream dispersion of radiophosphorous in a Michigan trout stream. Pap. Mich. Acad. Sci. Arts Lett. 48:57-64.

Cummins, K. W. 1962. An evaluation of some techniques for the collection and analysis of benthic samples with special emphasis on lotic waters. Amer. Midl. Natur. 67:477-504.

Cummins, K. W. 1974. Structure and function of stream ecosystems. BioScience 24:631-641.

Cummins, K. W. 1975. The ecology of running waters: Theory and practice. In Great Lakes Pollution from Land Use Activities, Proc. Sandusky River Basin Symp., Joint Comm. Int. Ref. Gp., edited by D. B. Baker, W. B. Jackson, and B. L. Prater, pp. 227-293. Washington, D. C.: U.S. Govt. Printing Office.

Cummins, K. W., and M. J. Klug. 1979. Feeding ecology of stream invertebrates. Ann. Rev. Ecol. Syst. 10:147-172.

Cummins, K. W., M. J. Klug, R. G. Wetzel, R. C. Petersen, K. F. Suberkropp, B. A. Manny, J. C. Wuycheck, and F. O. Howard. 1972. Organic enrichment with leaf leachate in experimental lotic ecosystems. BioScience 22:719-721.

Fisher, S. G. 1977. Organic matter processing by a stream-segment ecosystem: Fort River, Massachusetts, U.S.A. Int. Rev. Ges. Hydrobiol. 62:701-727.

Fisher, S. G., and G. E. Likens. 1973. Energy flow in Bear Brook, New Hampshire: an integrative approach to stream ecosystem metabolism. Ecol. Monogr. 43:421-439.

Hynes, H. B. N. 1963. Imported organic matter and secondary productivity in streams. Proc. 16th Internat. Congress Zool. 3:324-329.

Hynes, H. B. N. 1975. The stream and its valley. Verh. Internat. Verein. Limnol. 19:1-15.

Leopold, L. B., M. G. Wolman, and J. P. Miller. 1964. Fluvial Processes in Geomorphology. San Francisco: Freeman.

Manny, B. A., and R. G. Wetzel. 1973. Diurnal changes in dissolved organic and inorganic carbon and nitrogen in a hardwater stream. Freshwat. Biol. 3:31-43.

Merritt, R. W., and K. W. Cummins, eds. 1978. An Introduction to the Aquatic Insects of North America. Dubuque, Iowa: Kendall-Hunt.

Merritt, R. W., and D. L. Lawson. 1979. Leaf litter processing in floodplain and stream communities. In Strategies for Protection and Management of Floodplain Wetlands and Other Riparian Ecosystems, Proc. Symp. Forest Service, edited by R. R. Johnson and J. F. McCormick. USDA Tech. Rep. WO-12.

Minshall, G. W. 1978. Autotrophy in stream ecosystems. BioScience 28:767-771.

Odum, H. T. 1956. Primary production in flowing waters. Limnol. Oceanogr. 1:102-117.

Petersen, R. C., and K. W. Cummins. 1974. Leaf processing in a woodland stream. Freshwat. Biol. 4:343-368.

Rau, G. 1978. Carbon-13 depletion in a subalpine lake: carbon flow implications. Science 201:901-902.

Ross, H. H. 1963. Stream communities and terrestrial biomes. Arch. Hydrobiol. 59:235-242.

Russell-Hunter, W. D. 1970. Aquatic Productivity. New York: Macmillan Co.

Sedell, J. R., F. J. Triska, J. D. Hall, N. H. Anderson, and J. L. Lyford, Jr. 1974. Sources and fates of organic inputs in coniferous forest streams. In Integrated Research in the Coniferous Forest Biome, edited by R. H. Waring and R. L. Edmonds, pp. 57-69. Univ. of Washington, Coll. Forest Resources, Conif. For. Biome Bull. 5.

Strahler, A. N. 1957. Quantitative analysis of watershed geomorphology. Trans. Amer. Geophys. Union 83:913-920.

Suberkropp, K., and M. J. Klug. 1976. Fungi and bacteria associated with leaves during processing in a woodland stream. Ecology 57:707-719.

Swanson, F. J., and G. W. Lienkaemper. 1978. Physical consequences of large organic debris in Pacific Northwest streams. USDA Forest Service, Gen. Tech. Rep. PNW-69. Pacific Northwest Forest and Range Expt. Sta., Portland, Oregon.

Vannote, R. L., G. W. Minshall, K. W. Cummins, J. R. Sedell, and C. E. Cushing. 1980. The river continuum concept. Can. J. Fish Aquat. Sci. 37:130-137

Wallace, J. B., and R. W. Merritt. 1980. Filter-feeding ecology of aquatic insects. Ann. Rev. Ent. 25:103-132.

Ward, G. M., and K. W. Cummins. 1979. Effects of food quality on growth of a stream detritivore, Paratendipes albimanus (Meigen) (Diptera: Chironomidae). Ecology 60:57-64.

Webster, J. R. 1975. Analysis of potassium
and calcium dynamics in stream ecosystems on three southern Appalachian
watersheds of contrasting vegetation.
Ph.D. thesis, University of Georgia,
Athens.

Wiggins, G. B., and R. J. Mackay. 1979.
Some relationships between systematics
and trophic ecology in Nearctic aquatic
insects, with special reference to
Trichoptera. Ecology 59:1211-1220.

Appendix

FORTIETH ANNUAL BIOLOGY COLLOQUIUM

Theme
Forests: Fresh Perspectives from Ecosystem Analysis

Dates
April 27-28, 1979

Place
Oregon State University, Corvallis, Oregon

Colloquium Committee
Jerry F. Franklin, James D. Hall, J. Ralph Shay, Richard H. Waring, Donald B. Zobel

Standing Committee for the Biology Colloquium
John L. Fryer, John C. Gordon, Norman E. Hutton, Charles E. King, Betty E. Miner, Thomas C. Moore, Dale N. Moss, James E. Oldfield, Theran D. Parsons, Henry Van Dyke, B. J. Verts, David L. Willis, Margy J. Woodburn

Colloquium Speakers, 1979
Daniel B. Botkin, George C. Carroll, Kermit Cromack, Jr., Kenneth W. Cummins, Jerry F. Franklin, W. F. Harris, James A. MacMahon, D. McGinty, R. V. O'Neill, Dennis Parkinson, D. E. Reichle, Dan Sanantonio, Wayne T. Swank, Frederick J. Swanson, Frank J. Triska, Jack B. Waide, Richard H. Waring

Sponsors
Agricultural Experiment Station
College of Science
Environmental Health Science Center
Environmental Protection Agency
Phi Kappa Phi
Research Council
School of Forestry
Sigma Xi

Hayne 1949a   Rasmussen & Damon 1943

Kendeigh 1944   Hickey 1955

Cole 1946a

Preston 1948